International Antitrust Cartel Handbook

AMERICAN**BAR**ASSOCIATION

Antitrust Law Section

Printed in the United States of America.

23 22 21 20 19   5 4 3 2 1

ISBN: 978-1-64105-513-0

Discounts are available for books ordered in bulk. Special consideration is given to state bars, CLE programs, and other bar-related organizations. Inquire at Book Publishing, ABA Publishing, American Bar Association, 321 N. Clark Street, Chicago, Illinois 60654-7598.

www.shopABA.org

CONTENTS

Chapter III

FOREWORD

The Section of Antitrust of the American Bar Association proudly presents the *International Antitrust Cartel Handbook, First Edition*. Cartel issues arise in a variety of settings and industries and increasingly without regard to jurisdictional boundaries. Markets are more interconnected today than ever before. As a result, enforcement agencies around the world have begun to more rigorously enforce anti-cartel laws and to coordinate their respective enforcement efforts.

Navigating competition law across jurisdictions can be challenging for both competition law practitioners and in-house counsel. The *International Antitrust Cartel Handbook* was prepared by individuals experienced in both prosecuting and defending cartel matters around the world to be your guide. The *Handbook* reflects years of dedicated effort by Section members who have closely followed and in some instances guided the evolution of the applicable law. It is our hope that it will be a lasting resource for readers who face cartel enforcement efforts in multiple jurisdictions.

The Section is deeply grateful to the many members who generously contributed their wisdom and time to completing this prodigious undertaking. The project's chairs, Adam Hemlock and John Terzaken, along with Kayleigh Golish, deserve special mention for their tireless efforts and determination to make this project a success.

March 2019

Deborah A. Garza
Chair, Section of Antitrust Law
American Bar Association
2018-2019

PREFACE

This first edition of the *International Antitrust Cartel Handbook* is a vital reference for both new and experienced antitrust practitioners navigating the increasingly complex global cartel enforcement environment. Globalization is the overarching theme of modern cartel enforcement. Many jurisdictions have granted their competition authorities broad jurisdictional reach and provided them with aggressive investigative tools, such as wiretap authority and compulsory process. There is also a burgeoning movement to criminalize cartel activity in places where it has previously been regarded as wholly or principally a civil or administrative matter. And the global proliferation of leniency programs continues to radically destabilize cartels, creating powerful incentives for institutions to turn against their co-conspirators.

In this constantly evolving and ever more crowded regulatory environment, the United States remains among the world's leading jurisdictions for cartel enforcement. Cartel enforcement in the United States has remained a priority regardless of changes in administration or in the leadership of the Department of Justice's Antitrust Division. The Division's efforts continue to be marked by transparency in policy and predictability in results, themes that both fit with traditional notions of due process and create the kind of environment in which the Division's Leniency Program functions best. In its dealings with its partners abroad, the Division continues to try to lead by example and advocate its policy views while remaining cognizant of the comity considerations that are essential to what is increasingly a cooperative regime of global cartel enforcement.

The *International Antitrust Cartel Handbook* brings together leading cartel practitioners from around the world to address the critical issues that arise throughout the lifecycle of a cartel investigation and prosecution. The contributing drafters boast substantial experience with cartel investigations and many have served in senior positions in government. They know both what the law says and how it is actually enforced, and we think you will find their comprehensive and practical guidance invaluable. The Handbook seeks to provide both breadth of coverage and analytical depth suitable for a wide range of practitioners, including everyone from those who may find themselves on the front line of a government inquiry or internal investigation; to those awaiting their day in court to contest a criminal indictment; to those simply preparing to counsel a client on the basic "do's and don'ts" of engaging with competitors.

We express our thanks and gratitude to the many distinguished contributors to this book, as well as the members of the ABA Antitrust Section's Cartel and Criminal Practice Committee, which was the driving force behind this publication. Our particular thanks go to the editorial chairs, Adam Hemlock and John Terzaken, and to the contributors to this book, Melanie Aitken, Elizabeth Avery, Alf-Henrik Bischke, Rachel Brass, Emma Burnham, Jeremy Calsyn, Philippe Chappatte, Cecil Chung, Eva Cole, Shi Da, Darin M. Sands, Emrys Davis, Nele Dhondt, Frederico Carrilho Donas, Bo Du, Brandon Duke, Clay Everett, Andre Geverola, Kayleigh Golish, Yvonne Hsieh, Ryuta Kawai,and Chen Ma. Our thanks also to Books & Treatises Committee co-chair Leo Caseria and members Brandon Bigelow and Kevin Walsh for their editorial comments. Finally, this book would not have been possible without the tireless efforts of the document processing and support staff at Weil, Gotshal & Manges LLP and Simpson Thacher & Bartlett LLP.

March 2019   Brent Justus & Lindsey Vaala
                    Co-Chairs, Cartel & Criminal Practice Committee
                                            Section of Antitrust Law
                                         American Bar Association
                                                      2018-2019

CHAPTER I

SECTION 1 OF THE SHERMAN ACT
AND THE PER SE RULE

This chapter provides an overview of Section 1 of the Sherman Act and analyzes the criminal ramifications of per se violations of the Sherman Act, including price fixing, bid rigging, and allocation of markets or customers. This chapter also discusses the international reach of the Sherman Act and the application of the Sherman Act to corporate entities, and concludes with a review of other types of anticompetitive conduct that can lead to criminal liability.

A. Section 1 of the Sherman Act and the Per Se Rule

Enacted in 1890, the Sherman Act[1] is the United States' primary federal antitrust statute. It contains two principal substantive provisions: Section 1 and Section 2. Section 1 broadly prohibits agreements between distinct actors that unreasonably restrain trade.[2] It provides: "Every contract, combination in the form of trust or otherwise, or conspiracy, in restraint of trade or commerce among the several States, or with foreign nations, is declared to be illegal."[3]

Section 1 imposes both criminal and civil liability for violations. For criminal violations, Section 1 provides:

> Every person who shall make any contract or engage in any combination or conspiracy hereby declared to be illegal shall be deemed guilty of a felony, and, on conviction thereof, shall be punished by fine not exceeding $100,000,000 if a corporation, or, if any other person, $1,000,000, or by imprisonment not exceeding 10 years, or by both said punishments, in the discretion of the court.[4]

---

1.   15 U.S.C. §§ 1-7.
2.   Section 2 of the Sherman Act prohibits unilateral action and combinations and conspiracies that monopolize or attempt to monopolize trade or commerce. 15 U.S.C. § 2.
3.   15 U.S.C. § 1.
4.   *Id.*

The Supreme Court has explained that, despite its literal wording, Section 1 does not prohibit *every* type of agreement in restraint of trade.[5] Rather, Section 1 only prohibits agreements that restrain trade unreasonably.[6] To determine whether a restraint of trade is unreasonable, and thus prohibited by the Sherman Act, courts have traditionally applied one of two modes of analysis: the rule of reason and the per se rule of illegality.[7] The rule of reason is the presumptive test under Section 1.[8] Courts applying the rule of reason conduct a detailed analysis of the challenged conduct by weighing its perceived anticompetitive effects against its procompetitive efficiencies.[9]

The per se rule of illegality is an exception to the rule of reason, under which certain conduct is considered categorically anticompetitive and therefore illegal under Section 1 without extensive analysis.[10] Application

---

5.   *See* Am. Needle, Inc. v. NFL, 560 U.S. 183, 189 (2010) ("[E]ven though, 'read literally,' § 1 would address 'the entire body of private contract,' that is not what the statute means."); Texaco Inc. v. Dagher, 547 U.S. 1, 5 (2006) ("This Court has not taken a literal approach to this language, however.").

6.   Standard Oil Co. v. United States, 221 U.S. 1, 58-60 (1911); *see also* Leegin Creative Leather Prods. v. PSKS, Inc., 551 U.S. 877, 885 (2007) ("While § 1 could be interpreted to proscribe all contracts . . . the Court has never taken a literal approach to its language . . . Rather, the Court has repeated time and time again that § 1 outlaws only unreasonable restraints.") (citations omitted); State Oil Co. v. Khan, 522 U.S. 3, 10 (1997) ("[T]his Court has long recognized that Congress intended to outlaw only unreasonable restraints.").

7.   In recent decades, courts have also begun to apply an intermediate standard of analysis, often referred to as the "quick look" or "truncated rule of reason analysis." This method of analysis is often used when a full-scale rule of reason analysis is inappropriate, but the challenged conduct would not trigger traditional per se treatment. *See* JULIAN O. VON KALINOWSKI ET AL., ANTITRUST LAWS AND TRADE REGULATION § 12.01(3) (2d. ed. 2018).

8.   *Dagher*, 547 U.S. at 5 ("[T]his Court presumptively applies rule of reason analysis."); Business Elecs. Corp. v. Sharp Elecs. Corp., 485 U.S. 717, 726 (1988) ("[T]here is a presumption in favor of a rule-of-reason standard.").

9.   Nat'l Soc'y of Prof'l Eng'rs. v. United States, 435 U.S. 679, 691 (1978) (explaining that the "the inquiry mandated by the Rule of Reason is whether the challenged agreement is one that promotes competition or one that suppresses competition").

10.   N. Pac. Ry. Co. v. United States, 356 U.S. 1, 5 (1958) ("[T]here are certain agreements or practices which because of their pernicious effect on

of the per se rule is limited to conduct whose "surrounding circumstances make the likelihood of anticompetitive conduct so great as to render unjustified further examination of the challenged conduct."[11] The per se rule typically applies to horizontal price-fixing, [12] bid-rigging, [13] and market-allocation agreements among competitors.[14] Such agreements are considered per se illegal under Section 1 without regard to the offender's market power or the conduct's anticompetitive effects or procompetitive benefits.[15] At times, courts have also applied the per se rule to tying

---

competition and lack of any redeeming virtue are conclusively presumed to be unreasonable and therefore illegal without elaborate inquiry as to the precise harm they have caused or the business excuse for their use.")

11.   NCAA v. Bd. of Regents, 468 U.S. 85, 103-04 (1984).

12.   Ariz. v. Maricopa Cnty. Med. Soc'y, 457 U.S. 332, 347 (1982) ("We have not wavered in our enforcement of the per se rule against price fixing."). Per se treatment is not limited to agreements that literally *fix* the final price charged to customers. Rather, courts will apply per se treatment to various types of horizontal agreements insofar as they directly affect prices. *See, e.g.,* Catalano, Inc. v. Target Sales, 446 U.S. 643, 648 (1980) ("An agreement to terminate the practice of giving credit is thus tantamount to an agreement to eliminate discounts, and thus falls squarely within the traditional per se rule against price fixing.").

13.   United States v. Bensinger Co., 430 F.2d 584, 589 (8th Cir. 1970) (holding that a bid-rigging agreement "is a price-fixing agreement of the simplest kind, and price-fixing agreements are per se violations of the Sherman Act.").

14.   United States v. Topco Assocs., 405 U.S. 596, 608 (1972) ("One of the classic examples of a per se violation of § 1 is an agreement between competitors at the same level of the market structure to allocate territories in order to minimize competition.").

15.   United States v. Socony-Vacuum Oil Co., 310 U.S. 150, 226 n.59 (1940) ("Whatever economic justification particular price-fixing agreements may be thought to have, the law does not permit an inquiry into their reasonableness. They are all banned because of their actual or potential threat to the central nervous system of the economy."); *In re* Cardizem CD Antitrust Litig., 332 F.3d 896, 909 (6th Cir. 2003) ("[T]he virtue/vice of the per se rule is that it allows courts to presume that certain behaviors as a class are anticompetitive without expending judicial resources to evaluate the actual anticompetitive effects or procompetitive justifications in a particular case.").

agreements[16] and horizontal group boycotts[17]; however, the per se rule will only apply to such conduct under certain circumstances. The Supreme Court has held that the per se rule no longer applies to vertical group boycotts[18] or vertical price restraints.[19]

Once a plaintiff or prosecutor demonstrates that a defendant has engaged in conduct that is per se illegal, liability attaches, and courts are not required to undertake a detailed inquiry into the conduct's precise harm or business purpose.[20] Nor do courts engage in the balancing test as performed in regard to rule of reason matters.[21] Accordingly, litigation involving per se illegal conduct, at least with respect to liability, centers on whether an illegal agreement exists, rather than on the agreement's purpose or effects.[22]

B. Elements of the Offense

To establish a violation of Section 1, a plaintiff must prove three elements: (1) the existence of concerted action among at least two distinct actors, (2) that unreasonably restrains trade, and (3) that affects interstate or foreign commerce of the United States.[23] Because this Handbook concerns criminal cartel activity presumed to be unreasonable under the per se rule, this chapter focuses on the first element of a Section 1 offense: the existence of concerted action between distinct actors, otherwise known as the element of agreement.

---

16.   *See* Eastman Kodak Co. v. Image Tech. Servs., 504 U.S. 451, 462 (1992) (holding that per se rule may apply to tying arrangements, but only when the party imposing the tie has market power in the tying product market).

17.   FTC v. Superior Court Trial Lawyers Ass'n, 493 U.S. 411, 432 (1990) ("Respondents' boycott thus has no special characteristics meriting an exemption from the per se rules of antitrust law.").

18.   NYNEX Corp. v. Discon, Inc., 525 U.S. 128, 135 (1998).

19.   Leegin Creative Leather Prods. v. PSKS, Inc., 551 U.S. 877, 907 (2007).

20.   Nw. Wholesale Stationers, Inc. v. Pac. Stationery & Printing Co., 472 U.S. 284, 289 (1985).

21.   *Id.*

22.   However, a plaintiff seeking damages in a private civil action must also prove the existence and extent of antitrust injury. *See* Bigelow v. RKO Radio Pictures, Inc., 327 U.S. 251, 264 (1946).

23.   T.W. Elec. Serv. v. Pac. Elec. Contractors Ass'n, 809 F.2d 626, 632-33 (9th Cir. 1987).

Section 1 does not prohibit unilateral activity by a single actor or between actors within the same firm.[24] Rather, to establish a Section 1 violation, there must be concerted activity between "separate economic actors pursuing separate economic interests."[25] The determination of whether conduct involves separate actors does not turn on legal formalities, but on "a functional consideration of how [the parties] actually operate."[26] Actions undertaken by a single corporation and its employees, agents, unincorporated divisions, or wholly owned subsidiaries are generally considered unilateral and will not give rise to Section 1 liability.[27] The same is true for the actions of a fully integrated joint venture.[28] However, business arrangements that join together "independent centers of decision making," such as nonintegrated joint ventures, professional organizations, and trade groups, are capable of engaging in concerted activity under Section 1.[29]

Concerted activity (i.e., a "contract," "combination," or "conspiracy") occurs when there is "a conscious commitment to a common scheme designed to achieve an unlawful objective."[30] Put differently, distinct actors must share "a unity of purpose or a common design and understanding, or a meeting of minds."[31] An express agreement need not be proved to establish a violation Section 1.[32] Concerted activity may be

---

24.   Fisher v. City of Berkeley, 475 U.S. 260, 266 (1986) ("Even where a single firm's restraints directly affect prices and have the same economic effect as concerted action might have, there can be no liability under § 1 in the absence of agreement."). Unilateral activity is subject to scrutiny under Section 2 of the Sherman Act. 15 U.S.C. § 2.

25.   Am. Needle, Inc. v. NFL, 560 U.S. 183, 184 (2010) (quoting Copperweld Corp. v. Indep. Tube Corp., 467 U.S. 752, 769 (1984)).

26.   *Id.*

27.   *Copperweld*, 467 U.S. at 769-74 (rejecting the doctrine of intra-enterprise conspiracy).

28.   Texaco Inc. v. Dagher, 547 U.S. 1, 5-6 (2006).

29.   *Am. Needle*, 560 U.S. at 183-84.

30.   Monsanto Co. v. Spray-Rite Serv. Corp., 465 U.S. 752, 764 (1984) (citation omitted).

31.   Am. Tobacco Co. v. United States, 328 U.S. 781, 810 (1946).

32.   United States v. Gen. Motors Corp., 384 U.S. 127, 142-43, (1966) ("[I]t has long been settled that explicit agreement is not a necessary part of a Sherman Act conspiracy—certainly not where, as here, joint and collaborative action was pervasive in the initiation, execution, and fulfillment of the plan.").

accomplished tacitly, even without verbal or written communication.[33] Similarly, offenders need not have identical motives,[34] nor is it a defense that a party simply acquiesced in illegal conduct or was coerced into participating.[35] When a conspiracy is alleged, Section 1 does not require that the parties take any overt act in furtherance of the conspiracy or have the means of accomplishing its goals.[36] The act of conspiring is itself sufficient to constitute concerted activity under Section 1.

Section 1 does not, however, prohibit competitors from engaging in parallel conduct based on independent business judgement, so long as it is not purely based on concerted activity. This so-called conscious parallelism is not itself unlawful,[37] and courts recognize that prices among competitors may rise or coalesce in concentrated markets without the presence of concerted activity.[38]

---

33.   Esco Corp. v. United States, 340 F.2d 1000, 1007 (9th Cir. 1965) ("A knowing wink can mean more than words.").

34.   Spectators' Commc'n Network v. Colonial Country Club, 253 F.3d 215, 220 (5th Cir. 2001) ("Antitrust law has never required identical motives among conspirators, and even reluctant participants have been held liable for conspiracy.").

35.   MCM Partners v. Andrews-Bartlett & Assocs., 62 F.3d 967, 973 (7th Cir. 1995) ("[T]he 'combination or conspiracy' element of a section 1 violation is not negated by the fact that one or more of the co-conspirators acted unwillingly, reluctantly, or only in response to coercion."); United States v. Paramount Pictures, 334 U.S. 131, 161 (1948) ("[A]cquiescence in an illegal scheme is as much a violation of the Sherman Act as the creation and promotion of one").

36.   United States v. Socony-Vacuum Oil Co., 310 U.S. 150, 226 n.59 (1940) ("[I]t is likewise well settled that conspiracies under the Sherman Act are not dependent on any overt act other than the act of conspiring.").

37.   Blomkest Fertilizer, Inc. v. Potash Corp. of Saskatchewan, Inc., 203 F.3d 1028, 1032-33 (8th Cir. 2000) ("Evidence that a business consciously met the pricing of its competitors does not prove a violation of the antitrust laws.").

38.   *In re* Flat Glass Antitrust Litig., 385 F.3d 350, 359 (3d Cir. 2004) ("[F]irms in a concentrated market may maintain their prices at supracompetitive levels, or even raise them to those levels, without engaging in any overt concerted action.").

C. Per Se Conduct Most Likely to Be the Subject of Criminal Charges

Most criminal antitrust prosecutions involve price fixing, bid rigging, or allocation of markets or customers, each a per se violation of the Sherman Act. Each of these kinds of collusion can be prosecuted by the U.S. Department of Justice (DOJ) Antitrust Division (either on its own or in conjunction with other federal agencies, depending on the nature of the conduct) if the crimes occurred, at least in part, within the previous five years.[39]

1. Price Fixing

Price fixing is an agreement among competitors to raise, fix, or otherwise maintain the price at which they sell their goods or services. A price-fixing conspiracy does not necessarily mean that competitors in a given market charge the exact same price[40]; nor for that matter does a price-fixing scheme have to involve every competitor in a given market or industry.[41]

Price fixing takes numerous forms, but any agreement that restricts price competition violates the law, and many such agreements constitute criminal offenses as per se violations of Section 1 of the Sherman Act. In addition to explicit agreements among competing entities on the price or prices those competitors will charge their customers, other kinds of price-fixing agreements include agreements to hold prevailing prices firm, adopt a standard formula for computing the prices of products or services made

---

39. The DOJ has published a short but comprehensive overview of per se violations of the Sherman Act prosecuted by the Antitrust Division. U.S. DEP'T OF JUSTICE, ANTITRUST PRIMER: PRICE FIXING, BID RIGGING, AND MARKET ALLOCATION: WHAT THEY ARE AND WHAT TO LOOK FOR (2015), *available at* https://www.justice.gov/atr/price-fixing-bid-rigging-and-market-allocation-schemes.

40. *See, e.g., In re* Generic Pharm. Pricing Antitrust Litig., 338 F. Supp. 3d 404, 442 (E.D. Pa. 2018) ("[T]he Third Circuit has found that a showing of parallel pricing requires only evidence that defendants 'acted similarly,' and not evidence that they charged the same prices or engaged in identical conduct.") (quoting Petruzzi's IGA Supermarkets Inc. v. Darling-Delaware Co., Inc., 998 F.2d 1224, 1243 (3d Cir. 1993)).

41. *See* Ohio v. Am. Express Co., 138 S. Ct. 2274, 2290 n.10 (2018) (noting that the horizontal agreement in *Topco* "was unreasonable *per se*, even though the agreement did not extend to every competitor in the market").

or offered by different competitors, establish or maintain price discounts, fix credit or rebate terms, and refrain from advertising prices of competing products.

2. Bid Rigging

Rigging bids is a practice where competitors manipulate the process in which public and private entities purchase goods and services by soliciting competing bids.[42] Almost all kinds of bid-rigging schemes include an agreement among some or all of the bidders that predetermines the winning bidder, or that limits or eliminates competition among the conspiring vendors. Moreover, buy-side price fixing is per se illegal.

Bid rigging typically involves an agreement among competitors prior to the commencement of the bidding process or auction. Specific types of bid rigging include the following: bid suppression (where competitors agree to refrain from bidding on a particular job or contract, or withdraw a previously-submitted bid so that the agreed-upon winner will be selected), "complimentary" bidding (also known as "cover" or "courtesy" bidding, where competitors intentionally submit bids that are either too high, or impose too many terms on the purchaser to cause the buyer to reject the bid, in an effort to present an appearance of bid competition), and bid rotation (also known as "round robin" bidding, which involves bidders all submitting bids, but includes an agreement among the bidders that a certain bidder will make the lowest bid for that specific proposal, and in turn, that winning bidder submits an artificially high bid at the following auction).

3. Market or Customer Allocation

Schemes to divide or allocate markets or customers are agreements in which competing entities allocate specific customers (or types of customers), products, or sales territories among themselves. Examples of such agreements are those in which one competitor will be allowed to sell

---

42.   *In re* London Silver Fixing, Ltd., Antitrust Litig., 213 F. Supp. 3d 530, 558 (S.D.N.Y. 2016) ("Claims for bid rigging . . . typically involve competitors conspiring to raise prices for purchasers—often, but not always, governmental entities—who acquire products or services by soliciting competing bids.") (citing Gatt Commc'ns, Inc. v. PMC Assocs., L.L.C., 711 F.3d 68, 72–74 (2d Cir. 2013), and State of New York v. Hendrickson Bros., Inc., 840 F.2d 1065 (2d Cir. 1988))).

to (or bid on contracts put out by) a particular type of customer; in return, that company or person will not sell to (or bid on contracts put out by) other types of customers that have, by agreement, been allocated to another competitor. Other examples of illegal allocation or division schemes involve agreements where competitors agree to sell only to customers in an agreed-upon geographic area, and will refuse to sell to (or quote intentionally high prices to) customers or bidders allocated to other conspirators.[43]

D. Select Criminal Legal Principles

1. *Exchange of Information among Competitors*

Exchanges of information, without more, are not prosecuted as criminal violations of the Sherman Act, even if they involve the exchange of competitively sensitive information by competitors.[44] However, exchanges of competitively sensitive information may provide circumstantial evidence of per se illegal agreements concerning prices, customers, or output. "Competitively sensitive information" refers to confidential, nonpublic information that would not normally be shared with competitors in a competitive marketplace, such as pricing plans.[45]

---

43. United States v. Topco Assocs., Inc., 405 U.S. 596, 608 (1972) ("One of the classic examples of a per se violation of § 1 is an agreement between competitors at the same level of the market structure to allocate territories in order to minimize competition."); Procaps S.A. v. Patheon Inc., 36 F. Supp. 3d 1306, 1323 n.6 (S.D. Fla. 2014) ("*Topco* is the 40-year-old-seminal case that stands for the rule that allocating territories to minimize competition at the retail level is a horizontal restraint constituting a *per se* violation of section 1 of the Sherman Act.").
44. *See, e.g.*, United States v. Citizens & S. Nat'l Bank, 422 U.S. 86, 113 (1975) ("[T]he dissemination of price information is not itself a *per se* violation of the Sherman Act").
45. *See, e.g.*, U.S. Dep't of Justice, Bus. Review Letter to CyberPoint Int'l (Oct. 2, 2014), *available at* https://www.justice.gov/atr/response-cyberpoint-international-br-request-business-review-letter (defining "competitively sensitive information" to include "recent, current and future prices, cost data, or output levels.").

a.   Price Information

The Supreme Court has repeatedly held that sharing of price information among competitors, standing alone, is not per se illegal under Section 1 of the Sherman Act.[46] If there is no underlying agreement to fix or maintain prices, exchanges of pricing information are not necessarily unlawful. "It is not unlawful for a person to obtain information about competitors' prices, or even to exchange information about prices, unless done pursuant to an agreement or mutual understanding . . . ."[47]

However, evidence of frequent exchanges of price information may in some cases support a prosecution for price fixing.[48] If appropriate market conditions are present, exchanges of information concerning future prices may provide circumstantial evidence of a price-fixing agreement.[49]

---

46.   *See Citizens & S. Nat'l Bank*, 422 U.S. at 113; United States v. Container Corp., 393 U.S. 333, 339 (1969); Cement Mfrs. Protective Ass'n v. United States, 268 U.S. 588, 604-06 (1925); Maple Flooring Mfrs. Ass'n v. United States, 268 U.S. 563, 582-83 (1925).

47.   United States v. United States Gypsum Co., 438 U.S. 422, 441 n.16 (1978) ("The exchange of price data and other information among competitors does not invariably have anticompetitive effects . . . . For this reason, we have held that such exchanges of information do not constitute a *per se* violation of the Sherman Act.").

48.   *See, e.g., In re* Coordinated Pretrial Proceedings in Petroleum Prods. Antitrust Litig., 906 F.2d 432, 447 n.13 (9th Cir. 1990) ("[I]nformation exchanges help to establish an antitrust violation only when either (1) the exchange indicates the existence of an express or tacit agreement to fix or stabilize prices, or (2) the exchange is made pursuant to an express or tacit agreement that is itself a violation of § 1 under a rule of reason analysis.").

49.   United States v. Container Corp., 393 U.S. 333, 336-37 (1969) (informal agreement to provide price information may, under appropriate market conditions, constitute circumstantial evidence of an agreement to stabilize prices); King & King Enter. v. Champlin Petroleum Co., 657 F.2d 1147, 1152 (10th Cir. 1981) (finding that exchange of price information may serve as basis for inferring price fixing where effect of such exchange is to stabilize prices); Penne v. Greater Minneapolis Area Bd. of Realtors, 604 F.2d 1143, 1148-49 (8th Cir. 1979) (reversing summary judgment because non-moving party showed possible connection between information exchanges and alleged conspiracy to fix brokerage fees).

b. Nonprice Information

Prosecutions predicated solely on the exchange of nonprice information among competitors are rare. Some nonprice information—such as product development or production plans—is competitively sensitive, and exchange of such information could lead to illegal coordination of competitive behavior. Agreements to engage in such coordination may be inferred in certain cases—when appropriate plus factors are present—from the exchange of competitively sensitive nonprice information such as product or production plans.

2. Direct and Circumstantial Evidence

The central question in criminal antitrust prosecutions is whether there was an agreement in restraint of trade among the defendants. An agreement may be reflected in documents, or there may be direct testimony that an agreement existed. In other cases, however, the prosecutors must rely on circumstantial evidence of the parties' actions to establish "a unity of purpose or a common design and understanding, or a meeting of the minds" to fix prices, rig bids, or engage in some other per se illegal conduct.[50]

As a result of the Antitrust Division's Corporate Leniency Policy, the DOJ has increasingly been able to develop direct evidence of international cartel violations in the form of direct testimony of cooperating witnesses. In addition, documents produced to the government by leniency applicants play a vital role in proving the prosecution's case.[51]

In cases where direct evidence is not available, or to supplement the available direct evidence, the government may prove the existence of an illegal agreement from circumstantial evidence of the defendants' parallel pricing or other parallel behavior. Parallel pricing is not itself illegal; it may arise from normal patterns of pricing in competitive oligopolistic markets.[52]

Parallel pricing or other parallel behavior may, however, be indicative of illegal agreements when certain other "plus factors" are present. However, "[w]hen the government attempts to prove existence of a

---

50. *See, e.g.*, Am. Tobacco Co. v. United States, 328 U.S. 781, 810 (1946).
51. *See* United States v. Mitsubishi Corp., No. 00-033 (E.D. Pa. 2001) (government able to prove defendant's guilt through documents, despite lack of cooperation from witnesses).
52. Theatre Enters. v. Paramount Film Distrib. Corp., 346 U.S. 537 (1954) ("Conscious parallelism" does not, by itself, violate the Sherman Act).

conspiracy by circumstantial evidence [alone], each link in the inferential chain must be clearly proven."[53]

In particular, Sherman Act violations have been found, relying on evidence of parallel competitive behavior coupled with evidence of market or other factors that "exclude the possibility of independent action."[54] While "conscious parallelism" alone does not evidence a Sherman Act violation,[55] an unlawful agreement may be inferred from "proof that the defendants got together and exchanged assurances of common action or otherwise adopted a common plan even though no meetings, conversations, or exchanged documents are shown."[56] Courts have also credited various plus factors as supporting the inference of a conspiracy. The most significant plus factor is whether the conduct at issue was contrary to the independent self-interest of the alleged conspirators. If challenged actions would be rational only if undertaken jointly, that is circumstantial evidence indicative of a "meeting of the minds."[57]

3. Scope of Conspiracy

The determination of a conspiracy's scope affects the liability of a defendant for co-conspirators' actions, the application of the statute of limitations, the calculation of a fine based on the volume of commerce, the determination of individual sentences, and other important considerations in criminal antitrust cases.

The essence of a single conspiracy is a common goal among the conspirators. A single agreement, even if it is an agreement to commit

---

53. United States v. Galvan, 693 F.2d 417, 419 (5th Cir. 1982).
54. *See, e.g.*, Blomkest Fertilizer, Inc. v. Potash Corp. of Saskatchewan, 203 F.3d 1028, 1031-32 (8th Cir. 2000).
55. Bell Atlantic Corp. v. Twombly, 550 U.S. 544, 553–54 (2007) ("Even 'conscious parallelism,' a common reaction of 'firms in a concentrated market [that] recognize[e] their shared economic interests and their interdependence with respect to price and output decisions' is 'not in itself unlawful.'") (quoting Brooke Grp. Ltd. v. Brown & Williamson Tobacco Corp., 509 U.S. 209, 227 (1993)) (alterations in original).
56. Lifewatch Servs. Inc. v. Highmark Inc., 902 F.3d 323, 333 (3d Cir. 2018).
57. *Blomkest Fertilizer*, 203 F.3d at 1031–32 (price-fixing agreement inferred based on evidence of price information exchange and conclusion that in the industry at issue it would be against the participants' individual interests to exchange information in the absence of an agreement to coordinate pricing).

several crimes, constitutes a single conspiracy. [58] Just as single conspiracies can be identified by the pursuit of a common goal, multiple conspiracies can be identified by distinct, illegal ends to each of the conspirators' agreements. Simply put, "multiple agreements to commit separate crimes constitute multiple conspiracies."[59]

The so-called wheel, or hub-and-spoke, conspiracy exists where one central figure, the hub, conspires with several others, the spokes. The question becomes whether these individual conspiracies are bound together to create one overarching conspiracy with a single illegal objective and mutual awareness. In *Kotteakos v. United States*,[60] one individual (Brown) made fraudulent applications for loans from the Federal Housing Authority on behalf of numerous other individuals, most of whom had no connection with each other.[61] The Supreme Court held there was not one single conspiracy because each of these transactions was independent of the other and there was no common plan.[62]

By contrast, a hub-and-spoke conspiracy was found to exist in *United States v. Apple, Inc.*[63] In that case, the court found that Apple had organized a per se illegal price-fixing conspiracy among book publishers through its vertical pricing agreements with the publishers for ebooks, which each contained most-favored nations clauses.[64] In affirming the district court's decision, the Second Circuit held that the vertical agreements between Apple and the publishers facilitated an agreement between the publishers.[65]

The scope of a conspiracy has a number of practical implications. First, the issue of whether a single or multiple conspiracies existed may impact whether the statute of limitations bars the prosecution of certain agreements. A Sherman Act conspiracy begins when an agreement to restrain competition is formed. [66] The conspiracy continues until its

58. United States v. Broce, 488 U.S. 563, 570-71 (1989) (a continuous, cooperative effort to rig bids for highway construction over 25 years was a single conspiracy pursuant to the Sherman Act).
59. *Id.* at 571.
60. 328 U.S. 750 (1946).
61. *Id.* at 753.
62. *Id.* at 773-74, 777; *see also* Blumenthal v. United States, 332 U.S. 539, 558 (1947) (discussing *Kotteakos*).
63. 952 F. Supp. 2d 638 (S.D.N.Y. 2013), *aff'd*, 791 F.3d 290 (2d Cir. 2015).
64. *Id.* at 664.
65. United States v. Apple, Inc., 791 F.3d 290 (2d Cir. 2015).
66. United States v. Miller, 771 F.2d 1219, 1226 (9th Cir. 1985) (citing United States v. Inryco, Inc., 642 F.2d 290, 293 (9th Cir. 1981)).

purpose has been achieved or abandoned.[67] The statute of limitations on Sherman Act conspiracies "does not begin to run so long as the co-conspirators continue to engage in overt acts designed to accomplish the objectives of the conspiracy."[68] Thus, if multiple conspiracies existed, and the agreement was achieved or abandoned beyond the reach of the statute of limitations, the DOJ will not be able to prosecute it.

Second, the issue of whether a single or multiple conspiracies were in place will also affect the way the DOJ is able to charge any alleged violations of the Sherman Act. Charging a defendant with separate counts based on the same conduct is generally prohibited as "multiplicitous," as it can result in consecutive sentences for the same conduct.[69] A single act, however, can constitute two offenses if each offense requires proof of a fact that the other does not.[70] Thus, a single conspiracy can result in convictions and resulting consecutive sentences for violating multiple statutes, including violations of multiple sections of the Sherman Act.[71]

Third, upon conviction for price fixing or a guilty plea, the DOJ imposes a fine for violations of the Sherman Act. The manner in which the DOJ calculates the volume of commerce may have a significant impact on the amount of any potential fine. A determination of whether a single or multiple conspiracies are in place may also have an impact on the amount of any fine.

---

67. *Id.* at 1226.
68. *Id.* Note that the commission of overt acts is used in this context only as evidence that the agreement has not expired, as an overt act in the furtherance of a conspiracy is not a necessary element of a Sherman Act violation. *Id.*
69. United States v. Walker, 653 F.2d 1343, 1350-51 (9th Cir. 1981); *see also* United States v. Rose, 570 F.2d 1358, 1362-63 (9th Cir. 1978). In *Rose*, the court held that it was "[m]ultiplicitous to sentence a defendant consecutively for both making a false statement, in violation of 18 U.S.C. § 1001, and importing merchandise into the United Stated by means of a false statement, forbidden by 18 U.S.C. § 542, where both were based on a single false statement to customs officials that defendant only had two cameras to declare." *Rose*, 570 F.2d at 1362-63.
70. *Walker*, 653 F.2d at 1351 (citing United States v. Blockburger, 284 U.S. 299, 304 (1932)).
71. *Id.*; *see also* Am. Tobacco Co. v. United States, 328 U.S. 781, 815-16 (1946) (upholding convictions for violations of both sections 1 and 2 of the Sherman Act, though both were based on a single conspiratorial agreement).

Fourth, the Fifth Amendment's protection against "double jeopardy" acts to shield the defendants from having to defend themselves more than once for the same alleged criminal acts.[72] This prohibition against double jeopardy acts to prevent the government from making repeated attempts to convict a defendant in successive prosecutions based on the same transactions or same course of conduct.[73] Thus, a defendant indicted and acquitted of a single conspiracy in one case may raise a double jeopardy defense if subsequently indicted for charges based upon the same conspiracy.[74] No such protection exists if the government seeks to prosecute a defendant for charges arising from separate and distinct conspiracies.

4. Statute of Limitations

The statute of limitations applicable to criminal conspiracies violating Section 1 of the Sherman Act is five years.[75] The five-year statute of limitations begins to run after the underlying conspiratorial agreement is "complete."[76] A Sherman Act conspiracy is actionable any time after the agreement to restrain competition is formed, and "it remains actionable until its purpose has been achieved or abandoned."[77] "[O]nce a conspiracy has been established, it is presumed to continue until there is an affirmative showing that it has been abandoned."[78] Withdrawal is an affirmative defense that "requires a showing that a defendant affirmatively acted to defeat or disavow the conspiracy's purpose."[79]

5. Intent

"[I]ntent is a necessary element of a criminal antitrust violation."[80] Whereas parties may be held liable for damages or injunctive relief based solely on the effect that their actions have on competition—regardless of

---

72.   United States v. Am. Honda Motor Co., 271 F. Supp. 979, 981, 987 (N.D. Cal. 1967).
73.   *Id.* at 987-88.
74.   *Id.* at 986.
75.   18 U.S.C. § 3282.
76.   *See* United States v. Kissel, 218 U.S. 601, 610 (1910).
77.   United States v. Northern Imp. Co., 814 F.2d 540, 542 (8th Cir. 1987) (quotations omitted).
78.   United States v. Hayter Oil Co., 51 F.3d 1265, 1270-71 (6th Cir. 1995).
79.   United States v. True, 250 F.3d 410, 425 (6th Cir. 2001).
80.   United States v. United States Gypsum Co., 438 U.S. 422, 443 (1978).

their intent [81] —criminal prosecution is only appropriate where the defendants acted with "specific intent."[82] Like the other elements of the offense, intent in a criminal antitrust case must be proven "beyond a reasonable doubt."

In *United States v. United States Gypsum Co.*,[83] the trial court in a criminal price-fixing case instructed the jury that the defendants could be convicted of price fixing so long as the jury found that their exchanges of prices resulted in higher prices. [84] The Supreme Court rejected that instruction, and overturned the defendants' convictions, holding that intent is a necessary element of a criminal antitrust claim that "must be established by evidence and inferences drawn therefrom." [85] It is not necessary for the government to prove that the conduct at issue actually produced anticompetitive effects, but it is necessary for the government to prove that producing such effects was a purpose of the charged conspiracy.[86]

After *Gypsum*, the defendants in many price-fixing cases have argued that it is necessary to charge the jury that they must find that the defendants acted with the specific intent to produce anticompetitive effects; those arguments have failed. [87] Courts have generally held that the intent requirement from *Gypsum* may be established in criminal cases charging per se violations of the antitrust laws by evidence that the defendant had a purpose to commit the offense. It is not necessary separately to establish a purpose to produce anticompetitive effects, since anticompetitive effects are the presumptive (and presumptively understood and intended) result

---

81. *See, e.g.*, Brooke Group v. Brown & Williamson Tobacco Corp., 509 U.S. 209 (1993) (damages liability for predatory pricing predicated solely on objective pricing factors and the likelihood of recoupment).

82. *United States Gypsum Co.*, 438 U.S. at 435.

83. 438 U.S. 422 (1978).

84. *Id.*

85. *Id.* at 435.

86. *Id.* at 444 n.21.

87. *See* United States v. Gillen, 599 F.2d 541, 545 (3d Cir. 1979) (rejecting defendants' argument and holding that in price-fixing case, no specific intent is required other than the intent to agree on prices or price levels); Untied States v. Continental Group, Inc., 603 F.2d 444, 461 (7th Cir. 1980) ("We conclude, therefore, that conviction of a felony for violating the Sherman Act does not require a showing of specific intent to product anticompetitive effects."); United States v. Alston, 974 F.2d 1206, 1213 (9th Cir. 1992) ("[T]he government need not prove specific intent to produce anticompetitive effects where a *per se* violation is alleged.").

of per se antitrust violations. As the Ninth Circuit explained, "[w]here *per se* conduct is found, a finding of intent to conspire to commit the offense is sufficient; a requirement that intent go further and envision actual anticompetitive results would reopen the very questions of reasonableness which the per se rule is designed to avoid."[88]

E. International Scope of the Sherman Act

With the rise in enforcement directed at international cartels, the courts have increasingly been asked to determine the extraterritorial reach of the Sherman Act and to grapple with its limits. Many cases involve prosecutions of companies or individuals located outside the United States, and agreements that were reached outside the United States. The question raised in such cases is what, if any, portion of that conduct is subject to regulation under U.S. antitrust law and sanction in the U.S. courts.

Early cases turned on the "general and almost universal rule . . . that the character of an act as lawful or unlawful must be determined wholly by the law of the country where the act is done."[89] Based on the logic of this rule, courts focused on the location of the act in violation of the statute. Given that the Sherman Act violation is complete when there is a meeting of the minds on a scheme to restrain trade, arguably all violations among parties located outside the United States were excluded from U.S. jurisdiction.

Modern jurisprudence, however, has moved away from a focus on the location of the acts underlying the violation. Courts in the United States instead focus on the effects of the conduct being challenged. As the Supreme Court explained in *Hartford Fire Insurance Co. v. California*,[90] it is now "well established by now that the Sherman Act applies to foreign conduct that was meant to produce and did in fact produce some substantial effect in the United States."[91] Courts have struggled to determine consistently what constitutes a "substantial effect in the United States" sufficient to justify application of the Sherman Act.

Congress cabined the extraterritorial effect of the Sherman Act through the Foreign Trade Antitrust Improvements Act (FTAIA), passed

---

88.   United States v. Brown, 936 F.2d 1042, 1046 (9th Cir. 1991) (citation omitted).

89.   Am. Banana Co. v. United Fruit Co., 213 U.S. 347, 356 (1909).

90.   509 U.S. 764 (1993).

91.   *Id.* at 796.

in 1982.[92] The FTAIA's underlying presumption is that the Sherman Act does not apply to conduct "involving [non-import] commerce with foreign nations."[93] The FTAIA recognizes an exception, however, for conduct that produces "direct, substantial and reasonably foreseeable effects" on U.S. commerce.[94] The Sherman Act will apply to that type of foreign conduct.

Cases addressing and applying this FTAIA exception have abounded in recent years. The most common fact pattern, which has produced conflicting decisions, involves agreements to fix the prices of component parts sold to customers outside the United States that are incorporated into finished goods ultimately sold in the United States.

In *United States v. LSL Biotechnologies*, [95] the Ninth Circuit considered a case challenging an agreement between two tomato seed companies allegedly to allocate markets for certain tomato seeds between them. The seeds were primarily sold in Mexico, where most of the tomatoes were grown, but the vast majority of the resulting tomatoes were sold in the United States.[96] Federal prosecutors argued that the agreement produced a clear and demonstrable effect on the prices charged for certain tomatoes sold in the United States, but the Ninth Circuit held that such an effect was not sufficient to allow application of the Sherman Act to the agreement at issue because the sales directly affected by the agreement were all made in Mexico.[97] The Ninth Circuit explained that "an effect is 'direct' if it follows as an *immediate consequence* of the defendant's activity," i.e., it proceeds "without deviation or interruption."[98] Because the effects in the United States were only indirect effects, the FTAIA barred the suit.[99]

Ten years later, the Seventh Circuit sitting en banc in *MinnChem, Inc. v. Agrium, Inc.* [100] interpreted the FTAIA in a very different fashion. *Minnchem* involved claims that potash suppliers had conspired to restrict the global supply of potash and to coordinate prices charged for potash sold outside the United States.[101] Although there were no allegations that

---

92.   15 U.S.C. § 6a.
93.   *Id.*
94.   *Id.*
95.   379 F.3d 672 (9th Cir. 2004).
96.   *Id.* at 674.
97.   *Id.* at 683.
98.   *Id.* at 680.
99.   *Id.* at 683.
100. 683 F.3d 845 (7th Cir. 2012) (en banc).
101. *Id.* at 850.

the defendants had agreed on prices to be charged in the United States, the Seventh Circuit found that the alleged conspiracy "directly" affected U.S. commerce by restricting production of the product globally, which directly affected the supply—and thus the price—of the product in the United States.[102] In reaching that conclusion, the Seventh Circuit held that an effect is direct for the purposes of the FTAIA if it bears a "reasonably proximate causal nexus" with the foreign anticompetitive conduct, i.e., the effect is not "too remote."[103]

In either formulation, there remains substantial room for argument concerning the application of the Sherman Act to foreign cartels, particularly those involving component parts. For example, in *United States v. AU Optronics Corp.*,[104] the Ninth Circuit applied the stricter "follows as an immediate consequence" test and held that the Sherman Act applied to a cartel to fix the prices of TFT-LCD panels sold outside the United States.[105] In that case, the court upheld the conviction of a foreign company for participating in that cartel, concluding that sales of component TFT-LCD panels outside the United States at artificially high prices produced sufficient "direct" effects on the prices of finished goods (e.g., monitors) sold in the United States for the Sherman Act to apply.[106] In reaching that decision, the Ninth Circuit relied heavily on testimony concerning the close relationship between the prices charged for the component panels outside the United States and the prices charged for the finished goods in the United States.[107]

The extraterritorial application of the Sherman Act remains a hotly debated—and litigated—issue of central importance to many international cartel investigations and prosecutions.

F. Principles of Corporate Criminal Liability

Corporations are generally responsible, even criminally, for the acts of their employees acting within the scope of their authority. In certain limited circumstances, however, a corporate defendant may be able to argue that the actions of an employee should not be imputed to it.

Under common law agency principles, there are generally two requirements in order for the actions of an employee to be attributed to a

---

102. *Id.* at 863.
103. *Id.* at 856–57.
104. 778 F.3d 738 (9th Cir. 2015)
105. *Id.* at 759.
106. *Id.*
107. *Id.*

corporation. First, the illegal actions of the employee must have been within the scope of the employee's responsibilities and authority from the corporation. [108] Courts generally find this element satisfied if the employee's illegal actions were directly related to the performance of the duties assigned to the employee by the corporation.[109] Thus, for instance, agreements in restraint of trade concerning the sales activities of the corporation are likely to be attributed to the corporation if the liable employees had responsibilities relating to the sales functions of the corporation. The "authority" of employees has been construed broadly. For example, corporations have been held criminally liable for antitrust violations committed by low level employees.[110]

The second requirement for attributing the actions of an employee to a corporate employer under common law agency principals is that the employee must have acted with an intent to benefit the corporation.[111] Employers are typically found liable for criminal antitrust violations committed by their employees who acted with the intent of benefitting their employers by securing business for the corporation or increasing prices charged by the corporation. However, in certain cases, it may still be possible to argue that the corporation is not criminally liable for the actions of a rogue employee seeking to advance only his or her personal interests.[112]

G. Other Federal Offenses Charged in Criminal Antitrust Prosecutions

The DOJ Antitrust Division Manual states that "[i]n addition to the Division's criminal enforcement activities under the Sherman Act, the Division investigates and prosecutes offenses that arise from conduct accompanying the antitrust violations or otherwise impact the competitive process, as well as offenses that involve the integrity of the investigative

---

108. *See, e.g.*, RESTATEMENT (SECOND) OF AGENCY § 219 (1958).
109. *See, e.g.*, United States v. Automated Med. Lab., 770 F.2d 399, 407 (4th Cir. 1985).
110. *See, e.g.*, United States v. Koppers Co., 652 F.2d 290, 298 (2d Cir. 1981).
111. *See* RESTATEMENT (SECOND) OF AGENCY § 219 (1958).
112. *See, e.g.*, United States v. Hilton Hotels Co., 467 F.2d 1000, 1004 (9th Cir. 1972).

process."[113] Nearly all of these offenses fall under Title 18 of the U.S. Code.

Title 18 offenses arising from conduct accompanying a Sherman Act violation can include conspiracy;[114] various types of fraud, including bribery,[115] false statements,[116] and mail[117] or wire fraud;[118] money laundering;[119] and tax offenses.[120] Some recent Sherman Act investigations and prosecutions have also involved acts of conspiracy or bribery in violation of the Foreign Corrupt Practices Act.[121]

Title 18 offenses involving the integrity of the investigative process prosecuted by the Antitrust Division can include various types of obstruction of justice, including witness-tampering[122] and destruction or

---

113. ANTITRUST DIV., U.S. DEP'T OF JUSTICE, ANTITRUST DIVISION MANUAL (5th ed. 2012) (last updated Apr. 2018), *available at* https://www.justice.gov/atr/file/761166/download.

114. The general conspiracy statute, 18 U.S.C. § 371, prohibits conspiring to: (1) "commit any offense against the United States;" or (2) "defraud the United States, or any agency thereof in any manner or for any purpose." The Antitrust Division also prosecutes violations of 18 U.S.C. § 1349, attempt and conspiracy with respect to mail and wire fraud which covers individuals or entities who are not principal actors in a conspiracy can nevertheless be prosecuted under 18 U.S.C. § 2(a), which provides that "[w]hoever commits an offense against the United States or aids, abets, counsels, commands, induces or procures its commission, is punishable as a principal."

115. 18 U.S.C. § 201 (bribery of public officials and witnesses), § 666 (theft or bribery concerning programs receiving Federal funds).

116. 18 U.S.C. § 1001 (false statements or representations).

117. 18 U.S.C. § 1341 (mail fraud).

118. 18 U.S.C. § 1343 (wire fraud).

119. Money-laundering offenses prosecuted by the Antitrust Division can include violations of 18 U.S.C. § 1952 (interstate and foreign travel or transportation in aid of racketeering enterprise), § 1956 (laundering of monetary instruments), and § 1957 (engaging in monetary transactions in property derived from specified unlawful activity).

120. Tax offenses fall under Title 26 of the U.S. Code (the Internal Revenue Code), and offenses prosecuted by the Antitrust Division can include violations of 26 U.S.C. § 7201 (attempt to evade or defeat tax) and § 7206 (fraud and false statements in connection with tax returns and similar documentation filed with the IRS).

121. 15 U.S.C. § 78dd-1.

122. 18 U.S.C. § 1512 (tampering with a witness, victim, or an informant, with sub-section (c) of the statute prohibiting the destruction of documents to

falsification of records;[123] perjury[124] or false testimony before a grand jury or court;[125] and criminal contempt.[126]

In addition to investigating and prosecuting Title 18 offenses on its own, the Antitrust Division regularly works in partnership with other units of the Justice Department (including local U.S. Attorney's offices, the Criminal Division, and the Federal Bureau of Investigation) and as well as other federal agencies, including the Criminal Investigation Division of the Internal Revenue Service and the Defense Criminal Investigative Service of the Department of Defense, to investigate and prosecute Title 18 offenses that arise from conduct accompanying a Sherman Act violation or undermining the integrity of the investigative process.

H. Largest DOJ International Cartel Fines (Over $10 Million)

In 2004, Congress passed the Antitrust Criminal Penalty Enhancement and Reform Act (ACPERA), which, among other things, amended Section 1 by increasing the maximum criminal fine for corporations from $10 million to $100 million for each count.[127] Under the Comprehensive Crime Control Act and the Criminal Fine Improvements Act, authorities may also seek corporate fines for twice the gross gain derived from a Section 1 violation or twice the gross loss suffered by its victims.[128] The Antitrust Division typically relies on this provision when seeking fines above the $100 million maximum available under Section 1 of the Sherman Act.

The largest criminal fines obtained by the Antitrust Division have arisen in the context of international cartels.[129] This includes over 100

---

prevent the document's use in a governmental proceeding). Other obstruction of justice statutes prosecuted by the Antitrust Division are 18 U.S.C. § 1503 (influencing or injuring officer or juror generally), § 1505 (obstruction of proceedings before departments, agencies and committees), § 1509 (obstruction of court orders), and § 1510 (obstruction of criminal investigations).

123.   18 U.S.C. § 1519 (destruction, alteration, or falsification of records in Federal investigations and bankruptcy proceedings).

124.   18 U.S.C. § 1621 (perjury generally), § 1622 (subornation of perjury).

125.   18 U.S.C. § 1623 (false declarations before grand jury or court).

126.   18 U.S.C. § 402 (listing types of contempt constituting crimes).

127.   *See* Antitrust Criminal Penalty Enhancement and Reform Act of 2004 at § 215, Pub. L. No. 108-237, tit. II, 118 Stat. 661 (2004).

128.   18 U.S.C. § 3571(d).

129.   *See* U.S. Dep't of Justice, Sherman Action Violations Yielding a Corporate Fine of $10 Million or More (2016), *available at*

corporate fines that exceed Section 1's former $10 million maximum.[130] To date, the largest criminal fines imposed by the Antitrust Division for international cartel activity include:

- $500 million fine against AU Optronics Corporation of Taiwan (Taiwan) for conspiring to fix the prices of thin film liquid crystal display (LCD) panels (2012).[131]
- $470 million fine against Yazaki Corporation (Japan) for participating in multiple price-fixing and bid-rigging conspiracies related to automobile parts (2012).[132]
- $425 million fine against Bridgestone Corporation (Japan) for conspiring to fix prices, allocate sales, and rig bids for automotive anti-vibration rubber products (2014).[133]
- $400 million fine against LG Display Co., Ltd (Korea) and LG Display America for conspiring to fix prices in the sale of liquid crystal display (LCD) panels (2008-09).[134]

---

https://www.justice.gov/atr/sherman-act-violations-yielding-corporate-fine-10-million-or-more.

130. *Id.*
131. U.S. Dep't of Justice, Taiwan-Based AU Optronics Corporation Sentenced to Pay $500 Million Criminal Fine for Role in LCD Price-Fixing Conspiracy (Sept. 12, 2012), *available at* https://www.justice.gov/opa/pr/taiwan-based-au-optronics-corporation-sentenced-pay-500-million-criminal-fine-role-lcd-price.
132. U.S. Dep't of Justice, Yazaki Corp., Denso Corp. and Four Yazaki Executives Agree to Plead Guilty to Automobile Parts Price-Fixing and Bid-Rigging Conspiracies (June 30, 2012), *available at* https://www.justice.gov/opa/pr/yazaki-corp-denso-corp-and-four-yazaki-executives-agree-plead-guilty-automobile-parts-price.
133. U.S. Dep't of Justice, Bridgestone Corp. Agrees to Plead Guilty to Price Fixing on Automobile Parts Installed in U.S. Cars (Feb. 13, 2014), *available at* https://www.justice.gov/opa/pr/bridgestone-corp-agrees-plead-guilty-price-fixing-automobile-parts-installed-us-cars.
134. U.S. Dep't of Justice, LG, Sharp, Chunghwa Agree to Plead Guilty, Pay Total of $585 Million in Fines for Participating in LCD Price-fixing Conspiracies (Nov. 12, 2008), *available at* https://www.justice.gov/archive/opa/pr/2008/November/08-at-1002.html.

- $350 million fine against Société Air France and Koninklijke Luchtvaart Maatschappij, N.V. (France & the Netherlands) for conspiring to fix prices for air cargo transportation rates (2008).[135]
- $300 million fines against each of Korean Air Lines Co., Ltd. (Korea) and British Airway PLC (United Kingdom), for conspiring to fix prices for passenger and cargo flights (2007).[136]

---

135. U.S. Dep't of Justice, Major International Airlines Agree to Plead Guilty and Pay Criminal Fines Totaling More Than $500 Million for Fixing Prices on Air Cargo Rates (June 26, 2008), *available at* https://www.justice.gov/archive/opa/pr/2008/June/08-at-570.html.

136. U.S. Dep't of Justice, British Airways PLC and Korean Air Lines Co. Ltd. Agree to Plead Guilty and Pay Criminal Fines Totaling $600 million for Fixing Prices on Passenger and Cargo Flights (Aug. 1, 2007), *available at* https://www.justice.gov/archive/atr/public/press_releases/2007/224928.htm.

CHAPTER II

U.S. DEPARTMENT OF JUSTICE
INVESTIGATIONS

This chapter provides a general overview of U.S. Department of Justice (DOJ) investigations.

A. Antitrust Division

1. Overview

The DOJ Antitrust Division has primary jurisdiction over criminal violations of the antitrust laws. The Director of Criminal Litigation in charge of the Antitrust Division has supervisory authority over all investigations involving possible violations of the antitrust laws. [1] Criminal antitrust investigations typically are conducted by one of the Antitrust Division's criminal prosecuting offices. But in certain cases, U.S. Attorney's offices are permitted to conduct antitrust investigations with the approval and supervision of the Antitrust Division.[2] The Antitrust Division also may investigate non-antitrust crimes when those crimes are committed in connection with antitrust crimes or the investigation thereof (such as perjury or obstruction of justice), or when those crimes harm competition in the market.

2. Organization

The Antitrust Division has five criminal prosecuting offices: Chicago, New York, San Francisco, Washington Criminal I, and Washington Criminal II. Each office is supervised by a Chief, along with one or two Assistant Chiefs. Each office reports to the Director of Criminal Enforcement and the Deputy Assistant Attorney General for Criminal Enforcement.

---

1.   28 C.F.R. § 0.40(a).
2.   U.S. DEP'T OF JUSTICE, JUSTICE MANUAL § 7-1.000 (2018) [hereinafter *JUSTICE MANUAL*], *available at* https://www.justice.gov/jm/jm-7-1000-policy.

Each office has a designated geographic territory, as follows:[3]

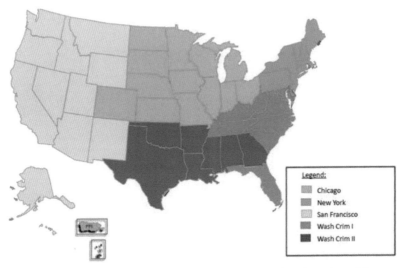

* District of Columbia is shared by Wash Crim I and Wash Crim II

The geographic territory of the offices typically determines where local and regional investigations are assigned. However, because the conduct and effects involved in international cartels usually are not limited to one locality, the assigned territories are not determinative in the assignment of international cartel investigations, which are assigned among the offices based on multiple factors, such as the location of the subjects, office capacity, and industry expertise.

B. Antitrust Division Investigative Tactics and Procedures

1. Sources of Investigations

There are many ways in which investigations may be initiated. Some of the more common sources of investigations are:

- Leniency Applicants: The Antitrust Division's highly successful leniency program incentivizes both corporate and individual cartel participants to self-report their conduct by applying for leniency.

---

3.   Image reprinted from U.S. DEP'T OF JUSTICE, ANTITRUST RESOURCE MANUAL (last updated Nov. 2017), *available at* https://www.justice.gov/jm/antitrust-resource-manual.

As described more fully below, leniency may result in immunity from prosecution for the reported conduct, as well as de-trebling any civil damages.[4]

- Employees and Former Employees: Employees may report their companies for antitrust violations. If the employee participated in the violation, the employee may apply for individual leniency that would cover that employee but not necessarily his employer. But there are also occasions where employees did not participate in the violation but are nevertheless aware of it. For example, a sales employee may be prohibited by superiors from competing for certain business, and may suspect that the prohibition is the result of an anticompetitive agreement. That employee may report his suspicions to the Antitrust Division.

- Customer Complaints: Customers may contact the Antitrust Division if they suspect that their suppliers are engaged in anticompetitive conduct. Government agencies and purchasing divisions of large companies may notice suspicious bidding and pricing patterns that suggest collusion, such as lockstep price increases or refusal to offer or negotiate pricing. The Antitrust Division works closely with many government agencies and inspector general offices to identify suspicious patterns or suspicious behavior among suppliers, such as similar arithmetic errors across purportedly independent bids or similar handwriting (for hard copy documents) or metadata (for electronic documents) on bids.

- Competitor Complaints: Cartels function best when there are a limited number of participants in an industry. Accordingly, cartel members may act in concert to try to keep out new entrants in the market. A company may contact the Antitrust Division if it has received an invitation to join a cartel, or if it suspects that its competitors are keeping it from entering the market in order to protect an existing cartel.

- News Reports: The Antitrust Division may initiate an investigation when staff learns of suspicious behavior from the news. This may occur when the media reports on lockstep price increases, or when the media reports on severe price increases or supply shortages for a particular good.

---

4.   *See* Antitrust Div., U.S. Dep't of Justice, Leniency Program (updated Feb. 2, 2017), *available at* https://www.justice.gov/atr/leniency-program.

- Civil Investigations and Litigation: The Antitrust Division has in the past initiated criminal investigations based on information initially learned in civil matters. For example, if witnesses or documents in a civil investigation, such as a merger investigation, indicate possible cartel activity, a criminal investigation may be opened. In addition, the Antitrust Division monitors private antitrust claims to determine whether an investigation is appropriate.

- Other Enforcement Agencies: The Antitrust Division routinely receives referrals from other agencies, such as the Federal Bureau of Investigation (FBI), U.S. Attorney's offices, inspector general's offices, and state attorney general's offices. In addition, the Antitrust Division has worked closely with foreign jurisdictions to develop their own cartel enforcement regimes. This investment of resources is paying off for the Antitrust Division, as dawn raids or other investigative activities in foreign jurisdictions have led to leniency applications in the United States.

Finally, the Antitrust Division maintains a complaint line that allows any member of the public to report—anonymously if necessary—anticompetitive conduct.[5] The Antitrust Division typically follows up on complaints received via the complaint line, and seeks information to corroborate the complaint. In situations where corroboration is obtained, the Antitrust Division may open an investigation.

2. *Investigation Procedures and Practices*

When a lead indicates a possible criminal violation of the Sherman Act, Antitrust Division staff will request approval to open an investigation. The staff does not begin a formal investigation until the front office determines that an investigation should proceed and resources should be committed.[6] Prior to the opening of an investigation, an attorney typically develops information from the complainant and from public or governmental sources.[7] The attorney then submits a recommendation to open an investigation to the Director of Criminal Enforcement and the

---

5.   *See* Antitrust Div., U.S. Dep't of Justice, Report Violations (updated Jan. 29, 2018), *available at* https://www.justice.gov/atr/report-violations.

6.   ANTITRUST DIV., U.S. DEP'T OF JUSTICE, ANTITRUST DIVISION MANUAL at III-6 (5th ed. 2012) (last updated Apr. 2018) [hereinafter *ANTITRUST DIV. MANUAL*], *available at* https://www.justice.gov/atr/file/761166/download.

7.   *Id.*

Deputy Assistant Attorney General for Criminal Enforcement, who will approve or deny the recommendation. Except under unusual circumstances that require prior approval, the attorney will not communicate, prior to the approval of an investigation, with individuals besides the complainant, including customers, potential victims or affected parties, or individuals and corporations that may be implicated in the alleged violation.[8]

As part of this process, the Antitrust Division and the Federal Trade Commission (FTC) clear proposed investigations with each other before they are opened.[9] The purpose of this clearance procedure is to ensure that both agencies are not investigating the same conduct and to avoid burdening the parties under investigation and potential witnesses with duplicative requests.

The Antitrust Division conducts two types of investigations based on the quality of the initial information or evidence: (1) preliminary investigations and (2) inquiries and grand jury investigations.

a. Preliminary Investigations or Inquiries (PIs)

When the Antitrust Division receives a report of suspicious activity that is not supported by a sufficient basis for a grand jury investigation, it may initiate a preliminary investigation, or "PI." Generally, the factors considered in authorizing a preliminary investigation include (1) whether there is reason to believe that an antitrust violation may have been committed; (2) what amount of commerce is affected; (3) if the investigation will duplicate or interfere with other efforts of the Antitrust Division, the FTC, a U.S. Attorney, or a state attorney general; and (4) whether allocating resources fits within the needs and priorities of the Antitrust Division.[10]

A preliminary investigation allows Antitrust Division staff to obtain evidence via voluntary means, but does not allow the staff to compel the production of evidence. At this stage, staff may conduct interviews with market participants, such as customers and competitors, to try to validate the information it has received, and may request documents from various parties. Staff also may obtain assistance from a federal law enforcement agency, such as the FBI, at this stage.

---

8.   *Id.* at III-6-7.
9.   *Id.* at III-10-11.
10.   *Id.* at III-7.

On occasion, a PI may involve compulsory process. When the victim is a government agency, that agency's inspector general may have subpoena authority. In this situation, the inspector general's office may issue a subpoena to the companies that are also the subjects of the preliminary investigation, and may work closely with the Antitrust Division during the course of the investigation. When conducting investigations with inspectors general, the Antitrust Division typically makes it known to the subjects that it is conducting a criminal investigation of the same conduct.

b.   Grand Jury Investigations

When the Antitrust Division has credible evidence of illegal activity, it will open a grand jury investigation. The Antitrust Division may open the grand jury investigation after conducting a PI, or may open the grand jury investigation without a PI if the initial information is sufficiently credible and involves a substantial federal interest. [11] Typically, information is found to be credible if it comes from a percipient witness or participant in the conduct, and is accompanied by some corroborating evidence. A substantial federal interest exists where the conduct has a not insignificant effect on interstate or import commerce, or where the federal government is the victim.

Grand jury authority allows the Antitrust Division to issue, through the grand jury, subpoenas compelling testimony (subpoena ad testificandum) or the production of documents (subpoena duces tecum). Subpoena recipients typically receive substantial time to comply with subpoenas, but in certain rare circumstances when there is a risk of flight or destruction or fabrication of evidence, subpoenas may require speedy compliance, usually within one day.[12] In addition, Division staff typically will agree to rolling productions of documents and will extend subpoena deadlines accordingly.

Subpoenas duces tecum also may be issued to individuals or to sole proprietors, who are treated as individuals. Although the contents of voluntarily created, preexisting documents are not protected by the Fifth Amendment privilege, [13] an individual may claim Fifth Amendment protection from the act of producing the documents if the production would implicitly concede the existence of the documents, the individual's

---

11.   *Id.* at III-12-13.
12.   *Id.* at III-85.
13.   Fisher v. United States, 425 U.S. 391, 409-10 (1976).

possession of the documents, or the authenticity of the documents.[14] However, a custodian of records may not claim a Fifth Amendment protection against production of documents.[15]

At the early stages of grand jury investigations, individuals typically are identified as witnesses or subjects. Subjects are individuals whose conduct is within the scope of the investigation.[16] In other words, these are individuals who have possible criminal exposure. These categories are not static—the determination is made based on the information available at a given time and may change as the evidence develops. Therefore, it would be advisable to confirm the status of an individual at various points during the investigation.

During the course of the investigation, the Antitrust Division may identify the targets of the investigation. Targets should be considered the likely defendants.[17] These individuals often are the most culpable participants of the antitrust conspiracy. The Antitrust Division typically issues target letters to individuals and companies where there is a likelihood of indictment.[18] The target letter typically is issued later in the investigation once sufficient evidence has been collected to believe that an indictment is likely.[19]

c.   Foreign-Located Evidence

Grand jury subpoenas in Division investigations typically do not call for the production of foreign-located evidence. However, courts have held that certain evidence may be obtained via grand jury subpoena even if it is located outside the country.[20] This is because a subpoena is executed with respect to a person rather than a place, and therefore operates domestically

---

14.   *Id.* at 410.
15.   Braswell v. United States, 487 U.S. 99, 108-10 (1988).
16.   JUSTICE MANUAL, *supra* note 2, § 9-11.151.
17.   *Id.*
18.   *Id.* § 9-11.153.
19.   *See id.*; *see also* U.S. DEP'T OF JUSTICE, CRIMINAL RESOURCE MANUAL § 160 (sample target letter), *available at* https://www.justice.gov/jm/criminal-resource-manual-160-sample-target-letter.
20.   *See In re* Grand Jury Proceedings Bank of N.S., 740 F.2d 817, (11th Cir. 1984); *see also In re* Marc Rich & Co., 707 F.2d 663, (2d Cir. 1983).

so long as that person is subject to the Courts' jurisdiction.[21] In addition, grand jury subpoenas may be served on U.S. citizens or residents located in a foreign country.

The Antitrust Division may also obtain foreign-located evidence through the assistance of foreign jurisdictions. The United States has Mutual Legal Assistance Treaties (MLATs) with many countries[22] that provide for mutual cooperation between the United States and the other country in criminal matters. The following assistance may be obtained under an MLAT:

- serving judicial process or other documents;
- locating or identifying persons or objects;
- taking testimony from a person (either by an Antitrust Division attorney or a foreign government official);
- examining objects and locations;
- requesting searches and seizures;
- obtaining documents or electronic records;

---

21.   *See* Marc Rich & Co. v. United States, 707 F.2d 663, 668-670(2d Cir), cert. denied, 463 U.S. 1215 (1083); 9A Charles Alan Wright and Arthur R. Miller, Federal Practice and Procedure § 2456, at 417 (3d ed. 2008).

22.   The United States has MLATs in force with the following countries: Antigua and Barbuda, Argentina, Australia, Austria, the Bahamas, Barbados, Belgium, Belize, Bermuda, Brazil, Canada, Cyprus, Czech Republic, Denmark, Dominica, Egypt, Estonia, Finland, France (including St. Martin, French Guiana, French Polynesia, Guadeloupe, and Martinique), Germany, Greece, Grenada, Hong Kong, Hungary, India, Ireland, Israel, Italy, Jamaica, Japan, Latvia, Liechtenstein, Lithuania, Luxembourg, Malaysia, Malta, Mexico, Morocco, the Kingdom of the Netherlands (including Aruba, Bonaire, Curacao, Saba, St. Eustatius, and St. Maarten), Nigeria, Panama, Philippines, Poland, Portugal, Romania, Russia, Slovak Republic, Slovenia, St. Lucia, St. Kitts and Nevis, St. Vincent and the Grenadines, South Africa, South Korea, Spain, Sweden, Switzerland, Thailand, Trinidad and Tobago, Turkey, Ukraine, the United Kingdom (including Anguilla, the British Virgin Islands, the Cayman Islands, the Isle of Man, Montserrat, and Turks and Caicos), Uruguay, and Venezuela. U.S. DEP'T OF STATE, 2015 INTERNATIONAL NARCOTICS CONTROL STRATEGY REPORT (INCSR), *available at* http://www.state.gov/j/inl/rls/nrcrpt/2015/vol2/239045.htm. The United States also entered an MLAT with the European Union that supplements existing MLATs and creates new mutual legal assistance relationships between the United States and every member of the EU. *Id.*

- identifying, tracing, and freezing or confiscating proceeds or instrumentalities of crime;
- transferring persons in custody;
- freezing assets; and
- any other assistance not prohibited by the foreign law and specified in the applicable MLAT.[23]

MLATs may only be issued by the DOJ; they are not available to private parties. Under an MLAT, foreign governments also may request the assistance of the DOJ to obtain evidence located in the United States and produce that evidence to the foreign government.[24] Disclosure of confidential grand jury material may be permitted in connection with an MLAT request.[25]

Importantly, MLAT requests may toll the statute of limitations applicable to the offense.[26] Upon application by the DOJ, the district court supervising the grand jury investigating the offense must toll the statute of limitations if it finds that an official request has been made for foreign-located evidence and that it reasonably appears, or reasonably appeared at the time the request was made, that such evidence is, or was, in the foreign country.[27] The tolling begins when the official request is made and expires when the foreign government has taken "final action."[28] The tolling is for a maximum of three years, or six months if "final action" is taken before the statute of limitations has expired.[29]

The Antitrust Division also may obtain foreign-located evidence through a letter rogatory (also known as a "letter of request"). Letters rogatory are formal requests for judicial assistance made by a court in one country to a court in another country. Letters rogatory typically are used to obtain evidence that may not be accessible to a foreign litigant or defendant without court authorization. Accordingly, unlike MLAT

---

23. *See* Virginia M. Kendall & T. Markus Funk, *The Role of Mutual Legal Assistance Treaties in Obtaining Foreign Evidence*, 40 ABA Litig. J. 59, 59-60 (2014).
24. 18 U.S.C. § 3512.
25. *See* Fed R. Crim. P. 6(e)(3)(A)(ii) (for outgoing requests); Fed. R. Crim. P. 6(e)(3)(E)(iii) (for incoming requests).
26. 18 U.S.C. § 3292.
27. *Id.* § 3292(a).
28. *Id.* § 3292(b).
29. *Id.* § 3292(c).

requests, which are issued by the DOJ, letters rogatory must be issued by a court.

Although they are used primarily by private parties who do not have access to the MLAT process, letters rogatory may be used by the Antitrust Division in the absence of an MLAT with the country where the evidence is located. Compliance with a letter rogatory request is left to the discretion of the receiving court, and is based on principles of international comity, rather than treaty obligation. The procedure for obtaining the requested evidence will be based on the legal procedures of the receiving court, and may not necessarily be consistent with U.S. legal procedures. As with MLAT requests, letters rogatory may be issued by foreign countries to obtain evidence located in the United States.[30]

Finally, the Antitrust Division may obtain foreign-located evidence through the cooperation of private parties. Specifically, leniency agreements and plea agreements contain cooperation obligations that require parties to produce foreign-located documents in the United States and to use their best efforts to assist with the voluntary appearance of employees in the United States.[31] Such efforts, however, may be limited by the privacy laws of the foreign jurisdictions where the evidence is located.

d.   Use of Covert Methods

Evidence obtained covertly often is the most powerful evidence obtained by the Antitrust Division. As a result, the Antitrust Division actively pursues covert investigative methods where possible. In some cases, the Antitrust Division will conduct a significant covert investigation lasting weeks or months before approaching investigative subjects with knock and talk interviews, grand jury subpoenas and/or search warrants.

These covert methods include consensual recordings by cooperators, applications for pen register/trap and trace devices,[32] grand jury subpoenas or search warrants for telephone or electronic communication records,[33]

---

30.   28 U.S.C. §§ 1696, 1781, 1782.

31.   *See* Antitrust Div., U.S. Dep't of Justice, Model Corporate Conditional Leniency Letter ¶ 2 (Jan. 26, 2017) [hereinafter *Corporate Conditional Leniency Letter*], *available at* https://www.justice.gov/atr/page/file/926531/download; Antitrust Div., U.S. Dep't of Justice, Model Annotated Corporate Plea Agreement ¶ 13 (Aug. 29, 2016), *available at* https://www.justice.gov/atr/file/889021/download.

32.   18 U.S.C. § 3123.

33.   *Id.* § 2703.

and wiretaps under Title III of The Omnibus Crime Control and Safe Streets Act of 1968 (Wiretap Act).[34] The Antitrust Division uses evidence obtained relying upon these methods to verify allegations, develop additional investigative options, and develop evidence for trial.

The Antitrust Division's use of these methods rarely becomes public, since most successful investigations end in guilty pleas. However, in the prosecution of several individuals involved in the lysine conspiracy in the 1990s, the Antitrust Division publicly displayed as trial exhibits several covert videos conducted with the assistance of a cooperator.[35] Those videos showed the conspirators meeting at secret locations such as hotel rooms, using trade expos as cover, and engaging in hardcore cartel conduct.[36] This footage was powerful evidence of guilt, and the trial defendants were convicted.[37] In addition, in the prosecution of individuals involved in the marine hose conspiracy in the 2000s, the Antitrust Division displayed at trial covert video of a conspiracy meeting that was conducted in the United States shortly before the conspirators were arrested and charged.[38] Importantly, the video was obtained pursuant to a wiretap authorization issued by a U.S. court.[39]

e.   Search Warrants

The destruction of evidence is always a concern in criminal investigations. Accordingly, the Antitrust Division often will obtain a warrant to search for and to seize evidence of the criminal activity. Unlike in other jurisdictions, in the United States a court order (a "search warrant") is required to allow entry onto private premises to search for and seize evidence of a crime.[40] A court will issue the search warrant only when there is probable cause to believe (1) that a crime has been committed, and (2) that evidence of the crime is located in the premises to be searched.[41]

The government obtains a search warrant by filing with the court an application for a search warrant. The application for the warrant is

---

34.   *Id.* § 2516.
35.   United States v. Andreas, 216 F.3d 645, 653 (7th Cir. 2000).
36.   *Id.* at 653-54.
37.   *Id.* at 649.
38.   Memo. of the United States on Admissibility of Video and Tr. at 1, United States v. Northcutt, 2008 WL 5714535 (S.D. Fla. Sept. 29, 2008).
39.   *Id.* at n.1.
40.   FED. R. CRIM. P. 41.
41.   *Id.* § 41(c) (listing additional items that may be seized).

accompanied by an affidavit—typically executed by a law enforcement agent—setting forth the probable cause for the search.[42] Oral testimony may be accepted in lieu of the affidavit if reasonable under the circumstances.[43] The warrant, the application, and the supporting affidavit typically are sealed by the court to maintain the confidentiality of the investigation. These documents typically are unsealed at a later time, and produced in discovery after an indictment is filed.

f.   "Knock and Talk" Interviews

When an investigation goes "overt"—in other words, becomes known to the subjects of the investigation—the government typically does so with "knock and talk" interviews (also known as "drop-in" interviews) coupled with grand jury subpoenas, and, where appropriate, the execution of search warrants. Knock and talk interviews are unscheduled interviews with the subjects of the investigation, and are typically done simultaneously with each other. The purpose of these interviews is to try to obtain admissions from subjects before they have an opportunity to communicate with each other and coordinate their statements.

The interviews typically are performed by two federal law enforcement agents, or one agent with one Antitrust Division attorney. The interviews are non-custodial and voluntary. Often, they are conducted at an individual's home or another location outside of the office so that the interview and the identity of the interviewee remain unknown to potential co-conspirators. At times, when an interviewee is cooperative, the agent(s) may propose that the interviewee voluntarily consent to allow a search of the premises or to conduct consensually recorded calls to other co-conspirators. Accordingly, the Antitrust Division views knock and talk interviews not only as opportunities to obtain statements from subjects, but also as opportunities to proactively develop additional evidence of the conspiracy.

g.   Closing Investigations

The Antitrust Division does not typically announce the closure of investigations. However, parties on occasion have requested and received letters confirming that they are no longer being investigated.[44]

---

42.   *Id.* § 41(d).
43.   *Id.*
44.   *See JUSTICE MANUAL, supra* note 2, § 9-11.155.

h. Civil Investigative Demands

Civil Investigative Demands (CIDs) are the Antitrust Division's "compulsory process tool of choice" in *civil* antitrust investigations of potential anti-competitive activity.[45] The Antitrust Division possesses authority to issue CIDs pursuant to the Antitrust Civil Process Act of 1976 (ACPA), which authorizes the Assistant Attorney General in charge of the Antitrust Division to serve a CID on "any person" where there is "reason to believe" that person "may be in possession, custody, or control of any documentary material, or may have any information, relevant to a civil antitrust investigation."[46]

The Antitrust Division may issue a CID under the "reason to believe" standard even in the absence of "probable cause" to believe that any particular violation within the scope of its authority has occurred.[47] Between 2005 and 2014, the Antitrust Division issued 1,354 CIDs in non-merger investigations.[48]

(1) Decision to Issue a CID

Pursuant to the Antitrust Division's practice, a CID may be issued only after a section or field office has been authorized to conduct a preliminary investigation into a possible civil antitrust violation.[49] During the preliminary investigation stage, staff makes the initial determination as to whether to conduct the rest of the investigation as a civil CID investigation or a criminal grand jury investigation, a decision which is guided by the suspected conduct. "In general, current Antitrust Division policy is to proceed by criminal investigation and prosecution in cases involving horizontal, per se unlawful agreements such as price-fixing, bid rigging, and customer and territorial allocations," so-called "hardcore" antitrust violations.[50]; and "civil prosecution is used with respect to other suspected antitrust violations, including those that require analysis under the rule of

---

45.   *ANTITRUST DIV. MANUAL, supra* note 6, at III-45.
46.   15 U.S.C. § 1312(a).
47.   *ANTITRUST DIV. MANUAL, supra* note 6, at III-45. For a thorough discussion on the legislative history, the broad reach of the ACPA, and the Antitrust Division's practice, *see* ABA SECTION OF ANTITRUST LAW, DOJ CIVIL ANTITRUST PRACTICE AND PROCEDURE MANUAL 61-89 (2012).
48.   Antitrust Div., U.S. Dep't of Justice, Workload Statistics FY 2005-2014, at 3-4, *available at* https://www.justice.gov/atr/file/630706/download.
49.   *ANTITRUST DIV. MANUAL, supra* note 6, at III-58.
50.   *Id.* at III-12.

reason as well as some offenses that historically have been labeled 'per se' by the courts."[51] Antitrust Division policy indicates that civil, rather than criminal, investigation may be appropriate even where the suspected conduct may appear to be a per se or hardcore violation of law in cases where:

- the case law is unsettled or uncertain;
- there are truly novel issues of law or fact presented;
- confusion reasonably may have been caused by past prosecutorial decisions; or
- there is clear evidence that the subjects of the investigation were not aware of, or did not appreciate, the consequences of their action.[52]

In contrast, evidence of serious cartel activity, such as "clandestine activity, concealment, and clear knowledge on the part of the perpetrators of the wrongful nature of their behavior" would argue in favor of criminal prosecution.[53] If the CID investigation uncovers evidence that establishes that a criminal prosecution is warranted, a grand jury investigation would then be pursued and the Antitrust Division would cease further investigation by CID.[54]

(2) Scope of CID Requests

CIDs may require the recipient to produce documentary material, answer written interrogatories, give oral testimony, produce products of discovery from other matters, or to furnish any combination thereof.[55] The

51.   *ANTITRUST DIV. MANUAL, supra* note 6, at III-12.
52.   *Id.*
53.   R. Hewitt Pate, Assistant Att'y Gen., Antitrust Div., U.S. Dep't of Justice, Vigorous and Principled Antitrust Enforcement: Priorities and Goals, Address Before the Antitrust Section of the American Bar Association Annual Meeting (Aug. 12, 2003), *available at* https://www.justice.gov/atr/speech/vigorous-and-principled-antitrust-enforcement-priorities-and-goals.
54.   *ANTITRUST DIV. MANUAL, supra* note 6, at III-46. Materials and information gathered through the CID may still be used in a subsequent criminal prosecution by the Antitrust Division and are not restricted to the pending investigation. *See* 15 U.S.C. § 1313(d)(1); 28 C.F.R. §§ 49.1-49.4; *ANTITRUST DIV. MANUAL, supra* note 6, at III-61-63.
55.   15 U.S.C. § 1312(a).

ACPA provides that the scope of any request may be comparable to and not exceed the standards applicable to grand jury subpoenas and discovery requests under the Federal Rules of Civil Procedure.[56] All CIDs are required to identify the "conduct constituting the alleged antitrust violation" and the applicable statute that is potentially being violated.[57]

C. Antitrust Division Leniency Policies

One of the most effective generators of cartel investigations and prosecutions is the Antitrust Division's leniency program, first implemented in 1978.[58] Substantial revisions introduced through the Corporate Leniency Policy in 1993 and Leniency Policy for Individuals in 1994 resulted in the current program.[59] Today, if the conditions of the Antitrust Division's leniency program are met, a corporation may avoid a criminal conviction or imposition of fines and an individual may avoid a criminal conviction, a prison term, or the imposition of fines by being the *first* to confess to participation in a criminal antitrust cartel.[60] Even those that cannot take full advantage of the leniency program because they are not the first to confess a violation may still benefit from significantly reduced penalties under certain conditions.

These incentives, combined with the increased certainty of treatment that the policy affords, destabilize cartels by increasing the likelihood that one of its members will confess to the Antitrust Division in order to win the race to be first. In 2011, the Antitrust Division calculated that "[p]rosecutions assisted by leniency applicants accounted for over 90 percent of the total commerce affected by all the cartels prosecuted by the Division since 1999."[61]

---

56. 15 U.S.C. § 1312(c).
57. 15 U.S.C. § 1312(b).
58. *See* Antitrust Div., US. Dep't of Justice, Leniency Program, *available at* https://www.justice.gov/atr/leniency-program; Antitrust Div., U.S. Dep't of Justice, Frequently Asked Questions About the Antitrust Division's Leniency Program and Model Leniency Letters (updated Jan. 26, 2017) [hereinafter *Leniency Program FAQs*], *available at* https://www.justice.gov/atr/page/file/926521/download.
59. *Leniency Program FAQs*, *supra* note 58, at 1 n.1.
60. *Id.* at 1.
61. Gregory J. Werden, Recidivism Eliminated: Cartel Enforcement in the United States Since 1999, Speech Before the Georgetown Global Antitrust Enforcement Symposium (Sept. 22, 2011), *available at* https://www.justice.gov/atr/file/518331/download.

1. Corporate Leniency Policy

The Antitrust Division's policy is to criminally prosecute when there is evidence of hardcore cartel activity.[62] Under the Corporate Leniency Policy, however, a corporation can avoid being criminally charged and fined by being the first to confess involvement in criminal antitrust cartel activity, fully cooperating with the Antitrust Division's investigation of the reported conduct, and meeting other specified conditions.[63] Leniency, also referred to as "amnesty," is only available to the first corporate confessor.[64] Subsequent corporate cooperators are not eligible for leniency, though they may be able to obtain some favorable treatment through a sentencing recommendation or through the Antitrust Division's "Leniency Plus" policy.[65] Any leniency agreement only binds the Antitrust Division and does not bind other federal or state prosecutors, though practice indicates that prosecution by another agency after a successful leniency application is unlikely.[66] Nevertheless, leniency applicants with exposure for both antitrust and non-antitrust crimes should report all crimes to the relevant prosecuting agencies.[67] The Leniency Program does not protect applicants from criminal prosecution by other prosecuting agencies for offenses other than Sherman Act violations.[68] In addition, a leniency application does not discharge prior reporting obligations to other prosecuting agencies, nor does it insulate the leniency applicant from the consequences of violating earlier agreements not to commit crimes.[69]

---

62. *See* R. Hewitt Pate, Assistant Att'y Gen., Antitrust Div., U.S. Dep't of Justice, Vigorous and Principled Antitrust Enforcement: Priorities and Goals, Address Before the Antitrust Section of the American Bar Association Annual Meeting (Aug. 12, 2003), *available at* https://www.justice.gov/atr/speech/vigorous-and-principled-antitrust-enforcement-priorities-and-goals.

63. Antitrust Div., U.S. Dep't of Justice, Corporate Leniency Policy (Aug. 10, 1993) [hereinafter *Corporate Leniency Policy*], *available at* https://www.justice.gov/atr/file/810281/download; *see* ANTITRUST DIV. MANUAL, *supra* note 6, at III-95-96.

64. *Leniency Program FAQs, supra* note 58, at 5; ANTITRUST DIV. MANUAL, *supra* note 6, at III-96.

65. *See* ANTITRUST DIV. MANUAL, *supra* note 6 at III-102.

66. *Leniency Program FAQs, supra* note 58, at 7-8.

67. *Id.* at 7.

68. *Id.*

69. *Id.*

a. Type A and Type B Leniency

The Corporate Leniency Policy provides two avenues for leniency, depending on whether or not the Antitrust Division initiated an investigation prior to receipt of a leniency request. If the Antitrust Division has not yet begun an investigation, the first corporate confessor will be granted "Type A" leniency if it meets the following six conditions:

- at the time the corporation comes forward to report the illegal activity, the Antitrust Division has not received information about the illegal activity being reported from any other source;
- the corporation, upon its discovery of the illegal activity being reported, takes prompt and effective action to terminate its part in the activity;
- the corporation reports the wrongdoing with candor and completeness and provides full, continuing, and complete cooperation to the Antitrust Division throughout the investigation;
- the confession of wrongdoing is truly a corporate act, as opposed to isolated confessions of individual executives or officials;
- where possible, the corporation makes restitution to injured parties;[70] and
- the corporation did not coerce another party to participate in the illegal activity and clearly was not the leader in, or originator of, the activity.[71]

If the Antitrust Division is already aware of illegal activity, a corporation will be granted "Type B" leniency if the following seven conditions are met:

- the corporation is the first one to come forward and qualify for leniency with respect to the illegal activity being reported;
- the Antitrust Division, at the time the corporation comes in, does not yet have evidence against the company that is likely to result in a sustainable conviction;

---

70. The restitution requirement is discussed in the *Leniency Program FAQs*, *supra* note 58, at 18-19.
71. *Corporate Leniency Policy*, *supra* note 63, at 1-2; *see* ANTITRUST DIV. MANUAL, *supra* note 6, at III-97.

- the corporation, upon its discovery of the illegal activity being reported, takes prompt and effective action to terminate its part in the activity;
- the corporation reports the wrongdoing with candor and completeness and provides full, continuing, and complete cooperation that advances the Antitrust Division in its investigation;
- the confession of wrongdoing is truly a corporate act, as opposed to isolated confessions of individual executives or officials;
- where possible, the corporation makes restitution to injured parties; and
- the Antitrust Division determines that granting leniency would not be unfair to others, considering the nature of the illegal activity, the confessing corporation's role in it, and when the corporation comes forward.[72]

The burden imposed by the last condition for Type B leniency depends on how far along the Antitrust Division's investigation has progressed prior to an applicant coming forward. Antitrust Division policy provides that the "burden will increase the closer the Division comes to having evidence that is likely to result in a sustainable conviction."[73] The Antitrust Division will not grant leniency under either Type A or Type B if the corporate applicant coerced another party to participate in the cartel or if it was the leader or cartel originator.[74] Disqualification under this policy only applies where there is a single ringleader of a conspiracy; where there are two ringleaders, either may be eligible for leniency if it is the first in the door.[75]

b.   Corporate Directors, Officers, and Employees

If a corporation qualifies for Type A leniency, "all [current] directors, officers, and employees of the corporation who admit their involvement in the illegal antitrust activity as part of the corporate confession will also

---

72.   *Corporate Leniency Policy, supra* note 63, at 2-3; *see* ANTITRUST DIV. MANUAL, *supra* note 6, at III-97-98.
73.   *Corporate Leniency Policy, supra* note 63, at 3; *see* ANTITRUST DIV. MANUAL, *supra* note 6, at III-98.
74.   *Leniency Program FAQs, supra* note 58, at 15-16; *see Corporate Conditional Leniency Letter, supra* note 31, at 2.
75.   *Leniency Program FAQs, supra* note 58, at 16.

receive leniency if they admit their wrongdoing with candor and completeness and continue to assist the Division throughout the investigation." [76] "Current" is defined as of the time the conditional leniency letter is signed by the Antitrust Division. [77]

If a corporation only qualifies for Type B leniency, or fails to qualify for leniency, the Corporate Leniency Policy provides that the "directors, officers, and employees who come forward with the corporation will be considered for immunity from criminal prosecution on the same basis as if they had approached the Division individually."[78] Notwithstanding this language, in practice "the Division ordinarily provides leniency to all qualifying current employees of Type B applicants in the same manner it does for Type A applicants."[79] The Antitrust Division nevertheless may exercise its discretion to exclude from the protections that the conditional leniency letter offers those current directors, officers, and employees who are determined to be highly culpable.[80]

Notably, former employees are not automatically covered under a corporation's leniency application.[81] To the contrary, in 2017 the Antitrust Division issued updated FAQs making clear that "[f]ormer directors, officers, and employees are presumptively excluded from any grant of corporate leniency."[82] However, the FAQs provided that at "the Division's sole discretion, specific, named former directors, officers, or employees may receive nonprosecution protection under a corporate conditional leniency letter or by a separate nonprosecution agreement."[83] Former employees may be covered at the Antitrust Division's discretion if they are providing substantial, non-cumulative cooperation or if their cooperation is necessary to perfect the corporation's leniency application.[84]

The Model Corporate Conditional Leniency Letter specifies a number of conditions an individual must satisfy to meet the Antitrust Division's requirement of truthful cooperation, including: (1) producing all requested documents and records; (2) making himself or herself available for

---

76. *Antitrust Div. Manual*, *supra* note 6, at III-98.
77. *Leniency Program FAQs*, *supra* note 58, at 21.
78. *Corporate Leniency Policy*, *supra* note 63, at 4; *see Antitrust Div. Manual*, *supra* note 6, at III-98.
79. *Antitrust Div. Manual*, *supra* note 6, at III-98.
80. *Leniency Program FAQs*, *supra* note 58, at 21.
81. *Id.* at 22.
82. *Id.*
83. *Id.*
84. *Id.*

interviews; (3) truthfully responding to all investigation inquiries without withholding any information; (4) voluntarily providing materials relevant to the investigation that were not requested; and (5) truthfully testifying at trial or a grand jury proceeding if called upon.[85]

The Antitrust Division reserves the right to decline to grant leniency or revoke conditional leniency for a corporate director, officer, or employee if the Antitrust Division determines that (1) the individual failed to comply fully with his or her obligations under the letter; (2) the individual caused the corporate leniency applicant to be ineligible for leniency for failure to take prompt corrective action upon discovery of anticompetitive activity, by coercing another to participate in anticompetitive activity, or by being the leader or organizer of the cartel; (3) the individual continued to participate in the cartel activity after being notified to stop by the corporation; or (4) the individual attempted to obstruct an investigation of the reported cartel activity at any time, even prior to the decision to report the corporation's conduct to the Antitrust Division.[86] Generally, before a final decision is made to revoke an individual's conditional leniency, the Antitrust Division will provide counsel an opportunity to meet and discuss the proposed revocation.[87]

c.   Procedure for a Leniency Application

If a corporation discovers information concerning possible criminal cartel activity and wishes to be first to apply for leniency, a leniency application may be initiated prior to completing an internal investigation or obtaining sufficient information to determine that the corporation has committed a criminal violation, the admission of which is ultimately required to obtain leniency. The Antitrust Division encourages a race to early reporting through its "marker" system, which allows an applicant to provide limited information and hold its place in line (a "marker") while it investigates and perfects a leniency application.[88] A leniency application and marker request is initiated by calling the Antitrust Division's Director or Deputy Assistant Attorney General for Criminal Enforcement and reporting the possible criminal violation.[89]

---

85.   *Corporate Conditional Leniency Letter, supra* note 31, at 5-7.
86.   *Id.* at 7; *see Leniency Program FAQs, supra* note 58, at 20-21.
87.   *Corporate Conditional Leniency Letter, supra* note 31, at 7; *e, supra* note 58, at 20-21.
88.   *Leniency Program FAQs, supra* note 58, at 2.
89.   *Id.* at 2. Leniency applications may be made to the Director or Deputy Assistant Attorney General for Criminal Enforcement at (202) 514-3543.

To obtain a marker, counsel must: (1) report that he or she has uncovered some information or evidence indicating that his or her client has engaged in a criminal antitrust violation; (2) disclose the general nature of the conduct discovered; (3) identify the industry, product, or service involved in terms that are specific enough to allow the Antitrust Division to determine whether leniency is still available and to protect the marker for the applicant; and (4) identify the client.[90] Although the bar for obtaining a marker is low, "it is not enough for counsel to state merely that the client has received a grand jury subpoena or has been searched during a Division investigation and that counsel wants a marker to investigate whether the client has committed a criminal antitrust violation."[91] However, it is possible in limited circumstances for counsel to obtain a short-term anonymous marker without identifying the client.[92]

Following issuance of a marker, an applicant will typically be given rolling thirty-day periods to conduct its investigation and proffer Findings to the Antitrust Division. There is no uniform proffer for leniency; the requirements will depend on the facts of the investigation. But through the course of proffered information, the applicant must present evidence sufficient to support an admission to participation in a criminal antitrust violation.[93] Proffers are typically presented orally because written submissions are unlikely to be privileged in a future private damages action.

If an applicant can properly admit to a criminal antitrust violation and meets the conditions for leniency, the Assistant Attorney General will issue the applicant a conditional leniency letter. The conditional letter provides upfront assurances that the corporation will receive non-prosecution protection at the conclusion of the cartel investigation if it fulfills the requirements of the leniency program outlined in the letter.[94] A model letter is available on the Antitrust Division's website.[95] Once the requirements set out in the conditional leniency letter are met, the Antitrust Division will issue a final leniency letter notifying the corporation that it has been granted unconditional leniency. Typically, the final leniency letter will not be issued until the close of the investigation and after any prosecution of co-conspirators.[96]

---

90. *Id.* at 3.
91. *Id.*
92. *Id.* at 3 n.6.
93. *Id.* at 6.
94. *Id.* at 24-25.
95. *Corporate Conditional Leniency Letter, supra* note 31, at 5.
96. *Leniency Program FAQs, supra* note 58, at 24.

d.   Additional Leniency Policies

Although Type A and Type B leniency are only available to the first qualifying corporation, later applicants who confess early to criminal cartel activity and cooperate with the Antitrust Division may obtain favorable treatment for their company or executives through plea agreement negotiations.[97] For example, the Antitrust Division may file a downward departure motion for substantial assistance,[98] or recommend a lesser sentence or fine[99]; the earlier the plea, the greater the likelihood that the defendant will be able to obtain an acceptance of responsibility reduction in calculating the applicable range under the *U.S. Sentencing Guidelines*.[100]

While a corporation that approaches the Antitrust Division early in an investigation is in the best position to provide substantial assistance, being the first mover is not enough to earn significant sentencing credit. The Antitrust Division will evaluate the nature, extent, timing, and value of cooperation provided by each cooperating company.[101] If one company begins to cooperate later than another but provides greater cooperation, the Antitrust Division has stated that it may recommend a larger substantial assistance departure for that later company.[102]

If the applicant has knowledge of a different cartel it also may be eligible for favorable treatment under the Antitrust Division's Leniency Plus policy. In any event, counsel for any applicant involved in multiple cartels should also be aware of the repercussions of failing to disclose all potential cartel activity under the Antitrust Division's Penalty Plus policy.

---

97.   *See* ABA SECTION OF ANTITRUST LAW, CRIMINAL ANTITRUST LITIGATION HANDBOOK 74-83 (2006) for a thorough discussion on plea agreement negotiations with the Antitrust Division.

98.   U.S. SENTENCING COMM'N, U.S. SENTENCING GUIDELINES MANUAL §§ 5K1.1, 8C4.1 (2016) [hereinafter *SENTENCING GUIDELINES*].

99.   *Id.* § 1B1.8.

100. *Id.* §§ 3E1.1, 8C2.5(g)(2)-(3).

101. Brent Snyder, Deputy Assistant Att'y General, Antitrust Div., U.S. Dep't of Justice, Individual Accountability for Antitrust Crimes, Remarks as Prepared for the Yale School of Management Global Antitrust Enforcement Conference (Feb. 19, 2016), *available at* https://www.justice.gov/opa/file/826721/download.

102. *Id.*

(1) Leniency Plus

Leniency Plus is available to leniency applicants who lost the race to confess anticompetitive activity related to one cartel but who self-report other information about a second cartel.[103] Multiple cartel situations are common. Frequently, over half the international cartel investigations pending before a grand jury at a given time are attributed to information obtained during an investigation of a separate market.[104]

Leniency Plus offers Type A or Type B leniency related to a corporation's disclosure of the second cartel and a discount at sentencing related to disclosure concerning the first.[105] The sentencing reduction, or "rewards," available to an Leniency Plus applicant are not uniform. They may typically include a reduction in the scope of affected commerce used to calculate a company's *Sentencing Guidelines* fine range, a substantial cooperation discount, a low starting point within the *Sentencing Guidelines* for application of a cooperation discount, or favorable treatment for company executives.[106] The size of the Leniency Plus

103.   Scott D. Hammond, Deputy Assistant Att'y Gen., Antitrust Div., U.S. Dep't of Justice, When Calculating The Costs And Benefits Of Applying For Corporate Amnesty, How Do You Put A Price Tag On An Individual's Freedom?, Speech Before the American Bar Association Criminal Justice Section's Fifteenth Annual National Institute on White Collar Crime (Mar. 8, 2001) [hereinafter Hammond, Price Tag], *available at* https://www.justice.gov/atr/speech/when-calculating-costs-and-benefits-applying-corporate-amnesty-how-do-you-put-price-tag.

104.   *See id.*; Scott D. Hammond, Deputy Assistant Att'y Gen., Antitrust Div., U.S. Dep't of Justice, An Overview Of Recent Developments In The Antitrust Division's Criminal Enforcement Program, Speech Before the American Bar Association Midwinter Leadership Meeting (Jan. 10, 2005), *available at* https://www.justice.gov/atr/speech/overview-recent-developments-antitrust-divisions-criminal-enforcement-program.

105.   In Amnesty Plus cases, the Division will issue a "Dual Investigations" Conditional Leniency Letter that expressly excludes the non-leniency conduct from letter. *See* Antitrust Div., U.S. Dep't of Justice, Model Dual Investigations Leniency Letter (Jan. 26, 2017), *available at* https://www.justice.gov/atr/page/file/926516/download.

106.   *See* Scott D. Hammond, Deputy Assistant Att'y Gen., Antitrust Div., U.S. Dep't of Justice, Measuring the Value of Second-In Cooperation in Corporate Plea Negotiations, Speech Before the American Bar Association Antitrust Section 2006 Spring Meeting (Mar. 29, 2006) [hereinafter Hammond, Value of Second-In Cooperation], *available at* https://www.justice.gov/atr/file/518436/download.

reduction varies and depends on the Antitrust Division's consideration of the following factors (1) the strength of the evidence supplied by the applicant; (2) the potential significance of the newly reported violation in terms of geographic scope and number of individuals and entities involved; and (3) the likelihood that the Antitrust Division would have discovered the second cartel absent self-reporting.[107] Among these factors, the first two are given the most weight.[108] On the high end of the reduction scale, one Leniency Plus applicant received a 59 percent reduction from the minimum criminal fine it would have otherwise received, which reflected a $70 million reduction in criminal penalties.[109]

Given the frequency with which multiple cartel situations arise, Antitrust Division staff investigating a cartel routinely ask an "omnibus question" at the conclusion of a witness interview, inquiring whether the witness has information about any additional cartel activity.[110] Disclosing additional cartel activity may result in favorable treatment; at the same time, the failure to disclose information about further cartel activity may result in significant negative repercussions under the Antitrust Division's Penalty Plus policy.[111]

(2) Penalty Plus

Under the Penalty Plus policy, a company that knows of and elects not to self-report activity in a second cartel may face harsh consequences from the Antitrust Division. Under the policy, the Antitrust Division will seek sentencing enhancements when a company is convicted of an antitrust offense that it failed to report when resolving other cartel conduct.

The severity of the Penalty Plus enhancement the Antitrust Division seeks depends on the reason the company failed to report the additional antitrust offense.[112] If a company conducts an internal investigation and fails to discover the additional offense but, after the Antitrust Division discovers that conduct, agrees to plead guilty and cooperate with respect to that offense, the Antitrust Division would begin any downward adjustment for that cooperation from a higher point in the *Sentencing Guidelines* range for the additional offense.[113] If a company made no

---

107.   *Leniency Program FAQs, supra* note 58, at 10.
108.   *Id.*
109.   Hammond, Value of Second-In Cooperation, *supra* note 106.
110.   *ANTITRUST DIV. MANUAL, supra* note 6, at III-102.
111.   Hammond, Price Tag, *supra* note 103.
112.   *Leniency Program FAQs, supra* note 58, at 11.
113.   *Id.*

meaningful effort to conduct an internal investigation or was aware of the additional conduct but elected not to report it, the Antitrust Division will seek a more severe Penalty Plus enhancement and will likely recommend that the district court impose probation on the company.[114]

In the most egregious cases, the Antitrust Division will recommend that the district court consider the company's failure to report the additional offense as an aggravating sentencing factor which warrants a fine at the top end of the *Sentencing Guidelines* range or an upward departure and a sentence above the *Sentencing Guidelines* range. In such cases, the Antitrust Division may also recommend that the district court appoint an external monitor to ensure that the company develops an appropriate culture of corporate compliance.[115]

(3) *Affirmative Leniency*

On rare occasions, the Antitrust Division will employ an affirmative leniency strategy in situations where the Antitrust Division reasonably suspects cartel activity before anyone self-reports. In this situation, the Antitrust Division may elect to approach a suspect company and offer leniency in exchange for cooperation.[116] The Antitrust Division's overture gives the company a head start in the leniency race. The affirmative leniency strategy is employed with caution for fear of tipping off a cartel about an investigation. Typically, the Antitrust Division will only approach a company with an affirmative leniency offer if that company previously proved trustworthy through another leniency application or other cooperation.[117]

e. Benefits

(1) *De-trebled Damages for Leniency Applicants*

With the goal of encouraging cooperation with the Antitrust Division and to provide cooperating parties with more predictability about what that cooperation will entail, Congress passed the Antitrust Criminal Penalty Enhancement and Reform Act (ACPERA) in 2004.[118] Pursuant to

---

114. *Id.*
115. *Id.*
116. Hammond, Value of Second-In Cooperation, *supra* note 106.
117. *Id.*
118. The statute has been extended through 2020. Pub. L. 111-190, § 1, 124 Stat. 1275, 1275.

ACPERA, a leniency applicant who provides "satisfactory cooperation" to civil plaintiffs can avoid the treble damages and joint and several liability provisions of the Sherman Act in any follow-on civil action. In such circumstances, a leniency applicant is liable only for actual damages from its own affected sales.

ACPERA fails to explain, however, exactly what constitutes "satisfactory cooperation." The statute states only that satisfactory cooperation "shall include . . . a full account to the claimant of all facts known to the applicant . . . that are potentially relevant to the civil action," as well as "all documents or other items potentially relevant."[119] Further, the applicant must also make best efforts to make individual employees available for "interviews, depositions or testimony." Under the 2010 amendments to ACPERA, the court must now also consider the "timeliness" of the applicant's cooperation in determining whether the limits to civil liability shall apply.

(2) Leniency Applicant Confidentiality Policy

Though eventually the leniency applicant's identity is likely to be revealed in the course of civil litigation, the Antitrust Division "holds the identity of leniency applicants and the information they provide in strict confidence, much like the treatment afforded to confidential informants."[120] The Antitrust Division will only identify the applicant (1) if the applicant reveals its leniency status; (2) after reaching agreement with the applicant to make the disclosure; or (3) if they are ordered by a court to do so.[121]

A leniency applicant also has an obligation to maintain the confidentiality of its application and the Antitrust Division's investigation. There is a risk of obstruction resulting from unauthorized disclosures.[122] As such, applicants are encouraged to discuss to whom, and how and when, information may be shared about their application.

f.   Drawbacks

While the benefits of being the leniency applicant discussed above can be substantial, there are potential drawbacks as well. The most obvious potential draw-back is the danger of exposing the applicant to an

119.   Pub. L. 108-237, § 213(b), 118 Stat. 661, 666; 15 USC § 1 note.
120.   *Leniency Program FAQs, supra* note 58, at 28.
121.   *Id.*
122.   *Id.* at 15.

investigation that may otherwise never occur, with the additional risk and legal costs that come with such a step. This includes the threat of investigations being launched by enforcement authorities outside of the United States and related civil litigation.

There are also risks that arise from the ambiguity of what "substantial cooperation" entails, both in terms of the timing of the cooperation and the substance of the cooperation. This is particularly true in the context of a relationship between adverse parties in the civil litigation context, where the evaluation of whether cooperation was sufficient cannot be done until it is too late for the leniency applicant to change course. The result is that leniency applicants are often incentivized to engage in early settlements with civil plaintiffs to mitigate the uncertainty created by the ambiguity.

2. Leniency Policy for Individuals

Leniency is also available to individuals who participated in cartel activity. In 1994, the Antitrust Division instituted its Individual Leniency Policy, so that individual cartel participants may earn leniency on their own accord even if their employer does not do so. Individual leniency is not available if the individual's employer has applied for corporate leniency; the individual's eligibility for leniency in that case will be based on his employer's leniency application under the Corporate Leniency Policy. [123] This individual option may be most valuable to former employees who participated in cartel activity, because former employees are not automatically covered under corporate leniency agreements.

The requirements of the Individual Leniency Policy largely track Part A of the Corporate Leniency Policy:

- At the time the individual comes forward to report the activity, the Antitrust Division has not received information about the activity being reported from any other source.
- The individual reports the wrongdoing with candor and completeness and provides full, continuing, and complete cooperation to the Antitrust Division throughout the investigation.

---

123. *Leniency Program FAQs, supra* note 58, at 22.

- The individual did not coerce another party to participate in the activity and clearly was not the leader in, or the originator of, the activity.[124]

As with the Corporate Leniency Policy, an individual will be ineligible for leniency based on a leadership role if he or she is clearly the single leader or organizer of the conduct.[125] Where a conspiracy has multiple leaders or organizers, any of those individuals may qualify for leniency.[126] Unlike Part B of the Corporate Leniency Policy, however, there is no leniency policy for individuals after an investigation has begun. Moreover, no current or former directors, officers, or employees, of a company that has applied for leniency under the Corporate Leniency Policy may be considered for leniency under the Individual Leniency Policy. [127] Nevertheless, on a case-by-case basis, the Antitrust Division will consider providing statutory or informal immunity to individuals who self-report and cooperate but are otherwise ineligible for individual leniency.[128]

a.   "Carve-Outs" and Individual Liability

Individual cartel participants who are unable to obtain leniency either individually or through their employer potentially are subject to prosecution. The Antitrust Division views imprisonment as the most effective way to deter and punish cartel activity, and will seek to prosecute the most culpable individual participants who are not covered by leniency. [129] Although corporate prosecutions typically receive greater

---

124.   Antitrust Div., U.S. Dep't of Justice, Leniency Policy for Individuals, *available at* https://www.justice.gov/atr/individual-leniency-policy; Antitrust Div., U.S. Dep't of Justice, Model Individual Conditional Leniency Letter, *available at* https://www.justice.gov/atr/page/file/926526/download.
125.   *Leniency Program FAQs, supra* note 58, at 23-24.
126.   *Id.*
127.   *Id.* at 22.
128.   *Id.* at 23.
129.   Scott D. Hammond, Deputy Assistant Att'y Gen., Antitrust Div., U.S. Dep't of Justice, Recent Developments, Trends, and Milestones in the Antitrust Division's Criminal Enforcement Program, Speech Before the American Bar Association Section of Antitrust Law's 2008 Annual Spring Meeting (Mar. 26, 2008), *available at* http://www.justice.gov/atr/speech/recent-developments-trends-and-milestones-antitrust-divisions-criminal-enforcement.

publicity, in each of the last ten years, the Antitrust Division has filed more cases against individuals than against companies.[130] Moreover, the average prison time imposed on individuals has increased steadily over the years, and in the last five-year period has averaged 24 months.[131]

Corporations who lose the leniency race but cooperate with the investigation and plead guilty to the offense will receive the benefit of many of its employees being covered by the non-prosecution provision of the corporate plea agreement. The most culpable employees in these companies are not covered by this provision; they are "carved out" of the plea agreement. In the past, the carveouts were named in the publicly filed plea agreement. This practice was subject to complaints from defense counsel who argued that the reputations of carveouts were being unnecessarily damaged.[132]

In 2013, the Antitrust Division changed its practice, and has since filed the names of the carveouts in a sealed attachment to the plea agreement.[133] The Antitrust Division also limits carveouts to potential targets of the investigation,[134] and makes carveout determinations on a case-by-case basis depending on the culpability and prosecutability of each individual,[135] rather than basing carveout decisions in part on the company's self-reporting and cooperation.[136] In practice, this means that the number of carveouts in each corporate plea agreement will be more case-specific than in the past.

---

130. *See* Antitrust Div., U.S. Dep't of Justice, Criminal Enforcement Trends Charts Through Fiscal Year 2017 (updated Mar. 12, 2018), *available at* https://www.justice.gov/atr/criminal-enforcement-fine-and-jail-charts.

131. *See id.*

132. *See, e.g.*, A. Paul Victor et al., *The Policy Case For Eliminating The Public Identification Of Carve-Outs In Antitrust Plea Agreements*, 104 ANTITRUST & TRADE REG. REP. 360 (BNA) (Mar. 15, 2013).

133. Snyder, Individual Accountability for Antitrust Crimes, *supra* note 101.

134. Bill Baer, Prosecuting Antitrust Crimes, Remarks before Georgetown University Law Center Global Antitrust Enforcement Symposium (Sept. 10, 2014), *available at* https://www.justice.gov/atr/file/517741/download.

135. JUSTICE MANUAL, *supra* note 2, § 9-27.220.

136. Snyder, Individual Accountability for Antitrust Crimes, *supra* note 101, at 14 ("The decision about who [sic] to carve out and ultimately prosecute is not the product of a formula derived from the timing of a corporate offender's decision to accept responsibility and cooperate.").

b.	Recent DOJ Policies on Individual Liability

In 2015, Deputy Attorney General Sally Yates issued a policy memorandum (the Yates Memo) to all DOJ attorneys to increase individual accountability in corporate criminal cases.[137] The memorandum explicitly excludes the Corporate Leniency Policy from its mandate that no corporate resolution provide protection for individuals, and in practice the Antitrust Division's carve-in policy for many corporate employees also has survived.[138] Nevertheless, even with its long history of pursuing culpable individuals, the Antitrust Division has implemented enhanced measures to identify and prosecute individual cartel participants.[139] These measures are resulting in closer analysis of carve-in/carve-out decisions, and may lead to a larger number of carveouts in corporate plea agreements.[140] In addition, under the Yates Memo, corporations are required to "provide all relevant facts about the individuals [within those companies] involved in corporate misconduct" to gain any cooperation credit.[141] These measures are designed to improve the DOJ's ability to identify and build cases against the most culpable individuals.

137.	Memo. from Sally Q. Yates, Deputy Att'y Gen., U.S. Dep't of Justice, Individual Accountability for Corporate Wrongdoing (Sept. 9, 2015), *available at* www.justice.gov/dag/file/769036/download.

138.	*Id.* at 5.

139.	Snyder, Individual Accountability for Antitrust Crimes, *supra* note 101, at 4 ("We have adopted new internal procedures to ensure that each of our criminal offices systematically identifies all potentially culpable individuals as early in the investigative process as feasible and that we bring cases against individuals as quickly as evidentiary sufficiency permits to minimize the risk that cases will be time-barred or that evidence will become stale from the passage of time.").

140.	Sally Q. Yates, Deputy Assistant Att'y Gen., Antitrust Div., U.S. Dep't of Justice, Speech Before the New York City Bar Association White Collar Crime Conference (May 10, 2016), *available at* https://www.justice.gov/opa/speech/deputy-attorney-general-sally-q-yates-delivers-remarks-new-york-city-bar-association ("[T]he Antitrust Division has recently announced that it is revamping its procedures to ensure that each of its criminal offices systematically identifies all potentially culpable individuals as early in the investigative process as possible.").

141.	Snyder, Individual Accountability for Antitrust Crimes, *supra* note 101; Yates, Individual Accountability for Corporate Wrongdoing, *supra* note 137, at 3.

The DOJ's enhanced focus on individual liability has affected specific aspects of the Antitrust Division's practice. For example, in Leniency Plus cases where a company under investigation reports a new conspiracy, the Antitrust Division will require full cooperation from employees to obtain protection under the company's leniency letter.[142] An individual who chooses to cooperate in the leniency investigation while refusing cooperation in the non-leniency investigation will not be covered by the company's leniency letter.[143]

In addition, former employees are no longer included in corporate plea agreements or leniency letters, with the exception of specific former employees who have demonstrated continuing cooperation with the investigation.[144] Rather than covering all former employees, the plea agreement or leniency letter will identify those specific employees who will be covered along with the current employees of the company.

Finally, superiors of the employees who commit the wrongdoing are receiving more scrutiny. These changes in practice have the net effect of increasing the number of culpable individuals potentially subject to prosecution. However, this should not have a significant effect on charging decisions. The Antitrust Division continues to follow the Principles of Federal Prosecution in deciding whether it is appropriate to prosecute a particular individual.[145]

3. Strategy

The need for a swift and comprehensive global strategy for applying for leniency is critical, with an ever-increasing numbers of countries in the global cartel enforcement community taking aggressive steps, often coordinated, to curb price-fixing conspiracies that cross borders in sometimes unpredictable ways.

Even if the conspiracy itself took place primarily in one jurisdiction, in most cases the direct and indirect impact of the conspiracy will spread to other jurisdictions. Reporting cartel activity in one jurisdiction will

---

142. Baer, Prosecuting Antitrust Crimes, *supra* note, 134 at 3-4 ("We recently have seen instances where counsel for an individual wanted to pick and choose where and how a client would cooperate—to confess to crimes in one market in hopes of qualifying for leniency, but not cooperate in another market, for which the client is culpable but not eligible for leniency. It does not work this way.").

143. *Id.*

144. Snyder, Individual Accountability for Antitrust Crimes, *supra* note 101.

145. *See JUSTICE MANUAL, supra* note 2, § 9-27.000.

likely lead to investigations that will begin a cascade of reporting by other conspirators in jurisdictions globally as those conspirators seek to benefit from some form of cooperation. Failing to immediately report not just in the primary jurisdiction, but also other impacted jurisdictions could substantially impair the leniency applicant's ability to reap the full rewards of fast reporting.

To determine whether a company should report in any particular jurisdiction, there a number of factors that must be considered. First and foremost, was there a violation of competition laws in the jurisdiction itself and does counsel have enough information to support a leniency application in a particular jurisdiction?

Second, what are the relative risks, costs and benefits of reporting in a particular jurisdiction? The analysis in every jurisdiction will be slightly different, but important considerations include: (1) the time period of the activity in question and the relative criminal and civil statutes of limitation; (2) the scope of potential civil litigation in each jurisdiction—this is increasingly relevant as private rights of action gain traction outside of the United States; (3) the amount of direct sales to the jurisdiction in question; and (4) an analysis of other reportable conduct and "Leniency Plus" considerations.

Once counsel settles on where to pursue leniency under a global strategy, he/she must also give critical thought as to how and when to seek markers in affected jurisdictions. As discussed above, a "marker" is given to leniency applicants for a limited period of time while counsel gathers the facts necessary to perfect the leniency application. The Antitrust Division requires the following to obtain a marker: (1) a report that some information or evidence has been obtained that indicates that the company has engaged in a criminal antitrust violation; (2) a disclosure of the general nature of the conduct in question; (3) the identification of the industry, product or service involved, with sufficient detail to allow the Antitrust Division to determine whether leniency is still available; and (4) the identification of the company in question.[146] The evidentiary standard for obtaining a marker from the Antitrust Division is relatively low, though it becomes higher if the Antitrust Division is already investigating the wrongdoing in question.[147]

Many other antitrust enforcement authorities utilize a marker system, though the amount of disclosure required to secure a marker differs by country, as does the amount of time for which a marker is granted, the

---

146. *Leniency Program FAQs, supra* note 58, at 3.
147. *Id.*

amount of cooperation required, the form of the application (written vs. oral), the number of companies allowed to secure markers after the first marker is granted, and prohibitions on applicants who engaged in certain activity (such as being a ringleader).[148]

4. Leniency Agreement Breaches

United States v. Stolt-Nielsen, S.A.[149] is the only reported case in which the Antitrust Division has attempted to revoke a conditional leniency letter. In that case, the Antitrust Division revoked the company's leniency because it believed that Stolt-Nielsen had falsely represented in the letter that it took "prompt and effective action" to terminate its participation in the conspiracy.[150] After notifying Stolt-Nielsen that it was in breach of the leniency letter and suspending Stolt-Nielsen's obligations under the letter, the Antitrust Division indicted Stolt-Nielsen.[151]

Stolt-Nielsen disputed that it had violated its obligations under the leniency letter and filed a motion to dismiss the indictment on the basis that the leniency letter barred prosecution.[152] The court held an evidentiary hearing to determine when Stolt-Nielsen "discovered" the reported conduct, and whether Stolt-Nielsen took "prompt and effective action" to terminate Stolt-Nielsen's participation in the anticompetitive conduct.[153] The court found that the leniency letter did not define the term "discovery," and did not identify the date upon which Stolt-Nielsen "discovered" the conduct covered by the leniency letter.[154] The court noted that the Antitrust Division defined "discovery" in a 1998 policy statement as occurring "at the earliest date on which either the board of directors or counsel for the corporation (either inside or outside) were first informed of the conduct at issue."[155] Accordingly, the court found that "discovery" occurred in January 2002, when Stolt-Nielsen's general counsel found a

---

148. To reduce the confusion around variations in marker policy across jurisdictions, some have called for a "One-Stop Shop" policy globally. *See* John M. Taladay, *Time for a Global "One-Stop Shop" for Leniency Markers*, 27 ANTITRUST 43 (Fall 2012).
149. 524 F. Supp. 2d 609 (E.D. Pa. 2007).
150. *Id.* at 616.
151. *Id.* at 615.
152. *Id.*
153. *Id.*
154. *Stolt-Nielsen*, 524 F. Supp. 2d at 617.
155. *Id.*

document that described a customer-allocation conspiracy and reported it to the Chairman.[156]

The court found that "prompt and effective action" was not defined in the leniency letter, and held that the plain meaning of the term did not require "immediate termination of all anticompetitive activity."[157] Rather, the court held, the term requires only that a "prompt and diligent process" be initiated.[158] The court found that Stolt-Nielsen had met this standard, because it had instituted a comprehensive and revised antitrust compliance policy by the end of February 2002.[159] The court found that, in connection with this new policy, Stolt-Nielsen distributed to employees and competitors an antitrust compliance handbook documenting the policy; held mandatory training on antitrust compliance in offices around the world; required all relevant employees to sign certifications of compliance with the policy; and informed competitors of the revised policy and its intention to comply with it.[160] The court further found that Stolt-Nielsen engaged in competition with its competitors beginning in March 2002, and that competitor communications during this period were non-conspiratorial in nature.[161] The court concluded that these actions were sufficient to show that Stolt-Nielsen took "prompt and effective action" to terminate its participation in the conspiracy.

Following the *Stolt-Nielsen* decision, the Antitrust Division revised its Model Conditional Leniency Letter to more clearly define the rights and obligations of the leniency applicant.[162] The Antitrust Division also issued an accompanying document answering frequently asked questions regarding the leniency program.[163] Although the Antitrust Division did not issue any other formal changes to the leniency program, practitioners have noted that leniency applications in recent years have taken more time during the marker phase before the Antitrust Division issues the conditional leniency letter.

---

156. *Id.*
157. *Id.*
158. *Id.*
159. *Stolt-Nielsen*, 524 F. Supp. 2d at 617.
160. *Id.* at 618.
161. *Id.* at 618-20.
162. David Vascott, *Scott Hammond on Stolt-Nielsen*, 2008 GLOBAL COMPETITION REV. 13 *available at* https://www.justice.gov/sites/default/files/atr/legacy/2008/07/09/234840.pdf.
163. *Leniency Program FAQs, supra* note 58.

5. Non-Leniency Investigations

The Antitrust Division also continues to enhance its capabilities to investigate antitrust conspiracies without the assistance of a leniency applicant. In a 2014 speech, then Assistant Attorney General Bill Baer stated that more than one-third of the Antitrust Division's investigations at that time began without a leniency applicant.[164] The Antitrust Division actively conducts outreach at government procurement and inspector general offices, and encourages those agencies to report suspicious conduct. The Antitrust Division also conducts outreach at law enforcement agencies and prosecutor's offices to educate them on how to identify a potential antitrust offense in the course of their investigations.

In addition, the Antitrust Division makes routine use of the "omnibus question" in witness interviews, asking whether the witness is aware of any other anticompetitive activity in addition to the conduct it is investigating. The Antitrust Division also makes use of "cartel profiling," targeting industries or companies that appear especially susceptible to anticompetitive activity.[165] The Antitrust Division is particularly sensitive to situations where culpable employees transfer to different divisions or business segments within a company, on the assumption that an individual willing to engage in anticompetitive activity will not limit that activity to only one business.

These methods of generating investigative leads may ultimately lead to Type B leniency applications, but are not dependent on an initial leniency applicant to begin the investigation.

6. Obstruction of Justice

To ensure effective prosecutions of cartel activity, the Antitrust Division will pursue obstruction of justice charges against companies and individuals that improperly interfere with the investigation. This can include making false statements, destroying, concealing, or withholding documents, and witness tampering.[166] If the Antitrust Division uncovers

---

164. Baer, Prosecuting Antitrust Crimes, *supra* note 134, at 2.
165. Hammond, Price Tag, *supra* note 103.
166. *See, e.g.*, 18 U.S.C. § 1001 (false statements); 18 U.S.C. § 1512 (tampering with a witness, victim, or informant); 18 U.S.C. § 1519 (destruction, alteration, or falsification of records in federal investigation).

obstructive conduct in an investigation—whether civil or criminal—it may pursue obstruction charges separate from any antitrust offense.[167]

For example, in 2012 a Japanese automobile parts manufacturer agreed to pay a $17.7 million criminal fine for price fixing as well as obstruction of justice.[168] Regarding obstruction, the Justice Department charged "that after the company and its executives and employees became aware that the FBI had executed a search warrant . . . a company executive directed employees to delete electronic data and destroy paper documents likely to contain evidence of antitrust crimes in the United States and elsewhere."[169] In addition, if an individual or a company has engaged in obstructive conduct, even if the Antitrust Division does not ultimately bring obstruction charges, it may seek sentencing enhancements for obstruction as part of the penalty for the antitrust offense.[170]

Obstruction of justice charges can also serve as the basis for extradition efforts. In 2010, the DOJ successfully extradited Ian Norris, a British national, who was alleged to have participated in an international conspiracy to fix carbon product prices.[171]

7. *International Enforcement Policy*

a.   1995 International Operations Guidelines

In 1995, the DOJ and FTC issued the *International Operations Guidelines*—an explanation of the respective agencies' international enforcement policies—in an attempt to provide guidance to businesses

---

167. *See, e.g.*, United States v. Higashida, No. 16-20641 (E.D. Mich. 2016) (individuals directed employees to delete and destroy communications with competitors).

168. Press Release, U.S. Dep't of Justice, Office of Public Affairs, Japanese Automobile Parts Manufacturer Agrees to Plead Guilty to Price Fixing and Obstruction of Justice (Oct. 30, 2012), *available at* https://www.justice.gov/opa/pr/japanese-automobile-parts-manufacturer-agrees-plead-guilty-price-fixing-and-obstruction.

169. *Id.*

170. *See* SENTENCING GUIDELINES, *supra* note 98, §§ 3C1.1, 8C2.5(e).

171. Press Release, U.S. Dep't of Justice, Office of Public Affairs, Former CEO of Morgan Crucible Co. Found Guilty of Conspiracy to Obstruct Justice (July 27, 2010), *available at* https://www.justice.gov/opa/pr/former-ceo-morgan-crucible-co-found-guilty-conspiracy-obstruct-justice.

engaged in international operations.[172] In January 2017, the DOJ and FTC issued updated *Antitrust Guidelines for International Enforcement and Cooperation.*[173] In particular, the revisions add a chapter on international cooperation in criminal investigations, update information concerning the application of U.S. antitrust law and the agencies' practice concerning actions involving foreign commerce, and include new examples of common issues that arise. [174]

b.   International Antitrust Cooperation

International enforcement cooperation on cartel investigations is, and has been, a top priority for the Antitrust Division. [175] International cooperation creates efficiencies for investigating agencies by facilitating the exchange of evidence and information and the coordination of public actions in ongoing investigations. It also assists the companies being investigated by, ideally, reducing the risk of conflicting outcomes and facilitating a consistent focus and swift resolution and focusing of investigations that involve multiple jurisdictions.[176]

The Antitrust Division advances its commitment to international cooperation by maintaining strong relationships with enforcement agencies globally and through its active cooperation in international organizations such as the Competition Committee of the Organization for Economic Cooperation and Development (OECD) and the International Competition Network (ICN).

Such cooperation is increasingly critical, as enforcement authorities beyond the traditional players of the U.S., the European Union (EU), and

---

172. U.S. DEP'T OF JUSTICE & FED. TRADE COMM'N, ANTITRUST ENFORCEMENT GUIDELINES FOR INTERNATIONAL OPERATIONS (Apr. 1995), *available at* https://www.justice.gov/atr/antitrust-enforcement-guidelines-international-operations.
173. U.S. DEP'T OF JUSTICE & FED. TRADE COMM'N, ANTITRUST GUIDELINES FOR INTERNATIONAL ENFORCEMENT AND COOPERATION (updated Jan. 13, 2017), *available at* https://www.justice.gov/atr/internationalguidelines/download.
174. *Id.*
175. *Id.*
176. *See* Leslie C. Overton, Deputy Assistant Att'y Gen., Antitrust Div., U.S. Dep't of Justice, International Antitrust Engagement: Benefits and Opportunities, Speech Before the Fifth Annual Chicago Forum on International Antitrust Issues (June 12, 2014), *available at* https://www.justice.gov/atr/file/517786/download.

Canada have begun to play more active roles in global enforcement initiatives. In 2014 alone, nineteen jurisdictions issued more than $6.5 billion in fines or penalties.[177]

c. Extradition

Up until the late 1990s, the DOJ often recommended against prison sentences for citizens of jurisdictions without extradition treaties with the United States.[178] Instead, to ensure cooperation, non-citizens were assured that cooperation would not lead to jail time. That changed in 1999,[179] primarily to ensure that U.S. executives were treated similarly to executives engaged in price fixing who happened not to be U.S. citizens.[180] Since that time, the Antitrust Division has taken an increasingly strong stance on seeking voluntary surrender or extradition and prison time for foreign nationals who are determined to have violated U.S. antitrust laws.[181]

---

177. William J. Baer, Assistant Att'y Gen., Antitrust Div., U.S. Dep't of Justice, Cooperation, Convergence, and the Challenges Ahead in Competition Enforcement, Speech Before the Georgetown Law 9th Annual Global Antitrust Enforcement Symposium (Sept. 29, 2015), *available at* https://www.justice.gov/opa/speech/assistant-attorney-general-bill-baer-delivers-remarks-ninth-annual-global-antitrust.

178. *See* Donald C. Klawiter & Jennifer M. Driscoll, *Sentencing Individuals In Antitrust Cases: The Proper Balance*, 23 ANTITRUST 75, 78 (2009).

179. *See* Scott Hammond, Deputy Assistant Att'y Gen., Antitrust Div., U.S. Dep't of Justice, Charting New Waters In International Cartel Prosecutions, Speech Before the Twentieth Annual National Institute On White Collar Crime (Mar. 2, 2006) [hereinafter Hammond, Charting New Waters], *available at* https://www.justice.gov/atr/speech/charting-new-waters-international-cartel-prosecutions.

180. *Id.*; *see also* Yoshiya Usami, *Why Did They Cross the Pacific? Extradition: A Real Threat to Cartelists*, AAI Working Paper No. 14-01 (2014), *available at* http://www.antitrustinstitute.org/content/aai-working-paper-no-14-01-why-did-they-cross-pacific-extradition-real-threat-cartelists (analyzing jurisdictional obstacles to extraditing foreign cartelists).

181. In April 2014, the DOJ announced that Germany agreed to the extradition of an Italian citizen, Romano Pisciotti, the first person ever to be extradited to the United States solely on the basis of price-fixing related antitrust charges. *See* Press Release, U.S. Dep't of Justice, Office of Public Affairs, First Ever Extradition on Antitrust Charges (Apr. 4, 2014), *available at* https://www.justice.gov/opa/pr/first-ever-extradition-antitrust-charge.

d. INTERPOL Red Notices for International Fugitives

In 2001, the Antitrust Division adopted a policy of placing fugitives on a "Red Notice" list maintained by INTERPOL. A Red Notice notifies the 184 member countries in INTERPOL that a particular individual is wanted by U.S. authorities and it can serve as a basis for an arrest with the goal of extradition. Even if the individual resides in a country without an extradition agreement with the United States, it nevertheless creates a risk that they will be extradited if they travel internationally.[182]

e. U.S. Travel Bans for Aliens Convicted of Antitrust Violations

In 1996, the Antitrust Division entered into a Memorandum of Understanding (MOU) with the Immigration and Naturalization Service (INS).[183] In that MOU, the INS declared that it "considers criminal violations of the Sherman Antitrust Act, 15 U.S.C. § 1, to be crimes involving moral turpitude, which may subject an alien to exclusion or deportation from the United States."[184] But the Antitrust Division and INS further agreed that as part of an antitrust plea agreement, for a "cooperating alien" in an antitrust case, the INS *may* defer an alien's deportation, waive an alien's inadmissibility, or grant parole.[185] The threat of deportation or of a U.S. travel ban for non-U.S. executives and the promise of relief can be a powerful tool for the Antitrust Division in persuading an individual to enter into a plea agreement. Accordingly, the immigration relief in the MOU typically is used by the Antitrust Division as an incentive for a foreign national who is outside the United States to submit voluntarily to U.S. jurisdiction and plead guilty.

---

182. *See* Hammond, Charting New Waters, *supra* note 179.
183. The INS ceased to exist on March 1, 2003, but the MOU remains effective and currently is administered by U.S. Immigration and Customs Enforcement.
184. Memo. of Understanding Between the Antitrust Div., U.S. Dep't of Justice and the Immigration and Naturalization Service, U.S. Dep't of Justice (Mar. 15, 1996), *available at* https://www.justice.gov/atr/memorandum-understanding-between-antitrust-division-united-states-department-justice-and.
185. *Id.*

f. U.S. Border Watches

Another tool at the Antitrust Division's disposal is a border watch, which notifies it if a foreign witness or defendant enters the country. This gives the Antitrust Division the opportunity to interview the witness or serve compulsory process, but also subjects the witness to potential obstruction charges if they lie about their knowledge of or participation in an antitrust conspiracy. Further, a witness identified through a watch list that is served with a subpoena to testify before a grand jury cannot leave the country without risking criminal contempt charges.[186] In addition, a fugitive defendant who is detained as a result of a border watch can be held through the conclusion of their criminal trial. Even if the witness or defendant never seeks to travel to the United States, the threat of detention and the related restrictions on travel can sometimes motivate individuals to voluntarily cooperate or accept guilty pleas.[187]

---

186. *Id.*
187. *Id.*

CHAPTER III

RESPONDING TO AN INVESTIGATION

This chapter provides a general overview of important considerations in responding to government cartel investigations and conducting parallel internal investigations.

A. General Principles

1. Immediate Considerations

When a client has been involved in potential cartel activity or is the subject of a cartel investigation, the most immediate strategic consideration is determining whether to apply for amnesty or leniency. In the United States and most other jurisdictions, the company that first alerts the government to a possible antitrust violation can avoid criminal liability completely. The first-in amnesty applicant in the U.S. also dramatically reduces its exposure to civil damages.

Speed is an important factor in considering whether to apply for amnesty or leniency, because competitors will likely be considering the same decision. In some cases, the first amnesty applicant has been only hours ahead of the second. The most immediate need when weighing this decision is to understand the facts so that if there is a potential violation, the company can attempt to be the first amnesty applicant (especially in the jurisdictions where the client faces the greatest exposure). If amnesty is not available, as is often the case when a government investigation has already been launched, the decision is whether to cooperate actively with the government to obtain a fine discount if a violation is found.

At the outset of an investigation, outside counsel should identify the point people within the client for the investigation—typically, the general counsel or someone in the legal group. Counsel and the client should also make an initial assessment of the geographic scope of the investigation and determine the point people in each jurisdiction. In the early stages, it is best to limit the size of the working group to the extent possible to avoid the possibility of leaks.

If a government investigation has not yet been launched, this group can consider whether to disseminate dawn raid or search warrant guidelines explaining how to respond to inquiries from government investigators and questions from the press. After the group has been established, counsel should begin to develop an understanding of the facts through interviews of a small number of employees and review of a targeted set of documents. It is important to direct interviewees to keep both the existence of the interview and its substance confidential. Where the identity of the individuals involved is unclear, sales personnel and management responsible for the products at issue may prove useful starting points.

Counsel should be prepared, even at this early stage, to answer the client's questions about the potential liability. Although detailed assessment of the risk is premature prior to investigation, counsel can explain the maximum penalties: in the United States, companies face criminal fines of up to $100 million or, in the alternative, twice the gain to the defendants or loss to customers resulting from the conspiracy (a number that may greatly exceed $100 million in some cases); employees face criminal fines of $1 million or twice the gain or loss, as well as a prison term of up to ten years.[1] In addition, in U.S. follow-on civil cases, the plaintiffs will generally be entitled to treble damages (or even higher damages in cases involving both direct and indirect purchasers). The process of complying with a government investigation and conducting follow-on litigation also entails considerable legal costs, likely over a period of several years, which are not reduced by amnesty. Where conduct raises issues in other jurisdictions, this exposure may be increased.

If amnesty is not available, companies have three basic options in responding to a government investigation. They can: (1) cooperate proactively; (2) passively respond to government requests; or (3) fight the investigation to the extent possible. The approach the company chooses depends on the facts discovered in the internal investigation and the company's approach to risk.

2.   *Basic Strategies*

a.   Proactive Cooperation

A strategy of proactive cooperation in the United States entails frequent contact with U.S. Department of Justice (DOJ) attorneys to provide relevant documents (located both inside and outside the United States) and proffers of facts relevant to the DOJ's investigation. This approach involves the production of both exculpatory and problematic

---

1.   15 U.S.C. § 1; 18 U.S.C. § 3751(b)-(d).

documents related to the conduct of interest. It requires counsel to follow the factual trail and keep the DOJ informed of the process and substance of the internal investigation. This strategy may be optimal when a company has found problematic activity and wishes to reduce its fine exposure, or if a company believes that it did not participate in the conduct at issue and can demonstrate its innocence through proactive production of documents and information. In practice, cooperation by the company also may result in constructive discussion of the government's priorities and views of the case. This approach also offers counsel the opportunity to effectively advocate its positions in the case, because it involves the disclosure of all relevant facts and generally facilitates productive relationships between the company and the DOJ.

b. Passive Cooperation

A passive cooperation strategy entails responding to the government's subpoena or informal requests but not proactively providing documents from outside the United States or extensive proffers to the government unless specifically requested. This strategy can be effective if the company is a peripheral player in the industry or did not seem to be involved in any problematic conduct. The goal of this approach is to minimize costs and avoid attention from the government. This strategy may be most attractive where the DOJ is relatively unlikely to indict.

c. Aggressive Opposition

A third option is to fight each step of the process. In this scenario, the client will consider contesting or resisting every request made by the DOJ to the greatest extent possible, thereby forcing the DOJ to invest the maximum amount of resources required to build its case. The risks of this strategy can be significant if damaging evidence can be obtained through other sources. This approach may result in an indictment of the company and ultimately a trial on the merits. If the company and the DOJ ultimately reach a negotiated resolution, the DOJ will insist on greater penalties than it would have otherwise. If the company is found guilty at trial, the amount of the judgment is likely to be much higher than the amount of a settlement negotiated through cooperation with the DOJ.

A strategy of noncooperation, though risky, may make sense when there is very little risk of liability, or when any potential negotiated resolution with the government is categorically unacceptable to a client.

Even in that case, passive cooperation without production of documents located outside the United States should be seriously considered.

B. Company Obligations

1. *Corporate Governance Issues*

a.   Mandatory Reporting and External Communications

Clients may be required to disclose the existence of a criminal antitrust investigation, for example, securities disclosures to investors. Experienced securities counsel should be consulted to advise on these issues, which can be complex and may vary by jurisdiction. It is important to discuss these issues openly with the DOJ so that it is not surprised by a disclosure that threatens to undermine the investigation or jeopardizes a leniency position. As to pending investigations in a non-amnesty setting, companies will not need to coordinate with the authorities as to the timing of the announcement, but the substance of any announcement should take into account the status of the government investigations and the various governments' likely reaction to the company's public statements.

Even if no law requires disclosure, the company may decide that it needs to make some sort of statement regarding the investigation to the press, investors, and customers—particularly if the fact that the company is under investigation is public knowledge. Counsel should be prepared to consult on these statements as necessary, and should be sure that the statements do not unnecessarily imply guilt on the part of the company or unnecessarily commit to a particular strategy regarding the investigation.

b.   Internal Communications

In addition to making public statements, the company will likely need to communicate internally about the investigation. One of the first internal communications is likely to be a document preservation notice. A company may also benefit from disseminating dawn raid guidelines. If the company communicates more broadly about the existence of an investigation, it should be sure to carefully tailor its message to avoid admissions of liability or discussions of strategic responses. The company may also wish to remind employees not to discuss the matter except with company lawyers—and to particularly avoid discussions with the press.

In addition, the individuals most likely to be of interest to the government (generally, sales personnel or other employees who have had contacts with competitors) should be contacted specifically. They should be instructed to involve counsel if they are contacted by the government, and further instructed that if they are contacted, they should answer the investigators' identifying questions in a polite way but should not answer substantive questions regarding competitor contacts or the business generally. The company should consider whether key past employees should be contacted as well, depending on the likelihood that the former employee was involved in competitor discussions and the terms on which the employee exited. Communications with former employees require care because these individuals may not feel loyalty to the company and may not take instruction on whether to keep information confidential. Therefore, it can be helpful to communicate with former employees on a "need to know" basis and establish a confidentiality agreement early.

The general employee and public communication plan should also be carefully considered to avoid the risk of expanding liability for the company in case of a leak. In these situations, a "no comment" approach is usually the best course, if possible.

2. Document Preservation

A company under government investigation should consider taking action to preserve documents immediately upon learning of the investigation. Preservation is critical for several reasons. First, a company that has received a subpoena from the DOJ is under a legal obligation to retain all relevant documents. Destruction of relevant materials can justify criminal charges of obstruction of justice, which can be brought even if a company or individual is completely innocent of any substantive antitrust offense.[2]

Second, criminal antitrust investigations often lead to follow-on civil litigation with private plaintiffs; if a company has not diligently preserved

---

2.   18 U.S.C. § 1512(c)(1). The statutory maximum is twenty years in prison and a fine of $250,000. Antitrust defendants have been charged with violations of this statute; for example, an executive of a Japanese automotive company in 2014 entered a plea agreement for violating this statute and agreed to serve a year and a day in jail. Plea Agreement, United States v. Fujitani, No. 14-20087 (E.D. Mich. Mar. 11, 2014). A charge of obstruction of justice served as a basis for extraditing a British defendant even though the defendant could not have been extradited for an antitrust offense alone. Norris v. United States [2008] UKHL 16, [2008] A.C. 920 (H.L.), Order for Extradition Pursuant to Section 93(4) of the Extradition Act 2003 (Sept. 22, 2008).

the documents relevant to that litigation, it may expose that company to a spoliation claim or may allow a court or jury to infer, from the document's absence, that its contents were damaging to the company.[3] These consequences can arise from a failure to preserve documents located outside the United States as well.[4]

Third, document preservation facilitates the large scale collection of documents that will almost certainly be required to comply with a government subpoena and, later, discovery in civil litigation. Finally, document preservation enables counsel to conduct a thorough and accurate investigation of the facts at issue, with confidence that all critical evidence has been preserved.

a.   Scope of Preservation

In general, preservation obligations are triggered by receipt of a grand jury subpoena from the DOJ (or by an imminent amnesty application). The subpoena lists the documents of interest to the government and can define the scope of the preservation requirement. The scope of any subpoena is likely to be quite broad, and as a general principle preservation should be broad as well—at least initially, until its scope can be narrowed. Preservation can begin broadly by preserving documents from potentially relevant employees for an extensive timeframe, and then narrow by reducing the number of employees and timeframe as the investigation develops and expand if needed based on the facts discovered by the investigation.

Because the risk involved with failing to preserve is so steep, broad preservation is generally considered prudent despite the information technology costs and burdens. At this early stage, counsel should understand the client's information technology systems; suspend relevant auto-delete and other preservation policies for relevant individuals and central files; and preserve back up files and information. In addition, counsel should instruct the information technology department to retain files and local data for individuals on the hold list who leave the company while the document hold is in place so that documents are not inadvertently destroyed. Moreover, since the obligation to preserve documents for civil litigation begins at the point that litigation is

---

3.   *See, e.g.*, Zubulake v. UBS Warburg LLC, 220 F.R.D. 212, 221 (S.D.N.Y. 2003).

4.   *See, e.g.*, Reino de Espana v. Am. Bureau of Shipping, 2006 WL 3208579, at *8 (S.D.N.Y. 2006).

reasonably anticipated, an early and broad preservation action helps protect clients against civil spoliation claims.

Preservation is likely to require close coordination with both legal and information technology personnel of the client. Preservation can be quite costly. Counsel should be prepared to demonstrate the consequences of failing to preserve that justify such an intrusive effort. It may be worthwhile, at this stage, to explain to the information technology employees that a large scale document collection will follow swiftly on the heels of the preservation. Counsel also may want to advise that preservation periods often last several years. Counsel and the client should consider ways to manage these substantial costs, including discussing limitations with the DOJ and stipulating to preservation date cut-offs with plaintiffs' counsel.

Finally, counsel and the client should be prepared to coordinate with lawyers in other jurisdictions to ensure that the company adheres to all applicable preservation obligations. Although a DOJ subpoena may only seek documents located in the United States, documents located outside the United States that may be relevant to the DOJ investigation should be preserved.

b. Preservation Notice

The preservation notice may be a client's first formal communication with its employees regarding the investigation. In that event, the notice should include some minimal background on the investigation—a statement to the effect that the company has received a subpoena and is reviewing the facts, that employees should avoid discussing the matter with each other or outside the company, that media inquiries should be directed to the public relations or legal departments, and that contacts with government investigators should be referred to counsel.

The notice should go to all individuals who may have relevant materials or who have the power to delete relevant documents, including personal assistants of the relevant employees where appropriate. The client should consider carefully the most effective source of the notice in the context of its organization. The notice should clearly indicate that the preservation obligation is important, and that failure to comply may result in significant penalties for both the company and the individual. It should also note that individuals receiving the notice are not necessarily suspected of any improper conduct, nor should receipt of the notice be taken as an indication that the individual is of interest in the investigation.

The substantive part of the notice should be simple and short, stating clearly what the employees cannot do (delete or destroy) to what categories of documents (all business-related documents, for example). The notice should clarify that a "document" is not only a paper document but also emails or any other sort of computer file, including images and recordings, files contained on external media, files stored in home offices, text messages, WeChat or WhatsApp messages, and the like. It should note that if an employee is unsure whether a document can be deleted, she should preserve it.

Finally, the notice should direct questions about the notice or the investigation to counsel (usually the in-house legal department). It may be helpful to develop sample talking points for questions employees may raise. Although preservation notices may seem routine to counsel, businesspeople who do not regularly participate in litigation may be upset or worried by them and may contact in-house counsel for a more detailed explanation at a time when in-house counsel are likely to be particularly busy.

3. Compliance Programs

After an investigation has been initiated, a client may conclude that upgrades to its antitrust compliance program (or the creation of an antitrust compliance program) are warranted. Upgrading the compliance program serves two purposes: it reduces the likelihood that employees will behave in a manner that will lead to future antitrust investigations, and might serve to persuade the government to treat the company more favorably during the immediate investigation. On the other hand, the failure to have a robust compliance policy can convince the government to insist on probation or the appointment of a compliance monitor if the company is found guilty or enters a plea agreement.

4. Employee Issues

During the course of an investigation, a company is likely to encounter several complex issues relating to its employees. If there is a divergence between the company's interests and the employee's interests, counsel for the company cannot advise or represent the employee. Investigations are likely to involve some inquiry into the activities of past employees, and can carry the real risk of prosecution and incarceration for individuals implicated in illegal activity. Relatedly, the company must decide how to treat employees who have behaved improperly. Finally, corporations must take into account that an investigation can limit the ability of its employees to travel internationally.

a.   Attorney-Client Privilege and Independent Counsel

Counsel for a company represents the company, not the individual employees who comprise it. Consequently, the company may elect to waive attorney-client privilege over the results of its internal investigations, including interviews with individual employees, without the permission or knowledge of those employees.[5] This principle requires that when interviewing employees, company counsel should make clear the boundaries of their representation, and explain the issues regarding privilege and the conditions under which it can be waived. A warning that the lawyer represents the company, not the individual, and that the company has the authority to unilaterally disclose the contents of an interview to authorities is known as an *Upjohn* warning. Counsel should give this warning clearly at the beginning of each internal interview and memorialize that the warning was given in an interview summary or memorandum.

The *Upjohn* warning serves two purposes: it protects outside counsel from claims of unethical conduct[6] and ensures that the company can introduce any useful findings from the interview, including any follow-up emails or information that an employee may provide.[7] It also ensures that the employee is treated fairly.

Company counsel should be prepared for the possibility that an individual may request personal advice during the course of an investigation—or that the company may decide that an individual needs the assistance of her or his own counsel. Even if it is very likely that the individual did not engage in problematic conduct, counsel for the company

---

5.   Upjohn Co. v. United States, 449 U.S. 383, 389-93 (1981).
6.   *See, e.g.,* United States v. Ruehle, 583 F.2d 600, 609 (9th Cir. 2009) (overturning district court presumption that, in the absence of any evidence to the contrary, a law firm conducting an internal investigation had improperly led an employee to believe that it represented both him and the company).
7.   *See, e.g., In re* Google, Inc., 462 F. App'x 975, 978-79 (Fed. Cir. 2012) (denying claim of privilege over employee email because there was no evidence, such as an *Upjohn* warning, to indicate that the email was made pursuant to an investigation by counsel).

cannot provide the individual with legal advice, and should inform the individual that she can consult her own lawyer.[8]

In addition to providing *Upjohn* warnings at interviews, counsel should be attuned to potential conflicts of interest. In general, U.S. lawyers are under an affirmative obligation to recommend that an employee obtain individual counsel in the event of such a conflict.[9] Typically, cartel cases involve divergence of interests between individuals and companies when the DOJ singles out an individual as a target of an investigation or a potential carve-out from any eventual resolution of the case against the company. In such a case, the DOJ will generally explain its position that company counsel cannot represent the individuals.

The DOJ's initial views on the necessity of individual counsel often become a point of advocacy. All things being equal, the company (and counsel) likely prefer to avoid individual representation because individual counsel will likely limit the company's access to the employee, who may be key to the investigation. For this reason, if counsel is comfortable that there is no conflict with the employee, counsel may attempt to explain to the DOJ why the individuals in question do not need individual representation—for example, because they did not participate in contacts, or lacked effective pricing authority. The DOJ has significant leverage on this question.[10] The consequence of company counsel losing such a motion can be disqualification of defense counsel altogether.[11] Generally, although these matters may be the subject of discussion with the DOJ, companies typically follow the DOJ's requests with respect to individual counsel. In the antitrust plea agreement context, many more individual employees retain independent counsel than are eventually carved out.

---

8. The company may engage "pool counsel" to handle questions from multiple employees who do not seem to have significant exposure. If there has been conduct that may be considered a violation, certain employees will likely need their own counsel.

9. *See, e.g.*, MODEL CODE OF PROF'L RESPONSIBILITY R. 1.7 & cmt. 8, 1.13(f).

10. *See* ANTITRUST DIV., U.S. DEP'T OF JUSTICE, ANTITRUST DIVISION MANUAL at IV-70 (5th ed. 2012) (last updated Apr. 2018) [hereinafter *ANTITRUST DIV. MANUAL*], *available at* https://www.justice.gov/atr/file/761166/download.

11. *See., e.g.*, United States v. Register, 182 F.3d 820, 834 (11th Cir. 1999) (holding, in part, that district court's disqualification of defendant's attorney due to conflict of interest was not abuse of discretion).

Counsel may provide the company with a list of recommended individual lawyers. The company should explain to the relevant employees (if applicable) that the DOJ has decided the employee possesses information relevant to the investigation and should have individual representation, that the separate representation does not necessarily imply that the employee will be charged with a crime, and (if true) that the company will pay the counsel's fees. Paying for an employee's counsel can help maintain the trust of the employee who may not be able to afford experienced antitrust counsel. Most companies pay for individual counsel, although the decision depends on the specific circumstances of each employee.

Where possible, a close working relationship between company and individual counsel is generally in the clients' common interest. Company and individual counsel should consider signing a joint defense agreement permitting them to exchange joint defense information without risking waiver of applicable privileges.

b. Former Employees

When the company learns of a government investigation, it should consider contacting former employees it believes to be relevant to alert them and explain that government investigators may contact them soon. Of course, it may be challenging to contact employees who left on bad terms or who now work for competitors. However, this issue is important because the DOJ (and the Federal Bureau of Investigation) may seek to contact directly these former employees to serve subpoenas and to receive information from the employee who may not think to contact counsel. Companies generally pay for individual counsel for former employees (as for current employees), although this decision depends on the specific situation of the former employee.

c. Government Prosecution

The United States prosecutes individuals for antitrust violations more frequently than any other country. In September 2015, the DOJ issued a memo entitled "Individual Accountability for Corporate Wrongdoing," which describes "seeking accountability from" (i.e., prosecuting or seeking guilty pleas from) individuals who commit antitrust violations as "[o]ne of the most effective ways to combat corporate misconduct."[12] It lays out six principles, some of which, if followed, would be expected to result in increased prosecutions and convictions of individuals.

The Yates memo states that prosecutors "should not resolve matters with a corporation without a clear plan to resolve related individual cases."[13] The Yates memo also provides that whenever a decision is made not to prosecute, it must be memorialized and formally approved.[14] In addition, the memo states that an absolute prerequisite to any credit for cooperation, such as amnesty benefits, is the provision of "all relevant facts relating to the individuals responsible for the misconduct."[15] Thus, if the DOJ believes that a company has provided all information about the company's conduct, but has not provided sufficient clarity about the actions of specific individuals at the company who engaged in the conduct, the Yates memo gives reason to believe that amnesty benefits could be withheld by the DOJ. Internal investigations must be robust enough to satisfy the DOJ that there has been a good-faith effort by the company to learn which employees are responsible for the behavior.[16]

The Yates memo also states that "culpable individuals" should not be released from liability "absent extraordinary circumstances or approved departmental policy."[17] Because the memo explicitly cites the Antitrust Division's Corporate Leniency Policy as an example of an approved policy, it seems unlikely that this language will lead to any formal change in DOJ antitrust enforcement policy, at least in the short term.[18] Finally, the Yates memo states that investigations "should focus on individuals from the inception" of an investigation.[19]

Because the DOJ Antitrust Division has a long history of prioritizing prosecution of individuals where possible in order to maximize deterrence from antitrust violations, the Yates memo may not significantly affect decision-making regarding individuals who are the focus of antitrust investigations. The Yates memo is important, however, because it affects how cooperation with the DOJ should proceed. A company considering

---

12. Memo. from Sally Q. Yates, Deputy Att'y Gen., U.S. Dep't of Justice, Individual Accountability for Corporate Wrongdoing (Sept. 9, 2015), *available at* www.justice.gov/dag/file/769036/download.
13. *Id.* at 6
14. *Id.* at 6.
15. *Id.* at 3
16. *Id.*
17. *Id.* at 5.
18. *Id.*
19. *Id.* at 4.

active cooperation with the DOJ should understand that this means providing specific information regarding the employees involved in the relevant conduct.

Throughout the investigation, if the company is cooperative, the DOJ will give preliminary indications of the employees in whom it is interested through its requests for interviews, follow-up requests for proffers, and requests for individual representation. The DOJ will identify the individuals who may be subject to prosecution if the company enters into plea negotiations. Generally, a corporate antitrust plea agreement will not only resolve the DOJ's antitrust case against the company but also provide a release from further prosecution to current employees, subject to continuing cooperation obligations.[20]

Certain individual employees may be carved out of a plea agreement. It is important to note that the simple fact that an individual has been carved out does not necessarily mean that that individual will be indicted in all cases. The DOJ's current practice is to provide the number of carved out employees in the plea agreement itself, while listing the individuals' names in a confidential annex to the plea agreement that is filed under seal.

If the company does not enter a plea and is indicted, the DOJ will typically indict several individuals as well.[21] If the government does decide to prosecute an individual, the individual will consider whether to attempt to negotiate a plea agreement, stand trial to defend the case, or (if the individual resides overseas) take the risk that he or she will not be extradited to the United States for trial.

---

20. *See, e.g.*, Plea Agreement, United States v. Mitsubishi Elec. Corp., No. 13-20710, at 15 (E.D. Mich. Nov. 6, 2013) (noting that the plea agreement covered directors, officers, and employees of Mitsubishi Electric); Plea Agreement, United States v. Omron Auto. Elecs. Co., No. 16-20182 (E.D. Mich. June 13, 2016) (no non-prosecution provision for individuals).

21. For example, in the well-known AU Optronics case, nine executives and managers were indicted alongside the company. Superseding Indictment, United States v. AU Optronics Corp., No. 09-110 (N.D. Cal. June 10, 2010). In two recent indictments in the auto parts cases, executives and companies were indicted simultaneously. Indictment, United States v. Maruyasu Indus. Co., No. 16-00064 (S.D. Ohio June 15, 2016) (indicting four executives with company); Indictment, United States v. Tokai Kogyo Co., No. 16-00063 (S.D. Ohio June 15, 2016) (indicting one executive with company).

d.   Internal Discipline

When an investigation reveals that an employee has behaved illegally or contrary to company policy, the company will need to consider whether to take adverse action against the employee. There are many options, including termination, moving the employee to a position in which he or she lacks pricing responsibility or contact with competitors, suspension, or adjustment of compensation. A practical consideration will be whether the employee is important to the ongoing defense of the company in the civil damages litigation or in ongoing investigations by regulatory authorities other than the DOJ. Local employment laws must also be considered.

If an individual is carved out of the company plea agreement, the DOJ will likely require that the company at least ensure that this employee is not in a position where he or she supervises other employees who would be sources of evidence in the DOJ's case against the carved out employee. There is a risk that taking no action against particularly culpable employees may cause the DOJ to believe that the company does not take its legal obligations seriously. To reduce this risk, the company should communicate with the DOJ to explain the reasoning for its employment decisions.

e.   International Travel

An employee located outside of the United States who may be the target of a U.S. government investigation will likely need to consider travel restrictions. This may affect the company's decision-making regarding the status of the employee.

Individuals may be placed on the Interpol Red Notice list at the request of the government that indicted or prosecuted the individual. This amounts to a formal request that all Interpol member states arrest the individual rather than permit entry into the country. The U.S. governments also may use border watches to identify relevant individuals (even individuals who have not been indicted) entering the United States. If an individual on this list attempts to enter or enters the United States, he or she may be served a subpoena for documents or testimony, the government may attempt to question the individual, or in rare cases the individual may be detained. Companies who have employees at risk of being on a border watch list should consider travel restrictions and should advise employees who travel how to handle the situation if visited by the U.S. government while traveling.

Finally, governments can formally request extradition of individuals indicted in absentia. As extradition generally requires dual criminality, and because the United States has generally been an outlier in the application of criminal antitrust laws to individuals, formal extraditions have historically been rare. However, as non-U.S. jurisdictions adopt more punitive approaches to individuals, and if the DOJ continues to seek extradition as a priority, extraditions may grow more common in the future.

C. Tools of DOJ Investigations

A typical cartel investigation is likely to be iterative: as the DOJ reviews the company's documents, interviews its employees, receives information from other competitors, and receives attorney proffers, it is likely to ask follow-up questions to confirm its understanding of various points or investigate new issues or theories. The best practice, as with all aspects of the investigation, is to log and record meticulously all interactions with the DOJ, including informal discussions between counsel and DOJ attorneys, document productions, attorney proffers, and employee interviews.

Counsel should also explain that the proceedings will generally be kept confidential; Rule 6(e) of the Federal Rules of Criminal Procedures provides for the confidentiality of grand jury proceedings in the United States, though there are exceptions. [22] Confidentiality rules vary by jurisdiction, so counsel should make sure the client understands the risks in the United States associated with making statements to the non-U.S. governments.

1. Search Warrants

As part of its investigation, the DOJ may obtain and execute a search warrant, which permits it to search the company's premises and copy or remove media. The warrant is also accompanied by a subpoena for

---

22. Disclosure can be made to various U.S. government personnel in connection with investigations, prosecutions, or national security or counterterrorism matters. In addition, a court can authorize disclosure in response to a request from a defendant challenging an indictment or in response to federal government requests for disclosure to foreign, state, tribal, or military officials if the investigation reveals evidence that the laws of those jurisdictions (or the Uniform Code of Military Justice) have been violated.

documents. The DOJ may sometimes use only a subpoena, rather than using a search warrant to forcibly remove large volumes of information.

It is good practice for companies to have a procedure in place in case the DOJ does execute a search warrant. Immediately after investigators arrive with a search warrant, employees should contact in-house counsel and other necessary management. Then, employees should ask to see the identification of the investigators and request a copy of the warrant, to be delivered to counsel immediately. Employees should familiarize themselves with the subject matter and scope of the warrant.

2. Subpoenas

The DOJ is likely to serve a subpoena at a relatively early stage of the investigation. If a subpoena is received, employees should contact management and in-house counsel quickly. Although the subpoena will require the quick production of significant amounts of documents and information, the company should be able to negotiate scope and timing of the subpoena with the DOJ. As discussed above, the company should also move quickly to understand the facts and consider its strategy. On its face, the subpoena will require the production of documents and the appearance of an employee before the grand jury to discuss the response to the subpoena; in practice, such grand jury testimony is rare, because companies discuss their response in detail with the DOJ. Individuals may also be served with subpoenas for fact testimony before the grand jury. These individuals may need individual counsel to quickly advise on the subpoena.

Receipt of a subpoena should prompt immediate discussion among counsel and information technology employees about how best to preserve the necessary documents. If a document preservation process is underway, counsel should verify that the subpoena does not require additions or modifications to the process.

Counsel will typically discuss the subpoena with the DOJ soon after it is received to understand the DOJ's particular areas of focus. At the same time, counsel should work closely with information technology personnel to understand the exact burden to the company associated with full compliance with the subpoena. Counsel may then wish to negotiate with the DOJ to narrow the scope of the subpoena, thus reducing the burden and expense of responding. Generally, counsel will want to explore any latitude it may have to reduce the time period, specific products, and geographic areas covered by the subpoena, and secure agreement for as narrow a set of search terms as possible (or even predictive coding) applied to as small a set of custodians and other document sources as possible. The subpoena will include a compliance certification that should be carefully considered before signing because it requires a statement under oath.

Although a company may be tempted to move to quash the subpoena, this effort is unlikely to succeed. The burden is on the recipient of a grand jury subpoena to demonstrate that it is unreasonable, and it cannot be quashed on the grounds of irrelevancy unless there is "no reasonable possibility that the category of materials the Government seeks will produce information relevant to the general subject of the grand jury's investigation."[23]

3. Interviews

The DOJ interviews employees both in informal sessions and in formal grand jury proceedings. Counsel can participate in the informal process but if individual counsel is involved the DOJ staff may not permit company counsel to attend. Counsel is not permitted to attend grand jury proceedings.

In addition to formal interviews, investigators may attempt to initiate informal conversations with an employee. Of course, from the perspective of a lawyer guiding a company through a DOJ investigation, the advice is that the employee should call counsel and should not answer substantive questions.

The more typical interview takes place before the DOJ staff. In these interviews, counsel can meet with the witness beforehand. If the company is cooperating, the DOJ staff may be willing to provide an outline of topics of interest. Before these interviews, counsel should verify the terms on which the interview is being conducted; in particular, counsel should seek a use immunity letter (also commonly referred to as a "queen for a day" letter) providing that the DOJ will not use the results of the interview in subsequent criminal prosecution of the interviewee, except in certain circumstances such as perjury or the impeachment of subsequent testimony. These letters also provide that the DOJ may use the information provided by the employee to further its investigation against the company and individuals including the interviewee.

Counsel, after becoming familiar with references to the employee in previous interviews with and proffers to the DOJ, as well as appearances by the employee in any "hot" documents likely to attract interest from the DOJ, should interview the employee internally before the DOJ interviews

---

23.   United States v. R. Enters., 498 U.S. 292, 293 (1991).

him or her. Typically, the DOJ will ask for an attorney fact proffer before interviewing the individual in order to understand the information the witness would provide in the interview.

At the interview, one company attorney should take detailed notes and memorialize the interview in a formal privileged memorandum.

D. Internal Investigations

1. *Organizing the Investigation*

International cartel investigations are complex, and counsel must make important decisions throughout the process regarding priorities in the investigation. The decisions can have ramifications in multiple jurisdictions. Further, the results of the investigation may remain relevant for years after the initial criminal aspects of the case have been resolved: in follow-on civil litigation, counsel will probably rely in part on work product from the criminal investigation. For these reasons, the substance and process of the investigation should be well documented.

2. *Preparing for and Conducting Interviews*

As soon as practicable, counsel should begin interviewing the employees most likely to have relevant information. Interviews are often the most critical fact-gathering component of the investigation; in addition, they allow counsel to assess the demeanor, knowledge, and consistency of the employees.

If the employees involved in the relevant behavior are unknown (as can be the case in the initial stages of an investigation), counsel may commence the interviews with the employees with the clearest responsibility for pricing. As the investigation gathers momentum, the identities of remaining employees with relevant information will become clearer.

Before interviewing employees, counsel should consider carefully the goal of the interview. Internal interviews in a cartel investigation often follow the funnel principle: they begin at a high level by asking open-ended questions of a relatively broad set of employees in order to ascertain the general boundaries of the conduct: how long did it last, in what jurisdictions, relating to what products or services, etc., pivoting to more detailed investigation of specific points later. In some other cases, the initial interviews may be quite narrow in scope—for example, where counsel is simply seeking enough information to obtain a leniency marker and believes the employee can provide such information. In the later stages, investigators are more likely to have specific questions.

Counsel typically begin the interview by giving the *Upjohn* warnings discussed earlier and discussing the employee's title, employment history, and job responsibilities, including the extent of the employee's authority over pricing. In many cases it is preferable to have more than one lawyer at the interview, so that one lawyer can concentrate on questioning while the other can take notes. To preserve privilege, these notes should detail the attorney's thoughts, mental impressions, and conclusions and not be a mere transcription of the interview.

Because beginning an interview by asking about competitor contacts may put an employee on the defensive, counsel may begin with more general questions about the nature of pricing within the industry and company or the overall competitive landscape of the industry. If and when competitor contacts are discussed, critical facts for counsel to establish include the frequency and duration of contacts, the identity of the participants (including individuals within the company who may have authorized but not directly participated in contacts), the subjects of the conversations, and the specific products or geographic areas affected. Counsel should understand whether agreements on price or output were actually reached, and how the behavior of the company and its competitors were altered after the contacts.

In many interviews, counsel will have questions for interviewees about specific documents uncovered during the review process. If such documents have been identified, it is advisable to ask the interviewee about them. If documents have not been reviewed yet or if they have been identified but cannot be discussed during the interview, counsel should consider letting the interview know that a further interview may be required.

Of course, each situation must be reviewed considering the specific facts of the matter. In some interviews, a different (potentially more aggressive) strategy or tone may be effective.

3. Document Collection, Review, and Production

Cartel investigations require large scale collection, review, and production of documents, to thoroughly investigate the conduct internally, to comply with government subpoenas, and to satisfy civil discovery obligations. Clients should expect an intrusive, burdensome, expensive, and lengthy process.

In addition to traditional documents, transactional or sales data are among the most critical "documents" in cartel cases. Production of this data can be among the most challenging aspects of the production process.

a. Document Collection

In many instances, counsel should begin the document collection efforts in the early stages as they work to negotiate the scope of a production. It is often fairly clear early on that there will be groups of individuals who will be of interest to the DOJ (such as pricing and sales personnel handling the products at issue). The DOJ typically refers to these individuals as custodians.

In a typical collection process, counsel or information technology personnel will discuss the collection with the individual custodians. In these discussions, the custodians may need to be reassured that the company is interested only in business-related documents; any purely personal documents will be deemed irrelevant and will not be produced. (The process in other jurisdictions, especially Europe, generally requires heightened sensitivity to privacy law issues, including if information in one jurisdiction is to be produced in another.) Many companies can generally collect electronic files without the direct involvement of a custodian; however, the custodian's identification of relevant documents that are not on the company's active servers can be helpful.

An e-discovery vendor in one or more jurisdictions is likely necessary to conduct at least some stages of the document review process, given the substantial volume of documents and the level of technical skill required. If the vendor does not perform the collection itself, it may be prudent to involve the vendor in the initial technical collection discussions.

b. Review Protocol

Document review procedures can be extremely expensive. Technical review strategies such as predictive coding can lower costs dramatically, but may also be subject to extensive negotiations with investigators who may be more comfortable with the older, more familiar process of utilizing search terms.

Given the size and complexity of cartel-related document productions, almost every production will utilize search terms or predictive coding (rather than assessing all documents by hand). The government and private plaintiffs in the U.S. demand (and in practice generally receive) a high degree of transparency regarding these processes. These negotiations are critical not only because they dramatically affect the cost of the document review process, but also because they are in some sense negotiations about the overall boundaries of the case—negotiations over time period, geographic scope, and products at issue often occur first in the context of negotiations over document production.

Counsel should expect to be significantly involved in the process of establishing search terms or establishing the predictive coding model. At this initial stage, the search term process is more intuitive and self-explanatory, and lends itself well to explicit negotiation where each side is aware of and agrees to the exact string of search terms used, although this is not a requirement in private civil litigation. For predictive coding, reviewers will manually review subsets of documents for responsiveness, and use their responses on those subsets to train the model on the sorts of documents considered responsive. The process is iterative: after coding the initial seed set, the reviewers will feed other sets of documents to the model and assess the model's conclusion; once the model has learned enough to code a high percentage of the documents correctly, it can be applied to an entire collection to determine initial responsiveness.

A host of technical problems can affect the client's review costs significantly. Counsel will likely work closely with the e-discovery vendor to help the client understand the costs and risks associated with various responses to these technical challenges.

After responsive documents are gathered through the search term/predictive coding process, the documents should be reviewed for content and privilege. It is often useful to capture a subset of "key" or "hot" documents: in cartel cases, these are generally documents referring to pricing discussions with competitors.

c. Translating Documents

International cartel cases often entail the review and production of a significant number of foreign-language documents. Investigators in the U.S. can insist on translation. It may be sensible, depending on the particular circumstances of the case, to ensure that counsel has staffed the case with lawyers with the most relevant language abilities, and of course, that competent translation services are available.

d. Document Production

Document productions in cartel cases are frequently made on a rolling basis. The exact contents of each production should be recorded so that the information can be accessed and understood several years later. Subpoenas and document requests contain instructions, often quite detailed, regarding the specific format of production. Counsel (and discovery advisors) should have a discussion with the DOJ's IT personnel to understand the government's production formatting requirements.

e.   Document Requests in Later Actions

After documents have been collected and reviewed in connection with a criminal investigation, and a final production to the DOJ has been completed, clients may wish to stop paying outside vendors to host those collections. Whatever action is taken in this regard should be meticulously documented in light of likely civil litigation which may require the production of a more expansive set of materials and data. Importantly, beyond the utility in subsequent civil litigation, preservation and documentation may be instrumental in protecting the client where future related conduct arises, especially in the event of an Leniency Plus scenario.

E.   Project Management and Legal Analysis

Managing a global cartel investigation requires procedural and substantive project management to quickly develop facts and analyze the application of the law to them, particularly to evaluate leniency options.

1.   Project Management

a.   Procedural Project Management

In a global investigation, implementing procedures for tracking communications and submissions is a key aspect of any project management plan. Outlined below are considerations for tracking communications and submissions to government authorities and among members of a joint defense group. In both cases, a systematic and clear procedural record of submissions and communications must be kept. Records are often maintained on two tracks: chronologically (e.g., memorializing all meetings with the government by date) and by topic (e.g., aggregating reverse-proffer information whether it came directly via the government or via the joint defense group).

(1) Government Submissions and Communications

Defendants should closely track their communications with and submissions to each governmental authority. It is good practice to memorialize every government meeting and communication with government authorities—formal and informal reverse-proffers, deferrals or agreements relating to subpoena compliance, and submissions to the government.

A project management plan should also address access to file issues. Leniency applicants and later arriving cooperators should take care to track their governmental submissions. Defendants should also consider requesting access to the evidence against them to the extent it is permitted.

(2) Individual and Co-Defendant Communications

It is also important to memorialize conversations between corporate and individual counsel and among co-defendants, which may provide insight into factual and legal analysis or a view into their communications with the government, including reverse-proffer information or the government's reaction to particular arguments. In addition, particularly for corporate counsel, it is also important to track documents provided to individual and co-defendants' counsel.

b. Substantive Project Management

A primary aspect of cartel investigation project management is managing the review of documents collected in the course of the investigation, both to meet the needs of the investigation and for production to government authorities.

(1) Managing Document Review

Document review is critical to developing the facts in any investigation. A typical cartel investigation focuses on several areas, including communications between competitors; meetings or the opportunity for meetings among competitors; and pricing and bidding documents, including internal communications setting pricing and external submissions to customers.

The repositories and media where documents focusing on these areas are located depend on factors such as corporate information technology structure and individual habits. However, a number of repositories and media are typical areas to focus on—for example, email, email-based schedulers or agendas, diaries and travel and expense reports, and pricing databases. However, technology continues to expand the available methods of communication, and telephone records, texts, chats, and other app- and web-based forms of communication may take on increasing importance. If improper communications exist, individuals may have used alternative forms of communication to conceal them.

(2) Marshalling Documentary Evidence & Interviewing Witnesses

One important and common way to cull documentary evidence into manageable and useful subsets is with chronologies. Chronologies can be helpful in mapping events, contracts or bids, or tracing the evidence related to a particular individual.

In addition to documentary evidence, investigations also rely upon witness interviews. Interview summaries can serve as a resource throughout the investigation and can help avoid the need to revisit issues with witnesses. To preserve privilege, interviews should not be recorded or transcribed and should contain an attorney's thoughts, mental impressions, and conclusions.[24] Interview memoranda should follow a standard format and expressly note that the summary: (i) is not a transcript or verbatim recitation and (ii) contains the thoughts, conclusions, and mental impressions of the attorney. It should also describe the *Upjohn* warning provided to the witness, the witness's understanding of that warning, and agreement to proceed.[25] Finally, witnesses should also be asked to keep interview discussions confidential. This serves to prevent waiver and also protect the integrity of the investigation.

2. Legal Analysis

As the facts particular to an investigation are developed, the legal implications of those facts should also be analyzed. While no investigation is the same, there are recurrent legal issues in cartel investigations that should be among those continually assessed during an investigation.

---

24.   *See* FED. R. CRIM. P. 26.2(f)(2) (defining a statement as "a substantially verbatim, contemporaneously recorded recital of the witness's oral statement that is contained in any recording or any transcription of a recording"); *see also* Palermo v. United States, 360 U.S. 343 (1959); ABA SECTION OF ANTITRUST LAW, CRIMINAL ANTITRUST LITIGATION HANDBOOK 184-93 (2d ed. 2006) [hereinafter *ABA CRIMINAL ANTITRUST LITIGATION HANDBOOK*].

25.   Upjohn Co. v. United States, 449 U.S. 383 (1981).

a. The Existence of an Agreement

The Sherman Act prohibits combinations and conspiracies "in restraint of trade."[26] The key to the existence of a combination or conspiracy is an agreement.[27] "No formal agreement is necessary to constitute an unlawful conspiracy."[28] An agreement "may be found in a course of dealing or other circumstances as well as in an exchange of words."[29] Mere attempts to agree are insufficient,[30] as are conspiracies that lack more than one participant or whose participants are part of the same economic enterprise, e.g., a company and its subsidiary, or a company and its employees,[31] and information exchanges alone, which are judged under the rule of reason but may also be used as evidence of conspiracy.[32] And unlike other areas of criminal law, proof of a Section 1 violation does not require an overt act in furtherance of the conspiracy.[33]

b. The Statute of Limitations

In addition to continually assessing evidence of an agreement, it is important to assess issues related to the statute of limitations. Criminal

26. 15 U.S.C. § 1.
27. *See ABA CRIMINAL ANTITRUST LITIGATION HANDBOOK, supra* note 24, at 261-63.
28. Am. Tobacco Co. v. United States, 328 U.S. 781, 809 (1946); *see also* United States v. Gen. Motors Corp., 384 U.S. 127, 142-43 (1966) ("[I]t has long been settled that explicit agreement is not a necessary part of a Sherman Act conspiracy.").
29. *Id.* at 810; *see also* Interstate Circuit, Inc. v. United States, 306 U.S. 208, 277 (1939) ("Acceptance by competitors, without previous agreement, of an invitation to participate in such a plan, the necessary consequence of which, if carried out, is a restraint of interstate commerce, is sufficient to establish an unlawful conspiracy under the Sherman Act.").
30. *See* United States v. Am. Airlines, 570 F. Supp. 654, 657 (N.D. Tex. 1983) ("Section 1 proscribes only actual combinations, contracts and conspiracies; it does not reach attempts."), *rev'd on other ground*, 743 F.2d 1114, 1119 (5th Cir. 1984).
31. *See* Copperweld Corp. v. Independence Tube Corp., 467 U.S. 752, 769 (1984); ABA SECTION OF ANTITRUST LAW, ANTITRUST LAW DEVELOPMENTS 30-40 (7th ed. 2012).
32. *See* ABA SECTION OF ANTITRUST LAW, ANTITRUST LAW DEVELOPMENTS 97-102 & n.586 (7th ed. 2012).
33. *See ABA CRIMINAL ANTITRUST LITIGATION HANDBOOK, supra* note 24, at 262 & n.20 (collecting cases).

violations of the Sherman Act are governed by a five-year statute of limitations.[34] The statute does not begin to run until the conspiracy's purpose has been achieved or it has been abandoned.[35] As a result, analysis of the limitations period depends upon (i) the timing of the last overt act in furtherance of or receipt of benefit from the conspiracy;[36] (ii) evidence of affirmative withdrawal from the conspiracy;[37] and (iii) circumstances that may toll the statute.[38]

c.   Corporate Entity Liability—Agency and Piercing the Corporate Veil

Two issues commonly arise in the context of corporate investigations: first, corporate liability for the acts of its employees and second, whether a parent entity is liable for the acts of a subsidiary's employees. Corporate defendants are liable for antitrust crimes through the acts of their agents.[39] But "[a] corporation is legally bound by an act of its agent only if the act is within the scope of the agent's employment or within the scope of the

---

34.   18 U.S.C. § 3282(a).

35.   *See* United States v. Inryco, Inc., 642 F.2d 290, 293 (9th Cir. 1981) (Sherman Act conspiracies "remain[] actionable until its purpose has been achieved or abandoned, and the statute of limitations does not run so long as the coconspirators engage in overt acts designed to accomplish its objectives.").

36.   *See ABA CRIMINAL ANTITRUST LITIGATION HANDBOOK, supra* note 24, at 320-26; United States v. Grimm, 2013 WL 6403072, at *4-5 (2d Cir. 2013) (finding that "when anticipated economic benefit continues, in a regular and ordinary course, well beyond the period 'when the unique threats to society posed by a conspiracy are present,' the advantageous interest payment is the *result* of a completed conspiracy, and is not in furtherance of one that is ongoing.") (citations omitted).

37.   *See ABA CRIMINAL ANTITRUST LITIGATION HANDBOOK, supra* note 24, at 326-31.

38.   The statutory period is not tolled by the initiation of a government investigation or grand jury impaneling; absent circumstances such as requests to foreign governments and situations where an individual defendant is a fugitive, it continues to run until indictment or information. *See* 18 U.S.C. § 3292(a)(1) (tolling during official requests for evidence in a foreign country); 18 U.S.C. § 3290 ("No statute of limitations shall extend to any person fleeing from justice.").

39.   United States v. Potter, 463 F.3d 9, 25 (1st Cir. 2006).

agent's actual or apparent authority, and the act is done knowingly and willfully."[40]

Jury charges relating to corporate liability are typically broad. Employers are "legally responsible" for conduct within an employee's actual or apparent authority even where the act is unauthorized or contrary to the employer's instructions so long as the conduct is done with the "hope" or "view of furthering the corporation's business" even if no benefit occurs or the result is adverse.[41]

A parent company generally is "not liable for the acts of its subsidiaries."[42] Where there is no evidence of parent-level involvement, parent entities can be held liable based upon (i) piercing the corporate veil or (ii) based upon principles of common-law agency. Veil piercing is a fact-intensive analysis, which requires a showing of "complete domination" by parent over the subsidiary and evidence that such control was used to commit wrong.[43] The scope and extent of common-law agency, in turn, depends upon "the terms of the agreement and the intention" of the parent and its subsidiary.[44] Designation as an agent for one purpose does not make the subsidiary an agent for every purpose.[45] Rather, liability turns on whether the subsidiary is an agent of the parent "for purposes of the type of conduct in question."[46]

d. Foreign Trade Antitrust Improvements Act

The Foreign Trade Antitrust Improvements Act (FTAIA) limits the application of U.S. antitrust law to foreign commerce.[47] Two areas fall under the Sherman Act and are not limited by the FTAIA: domestic

---

40. Jury Charge at 141-42, United States v. Mitsubishi, Crim. No. 00-033, (E.D. Pa. Feb. 5, 2001).
41. Court's Instruction to the Jury, United States v. Smigel, No. 00-362 (N.D. Tex. Oct. 15, 2001).
42. United States v. Bestfoods, 524 U.S. 51, 61 (1998).
43. WILLIAM MEADE FLETCHER, FLETCHER CYCLOPEDIA OF THE LAW OF CORPORATIONS § 43 (Carol A. Jones ed. 2006).
44. 2A C.J.S. AGENCY § 43 (2016).
45. *Id.*
46. RICHARD S. GRUNER, CORPORATE CRIMINAL LIABILITY AND PREVENTION § 5.02[2][a] (2005).
47. 18 U.S.C. § 6a; Hartford Fire Ins. Co. v. California, 509 U.S. 764, 796 (1993) (Sherman Act applies "to conduct that was meant to produce and did in fact produce some substantial effect in the United States.").

commerce and import trade or commerce.[48] The FTAIA then sets forth exceptions by which non-import, foreign trade or commerce can still fall under the Sherman Act. Namely, if their conduct has (A) a direct, substantial, and reasonably foreseeable effect on (i) U.S. import trade or commerce; (ii) U.S. domestic commerce; or (iii) or export trade or commerce and (B) that effect gives rise to a Sherman Act claim.[49]

F. Joint Defense Agreements

Counsel whose clients have a common interest often enter into a joint defense agreement to promote information sharing while maintaining attorney-client and work product privileges.

1. *Parties to Joint Defense Agreements*

In the context of cartel investigations, common interest often arises among counsel for co-defendants or among corporate counsel and counsel for individual employees or former employees.[50] However, whether or not a common interest exists is dependent upon factual and procedural circumstances. Aligned interests among entities and individuals may change over time depending upon their status in the investigation or civil litigation, and whether they are negotiating a resolution and cooperating or defending the allegations against them.

2. *Form and Terms*

Joint defense agreements can be formal, written, and signed documents or informal oral agreements.[51] If the parties enter into a written agreement, a number of terms should be considered. First, the agreement should outline the basis for common interest. Second, it should carefully address the scope of and any restriction associated with information sharing, including outlining that sharing information pursuant to the agreement will not waive any applicable privilege and that the parties may not share information disclosed by the joint defense group to those outside the group. Finally, the agreement should provide for withdrawal from the

---

48.   18 U.S.C. § 6a.
49.   *Id.*; F. Hoffman-La Roche Ltd. v. Empagran S.A., 542 U.S. 155, 162 (2004).
50.   *See ABA CRIMINAL ANTITRUST LITIGATION HANDBOOK, supra* note 24, at 30.
51.   *See* ABA SECTION OF ANTITRUST LAW, HANDBOOK ON ANTITRUST GRAND JURY INVESTIGATIONS 232 & n. 172 (3d ed. 2002).

joint defense group, while providing continuing confidentiality obligations and for the return of any documents.

G. Persuading the Antitrust Division Not to Indict

1. Preventing Indictment

Persuading the Antitrust Division to drop its investigation requires thoroughly addressing the factual and legal bases for the alleged wrongdoing. Practitioners must dissect the elements of a Sherman Act violation and marshal facts and legal analysis to show that there was not, or could not have been, an anticompetitive agreement. Additionally, legal bars, such as the FTAIA or the statute of limitations can prevent indictment.

Convincing the Antitrust Division of legal and factual hurdles to prosecution requires overcoming asymmetry of information. The Antitrust Division will look to verify counsel's arguments by reviewing the evidence for itself. Counsel must limit the burden on its client entailed in producing the evidence, while ensuring compliance with the Division's demands and production of sufficient evidence to support a defense of the accusations.

Persuasion can take many forms. Two of the most common forms are in-person meetings and white papers. The *Antitrust Division Manual* provides for meetings with Antitrust Division staff and the field office or section leadership.[52] Meetings with the Front Office, consisting of the Director of Criminal Enforcement and the Criminal Deputy Assistant Attorney General are typical, though the *Antitrust Division Manual* cautions that they are not an "absolute right," while meetings with the Assistant Attorney General occur "[o]nly in very unusual circumstances."[53] In addition to meetings, white papers outlining factual and legal positions are also common, particularly if Staff or the Front Office point to particular areas that are significant to their decision or to counter expected portions of Staff's recommendation memoranda.

2. Maintaining Privilege

Using evidence obtained from interviews to prevent indictment has particular privilege implications. Steps should also be taken to ensure memoranda summarizing witness interviews remain privileged. Counsel

---

52.   *ANTITRUST DIV. MANUAL, supra* note 10, at III-119.
53.   *Id.*

should limit the distribution of the memoranda and take care to limit the disclosure of facts memorialized in the memoranda.

Counsel often choose to proffer factual information—and factual information alone—rather than disclose entire interview memoranda or notes. Even oral proffers have been held to constitute waiver of witness interview notes. [54] Counsel should be mindful that waiver before a government authority may result in waiver of that subject matter in other investigations or civil suits.[55] Likewise, counsel should also be wary of subject matter waiver when choosing to disclose information.[56]

3. Resolution

There are a few alternative resolutions to a criminal antitrust investigation. First, and ideally, the Antitrust Division will act according to its policy and provide written notification to corporations and individuals targeted in the investigation that it has closed its case. [57] Second, in certain circumstances, corporate and individual defendants may be confronted with long periods of silence. Despite its inherent uncertainty, silence may be a positive sign that the Antitrust Division has focused its attention elsewhere as the statute of limitations ticks away. Silence is not always golden, however; it may mean the Antitrust Division is awaiting the fruits of an assistance request from another agency or, in the case of a foreign national, has indicted under seal and added the individual to a Red Notice list.[58] Third, although rare, there have been instances where the Antitrust Division entered into deferred prosecution or non-prosecution agreements.[59] Finally, the Antitrust Division has the option to refer the case to another enforcement agency, including other

---

54.   Gruss v. Zwirn, 2013 WL 3481350, at *12. (S.D.N.Y. 2013) (finding waiver after disclosure of witness interview summaries in a presentation to the SEC); SEC v. Vitesse Semiconductor Corp., 2011 WL 2899082, at *3 (S.D.N.Y. 2011) (finding waiver of interview notes following "very detailed" "witness-specific" oral summaries to the SEC).

55.   *See, e.g.*, United States v. Martin, 278 F.3d 988, 999-1000 (9th Cir. 2002) (upholding district court's denial of a motion to suppress, in part because the defendant's statements, though made to his lawyer, were not privileged).

56.   *See* FED. R. EVID. 502.

57.   *ANTITRUST DIV. MANUAL*, *supra* note 10, at III-21.

58.   *See* ABA SECTION OF ANTITRUST LAW, ANTITRUST LAW DEVELOPMENTS 987 (7th ed. 2012).

59.   *Id.* at 982-83.

agencies internationally, state agencies, its civil division or the Federal Trade Commission.[60]

H. International Cartel Investigations

A criminal investigation typically begins when a leniency applicant seeks amnesty in connection with a conspiracy, although it may also result from the Antitrust Division's independent investigative work or from private complaints. The Antitrust Division will then recommend a federal grand jury investigation and issue subpoenas for documents, although there has also been an increase in other investigative tactics such as "dawn raids." As a result of heightened international coordination, it is becoming increasingly common for international antitrust authorities to discuss investigative strategies and coordinate searches, service of subpoenas, drop-in interviews, and the timing of filing of charges.

Once an investigation is underway, a company can still benefit from cooperation with the Antitrust Division and may substantially decrease its criminal fines in exchange for cooperation and an agreement to plead guilty. "Leniency Plus" allows a company attempting to negotiate a plea in a current investigation to receive leniency in exchange for self-reporting involvement in a second, unrelated conspiracy. The company receives amnesty and is protected from receiving any fines or having any of its employees prosecuted criminally in connection with the second offense. The maximum jail term for antitrust offenders is 10 years, the maximum corporate fine is $100 million, and the maximum individual fine is either $1 million or double the loss or gain from the offense.[61]

In 2010, the Antitrust Division began investigating allegations that auto part manufacturers engaged in market allocation, bid rigging, and price fixing.[62] The investigation, which spans three continents and involves foreign enforcement agencies in the European Union, Canada, Mexico, Japan, Korea, and Australia,[63] has been described as the "largest

---

60.   *See* ANTITRUST DIV. MANUAL, *supra* note 10, at III-12-13.
61.   15 U.S.C. § 1.
62.   Press Release, U.S. Dep't of Justice, Corning International Kabushiki Kaisha to Pay $66.5 Million for Fixing Prices of Automotive Parts, (May 16, 2016) *available   at*   https://www.justice.gov/opa/pr/corning-international-kabushiki-kaisha-pay-665-million-fixing-prices-automotive-parts.
63.   Press Release, U.S. Dep't of Justice, Nine Automobile Parts Manufacturers and Two Executives Agree to Plead Guilty to Fixing Prices on Automobile Parts Sold to U.S. Car Manufacturers and Installed in U.S. Cars (Sept. 26,

criminal investigation the Antitrust Division has ever pursued."[64] It has resulted in record-breaking criminal fines,[65] obstruction of justice charges against a number of companies and individuals,[66] and prominent use of the "Leniency Plus" and "Penalty Plus" programs.[67]

The Antitrust Division has undertaken several other major investigations in recent years. In 2002, the Antitrust Division initiated an investigation into Dynamic Random Access Memory (DRAM) manufacturers as a result of claims by U.S. computer-makers that inflated DRAM pricing was causing lost profits and hindering the competitive market. The DRAM investigation resulted in criminal fines totaling $730 million,[68] as well as obstruction of justice charges.[69]

2013), *available at* https://www.justice.gov/opa/pr/nine-automobile-parts-manufacturers-and-two-executives-agree-plead-guilty-fixing-prices.

64. Press Release, U.S. Dep't of Justice, Two Japanese Auto Parts Companies, U.S. Subsidiaries, and Five Executives Indicted for Rigging Automotive Parts Bids (June 15, 2016), *available at* https://www.justice.gov/opa/pr/two-japanese-auto-parts-companies-us-subsidiaries-and-five-executives-indicted-rigging.

65. Press Release, U.S. Dep't of Justice, Yazaki Corp., DENSO Corp. and Four Yazaki Executives Agree to Plead Guilty to Automobile Parts Price-Fixing and Bid-Rigging Conspiracies (Jan. 30, 2012), *available at* https://www.justice.gov/opa/pr/yazaki-corp-denso-corp-and-four-yazaki-executives-agree-plead-guilty-automobile-parts-price.

66. Press Release, U.S. Dep't of Justice, NGK Insulators Ltd. to Pay $65.3 Million for Fixing Prices on Auto Parts (Sept. 3, 2015), *available at* https://www.justice.gov/opa/pr/ngk-insulators-ltd-pay-653-million-fixing-prices-auto-parts.

67. Press Release, U.S. Dep't of Justice, Bridgestone Corp. Agrees to Plead Guilty to Price Fixing on Automobile Parts Installed in U.S. Cars (Feb. 13, 2014), *available at* https://www.justice.gov/opa/pr/bridgestone-corp-agrees-plead-guilty-price-fixing-automobile-parts-installed-us-cars.

68. Press Release, U.S. Dep't of Justice, Sixth Samsung Executive Agrees to Plead Guilty to Participating in Price-Fixing Cartel (Apr. 19, 2007), *available at* https://www.justice.gov/archive/atr/public/press_releases/2007/222770.htm.

69. Press Release, U.S. Dep't of Justice, Elpida Memory Executive Agrees to Plead Guilty for Participating in DRAM Price-Fixing Conspiracy (Nov. 16, 2006), *available at* https://www.justice.gov/archive/opa/pr/2006/November/06_at_770.html.

In 2006, the Antitrust Division began an investigation of price fixing in the thin-film transistor liquid crystal display (TFT-LCD) industry, which resulted in over $1.39 billion in fines from eight companies; additionally, twenty-two executives were charged and thirteen imprisoned for jail terms ranging from six months to three years.[70] The investigation also resulted in the second time in more than a decade that corporate defendants in an international cartel went to trial: in March 2012, a jury returned guilty verdicts against Taiwanese corporation AU Optronics, its American subsidiary, and the former president and vice president for their participation in the conspiracy.[71]

In 2012, the Antitrust Division launched an investigation into the alleged manipulation of the London InterBank Offered Rate (LIBOR), a benchmark rate for short-term interest rates that forms the basis of many loans and contracts globally. Many of the banks implicated in the LIBOR investigation were charged in a separate, but related, investigation into alleged manipulation of the Foreign Exchange (FX) spot market.[72] In 2013, the Royal Bank of Scotland PLC, one of the banks implicated in the investigations, was named a defendant in criminal antitrust charges brought by the Antitrust Division and entered into a deferred prosecution agreement as a result of the ongoing LIBOR investigation, marking the first time a financial services firm had been held criminally liable under antitrust laws for a trader-based market manipulation scheme.[73] Similarly, the Antitrust Division's announcement that Switzerland's UBS AG, another bank implicated in the investigations, had violated its non-prosecution agreement ("NPA") represented "the first time in recent

70. Press Release, U.S. Dep't of Justice, AU Optronics Corporation Executive Sentenced for Role in LCD Price-Fixing Conspiracy (Apr. 29, 2013), *available at* https://www.justice.gov/ opa/pr/au-optronics-corporation-executive-sentenced-role-lcd-price-fixing-conspiracy.

71. Press Release, U.S. Dep't of Justice, Criminal Program Update 2013 (Spring 2013), *available at* https://www.justice.gov/atr/public-documents/division-update-spring 2013/criminal-program.

72. Press Release, U.S. Dep't of Justice, Five Major Banks Agree to Parent-Level Guilty Pleas (May 20, 2015), *available at* https://www.justice.gov/opa/pr/five-major-banks-agree-parent-level-guilty-pleas.

73. *See* Deferred Prosecution Agreement, United States v. The Royal Bank of Scotland PLC, No. 13-00074 (D. Conn. Apr. 12, 2013).

history that the Department of Justice has found that a company breached an NPA over the objection of the company."[74]

---

74.   Loretta Lynch, U.S. Att'y Gen., Remarks at a Press Conference on Foreign Exchange Spot Market Manipulation (May 20, 2015), *available at* http://www.justice.gov/opa/speech/attorney-general-lynch-delivers-remarks-press-conference-foreign-exchange-spot-market.

CHAPTER IV

PARALLEL PROCEEDINGS

Worldwide anti-cartel enforcement activity has surged to remarkable levels in the past two decades. Perhaps the single most significant factor in this growth has been the adoption of amnesty programs by the most active enforcers in anti-cartel efforts globally, including the United States. The expansion of these programs has led not only to a rise in criminal and civil prosecutions worldwide, but also to an increase in private civil lawsuits whose scope reflects the international nature of cartel activities and government enforcement against such activities. This chapter addresses parallel public enforcement and private litigation proceedings and investigates how these parallel streams impact leniency agreements, information sharing and disclosures, collateral estoppel, the role of enforcement agencies in private litigation, and constitutional considerations.

A. Coordinated Investigations and Leniency Agreements

1. U.S. Department of Justice Policies on Parallel Proceedings

With simultaneous cartel investigations across multiple jurisdictions now commonplace, the U.S. Department of Justice (DOJ) Antitrust Division has made cooperation among international enforcement authorities a "top priority."[1] The DOJ seeks to collaborate with foreign governments investigating the same conduct.[2] Recognizing that the "greatest challenge in investigating and prosecuting cross-border cartels is

---

1.   U.S. Dep't of Justice, Division's International Program Enhances Enforcement and Cooperation, Division Update Spring 2016 (Apr. 11, 2016), *available at* https://www.justice.gov/atr/division-operations/division-update-2016/division-international-program-enhances-enforcement-cooperation.

2.   U.S. Dep't of Justice & Fed. Trade Comm'n, Antitrust Enforcement Guidelines for International Operations § 4.2 (Apr. 1995) [hereinafter Antitrust Enforcement Guidelines], *available at* https://www.justice.gov/atr/antitrust-enforcement-guidelines-international-operations.

obtaining evidence and information located in other jurisdictions," the DOJ has said that cooperation with other competition authorities is an "effective" means to overcome this challenge. [3]   Such enhanced coordination is one reason the DOJ has been increasingly able to successfully detect and prosecute international cartels. Thus, the DOJ leadership encourages its staff "to be mindful of the international implications of [their] actions from the start of an investigation right through the remedial phase."[4]

The DOJ has developed close relationships with the competition authorities of many countries and collaborates both formally and informally in cartel investigations.[5] The DOJ has reached agreement with many foreign authorities on notifications, information sharing, and mutual support. Even in the absence of a formal agreement, general rules implemented by multilateral organizations, such as the Organization for Economic Co-operation and Development (OECD) and the International Competition Network (ICN), provide the basis for the DOJ's cooperation policies. [6] Regardless, the DOJ's default policy is to seek to work collaboratively with its foreign counterparts in investigations, including establishing ground rules for doing so on a "case-by-case basis."[7]

The DOJ takes into account issues of international comity when deciding whether to engage in proceedings parallel to those of foreign competition agencies. [8] Specifically, the DOJ considers whether any

---

3. U.S. Dep't of Justice, Contribution from the United States to Global Forum on Competition, Improving International Co-operation in Cartel Investigations at 4 (Jan. 31, 2012) [hereinafter Improving International Co-operation], *available at* https://www.justice.gov/sites/default/files/atr/legacy/2012/08/24/286282.pdf.

4. U.S. Dep't of Justice, Division Update Spring 2011, International Cooperation at an All-Time High (July 13, 2015), *available at* https://www.justice.gov/atr/public-documents/division-update-spring-2011/international-program-update-2011.

5. ANTITRUST ENFORCEMENT GUIDELINES, *supra* note 2, § 2.9; Improving International Co-operation, *supra* note 3, at 3.

6. ANTITRUST ENFORCEMENT GUIDELINES, *supra* note 2, § 2.9.

7. *Id.*; Christine A. Varney, International Cooperation: Preparing for the Future, Remarks as Prepared for the Fourth Annual Georgetown Law Global Antitrust Enforcement Symposium (Sept. 21, 2010), *available at* https://www.justice.gov/atr/speech/international-cooperation-preparing-future ("On a case-by-case basis too, cartel cooperation among competition enforcers also has increased significantly.").

8. ANTITRUST ENFORCEMENT GUIDELINES, *supra* note 2, § 3.2.

country's significant interests would be affected by initiating an investigation, bringing an action, or seeking particular remedies in a given case. The DOJ does so by weighing, among other factors, "the extent to which the enforcement activities of another country with respect to the same persons, including remedies resulting from those activities, may be affected; and [] the effectiveness of foreign enforcement as compared to U.S. enforcement action."[9] The DOJ also considers whether its actions "would interfere with or reinforce the objectives of the foreign proceeding, including any remedies contemplated or obtained by the foreign antitrust authority."[10]

After the DOJ has decided that a proceeding may be warranted, it will "ordinarily notify the antitrust authority in the cartel's home country" of the suspected anticompetitive conduct or potential enforcement action.[11] "If that authority were in a better position to address the competitive problem, and were prepared to take effective action to address the adverse effects on U.S. commerce, the [DOJ] would consider working cooperatively with the foreign authority or staying [its] own remedy pending enforcement efforts by the foreign country."[12] At this pre-investigative stage, cooperation efforts may include "the sharing of leads and background information about the relevant industry and actors, notification of initial investigative actions and the coordination of inspections and interviews."[13]

Once formal investigations are initiated, "much of the cooperation [the] DOJ engages in takes the form of formal requests for assistance pursuant to MLATs or letters rogatory."[14] Steps can also include "sharing of documents obtained by subpoena and search warrant; sharing of documents obtained from foreign defendants pursuant to plea agreements; jointly interviewing witnesses; joint document analysis; and conducting parallel and coordinated plea negotiations."[15] The DOJ also "seek[s] to develop coordinated investigative strategies, such as the simultaneous

---

9.   *Id.*
10.   *Id.*
11.   *Id.*
12.   *Id.*
13.   Improving International Co-operation, *supra* note 3, at 2.
14.   *Id.*
15.   Gary R. Spratling, Criminal Antitrust Enforcement Against International Cartels, Address Before the Advanced Criminal Antitrust Workshop (Feb. 21, 1997), *available at* https://www.justice.gov/atr/speech/criminal-antitrust-enforcement-against-international-cartels.

searches and arrests" of targets.[16] As the DOJ has explained, "information sharing and coordinating the timing and format of critical investigative steps across jurisdictions[] allow[s] each jurisdiction to more effectively execute its own investigation."[17]

When investigations are substantially complete, and "where a punishment by a non-[U.S.] enforcer satisfies the United States' deterrent interests," the DOJ has explained that "prosecutorial discretion may counsel against embarking on a separate action, or perhaps in favor of a reduced penalty, in the [United States]."[18] More recently, the DOJ has expressed interest in "greater discussion among [international] enforcers" to "help [] minimize the risk of inconsistent approaches and overlapping fines" when multiple jurisdictions engage in parallel proceedings.[19] As a result of these efforts by the DOJ, as well as global efforts through the ICN to address commerce that implicates multiple jurisdictions, entities facing such penalties are increasingly seeking or facilitating discussions among enforcers and engaging in advocacy to reduce the possibility of duplicative, unnecessary, or unwarranted punishment.

---

16. Rachel Brandenburger, Special Advisor, Antitrust Div., U.S. Dep't of Justice, International Cooperation: Where Next?, Remarks as Prepared for the Women's Competition Network at 9 (May 23, 2011), *available at* https://www.justice.gov/atr/file/518341/download; *see also* William Baer, Assistant Att'y Gen., Antitrust Div,. U.S. Dep't of Justice, Cooperation, Convergence, and the Challenges Ahead in Competition Enforcement, Remarks as Prepared for the Ninth Annual Global Antitrust Enforcement Symposium (Sept. 29, 2015), *available at* https://www.justice.gov/opa/ speech/assistant-attorney-general-bill-baer-delivers-remarks-ninth- annual-global-antitrust ("We coordinate searches and dawn raids.").

17. Antitrust Div., U.S. Dep't of Justice, Division's International Program Enhances Enforcement and Cooperation (Apr. 11, 2016), *available at* https://www.justice.gov/atr/division-operations/division-update- 2016/division-international-program-enhances-enforcement-cooperation.

18. Brandenburger, International Cooperation: Where Next?, *supra* note 16, at 7.

19. Brent Snyder, Deputy Assistant Att'y Gen., Antitrust Div., U.S. Dep't of Justice, Leniency in Multi-Jurisdictional Investigations: Too Much of a Good Thing?, Remarks as Prepared for Delivery at the Sixth Annual Chicago Forum on International Antitrust (June 8, 2015), *available at* https://www.justice.gov/sites/default/files/atr/legacy/2015/06/30/315474. pdf.

2. *International Leniency Programs*

In 1993, the DOJ adopted its Amnesty Program.[20] As of 2018, there are more than sixty jurisdictions with some form of leniency program and the landscape is continually evolving. [21] For example, in 2014, the Competition Authority of Kenya announced a new leniency program which makes companies and directors that voluntarily disclose the existence of anticompetitive practices eligible for reduced penalties.[22] The following year, Hong Kong released a new leniency policy which would shield the first cartel member to self-report anticompetitive conduct from pecuniary penalties. [23] At the same time, countries with established leniency programs seek to update and improve those regimes. In 2014 and 2015 alone, competition authorities in various jurisdictions updated their leniency programs to require applicants to unconditionally admit to cartel activity in exchange for reduced fines (Singapore); shorten the amount of time that cartel members have to self-report anti-competitive activity (Colombia); and prohibit leniency for repeat offenders of local anti-competition laws (South Korea).[24]

---

20.   Antitrust Div., U.S. Dep't of Justice, Corporate Leniency Policy (Aug. 10, 1993), *available at* https://www.justice.gov/atr/file/810281/ download.

21.   Org. for Econ. Co-operation & Dev. [OECD], *Challenges and Co-Ordination of Leniency Programmes* (2018), *available at* https://one.oecd.org/document/DAF/COMP/WP3(2018)1/en/pdf.

22.   Mugambi Mutegi, *Cartel firms get amnesty in new CAK regulation*, BUS. DAILY AFR. (Aug. 25, 2014), *available at* http://www.businessdailyafrica.com/Corporate-News/Cartel-firms-get-amnesty-in-new-CAK-regulation/-/539550/2429612/-/10y3f08/-/index.html.

23.   Press Release, Hong Kong Competition Commission, Competition Commission Publishes Enforcement Policy and Cartel Leniency Policy (Nov. 19, 2015), *available at* https://www.compcomm.hk/en/media/press/files/20151119_PressRel_Policy_Documents_Eng.pdf.

24.   *See* Competition Commission of Sing., CCS Guidelines on Lenient Treatment for Undertakings Coming Forward with Information on Cartel Activity, *available at* https://www.ccs.gov.sg/public-register-and-consultation/public-consultation-items/public-consultation-on-proposed-changes-to-ccs-guidelines?type=public_consultation; Carolina Prieto, *Decree 1523 of 2015 establishes new rules to apply for the leniency program in Colombia*, GLOBAL COMPLIANCE NEWS (Sept. 14, 2015), *available at* http://globalcompliancenews.com/decree-1523-of-2015-establishes-new-rules-to-apply-for-the-leniency-program-in-colombia/;

As a result of converging policies, the majority of leniency programs share common features, although the details of implementation differ.[25] These similarities allow actual or potential subjects of international cartel investigations to make decisions on a global scale about whether to self-report and cooperate with enforcement authorities. If the provisions of the leniency policy in one jurisdiction are so unattractive that they dissuade a potential applicant from applying there, that potential applicant may not self-report or cooperate in any jurisdiction.

In general, these programs offer guaranteed immunity from penalty to the first cartel member that cooperates with authorities, while simultaneously threatening severe penalties for those who fail to self-disclose. For instance, the European Commission offers complete immunity from fines to the first cartel member that reports and provides evidence of illegal conduct.[26] Those who fail to self-report face fines that not only take into account the duration of the conduct and the value of affected commerce, but also have a sufficient deterrent effect to both the infringer and others who might engage in anticompetitive behavior.[27] Similarly, Canada offers immunity from prosecution to the first cartel member to self-report anticompetitive conduct.[28]

Many jurisdictions, including those in Europe, South Korea and Japan, also offer incentives to cartel members who are not the first to report, self-report, and cooperate.[29] For example, the European Commission makes

Press Release, S. Kor. Fair Trade Commission, Prior Administrative Notice of Amendment to Public Notification on Leniency for Voluntary Reporting (Nov. 19, 2014), *available at* http://eng.ftc.go.kr.

25.　Michael G. Egge & Alexandra L. Shandell, *Managing the Risk of Tagbacks to Leniency Applicants in Cartel Investigations*, ANTITRUST SOURCE, Jun. 2012, at 3, *available at* http://www.americanbar.org/content/dam/aba/publishing/antitrust_source/jun12_egge_6_26f.authcheckdam.pdf.

26.　EUROPEAN COMM'N, CARTELS: LENIENCY (Apr. 1, 2016) [hereinafter CARTELS: LENIENCY], *available at* http://ec.europa.eu/competition/cartels/leniency/leniency.html.

27.　EUROPEAN COMM'N, GUIDELINES ON THE METHOD OF SETTING FINES IMPOSED PURSUANT TO ARTICLE 23(A)(A) OF REGULATION NO 1/2003, 2006 O.J. (C 210) 2, *available at* http://eur-lex.europa.eu/legal-content/EN/ALL/?uri=CELEX:52006XC0901(01).

28.　CANADIAN COMPETITION BUREAU, BULLETIN: LENIENCY PROGRAM § 3.1 (Sept. 29, 2010), *available at* http://www.competitionbureau.gc.ca/eic/site/cb-bc.nsf/eng/03288.html.

29.　*See* Egge & Shandell, *supra* note 25, at 3 (describing the general scope of the amnesty-plus program).

available to the second cooperator a discount in fines of up to 20 to 30 percent.[30] The DOJ also rewards timely cooperators with greater credit for cooperation than companies that only later accept responsibility for their wrongdoing, although the degree of credit awarded depends on, among other factors, the value of the evidence offered by the cooperating party.[31]

Details regarding leniency and other features of many of the most active jurisdictions can be found in Chapter IX.

3. Managing Information Disclosures Across Jurisdictions

Investigations into international cartels increasingly involve competition authorities in different jurisdictions sharing information, either via informal communication channels or formal agreements such as treaties. Managing how and what information is disclosed requires careful attention to differing privilege and confidentiality rules, many of which afford less robust attorney-client privilege and/or confidentiality protection than would be provided in the United States.

With the expansion of leniency programs, it has become more common for companies engaged in self-reporting to seek leniency in multiple jurisdictions. Permitting some degree of exchange of otherwise-confidential information with foreign enforcement agencies is a de facto requirement for leniency applicants and subsequent cooperators in many jurisdictions.

Notwithstanding agreements and treaties that encourage information sharing between signatories, jurisdictions will generally not share confidential information provided by a leniency applicant unless the leniency applicant consents, typically by written waiver. Under the DOJ's longstanding policy, the DOJ does not disclose to foreign authorities "information obtained from a leniency applicant unless the leniency applicant agrees first to the disclosure," but the DOJ expects leniency applicants to agree to such disclosures in the form of waiver letters.[32]

---

30. CARTELS: LENIENCY, *supra* note 26.
31. *See generally* Scott D. Hammond, Deputy Assistant Att'y Gen., Antitrust Div., U.S. Dep't of Justice, Measuring the Value of Second-In Cooperation in Corporate Plea Negotiations, Remarks Before The 54th Annual American Bar Association Section of Antitrust Law Spring Meeting (March 29, 2006), *available at* https://www.justice.gov/atr/speech/measuring-value-second-cooperation-corporate-plea-negotiations.
32. Scott D. Hammond, Deputy Assistant Att'y Gen., Antitrust Div., U.S. Dep't of Justice, Dispelling the Myths Surrounding Information Sharing,

These waivers typically fall into two categories: "procedural" and "full" waivers. In the leniency context, "procedural" waivers are limited in scope and apply only to the information necessary to coordinate key investigative steps between agencies, whereas "full" waivers permit the exchange of substantive information, including both information provided in the context of the leniency application itself and information subsequently provided by the applicant.[33]

Waivers of confidentiality typically only provide the amount and kind of confidentiality protection that would otherwise be required if the information had been directly received by the *receiving* agency.[34] Because such protections vary widely by jurisdiction, the decision of whether to grant a waiver has significant strategic implications. For example, the scope of the attorney-client privilege and work-product protections can differ (e.g. the Australian Federal Court recently ruled that the Australian Consumer and Competition Commission cannot prevent disclosure to other defendants in a cartel investigation notes taken by agency officials during proffer discussions.)[35] Likewise, substantial uncertainty exists in the European Union as to whether documents submitted by a leniency applicant must be disclosed to a private plaintiff in a subsequent suit for money damages.[36] Leniency applicants and subsequent cooperators therefore should consider carefully the potential for disclosure in the receiving jurisdiction.

## 4.	*Treaties and Formal Cooperation Agreements*

In today's global economy, antitrust criminal cartel investigations routinely involve foreign individuals and evidence. Therefore, antitrust enforcers are tasked with coordinating across borders to extract evidence and individuals for investigation and prosecution. The four categories of agreements most often used in cartel investigations—Antitrust Cooperation Agreements, Antitrust Mutual Assistance Agreements,

---

Speech Before the ICN Cartels Workshop (Nov. 20-21, 2004), *available at* http://www.justice.gov/atr/public/speeches/206610.htm.

33.	INT'L COMPETITION NETWORK, WAIVERS OF CONFIDENTIALITY IN CARTEL INVESTIGATIONS—EXPLANATORY NOTE 4, *available at* http://www.internationalcompetitionnetwork.org/uploads/library/doc1012.pdf.

34.	*Id.* at 3.

35.	ACCC v. Prysmian & Ors, SAD 145/2009.

36.	*See* C-360/09, Pfleiderer AG v. Bundeskartellamt, 2011 E.C.R. I-5186 (Eur. Ct. Justice).

Mutual Legal Assistance Treaties, and Extradition Treaties—are discussed here.

a.   International Antitrust Enforcement Assistance Act

The International Antitrust Enforcement Assistance Act of 1994 (IAEAA) authorizes the DOJ and the Federal Trade Commission (FTC) to enter into reciprocal cooperative agreements—(referred to as Antitrust Mutual Assistance Agreements (AMAAs)—with foreign antitrust agencies.[37] Congress passed the IAEAA in November 1994 in response to concerns that effective antitrust enforcement by U.S. and foreign agencies was hampered by the fact that a country's domestic confidentiality restrictions often bar the transmittal of important antitrust evidence to agencies in other jurisdictions.[38] Commentators observed that the DOJ and the FTC initially were eager to use the IAEAA to develop a "broad network" of AMAAs, including agreements with the European Union and its Member States.[39] However, such a network of agreements has yet to materialize. To date the United States has entered into only one agreement pursuant to the IAEAA—an AMAA with Australia that was finalized in April 1999—and there is no indication that the DOJ or the FTC have current plans to enter into additional AMAAs.[40]

---

37.   International Antitrust Enforcement Assistance Act of 1994, 15 U.S.C. §§ 6201-6211 (Supp. 1996).

38.   *See* H.R. REP. NO. 103-722, (Oct. 3, 1994); *see also* Anne K. Bingaman, International Antitrust: A Report from the Department of Justice, Address Before the Fordham Corporate Law Institute (Oct. 27, 1994), *available at* https://www.justice.gov/atr/speech/international-antitrust-report-department-justice (supporting enactment of IAEAA because improving international antitrust enforcement requires "continued progress in the areas of mutual assistance and procedural reciprocity").

39.   *See* Laraine L. Laudati and Todd J. Friedbacher, *Trading Secrets—The International Antitrust Enforcement Assistance Act*, 16 NW.J. INT'L L & BUS. 478, 479 & n. 4 (1995-1996) (noting that U.S. officials met with officials in EU Member States to promote the IAEAA and that the House and Senate Reports regarding the IAEAA "strongly allude" to agreements with the European Union and its Member States).

40.   Agreement on Mutual Antitrust Enforcement Assistance, Austl.-U.S., Apr. 27, 1999, *available at* https://www.justice.gov/sites/default/files/atr/legacy/2015/01/15/311076.pdf.

An AMAA allows a foreign antitrust authority to request the DOJ or the FTC to: (1) share information already in their possession;[41] or (2) use their investigative powers to collect new evidence. [42] In providing investigative assistance, the DOJ or the FTC may use its normal investigative powers,[43] or it may apply to a U.S. federal district court for an order compelling a private party to give testimony or produce documents or other evidence.[44]

In the criminal context, the IAEAA allows for confidential grand jury information to be shared with foreign authorities in limited circumstances. Although the IAEAA generally prohibits the disclosure of grand jury information in accordance with Federal Rule of Criminal Procedure 6(e), such information may be disclosed if the foreign antitrust authority demonstrates to a court that it has "particularized need" for the information.[45]

Critics of the IAEAA have pointed out that the Act's reciprocity provisions require many nations to revise their existing confidentiality and information sharing statutes in order to enter an AMAA with the United States, which these nations are reluctant to do.[46] U.S. and foreign agencies are therefore likely to continue to rely on other cross-border information sharing mechanisms to gather evidence.

b. Antitrust Cooperation Agreements

The DOJ's Antitrust Division and international agencies typically share information with each other pursuant to formal treaties, Antitrust Cooperation Agreements (ACAs), and matter-specific waiver letters

---

41.   15 U.S.C. § 6201.
42.   *Id.* § 6202(b).
43.   *Id.* § 6202(b).
44.   *Id.* § 6203(a).
45.   *Id.* § 6204(2). The text of the IAEAA provides no guidance as to what constitutes "particularized need" in this context. The drafters of the IAEAA "purposely [did] not specify any standard or criteria" on this point in order to afford courts with the "latitude to make this determination in accordance with the jurisprudence as it exists and as it may develop in the future." H.R. Rep. No. 103-722 at 17-18 (Oct. 3, 1994). Courts have yet to opine on the meaning of "particularized need" as it pertains to the IAEAA.
46.   *See* Peter J. White, *International Judicial Assistance in Antitrust Enforcement: The Shortcomings of Current Practices and Legislation, and the Roles of International Organizations*, 62 ADMIN. L. REV. 263, 273 & n.72 (2010).

executed by leniency applicants, subsequent cooperators, and other entities under investigation.[47] Most ACAs commit the signatory antitrust authorities to provide information already in their possession upon request and voluntarily, although this commitment does not supersede domestic laws that forbid the sharing of certain types of information.[48]

ACAs are "soft" commitments, subordinate to domestic laws and interests that establish protocols for and memorialize existing inter-agency relationships. Most ACAs commit the respective agencies to provide information that domestic law does not otherwise exempt from disclosure, and usually to consider seeking reciprocal waivers to enable the disclosure of information across jurisdictions. Because these agency agreements do not permit the disclosure of information that is shielded by domestic law, they do not independently allow the cross-border disclosure of otherwise-protected information without a waiver of some kind. Information that may typically be exchanged without a waiver includes non-public agency information specific to an investigation, general information regarding enforcement activities, and other publicly available information.[49]

It should be noted that in the absence of a waiver, agencies can still discuss non-confidential and publicly available information, share general information about deadlines, and trade views on market conditions and theories of harm.[50] However, many enforcement authorities prefer to have executed waivers in hand because they allow substantive discussions between authorities in different jurisdictions, the sharing of documents and data, and the close coordination of investigations.

c.   Mutual Legal Assistance Treaties

The United States has entered into mutual legal assistance treaties (MLATs) with approximately 80 other countries under which the United

---

47.   The United States is a party to ACAs with Brazil, Canada, Germany, Israel, Japan, Mexico, Australia, and the Commission. *See* ABA SECTION OF ANTITRUST LAW, INT'L ANTITRUST COOPERATION HANDBOOK 37 (2004) [hereinafter *INT'L ANTITRUST COOPERATION HANDBOOK*].

48.   *Id.* at 40.

49.   INT'L COMPETITION NETWORK, WAIVERS OF CONFIDENTIALITY IN CARTEL INVESTIGATIONS – EXPLANATORY NOTE, *supra* note 33, at 5.

50.   Leslie C. Overton, Deputy Assistant Att'y Gen., Antitrust Div., U.S. Dep't of Justice, International Antitrust Engagement: Benefits And Opportunities, Remarks at the Fifth Annual Chicago Forum on International Antitrust Issues 5 (June 12, 2014), *available at* https://www.justice.gov/atr/file/517786/download.

States and its co-signatory agree to assist one another in criminal law enforcement matters.[51] Although the specific terms of each treaty vary, they generally allow information to be shared with the criminal law enforcement authorities in each signatory's jurisdiction, and provide for mutual assistance in criminal law enforcement matters such as the conduct of searches, the taking of witness testimony, and service of documents. While MLATs apply generally to all criminal law enforcement matters, and the DOJ frequently employs the tools MLATs make available whenever necessary to investigate and prosecute cartel behavior, certain countries may not allow their use in antitrust cases if those countries do not view cartel conduct as criminal.[52]

The goal of MLATs is to "improve the effectiveness of judicial assistance and to regularize and facilitate its procedures." [53] Only government officials, most typically prosecutors, can resort to MLAT remedies.[54] In most cases, defense attorneys may not use MLATs to obtain evidence located in a foreign country and find the country's laws restrict access to such evidence.[55]

Certain MLATs apply only when the underlying offense is a crime in both the requesting country and the country providing assistance.[56] This "dual criminality" requirement may be implicated in the antitrust context, because relatively few countries have criminalized cartel or other collusive

---

51.　U.S. Dep't of Justice, Submission to Directorate for Financial and Enterprise Affairs, Organisation for Economic Co-Operation and Development, Discussion on How to Define Confidential Information at 7 (Oct. 29, 2013), *available at*, https://www.justice.gov/sites/default/files/atr/legacy/2015/04/02/311212.pdf.

52.　*INT'L ANTITRUST COOPERATION HANDBOOK*, *supra* note 47, at 10, 63-64. Some MLATs specifically carve out antitrust and competition matters regardless of whether the signatory recognizes cartel conduct as criminal. *Id.* at 9.

53.　*Id.* at 9.

54.　*Id.*

55.　*Id.*

56.　*See* Treaty Between the Government of the United States of America and the Government of Malaysia on Mutual Legal Assistance in Criminal Matters, Malay–U.S., art. 3, July 28, 2006, S. TREATY DOC. NO. 109-22, (stating that the requested state may refuse assistance if "the request relates to an act or omission that, if it had occurred in the requested state, would not have constituted an offence against the laws of the requested state punishable under the laws of that state by deprivation of liberty for a period of one year or more, or by a more severe penalty").

conduct.[57] In those jurisdictions, process crimes (such as obstruction of justice), fraud or bid rigging may satisfy the dual criminality requirement.[58] However, most MLATs do not use the requirement to deny or reduce the assistance available under the MLAT.[59]

The DOJ largely has avoided providing specific details publicly regarding its use of MLATs, although some details have emerged. One example is the "fax paper" cases, where the DOJ worked with Canadian antitrust authorities to charge six Japanese firms, two U.S. subsidiaries of Japanese firms, the U.S. subsidiary of a Swedish firm, five Japanese nationals, and one U.S. national with price-fixing in the fax paper market. The investigation involved extensive information sharing between the United States and Canada within the bounds of the applicable MLAT, and resulted in eight defendants pleading guilty.[60]

Signatories use MLATs in both the investigative and the prosecutorial phases of a criminal investigation typically by requesting a country to: (i) exercise a coercive power (such as forced witness testimony or

57.   ABA SECTION OF ANTITRUST LAW, HANDBOOK ON ANTITRUST GRAND JURY INVESTIGATIONS 266 (3d Ed. 2002), *INT'L ANTITRUST COOPERATION HANDBOOK*, *supra* note 47, at 63-64. As of the date of publication, the countries criminalizing antitrust violations include: Australia, Austria, Barbados, Brazil, Canada, Czech Republic, Cyprus, Denmark, Estonia, France, Germany, Greece, Hungary, Iceland, Indonesia, Ireland, Israel, Italy, Japan, Kenya, Latvia, Malta, Mexico, Norway, Poland, Romania, Russia, Slovakia, Slovenia, Spain, South Africa, South Korea, Taiwan, Thailand, United Kingdom, United States, and Zambia. *See* Gregory C. Shaffer, Nathaniel H. Nesbitt, and Spencer Weber Waller, *Criminalizing Cartels: A Global Trend?*, RESEARCH HANDBOOK ON COMPARATIVE COMPETITION LAW (2015), Veronica Pinotti and Martino Sforza, *Interplay Between Antitrust and Criminal Law in Europe*, BLOOMBERG LAW REPORTS ANTITRUST & TRADE (2011).

58.   *INT'L ANTITRUST COOPERATION HANDBOOK*, *supra* note 47, at 64.

59.   The MLAT between Switzerland and the United States expressly bans its application to antitrust proceedings. *See* Mutual Legal Assistance Treaty with Switzerland, Switz.–U.S., May 25, 1973, 27 U.S.T. 2019, (stating that the Treaty shall not apply to an investigation or proceeding "for the purpose of enforcing cartel or antitrust laws").

60.   Joel I. Klein, Acting Assistant Atty. Gen., Antitrust Div., U.S. Dep't of Justice, The Internationalization of Antitrust: Bilateral And Multilateral Responses, Remarks Before the European University Institute Conference of Competition (June 13, 1997), *available at* https://www.justice.gov/atr/speech/internationalization-antitrust-bilateral-and-multilateral-responses.

mandatory reporting by experts) and/or (ii) to obtain an order of a court or a search warrant.[61] This may include assistance with the following:

- taking testimony or statements of persons[62]
- providing documents, records, and evidence
- providing service of process
- locating and identifying persons of interest
- transferring persons in custody for testimony or other purposes
- executing requests for search and seizure[63]

Certain MLATs also commit the signatories to assist with the immobilization or forfeiture of assets, or contain catch-all provisions for "any other form of assistance not prohibited by the laws of the Requested State." [64] The scope of assistance available also depends on the specific MLAT, as some allow for assistance to be provided solely in accordance with domestic law, as permitted under the terms of the treaty, or both.[65]

d.   Extradition Treaties

Extradition treaties permit the signatories to request the transfer of individuals for prosecution in the requesting country. The United States is currently a party to over one hundred extradition treaties.[66] Under these treaties, the criminal offense must be sufficiently serious (punishable by at least a one-year jail sentence), and the extradition remedies are only available to the signatory governments, rather than individuals.[67]

Further, because extradition treaties, unlike most MLATs, do not waive or otherwise relax the dual criminality requirement, the offense must be "sufficiently serious" in both countries. Older extradition treaties

---

61.   *INT'L ANTITRUST COOPERATION HANDBOOK, supra* note 47, at 55.
62.   This assistance involves both the right to request that the person be compelled to testify and to request that the person voluntarily appear in the requesting state. *See INT'L ANTITRUST COOPERATION HANDBOOK, supra* note 47, at 60-61.
63.   *See* Mutual Legal Assistance Treaty Between the United States of America and the United Kingdom of Great Britain and Northern Ireland, U.K.–U.S., January 6, 1994, S. TREATY DOC. NO. 104-2, art 1.
64.   *Id., see also INT'L ANTITRUST COOPERATION HANDBOOK, supra* note 47, at 60.
65.   *INT'L ANTITRUST COOPERATION HANDBOOK, supra* note 47, at 58-59.
66.   *Id.* at 65.
67.   *Id.* at 67.

have a "list" system, with the crimes qualifying for extradition listed in the body of the treaty, but more recent treaties require "pure" dual criminality conduct that would constitute a serious offense in both the requesting and requested countries.[68] Certain treaties contain additional requirements if, for example, the offense occurred outside the requested country,[69] while others prohibit the use, or allow the country to exercise discretion not to use, the treaty against a national of the requested country.[70] Therefore, these treaties may only be used to extradite a national of the requesting country, or a foreign national located in the requested country.

Extradition treaties typically only permit extradition of the person of interest; however, some treaties also allow for the seizure of related evidence.[71] Given the number of alternative means to obtain evidence from other jurisdictions, and the historical difficulty seeking extradition in antitrust cases, this has not been a primary enforcement tool of U.S. antitrust agencies.

e.   Informal Information Sharing

International treaties and agreements have facilitated the sharing of information between jurisdictions investigating the same conduct. Informal cooperation, however, represents the most significant recent cooperative development. International enforcement authorities now increasingly cooperate informally because, as explained by former Canadian Commissioner of Competition Sheridan Scott, "[n]o amount of formal cooperation agreements can substitute for the ability to pick up the

---

68.   Julian M. Joshua, Peter D. Camesasca, Youngjin Jung, *Extradition and Mutual Legal Assistance Treaties: Cartel Enforcement's Global Reach*, 75 ANTITRUST L.J. 353, 364 (2008).

69.   *See* Extradition Treaty Between the Government of the United States of America and the Government of the Swiss Confederation, art. 1.2, Switz.– U.S., November 14, 1990, S. TREATY DOC. NO. 104-9 (stating "with respect to an offence committed outside the territory of the Requesting State, the Requested State shall grant extradition if: (a) its law would provide for the punishment of such an offense in similar circumstances; or (b) the person sought is a national of the Requesting State or is wanted for an offence against a national of the Requesting State").

70.   *See* Extradition Treaty Between the United States of America and France, art. 3.1, Fr.–U.S., April 23, 1996, S. TREATY DOC. NO. 105-13 ("[t]here is no obligation upon the Requested State to grant the extradition of a person who is a national of the Requested State").

71.   *INT'L ANTITRUST COOPERATION HANDBOOK*, *supra* note 47, at 67-68.

phone and informally talk something out with a foreign counterpart . . . ."[72]

Beyond sharing leads, informal cooperation includes sharing investigative strategies, offering wider access to people and evidence located within their borders, and coordinating their enforcement efforts.[73] Informal cooperation is effective because it circumvents the need to jump through legislative or judicial hoops or obtain prior approvals to cooperate regarding the initiation of compulsory process, the coordination of subsequent investigations, the exchange of status reports regarding their investigations, the sharing of investigative plans, and the discussion of their prosecutorial objectives. These exchanges now occur far more frequently, on both bilateral and multilateral bases.[74]

Cross-waivers by leniency applicants have permitted enforcement agencies to exchange a great deal of crucial substantive evidence, all on an informal basis. Reciprocal cross-waivers by amnesty applicants likewise have resulted in exchanges of far more information than that exchanged pursuant to formal agreements.[75]

---

72. Sheridan Scott, "C" Is For Competition: How We Get Things Done In A Globalized Business World, Remarks Before the Insight Conference (June 17, 2005), at 4-6.

73. *See* Scott D. Hammond, Dir. of Criminal Enforcement, U.S. Dep't of Justice, Beating Cartels At Their Own Game—Sharing Information In The Fight Against Cartels, Remarks Before the Inaugural Symposium on Competition Policy (Nov. 20, 2003) *available at* https://www.justice.gov/ atr/speech/beating-cartels-their-own-game-sharing-information-fight-against-cartels.

74. As an example, the DOJ cooperated "extensively" with the Japanese Fair Trade Commission in investigating and prosecuting Japanese companies and executives accused of fixing prices for auto parts. Leslie C. Overton, Deputy Assistant Atty Gen., U.S. Dep't of Justice, International Antitrust Engagement: Benefits and Opportunities, Remarks Before the Fifth Annual Chicago Forum on International Antitrust Issues (June 12, 2014), *available at* https://www.justice.gov/atr/file/517786/download.

75. These discussions and exchanges are facilitated by the relationships developed in enforcement agency working groups, particularly the International Competition Network (ICN) and its Cartel Working Group. *See Cartel*, INTERNATIONAL COMPETITION NETWORK, http://www.internationalcompetitionnetwork.org/working-groups/current/ cartel.aspx. The Organization for Economic Cooperation and Development is another forum through which international agencies continue to share information and develop best practices, including in the area of cartel

5. Cross-Border Evidentiary and Legal Issues—Blocking Statutes

In response to the extraterritorial application of U.S. antitrust law by U.S. enforcement agencies and courts, many nations passed "blocking statutes" which limit or prohibit the disclosure of certain information outside a country's borders.[76] Blocking statutes, which can act as serious hurdles to the free sharing of evidence between agencies in different jurisdictions, "have the general effect of refusing to enforce United States requests for production of documents located within the territory of the 'blocking' nation, and of preventing the enforcement of American judgments."[77] These statutes further demonstrate the importance of formal information sharing agreements to international criminal cartel enforcement.

In 1982, Congress passed the Foreign Trade Antitrust Improvements Act (FTAIA),[78] to clarify the Sherman Act's scope as applied to foreign conduct and commerce.[79] It generally excludes from the reach of the Sherman Act anticompetitive conduct that causes only foreign injury.[80] It accomplishes this by eliminating exporting and commercial activities taking place abroad as actionable conduct *unless* those activities adversely affect domestic commerce, imports to the United States, or exporting activities of one engaged in such activities within the United States.[81] The FTAIA can be distilled to two main principles salient in most cases implicating foreign conduct or markets. First, because the FTAIA exempts import trade, antitrust liability for import conduct remains unaltered, and the Sherman Act thus applies to any "import trade or import commerce" with foreign nations.[82] Second, the Sherman Act still applies to non-import

---

enforcement. *See Cartels and Anti-competitive Agreements*, ORGANIZATION FOR ECONOMIC COOPERATION AND DEVELOPMENT, *available at* http://www.oecd.org/competition/cartels/.

76. Kevin R. Roberts, *Extraterritorial Application of United States Antitrust Laws: Minimizing Conflicts*, 1 U. MIAMI INT'L & COMP. L. REV. 325, 345 (1991).

77. *Id.*

78. Pub. L. No. 97-290, 96 Stat. 1246 (codified at 15 U.S.C. § 6a).

79. F. Hoffmann-La Roche Ltd. v. Empagran S.A., 542 U.S. 155, 169 (2004).

80. *Id.* at 158.

81. *Id.* at 161; 15 U.S.C. § 6a.

82. 15 U.S.C. § 6a (excluding "import trade or import commerce"); United States v. Hui Hsiung, 778 F.3d 738, 751, 754 (9th Cir. 2015) ("[I]mport trade . . . does not fall within the FTAIA at all. It falls within the Sherman Act without further clarification or pleading.")

conduct if the conduct has a "direct, substantial, and reasonably foreseeable effect" on domestic markets.[83]

To determine whether conduct constitutes "import" trade or commerce, courts ask whether the defendants or their co-conspirators manufactured the products at issue abroad and sold them into the United States. Thus, in cases involving foreign cartel members, "transactions that are directly between [U.S.] purchasers and the defendant cartel members are the import commerce of the United States"[84] Direct sales to the United States by a defendant, however, may not necessarily be required. As the Third Circuit has held, the exemption of import commerce from the FTAIA "is not limited to importers, but also applies if the defendants' conduct is directed at an import market."[85]

For non-import trade, application of the domestic-effects exception of the FTAIA often turns on whether the effects on U.S. commerce can be said to be sufficiently "direct." Courts have differing standards, however, as to what this language requires. The Ninth Circuit maintains that conduct only has the requisite "direct" effect on U.S. commerce "if it follows as an immediate consequence of the defendant[s'] activity." [86] An effect, therefore, cannot be direct where it depends on "uncertain intervening developments." [87] Both the Second and the Seventh Circuits, however, interpret "direct" more liberally to "require only a reasonably proximate causal nexus"—rejecting the "immediate consequence" standard.[88] These

---

83.   *Hsiung,* 778 F.3d at 751; 15 U.S.C. § 6a.
84.   Minn-Chem, Inc. v. Agrium, Inc., 683 F.3d 845, 855 (7th Cir. 2012); *accord Hsiung,* 778 F.3d at 755 (concluding that "transactions between the foreign defendant producers of TFT-LCDs and purchasers located in the United States" are "import commerce"); Carrier Corp. v. Outokumpu Oyj, 673 F.3d 430, 438 & n. 3, 440 (6th Cir. 2012) (holding goods manufactured abroad and sold in the United States are "import commerce"); Motorola Mobility LLC v. AU Optronics Corp., 775 F.3d 816, 818 (7th Cir. 2015) (noting the exemption applies when "defendants conspired to sell LCD panels to Motorola in the United States at inflated prices").
85.   Animal Sci. Prods., Inc. v. China Minmetals Corp., 654 F.3d 462, 470-71 & n. -11 (3d Cir. 2011).
86.   United States v. LSL Biotechnologies, 379 F.3d 672, 680-81 (9th Cir. 2004) (holding possible harms to future innovation in development of tomato seeds insufficient to establish a direct effect on American commerce).
87.   *Id.; Hsiung,* 778 F.3d at 758-59.
88.   Lotes Co., Ltd. v. Hon Hai Precision Indus. Co., 753 F.3d 395, 398 (2d Cir. 2014); *Minn-Chem,* 683 F.3d at 857, 860.

circuits have adopted the more tort-like standard advocated by the DOJ to address Congress' "classic" concerns about "remoteness," or a "situation in which action in a foreign country filters through many layers and finally causes a few ripples in the United States."[89]

B. Parallel Civil Proceedings:

1. *Statutory Consequences of Decree or Order and Treble Damage Provisions of Antitrust Laws*

The consequences of a party's actions, words, or investigation strategies should be considered when that party faces exposure to civil penalties as a result of alleged anticompetitive offenses. The duality of both criminal and civil offenses propounded by the U.S. antitrust laws often results in criminal and civil cases proceeding on similar claims and alleged offenses. Accordingly, parties must consider the types of consent judgments or decrees they enter into with government authorities, statements made by any parties or individuals at plea allocutions, or other strategic commitments made during investigation proceedings and how they may ultimately invoke collateral estoppel, allow for the establishment of evidentiary records, or trigger expensive cost/fee provisions in state antitrust statutes.

Section 5 of the Clayton Act provides that a final judgment or decree in criminal or civil antitrust proceedings brought by the U.S. government "shall be prima facie evidence against such defendant in any action or proceeding brought by any other party" concerning the same subject matter.[90] Furthermore, "collateral estoppel" (or issue preclusion) applies in such parallel or subsequent proceedings.[91] Findings made by the FTC cannot be the basis for collateral estoppel, but may be used as prima facie evidence.[92]

Although Section 5(a) expressly does "not apply to consent judgments or decrees entered before any testimony has been taken," courts have long established that guilty pleas do not fall within this exclusion, and therefore can be used both as prima facie evidence and a basis for collateral estoppel

---

89. *Minn-Chem*, 683 F.3d at 857, 860; *see also Lotes*, 753 F.3d at 398.

90. 15 U.S.C § 16(a).

91. *Id.* The statute was amended in 1980 to clarify that it does not "impose any limitation on the application of collateral estoppel." *Id.*

92. 15 U.S.C § 16(a).

in other proceedings.[93] Convictions based on pleas of nolo contendere (which are not an admission of guilt but rather a consent to punishment), however, are viewed as "consent decrees" that cannot subsequently be used for such purposes in civil cases if entered before testimony has been taken.[94]

The common-law doctrine of collateral estoppel "precludes relitigation of issues actually litigated and necessary to the outcome of the first action."[95] While the precise definition and elements articulated by a particular jurisdiction should be consulted, in general "[t]he party asserting collateral estoppel must show that the estopped issue is identical to an issue actually litigated and decided in the previous action," and that the issue was "necessary to support the judgment in the prior action."[96] Disputes in follow-on antitrust litigation frequently center on whether the issues at stake in the actions are identical.

The legal elements of the criminal offense and those of the civil cause of action will often be the same given the dual grant of criminal and private rights of action by the Sherman and Clayton Acts, as well as the many state statutes modeled thereafter. The underlying factual basis asserted, however, may differ in certain important respects, or may not have been necessarily decided. Thus, for example, in subsequent civil litigation the parties can dispute the temporal scope of the conduct admitted or adjudged, or the product markets affected.[97]

---

93. United States v. Real Property Located at Section 18, 976 F.2d 515, 519 (9th Cir. 1992) ("a guilty plea may be used to establish issue preclusion in a subsequent civil suit"); City of Burbank v. Gen. Elec. Co., 329 F.2d 825, 834-36 (9th Cir. 1964); Stephen P. Freccero, *The Use and Effect of an Antitrust Guilty Plea in Subsequent Civil Litigation*, 22 COMPETITION: J. ANTI. & UNFAIR COMP. L. SEC. ST. B. CAL. 136, 138 (2013) ("There is no real dispute that a criminal conviction following a guilty plea qualifies as a final judgment within the meaning of Section 5 of the Clayton Act.") (collecting cases).

94. *See* North Carolina v. Alford, 400 U.S. 25, 35 n.8 (1970); Dalweld Co. v. Westinghouse Elec. Corp., 252 F. Supp. 939, 941-42 (S.D.N.Y. 1966).

95. Parklane Hosiery Co. v. Shore, 439 U.S. 322, 326 n.5 (1979)

96. Pool Water Prod. v. Olin Corp., 258 F.3d 1024, 1031 (9th Cir. 2001).

97. *See In re* TFT-LCD (Flat Panel) Antitrust Litig., 2012 WL 4858836, at *3 (N.D. Cal. 2012) (finding that prior criminal trial did not "necessarily decide[] that the conspiracy lasted for the entire time charged in the superseding indictment."); Stephen P. Freccero, *The Use and Effect of an Antitrust Guilty Plea in Subsequent Civil Litigation*, 22 COMPETITION: J. ANTI. & UNFAIR COMP. L. SEC. ST. B. CAL. 136, 141 (2013) ("There is no

If collateral estoppel is avoided, the Clayton Act's mandate that a judgment from government proceedings "shall be prima facie evidence" creates a rebuttable presumption in a private plaintiff's favor as to those issues previously decided—effectively shifting the burden of proof to the defendant.[98] This provision works in conjunction with the Federal Rules of Evidence, which afford private plaintiffs multiple avenues for introducing the prior judgment and associated documents or statements. Foremost, statements by a defendant in connection with the criminal proceedings, including a guilty plea and related agreements, are admissible party admissions under Rule 801(d)(2)(A) of the Federal Rules of Evidence.

The defendant's "own statements at [its] plea allocution, including [its] explicit and unambiguous agreement with the description of evidence given by the government" is generally admissible.[99] Moreover, Rule 803(22) of the Federal Rules of Evidence expressly permits the introduction of a final judgment of conviction "entered after a trial or guilty plea . . . to prove any fact essential to the judgment" as an exception to the hearsay rule.[100] Alternatively, because the record of a guilty plea carries a heightened standard of reliability and trustworthiness, it may be admitted under the "residual" exception to the hearsay rule.[101]

These statutory consequences can be particularly acute in the civil litigation context. The Clayton Act and many parallel state statutes allow successful plaintiffs to recover not only mandatory treble damages, but attorneys' fees and costs as well.[102]

---

real dispute that a criminal conviction following a guilty plea qualifies as a final judgment within the meaning of Section 5 of the Clayton Act.") (collecting cases)Freccero.

98. *See, e.g.,* Purex Corp. v. Procter & Gamble Co., 453 F.2d 288, 291 (9th Cir. 1971); Illinois v. Gen Paving Co., 590 F.2d 680, 681 (7th Cir. 1979).

99. SEC v. Berger, 244 F. Supp. 2d 180, 189 (S.D.N.Y. 2001).

100. FED. R. EVID. 803(22). A Sherman Act violation is punishable by imprisonment for up to 10 years. 15 U.S.C.§ 1.

101. FED. R. EVID. 807; *See, e.g., In re* Slatkin, 525 F.3d 805, 812 (9th Cir. 2008) (affirming summary judgment avoiding certain transfers by debtor during operation of Ponzi scheme based on undisputed evidence including debtor's plea agreement admitting to scheme).

102. 15 U.S. Code § 15(a). Various similarly modeled state antitrust statutes likewise provide for trebled recovery and attorney's fees. *See e.g.,* CAL. BUS. & PROF. CODE § 16750(A); N.Y. GEN BUS LAW § 340(5); MINN. STAT. § 325D.57.

2. Fifth Amendment Privilege

The Fifth Amendment of the U.S. Constitution provides for, among other things, a privilege against self-incrimination. [103] In general, the privilege provides that an individual may refuse to answer questions in either a civil or criminal case when the individual reasonably fears that the information sought could be used in a state or federal criminal proceeding. [104] In its most common usage, a witness invokes the Fifth Amendment to avoid having to give self-incriminating testimony during an interview, in a deposition, or on the witness stand. However, a person may also invoke the Fifth Amendment to avoid having to produce documents (for instance, in response to a discovery request) where the act of production would be testimonial in nature, i.e., where the witness, by producing the documents, "admits the documents exist, are in [the witness'] possession or control, and are authentic."[105]

The Fifth Amendment has limits, several of which may be relevant in a criminal antitrust investigation. First, with a narrow exception, the Fifth Amendment may not be invoked to avoid self-incrimination when the witness's only fear of prosecution is by a foreign sovereign. [106] Second, corporations do not have a Fifth Amendment privilege against self-incrimination. [107] Nor can a corporate representative invoke the privilege

---

103. U.S. CONST. amend. V.
104. Kastigar v. United States, 406 U.S. 441, 444-45 (1972); McCarthy v. Arndstein, 266 U.S. 34, 40 (1924).
105. *In re* Grand Jury Subpoena Dated April 18, 2003, 383 F.3d 905, 909 (9th Cir. 2004).
106. United States v. Balsys, 524 U.S. 666 (1998). The Supreme Court left the door open to fear of prosecution by a foreign sovereign falling within the privilege against self-incrimination in a narrow set of circumstances where the United States and the foreign jurisdiction have "substantially similar criminal codes" aimed at prosecuting international acts, and it can be shown the United States had granted immunity from domestic prosecution for the purpose of obtaining evidence to aid prosecutors in the foreign jurisdiction. *Id.* at 698. For a discussion of whether cooperation between antitrust enforcers of different jurisdictions should fall within the *Balsys* exception, see Dylan I. Ballard, *Mask for the Guilty and Shield for the Innocent: The Privilege Against Self-Incrimination in Federal and California Antitrust Cases*, 22 No. 2 COMPETITION: J. ANTITRUST & UNFAIR COMP. L. SEC. ST. B. CAL. 75 (2013).
107. Bellis v. United States, 417 U.S. 85, 89-90 (1974) (stating that "the privilege against compulsory self-incrimination should be 'limited to its

when asked to testify or produce records solely in that capacity, even if the information produced would be personally incriminating.[108] Third, a valid invocation of the Fifth Amendment privilege must occur before the statute of limitations to prosecute the invoking party for a criminal offense has run.[109]

Perhaps most significantly for purposes of concurrent proceedings, a finder of fact can draw different inferences from the invocation of the Fifth Amendment privilege, depending on whether the relevant proceedings are criminal or civil. In a criminal proceeding, a jury cannot draw an adverse inference from a defendant's invocation of her Fifth Amendment right.[110] However, civil juries in a federal court may infer that the withheld testimony or evidence would have been unfavorable to the invoking party if the party seeking the adverse inference can make two showings: (1) independent evidence supports the adverse inference; and (2) the party has a substantial need for the evidence sought from the witness, and a less burdensome way to obtain it does not exist.[111] Additionally, the invocation of Fifth Amendment privilege by a current or ex-employee of a corporate defendant can result in an adverse inference for the employer.[112]

It is worth noting that an adverse inference is not limited to situations in which a corporation's own employees invoke the Fifth Amendment. A *former* employee's invocation of the privilege can also result in an adverse inference against the former employer in civil litigation.[113] And the

---

historic function of protecting only the natural individual from compulsory incrimination through his own testimony or personal records.'" (quoting United States v. White, 322 U.S. 694, 701 (1944)).

108. *Id.* at 88.
109. *See In re* Ethylene Propylene Diene Monomer (EPDM) Antitrust Litig., 681 F. Supp. 2d 141, 149 n.7 (D. Conn. 2009) ("The applicable statute of limitations for criminal prosecutions is a potentially decisive consideration for evaluating whether witnesses' statements are privileged under the Fifth Amendment.").
110. Baxter v. Palmigiano, 425 U.S. 308, 327 (1976) (Brennan, J., concurring in part and dissenting in part).
111. Rudy-Glanzer v. Glanzer, 232 F.3d 1258, 1264-65 (9th Cir. 2000).
112. *See* Coquina Investments v. TD Bank, N.A., 760 F.3d 1300 (11th Cir. 2014); *see also* In re Polyurethane Foam Antitrust Litigation, WL 12747961 (N.D. Ohio 2015).
113. *See, e.g.,* Brink's Inc. v. City of New York, 717 F.2d 700, 710 (2d Cir. 1983) ("The fact that the invokers of the privilege are no longer employees of the defendant does not necessarily bar admittance of their refusals to testify as vicarious admissions of their former employer . . . .").

invocation of the Fifth Amendment privilege by a *third party* can also result in an adverse inference, provided that the offering party can satisfy certain legal standards.[114]

Parallel criminal and civil proceedings can present other unique challenges for defense counsel. For instance, a witness may be asked to supply information in civil discovery that would expose the witness to criminal liability while a related criminal investigation is ongoing. One possible way to avoid such a situation is to seek a stay of discovery in the civil action pending completion of any related criminal investigation. However, depending on the stage of the related criminal investigation, a court may not be inclined to stay all civil proceedings, particularly where some civil proceedings can be completed without prejudice to the defendants.[115]

Another challenge can arise if a witness who has previously invoked the Fifth Amendment to avoid criminal liability wishes to testify in a civil case *after* the statute of limitations for criminal liability has expired. In this

---

114. When the adverse inference is based on a third party's invocation of the privilege, courts generally look to the four-factor test established by the Second Circuit in LiButti v. United States, 107 F.3d 110, 123-24 (2d Cir. 1997), which considers (1) the nature of the relationship between the nonparty claiming privilege and the party against whom the adverse inference is sought; (2) the degree of control of the party over the nonparty; (3) the compatibility of the interests of the party and the nonparty; and (4) the role of the nonparty in the litigation. *See, e.g., In re* Urethane Antitrust Litig., 2013 WL 100250, at *1 (D. Kan. 2013) (holding the plaintiffs could not offer evidence that defendant's alleged co-conspirators in price-fixing conspiracy invoked the Fifth Amendment because no reason to believe third-party witnesses felt "any particular loyalty to [the defendant] many years after the end of the alleged conspiracy and [the third party's] own settlement with the plaintiffs").

115. *See* MANUAL FOR COMPLEX LITIGATION § 20.31 (4th ed. 2004) (stating that "[s]uspending all pretrial activities in civil litigation until the end of the criminal proceeding . . . may be inadvisable, since it may be possible to conduct major portions of the civil case's discovery program without prejudice before completion of the criminal proceedings."). *See also In re* Blood Reagents Antitrust Litigation, 756 F. Supp. 2d 623, 635-36 (E.D. Pa. 2010) (declining to stay all discovery in civil antitrust proceeding because stay was an "extraordinary remedy appropriate for extraordinary circumstances," related criminal grand jury investigation was still in its "infancy," and Fifth Amendment privilege issues could be handled on "case-by-case basis" as they arose).

case, courts have held that a witness may withdraw the assertion of the Fifth Amendment privilege provided that it would not cause undue prejudice to any party that opposes withdrawal of the invocation, and there is no evidence that the litigant is trying to "abuse, manipulate or gain an unfair strategic advantage over opposing parties."[116] In such a situation, the witness then typically will sit for a new deposition.

3. Debarment and Suspension

In addition to criminal and civil penalties for cartel activity, U.S. government agencies may suspend and/or debar a government contractor due to antitrust violations, if doing so is "in the public interest for the Government's protection."[117] Both sanctions can only be imposed "on the basis of adequate evidence."[118] Federal regulations explicitly prohibit the use of suspension and debarment "for purposes of punishment." Rather, they are to be used to protect the public by ensuring that the government only engages "responsible" contractors.[119] In the antitrust context, the government commonly employs both sanctions in cases involving bid rigging.[120]

Suspension temporarily disqualifies a firm from contracting with the U.S. government, typically until an investigation, litigation, or agency determination has resolved the debarment issue.[121] Agencies may suspend a contractor only when protection of the public interest demands "immediate action" based on "information sufficient to support the reasonable belief that a particular act or omission has occurred."[122] In the anti-cartel enforcement context, suspension typically takes place following an indictment for bid rigging, and may occur where the Antitrust Division has developed sufficient facts to indict, but has yet to do so.[123]

Debarment disqualifies a firm from contracting with the U.S. government for up to three years. Conviction for a criminal offense, including a criminal antitrust violation at the federal or state level, suffices

---

116. SEC v. Smart, 678 F.3d 850, 855 (10th Cir. 2012).
117. 48 C.F.R. § 9.402(b).
118. *Id.* § 9.407-1(b)(1).
119. *Id.* § 9.402(b); 2 C.F.R. § 180.125(c).
120. *See, e.g.*, Coleman Am. Moving Servs., Inc. v. Weinberger, 716 F. Supp. 1405 (M.D. Ala. 1989).
121. 48 C.F.R. §§ 9.407-1(a)-(b); 2 C.F.R. §§ 180.700, 180.760.
122. 48 C.F.R. §§ 9.407-1(b)(1); 2 C.F.R. § 180.700.
123. *See, e.g.*, Electron-Methods, Inc. v. United States, 728 F.2d 1471 (Fed. Cir. 1984).

for debarment.[124] Debarment is a common collateral consequence of a criminal conviction, but may be imposed even where an entity agrees to cooperate with the DOJ in exchange for leniency.[125] In addition, several U.S. states now have parallel suspension and debarment proceedings for violations of federal or state antitrust laws, either on a reciprocal basis (where the state debars or suspends *because of* the federal suspension or debarment), or an independent one.[126] A federal agency's debarment decision is reviewable in a district court under the Administrative Procedure Act, but only where the entity has exhausted any and all administrative remedies before pursuing judicial review.[127] Similarly, judicial review of state debarment decisions is governed by each state's laws.

4. Stays of Civil Proceedings

It is well-settled that courts may stay, or restrict discovery in, a private civil action pending the resolution of a parallel or related criminal action

---

124.   48 C.F.R. §§ 9.406-2(a).

125.   Am. Floor Consultants & Installations, Inc. v. United States, 70 Fed. Cl. 235 (2006).

126.   *See, e.g.,* MASS. GEN. LAWS ch. 29, § 29F(c)(2) ("Notwithstanding any other provision of this section, any contractor debarred or suspended by any agency of the United States shall by reason of such debarment or suspension be simultaneously debarred or suspended under this section, with respect to non-federally aided contracts; the secretary or the commissioner may determine in writing that special circumstances exist which justify contracting with the affected contractor."); MD. CODE ANN., STATE FIN. & PROC. § 16-203(c) ("A person may be debarred from entering into a contract with the State if the person, an officer, partner, controlling stockholder or principal of that person, or any other person substantially involved in that person's contracting activities has been debarred from federal contracts under the Federal Acquisition Regulations, as provided in 48 C.F.R. Chapter 1."); 62 PA. CONS. STAT. § 531(b)(9) ("The causes for debarment or suspension include. . .[d]ebarment by any agency or department of the Federal Government or by any other state."); N.J. ADMIN. CODE § 17:19-3.1(a)(13) ("In the public interest, the [Division of Property Management and Construction] may debar a firm or an individual for any of the following causes ... [d]ebarment or disqualification by any other agency of government").

127.   5 U.S.C. § 704.

if the interest of justice so requires.[128] Given the increased frequency of parallel criminal and private civil antitrust proceedings in the United States,[129] antitrust litigants often must choose between seeking a stay of the civil matter or consenting to or opposing a stay once sought, and if so, to what extent.

For example, a defendant involved in parallel criminal and civil antitrust litigations may move to stay the civil proceeding in order to avoid the dilemma of having to choose to waive the Fifth Amendment right against self-incrimination or potentially subject themselves to an adverse inference based upon their Fifth Amendment invocation. Those defendants, however, must weigh such considerations against the potential benefit of civil discovery, which is broader than that available in criminal cases.[130]

The DOJ may move to intervene in and seek a stay of private civil proceedings to protect its interests in its own related criminal investigation or prosecution.[131] In recent years, the DOJ increasingly has opted to do so, usually on the ground that a stay is required to maintain the secrecy of grand jury proceedings pursuant to Federal Rule of Criminal Procedure

---

128. Landis v. North American Co., 299 U.S. 248, 254-55 (1936). *See also* Microfinancial, Inc. v. Premier Holidays Int'l, Inc., 385 F.3d 72, 77 (1st Cir. 2004). It is equally well-settled, however, that courts need not stay the parallel civil action as a matter of due process. United States v. Kordel, 397 U.S. 1, 9-10 (1970); *In re* Plastics Additives Antitrust Litig., 2004 WL 2743591, at *5 (E.D. Pa. 2004); Walsh Sec., Inc. v. Cristo Prop. Mgmt., Ltd., 7 F. Supp. 2d 523, 526 (D.N.J. 1998).

129. Bradley S. Lui, et al., *Increased DOJ Intervention to Stay Discovery in Civil Antitrust Litigation*, ANTITRUST LITIGATOR, Spring 2009, at 1. This Section does not discuss stays in parallel criminal and civil antitrust actions brought by federal agencies, state entities and private plaintiffs, or foreign entities and private actors, which involve different considerations and analyses.

130. *See* Afro-Lecon, Inc. v. United States, 820 F.2d 1198, 1203 (Fed. Cir. 1987) (observing that the broad scope of civil discovery may be an "irresistible temptation" to the criminal defendant). For example, while civil defendants may serve interrogatories or depose witnesses, FED. R. CIV. P. 26-37, criminal defendants may not without leave of court, FED. R. CRIM. P. 15-16.

131. FED. R. CIV. P. 24; *see also, e.g.,* SEC v. Chestman, 861 F.2d 49, 50 (2d Cir. 1988) (per curiam); *In re* Air Cargo Shipping Servs., 2010 WL 5027536, at *1 (E.D.N.Y. 2010) (finding DOJ intervention appropriate in civil antitrust action for the purpose of obtaining a stay of discovery).

6(e) and/or to preclude those under investigation or indictment from using broad civil discovery.[132] In deciding whether to seek a stay, the DOJ generally considers whether civil discovery will lead to the disclosure of secret grand jury information or covert aspects of an investigation including spinoff investigations; expose the identities of government cooperators and lead to witness intimidation; give noncooperating subjects of a grand jury investigation a roadmap to the investigation, revealing its scope and direction; allow grand jury subjects or the defendants to use civil tools improperly to circumvent the limited discovery rules of the Federal Rules of Criminal Procedure to obtain material in defense of a grand jury investigation or criminal case; and whether potential witnesses will be deposed before the witness has been interviewed by the Antitrust Division or testified before the grand jury or at trial.[133] In certain cases, the DOJ may seek a limited stay that permits certain document discovery while staying any discovery of "conspiracy" related documents or any depositions.[134]

The private civil plaintiff must consider whether, and to what degree, to consent to or oppose a stay sought by the defendant, the DOJ, or both. In opposing stays, the plaintiffs have argued that they would be prejudiced by the inability to take depositions before memories fade, witnesses become unavailable, or a statute of limitations bars meritorious, yet-to-be-discovered claims.[135] Postponement may prove advantageous, however, if

---

132. Bradley S. Lui et al., *Increased DOJ Intervention to Stay Discovery in Civil Antitrust Litigation*, ANTITRUST LITIGATOR, Spring 2009, at 1, 20.

133. ANTITRUST DIV., U.S. DEP'T OF JUSTICE, ANTITRUST DIVISION MANUAL at III-109 (5th ed. 2012) (last updated Apr. 2018), *available at* https://www.justice.gov/atr/file/761166/download.

134. *See* Stipulation and Order by United States and Direct Purchaser Plaintiffs Regarding Discovery, *In re* Inductors Antitrust Litigation, 5:18-cv-00198 (N. D. Cal. Dec. 18, 2018); Pretrial Order No. 44, *In re* Generic Pharmaceuticals Pricing Antitrust Litigation, 16-MD-2724 (E.D. Penn. Feb. 9, 2018)

135. *See, e.g.*, Sanrio, Inc. v. Ronnie Home Textile Inc., 2015 WL 1062035, at *3 (C.D. Cal. 2015); Harper v. Cronk, 2013 WL 5200358, at *2 (D. Colo. 2013); Walsh Sec., Inc. v. Cristo Prop. Mgmt., Ltd., 7 F. Supp. 2d 523, 528 (D.N.J. 1998); Lee F. Berger and Sophia A. Vandergrift, *The Antitrust Division's Stay Practice in Civil Litigation Paralleling Criminal Investigations Is Good Policy*, ANTITRUST, Fall 2013, at 86, 88.

it allows the plaintiff in a civil case to use the guilty pleas, verdicts, testimony, or other evidence offered at the criminal trial.[136]

The party requesting the stay has the burden of showing that a stay is required in the interest of justice.[137] The court has discretion to decide whether to stay the civil proceeding in its entirety, postpone civil discovery, or impose protective orders and conditions. Courts have not adopted a uniform approach to evaluating a motion for stay, but generally employ a test which balances (1) the extent to which the issues in the criminal and civil case overlap; (2) the status of the case, including whether the defendant has been indicted; (3) the plaintiff's interest in proceeding expeditiously weighed against the prejudice to the plaintiff caused by a delay; (4) the private interests of and burdens on the defendants; (5) the interests of the court; and (6) the public interest.[138]

Given the fact-specific nature of the test, its application has led to diverse results, but a few generalizations can be drawn from the cases. The status of the case tends to be crucial to the court's inquiry, as the odds that a stay will be granted can vary greatly depending on the degree of criminal exposure or likelihood of criminal proceedings.[139] Courts, however, often

---

136. The outcome of criminal antitrust action ordinarily may be introduced as prima facie evidence of a defendant's guilt in a later civil proceeding, provided the result represents a final judgment. 15 U.S.C. §16(a). Evidence or guilty pleas obtained through government investigations likewise may aid the plaintiffs in negotiating civil settlements or litigating pretrial issues, *see, e.g., In re* Packaged Ice Antitrust Litig., 723 F. Supp. 2d 987, 1011 (E.D. Mich. 2010) (denying motion to dismiss where defendants' guilty pleas to conspiracy "in one market [were] suggestive of the plausibility of a conspiracy to commit the same illegal acts in another market").

137. Landis v. North American Co., 299 U.S. 248, 255-66 (1936).

138. *See, e.g.,* SEC v. Gerhardt, 2007 WL 1452236, at *2 (E.D. Mo. 2007); *see also* SEC v. Gilbertson, 2017 WL 5172313, at *1 (D. Minn. 2017), Garrett v. Cassity, 2011 WL 2689359, at *2 (E. D. Mo. 2011).

139. *See, e.g.,* SEC v. Dresser Indus., Inc., 628 F.2d 1368, 1375-76 (D.C. Cir. 1980) (strongest case for stay of discovery in civil case occurs during a criminal prosecution after indictment is returned because potential for self-incrimination is greatest during this stage); Sterling Nat'l Bank v. A-1 Hotels Int'l, Inc., 175 F. Supp. 2d 573, 578 (S.D.N.Y. 2001) (denying stay pending resolution of grand jury proceedings because "there is no way of measuring with any precision what questions defendants may refuse to answer, or what damage may be done to their position in the civil case by any assertions of privilege they choose to make"). *But see* SEC v. Schroeder, 2008 WL 152227, at *2 (N.D. Cal. 2008) (staying deposition

are reluctant to stay the entire civil action or impose indefinite or lengthy discovery delays in light of the competing interests among the parties, the court, and the public.[140] Rather, courts will limit stays to discovery in the civil proceeding, defining the limits on the type of discovery subject to the stay and/or the time period during which the stay will remain in place, based upon the circumstances of the case and often on the stipulation or recommendations of the parties.[141]

5. Protection of Grand Jury Secrecy and Production of DOJ Materials

Federal Rule of Criminal Procedure Rule 6(e) does not allow a litigant in a civil case to obtain materials relating to "matters occurring before the grand jury" in a parallel criminal case unless an exception applies. Such grand jury material may be disclosed "preliminarily to or in connection with a judicial proceeding." [142] Federal Rule of Criminal Procedure 6(e)(3)(E)-(G) details the procedure for petitioning a district court for such disclosure.

A litigant seeking disclosure of transcripts of grand jury testimony must make a "strong showing of particularized need" for them.[143] To carry

---

of the defendant in a civil action for four months to protect the defendant's Fifth Amendment rights during criminal investigation despite the fact no indictment has been issued).

140. *See* Green v. Cosby, 2016 WL 1312011, at *3 (D. Mass. 2016) ("By limiting both the time and subject matter covered in temporary deferrals of particular discovery, a Court can allow civil proceedings to progress as much as possible without prejudicing the relative interests of the litigants."); MANUAL FOR COMPLEX LITIGATION § 30.4 (4th ed. 2004) ("[A] general stay of all activities in the civil litigation pending completion of the criminal case will rarely be appropriate.").

141. *See, e.g.*, Four In One Co. v. SK Foods, L.P., 2010 WL 4718751, at *5-7 (E.D. Cal. 2010) (granting a "sixth month limited stay" in light of Fifth Amendment considerations but denying request for an "optional extension" of the stay); Order, *In re* Municipal Derivatives Antitrust Litig., Case No. 08-02516 (S.D.N.Y. May 27, 2010) (granting in part and denying in part DOJ's application to stay discovery); Order, *In re* Elec. Carbon Prods. Antitrust Litig., No. 03-02182 (D.N.J. Oct. 19, 2004) (granting in part DOJ's motion for a limited stay of discovery).

142. For an explanation of the rule's underlying rationale, *see* United States v. Procter & Gamble Co., 356 U.S. 677, 681 n.6 (1958).

143. United States v. Sells Eng'g, 463 U.S. 418, 443 (1983).

that burden, the petitioner must persuade the district court that the transcripts are (1) "needed to avoid a possible injustice in another judicial proceeding," (2) "that [the] need for disclosure is greater than the need for continued secrecy," and (3) "that [the] request is structured so as to cover only material so needed."[144]

While it is clear that grand jury transcripts constitute Rule 6(e) "matters occurring before a grand jury" to which the *Douglas Oil* disclosure standard applies, whether Rule 6(e) applies to materials generated in connection with a grand jury proceeding has yet to be decided by the Supreme Court. Every circuit court except the First Circuit has answered the question, but the answers continue to display a "striking lack of unanimity."[145]

6. Managing Parallel International Civil Proceedings

Parallel civil proceedings are no longer a limited phenomenon. With the global adoption of anti-cartel and leniency regimes there has also followed an expansion of global civil remedies for victims of anti-competitive conduct. To date approximately forty major jurisdictions have civil antitrust liability, and nearly half of those jurisdictions allow private parties to bring some form of class or collective action.[146]

---

144. Douglas Oil Co. v. Petrol Stops Northwest, 441 U.S. 211, 222 (1979). The desire to use the transcripts to impeach, or refresh the recollection, or test the credibility of a witness usually supplies the necessary "particularized need" *Id.* at 222 n.12 The need must be "actual," not theoretical. *In re* Special Grand Jury 89-2, 143 F3d 565, 571 (10th Cir. 1998).

145. *In re* John Doe Grand Jury Proceedings, 537 F. Supp. 1038, 1043 (D.R.I. 1982).

146. These jurisdictions include: Australia*; Austria; Belgium; Brazil; Canada*; China; Colombia*; the Czech Republic; Denmark*; Finland; France*; Germany; Greece*; Hong Kong; Hungary; India*; Indonesia; Ireland; Israel*; Italy*; Japan; Malaysia; Mexico*; Netherlands*; Nigeria*; Norway*; Poland*; Portugal*; Romania; Russia; Singapore; South Africa*; South Korea; Spain; Sweden*; Switzerland; Taiwan*; Turkey; Ukraine; the United Kingdom*; and the United States*. Jurisdictions denoted with (*) permit some form of class or collective action.

CHAPTER V

INDICTMENT AND PRETRIAL MOTIONS

This chapter addresses key procedural and substantive issues that arise in the context of charging decisions made by the U.S. Department of Justice (DOJ) Antitrust Division, and subsequent pretrial proceedings.

A. Indictments and Criminal Complaints

The Fifth Amendment states: "No person shall be held to answer for a capital, or otherwise infamous crime, unless on a presentment or indictment of a Grand Jury."[1] Rule 7 of the Federal Rules of Criminal Procedure requires that offenses punishable by imprisonment for more than one year must be prosecuted by indictment unless waived by a defendant.[2] As a matter of practice, defendants who plead guilty to antitrust offenses agree to be charged by information rather than indictment. All other defendants in criminal antitrust cases must be charged by indictment because violations of the Sherman Act are felonies punishable by prison terms of up to ten years.[3]

When the Antitrust Division is seriously considering charging corporations or individuals, it will usually advise them that they are "targets" of the investigation. A "target" is defined as a person against whom the prosecutor or the grand jury has substantial evidence linking that person to the commission of a crime and who, in the prosecutor's judgment, is a putative defendant.[4] As the staff of the Antitrust Division is finalizing its memorandum recommending an indictment, it will usually advise targets and give them an opportunity to make a presentation to the staff's section or office chief.[5] Putative defendants have no absolute right

---

1. U.S. CONST. amend. V.
2. FED. R. CRIM. P. 7(a)(1)(B), 7(b).
3. 15 U.S.C. § 1.
4. U.S. DEP'T OF JUSTICE, JUSTICE MANUAL § 9-11.151 (2018) [hereinafter JUSTICE MANUAL], available at http://www.usdoj.gov/jm/jm-9-11000-grand-jury#9-11.151.
5. ANTITRUST DIV., U.S. DEP'T OF JUSTICE, ANTITRUST DIVISION MANUAL at III-119 (5th ed. 2012) (last updated Apr. 2018) [hereinafter ANTITRUST DIV.

to be heard by Antitrust Division supervisory officials in Washington, but they ordinarily receive a chance to meet with the Director of Criminal Enforcement and the Deputy Assistant Attorney General for Criminal Enforcement.[6]

Indictments are normally public documents. But in cases involving foreign national individuals, sometimes the Antitrust Division will have indictments placed under seal on the basis that disclosure could hinder the apprehension of the defendant.[7] Also, on occasion, the Antitrust Division will charge an individual on an expedited basis by having an agent swear out a criminal complaint—a written statement of the essential facts constituting the offense charged, made under oath before a judicial officer, normally a magistrate judge.[8] If the complaint and accompanying affidavit establish probable cause that the defendant committed an offense, the judge must issue an arrest warrant.[9]

This procedure has been used in cases when the Antitrust Division learns that a foreign national who is a target of an investigation and on a border watch is entering the United States. The criminal complaint allows the Antitrust Division to move quickly—far more quickly than would be possible using a grand jury—to charge the individual and secure an arrest warrant so that the individual can be arrested before leaving U.S. jurisdiction.

For example, in a cartel investigation involving aftermarket auto lights, the Antitrust Division learned that an executive from Taiwan who was a target was scheduled to transit through Los Angeles International Airport (LAX) on his way to Mexico and Central America. The executive had rejected a plea offer and through his counsel had said he was considering staying in Taiwan beyond the reach of U.S. prosecutors.[10] The executive was arrested at LAX on the basis of a criminal complaint

---

MANUAL], *available at available at* https://www.justice.gov/atr/file/761166/download.

6.   *Id.*

7.   *See, e.g.,* Indictment, United States v. Isawa, No. 15-00163 (N.D. Cal. Mar. 12, 2015), *available at* https://www.justice.gov/atr/case/us-v-takuro-isawa.

8.   FED. R. CRIM. P. 4.

9.   *Id.*

10.   *See* Sentencing Memo. at 2, United States v. Hsu, No. 11-00488 (N.D. Cal. Jan. 15, 2013).

obtained that same day.[11] Because he was in custody, he was entitled to have within fourteen days a preliminary hearing before a magistrate judge to determine whether probable cause existed to believe he committed the violation.[12] The Antitrust Division chose instead to obtain a grand jury indictment seven days later.[13]

Rule 7(c)(1) of the Federal Rules of Criminal Procedure requires that an indictment be a "plain, concise, and definite written statement of the essential facts constituting the offense charged."[14] It need only contain enough information to allow the defendant to prepare a defense and invoke the Double Jeopardy Clause if the defendant is charged in a separate case for the same conduct. An indictment must describe with reasonable particularity the conduct alleged to constitute the offense, but need not contain evidentiary detail, such as the contents of key documents.[15]

A grand jury consists of sixteen to twenty-three members who are summoned by the court.[16] Unlike trial juries, grand juries conduct their business in secret.[17] At least sixteen jurors must be present for a quorum; no business may be conducted in the absence of a quorum. At least twelve jurors must concur to return an indictment.[18]

Grand juries generally sit for no more than eighteen months, but may have their terms extended to as much as twenty-four months.[19] Given the size and scope of criminal antitrust matters, particularly international cartel cases, the Antitrust Division will often petition a court to empanel a grand jury to concentrate exclusively on a single, large investigation.

---

11. *See* Criminal Complaint, United States v. Hsu, No. 11-70758 (N.D. Cal. July 12, 2011), *available at* https://www.justice.gov/atr/case-document/file/498951/download.

12. FED. R. CRIM. P. 5.1(a).

13. *See* Indictment, United States v. Hsu, No. 11-0488 (N.D. Cal. July 19, 2011), *available at* https://www.justice.gov/atr/case-document/file/494446/download.

14. FED. R. CRIM. P. 7(c)(1).

15. *See* ABA SECTION OF ANTITRUST LAW, CRIMINAL ANTITRUST LITIGATION HANDBOOK 7-15 (2d ed. 2006) [hereinafter *ABA CRIMINAL ANTITRUST LITIGATION HANDBOOK*] (explaining an example of a typical charging document in an antitrust case).

16. FED. R. CRIM. P. (a)(1); *see also* ABA SECTION OF ANTITRUST LAW, HANDBOOK ON ANTITRUST GRAND JURY INVESTIGATIONS (3d ed. 2002) (describing grand jury process).

17. FED. R. CRIM. P. 6(e).

18. FED. R. CRIM. P. 6(f).

19. FED. R. CRIM. P. 6(g).

Alternatively, it may secure time in front of a regular, sitting grand jury that is hearing testimony and returning indictments in cases involving all types of federal crimes that U.S. Attorney's Offices handle.

Antitrust Division staff have broad discretion in how they present evidence to a grand jury. They may use subpoenas to compel non-cooperating witnesses to testify before the grand jury. Often they will interview a cooperating witness outside of the grand jury in a less formal office setting; but they may attempt to "lock in" the interviewee before the grand jury if they are concerned that he or she might equivocate or backslide if called to testify at trial. Because grand jury testimony is delivered under oath and transcribed, it can be used more effectively than interview notes to impeach witnesses at trial and it may be admissible as substantive evidence.[20]

Once staff has received approval from DOJ officials to seek an indictment, it will present the case to the grand jury for decision. In seeking an indictment, staff attorneys will walk through the allegations of the indictment in detail and give a presentation on the applicable law. They also will provide a summary of the evidence relevant to the proposed charges. Normally, an FBI or other case agent will summarize all of the important evidence including the key documents, a review of the relevant testimony of witnesses who appeared before the grand jury, and a summary of the relevant statements of witnesses who were interviewed outside of the grand jury. Because the grand jury can rely on hearsay in determining whether to vote out an indictment, it can rely on agent summaries of witnesses the grand jurors never saw.[21]

If the grand jury votes to indict, it returns the indictment in open court to a magistrate judge.[22] The magistrate judge then issues appropriate warrants or summonses to compel the defendant's appearance at an arraignment.[23]

---

20.   *See* FED. R. EVID. 801(d)(1).
21.   *See* United States v. Calandra, 414 U.S. 338, 343-44 (1974); JUSTICE MANUAL, *supra* note 4, § 9-11.232.
22.   FED. R. CRIM. P. 6(f).
23.   FED. R. CRIM. P. 9.

B. Discovery under Federal Rule of Criminal Procedure 16 and Other Rules

1. DOJ and Antitrust Division Policy on Discovery in Criminal Cases

In response to the government's failure to meet its discovery obligations in a particular high-profile case (involving former Senator Ted Stevens), in April 2009 the DOJ created a working group to review policies on criminal case management and discovery.[24] In January 2010, the Office of the Deputy Attorney General issued three memoranda to all criminal prosecutors that provide guidance on discovery practices.[25] The memoranda direct each U.S. Attorney's Office and DOJ litigating component, including the Antitrust Division, to develop discovery policies. The Antitrust Division issued its *Criminal Discovery Policy* in March 2010.[26] The DOJ memos and the *Criminal Discovery Policy* provide guidance on how federal prosecutors are required to meet their discovery obligations as established by Federal Rules of Criminal Procedure 16 and 26.2, the Jencks Act,[27] *Brady v. Maryland*,[28] *Giglio v. United States*,[29] and the *Justice Manual*.[30]

Antitrust Division staff handling criminal cases, including international cartel prosecutions, are required to follow the *Criminal Discovery Policy*. This policy reflects the DOJ's goal that prosecutors "avoid lapses that can result in consequences adverse to the Department's

---

24. *See* U.S. Dep't of Justice, A Commitment to Serving Justice: Enhanced Discovery and Training Resources (2012), *available at* https://www.justice.gov/opa/blog/commitment-serving-justice-enhanced-discovery-and-training-resources.

25. *See, e.g.*, Memo. from Deputy Att'y Gen. David W. Ogden, U.S. Dep't of Justice, Guidance for Prosecutors Regarding Criminal Discovery (Jan. 4, 2010), *available at* https://www.justice.gov/archives/dag/memorandum-department-prosecutors.

26. *See* Memo. from Christine A. Varney to Antitrust Division Criminal Attorneys, Antitrust Division Criminal Discovery Policy (Mar. 31, 2010) [hereinafter *Antitrust Division Criminal Discovery Policy*], *available at* https://www.justice.gov/sites/default/files/atr/legacy/2015/04/24/313434.pdf.

27. 18 U.S.C. § 3500.

28. 373 U.S. 83 (1963).

29. 405 U.S. 150 (1972).

30. *Justice Manual*, *supra* note 4, § 9-5.001.

pursuit of justice."[31] The policy states that it is Antitrust Division practice "to provide discovery beyond what the rules, statutes, and case law mandate," "to err on the side of disclosure when faced with a close call on whether to disclose materials," and to "provide discovery beyond what is legally required whenever and wherever possible."[32]

The policy recognizes that local criminal rules and standard practice of U.S. Attorney's Offices vary across districts.[33] The Antitrust Division has criminal enforcement offices in just four cities: Washington, New York, Chicago, and San Francisco. As a result, staff often file cases outside of their home jurisdictions. The policy requires Antitrust Division attorneys to follow local discovery practices unless the staff, "after consultation with the USAO, prefers to provide more or earlier disclosure than called for by USAO policy."[34] Staff are specifically required to consult with the local U.S. Attorney's Office and court clerk to ensure that they are following local district practices on such things as the forms that must accompany indictments, the timing of arraignments, ministerial details such as photographing and fingerprinting of defendants, and timetables for pretrial criminal discovery and motions practice.[35]

2. Federal Rule of Criminal Procedure 16

International cartel cases typically involve massive amounts of information—often totaling many millions of documents.[36] Rule 16 of the Federal Rules of Criminal Procedure covers several categories of material that the government is required to produce in criminal discovery. The most important of these categories in antitrust cases is addressed in Rule 16(a)(1)(e), which requires the government to produce to the defendants upon request documents and other materials in the government's possession that are "material to preparing the defense," that the

31. Memo. from Deputy Att'y Gen. David W. Ogden, U.S. Dep't of Justice, Guidance for Prosecutors Regarding Criminal Discovery (Jan. 4, 2010), *available at* https://www.justice.gov/archives/dag/memorandum-department-prosecutors.
32. *See Antitrust Division Criminal Discovery Policy, supra* note 26, at 2.
33. *Id.* at 4.
34. *Id.*
35. *See ANTITRUST DIV. MANUAL, supra* note 6, at IV-63-64.
36. *See, e.g.,* Order Denying Defts.' Mot. to Compel Discovery at 2, United States v. AU Optronics, No. 09-00110 (N.D. Cal. Dec. 23, 2011) (referring to government production of discovery totaling 37 million documents in a prosecution of an international cartel involving TFT-LCD panels).

government intends to use in its case-in-chief at trial, or that were obtained from or belong to the defendant.[37]

Antitrust Division policy requires staff typically to begin making Rule 16 discovery material available immediately after indictment without waiting to receive a formal defense request.[38] The Antitrust Division tends to interpret its obligations under Rule 16 broadly. Normally, it will not attempt to parse the documents it has secured during a grand jury investigation to separate information that is "material" to the defense from what is not. Instead, it will produce all of the pre-existing documents it has seized or subpoenaed during an investigation without holding anything back.

As stated in the *Criminal Discovery Policy*: "It is not unusual in Division investigations for staff to obtain hundreds of boxes of documents and extremely large electronic productions, which makes a thorough review of all of these materials for possible discoverable information difficult and time consuming." [39] The policy recommends that staff consider producing *all* of the materials "to eliminate the possibility that there will be a later discovery by Division staff of something that could arguably be discoverable information that was not disclosed."[40] The policy also recommends that staff consider providing indices of the material produced, stating that this approach may promote pretrial resolution of the case and improve the government's ability to defend against claims that the government is "purposely dumping a huge number of documents on the defense in an effort to obfuscate—not further—meaningful disclosure."[41]

3. *Jencks Act and Rule 26.2*

The Jencks Act requires the government to produce to the defendants the pretrial "statements" of a government witness. [42] But it limits the government's discovery obligations in several ways. Witness "statements" include only grand jury testimony or statements that a witness signs or otherwise adopts or approves and are substantially verbatim recordings.[43]

---

37.   FED. R. CRIM. P. 16(a)(1)(e).
38.   *See ANTITRUST DIV. MANUAL, supra* note 6, at IV-64.
39.   *Antitrust Division Criminal Discovery Policy, supra* note 26, at 5.
40.   *Id.*
41.   *Id.*
42.   18 U.S.C. § 3500.
43.   18 U.S.C. § 3500(e); FED. R. CRIM. P. 26.2(f).

They must relate to the subject matter of the witness's testimony.[44] They must be produced only after the witness has testified on direct examination at trial.[45] And the production obligation is triggered only by a defendant's timely request that is sufficiently precise to identify the statements sought.[46] There is a substantial body of law parsing each of these requirements in cases where the government resisted production of materials or defendants alleged that the government had failed to comply with the Jencks Act.[47]

At one time, the Antitrust Division had no uniform policy on whether staff were required to produce witness interview notes.[48] Some staff resisted production of witness interview notes taken by attorneys, paralegals, and agents because the notes did not fall within the strict definition of what constitutes Jencks Act materials. Some staff also resisted early production of Jencks Act materials.[49] The Antitrust Division has now clarified its policy on production of witness interview notes. Division policy now makes clear that staff are required to provide discovery that goes beyond the strict requirements of the Jencks Act.[50] It requires staff to disclose *all* interview memoranda of testifying trial witnesses, even though the memoranda are not signed or adopted by the witnesses.[51] It also notes that agreements are often reached to provide Jencks Act materials to the defendants at "some reasonable time prior to trial."[52] It directs staff to consult with the local U.S. Attorney's Office about how soon before trial Jencks material is typically produced and to comply with the local practice for the district or the court absent a "significant reason" to do otherwise.[53]

---

44.   18 U.S.C. § 3500(b); FED. R. CRIM. P. 26.2(a).

45.   18 U.S.C. § 3500(a); FED. R. CRIM. P. 26.2(a).

46.   18 U.S.C. § 3500(b); FED. R. CRIM. P. 26.2(a).

47.   *See Discovery and Access to Evidence*, 43 GEO. L.J. ANN. REV. CRIM. PROC. 377, 406-12 (2014) (collecting cases); *ABA CRIMINAL ANTITRUST LITIGATION HANDBOOK, supra* note 15, at 189-92 (discussing what constitutes a Jencks Act statement and when a statement is related to the subject matter of a witness's testimony).

48.   *See* ABA SECTION OF ANTITRUST LAW, ANTITRUST LAW DEVELOPMENTS 1000-01 (7th ed. 2012).

49.   *Id.* at 1001.

50.   *ANTITRUST DIV. MANUAL, supra* note 5, at IV-67.

51.   *Id.*

52.   *Id.*

53.   *Id.*

4. *Brady and Giglio*

Brady v. Maryland,[54] *Giglio v. United States*,[55] and several related cases impose a constitutional obligation on prosecutors to disclose to the defense all evidence in the government's possession that is material either to the defendant's guilt or to punishment. DOJ policy requires prosecutors to take a broad view of their *Brady* and *Giglio* obligations, to err on the side of disclosure in close cases, and to go beyond that which is constitutionally and legally required so as to ensure that trials are fair.[56]

C. Pretrial Motions

1. *Procedural Motions*

a. Motion to Modify Conditions of Release

Section 3142 of the Bail Reform Act of 1984 governs conditions of pretrial release.[57] The arraigning judicial officer must impose the least restrictive bail conditions that will reasonably assure the defendant's appearance at trial.[58] The court will typically order the defendant's pretrial release on personal recognizance or an unsecured appearance bond, unless it determines that such release will not reasonably assure the defendant's appearance at trial.[59] The government has the burden of proving a defendant's flight risk by a preponderance of the evidence.[60]

In assessing flight risk and determining conditions of release, the court may look to whether the defendant is a non-U.S. citizen.[61] The court must also consider "the nature and circumstances of the offense charged," "the weight of the evidence against" the defendant, and "the history and characteristics of" the defendant.[62] Consideration of the nature of the

---

54. 373 U.S. 83 (1963).
55. 405 U.S. 150 (1972).
56. *JUSTICE MANUAL*, *supra* note 4, § 9-5.001(C).
57. 18 U.S.C. § 3142.
58. 18 U.S.C. § 3142(b)-(c).
59. *See* 18 U.S.C. § 3142(b); *ABA CRIMINAL ANTITRUST LITIGATION HANDBOOK*, *supra* note 15, at 47.
60. *See* United States v. Townsend, 897 F.2d 989, 994 (9th Cir. 1990); United States v. Motamedi, 767 F.2d 1403, 1406 (9th Cir. 1985).
61. *See Townsend*, 897 F.2d at 994-96.
62. 18 U.S.C. § 3142(g).

offenses charged involves consideration of the penalties.[63] The weight of the evidence is the least important factor under Section 3142.[64] Among the history and characteristics to consider are the defendant's "character, physical and mental condition, family ties, employment, financial resources, length of residence in the community, community ties, past conduct, history relating to drug or alcohol abuse, criminal history, and record concerning appearance at court proceedings."[65]

Courts often impose travel restrictions on defendants who pose flight risks.[66] The Antitrust Division generally considers a foreign individual defendant in an international cartel case to be a serious flight risk who warrants additional conditions of release under Section 3142(c). [67] Extradition also plays a role in the Antitrust Division's assessment of a defendant's flight risk. If the defendant is from a country with no extradition agreement with the United States, the Antitrust Division will argue there is serious flight risk because the court cannot compel the defendant to return to the United States once he leaves.[68]

Even if the defendant is from a country with an extradition agreement with the United States, the Antitrust Division may argue that extradition is a lengthy process with no guarantee of success and that most extradition treaties with the United States do not list antitrust crimes as extraditable offenses. Additionally, the Antitrust Division may argue that a waiver of

---

63. *Townsend*, 897 F.2d at 994.
64. United States v. Beker, No. 07-0765 (N.D. Cal. 2010).
65. 18 U.S.C. § 3142(g).
66. *See* 18 U.S.C. § 3142(c)(1)(B)(iv).
67. *See* United States' Opp. to Deft.'s Mot. to Modify Conditions of Pretrial Release, United States v. Hsu, No. 11-0488 (N.D. Cal. Jan. 25, 2012); United States' Mot. for Relief from Nondispositive Pretrial Orders of Magistrate Judge, United States v. AU Optronics Corp., No. 09-0110 (N.D. Cal. Aug. 10, 2010); United States' Opp. to Mots. to Modify Release Conditions by Defts.., United States v. AU Optronics Corp., No. 09-0110 (N.D. Cal. Aug. 6, 2010).
68. United States' Opp. to Deft.'s Mot. to Modify Conditions of Pretrial Release at 2; United States' Mot. for Relief from Nondispositive Pretrial Orders of Magistrate Judge at 5; United States' Opp. to Mots. to Modify Release Conditions by Defts. at 13; United States' Reply in Support of Mot. for Conditions of Pretrial Release at 3-4, United States v. AU Optonics Corp., No. 09-0110 SI (N.D. Cal. July 26, 2010); United States' Mot. for Conditions of Pretrial Release for Deft. at 12, United States v. AU Optronics Corp., No. 09-0110 (N.D. Cal. July 26, 2010).

extradition executed prior to the initiation of an extradition proceeding is generally unenforceable.

In addressing the nature and circumstances of the offense factor, the Antitrust Division typically argues that a foreign defendant has strong incentives to stay in his home country and not to appear at trial because criminal violations of the Sherman Act are felonies that carry maximum penalties of ten years in prison and substantial fines. In addressing the history and characteristics factor, the Antitrust Division takes the position that a defendant's voluntary appearance at arraignment has no predictive values and cannot reasonably assure the defendant's appearance at a trial that is years away.

Additionally, the Antitrust Division views a defendant's access to substantial financial resources outside of the United States as heightening the risk that the defendant will not return for trial if allowed to travel freely.[69] Access to such resources suggests that the defendant can easily pay off any bonds set in the case and continue to live comfortably in his home country.[70] The Antitrust Division also views negatively the fact that a defendant has substantial family, employment, financial, and residential ties to the defendant's home country, but minimal ties to the United States.[71]

The government typically will request that release conditions include the surrender of a defendant's passport, that the defendant not be allowed to apply for any other travel documents during the pendency of the case, and that the defendant's travel be restricted to the jurisdiction of the district court in which the case is pending.[72] The government generally will not oppose a defendant's request for temporary travel to visit family members or to attend work-related conferences within the United States.[73] The government will oppose a defendant's request for international travel, however, even if it is to visit ailing family members or to attend investors' conferences.[74]

---

69. *Id.*
70. *Id.*
71. *Id.*
72. *Id.*
73. *See* Deft.'s Unopposed Application and Order for Temporary Travel at 2, United States v. AU Optronics Corp., No. 09-0110 (N.D. Cal. Oct. 13, 2010); Deft.'s Unopposed Application and Order for Temporary Travel at 2, United States v. AU Optronics Corp., No. 09-0110 (N.D. Cal. Aug. 18, 2010).
74. *See* United States' Opp. to Deft.'s Mot. for Travel Pass at 18-21, United States v. AU Optronics Corp., No. 09-0110 (N.D. Cal. Aug. 24, 2010).

b. Motion for Severance from Other Defendants

Rule 8 of the Federal Rules of Criminal Procedure allows joinder of charges or defendants in the same charging document.[75] Rule 8(b) permits joinder of defendants in the same indictment when the defendants "are alleged to have participated in the same act or transaction, or in the same series of acts or transactions, constituting an offense or offenses."[76] Because cartel violations are conspiracies, the Antitrust Division routinely joins all alleged conspirators in a single indictment. This is a common and regularly upheld charging practice.[77]

Rule 14 of the Federal Rules of Criminal Procedure permits courts to address prejudicial joinder of charges or defendants by ordering separate trials of counts, by severing the defendants, or "any other relief that justice requires."[78] On occasion, the defendants in cartel cases seek severance under Rule 14, arguing that they will be prejudiced by having to go to trial with their codefendants. For example, the defendants have argued that they would be prejudiced by a "spillover effect" of evidence that codefendants or representatives of corporate codefendants allegedly took steps to destroy evidence when they became aware of the government investigation.[79] In ruling on Rule 14 motions, trial courts have broad discretion to balance the interests of judicial economy against the risks of prejudice to parties.[80] In practice, courts rarely find that the risk of spillover effects constitutes sufficient prejudice to grant severance motions.[81] Instead, they normally rule that they can prevent harm to the defendants by issuing limiting instructions.[82]

---

75. FED. R. CRIM. P. 8.
76. FED. R. CRIM. P. 8(b).
77. *See Joinder and Severance*, 43 GEO. L.J. ANN. REV. CRIM. PROC. 332, 338-39 nn.986-87 (2014) (collecting cases).
78. FED. R. CRIM. P. 14(a).
79. *See* Mot. for Severance from Defendant Corporations, United States v. AU Optronics, No. 09-00110 (N.D. Cal. Jan. 3, 2012); Deft.'s Mot. for Severance, United States v. AU Optronics, No. 09-00110 (N.D. Cal. Dec. 26, 2011).
80. *See Joinder and Severance*, *supra* note 77, at 349.
81. *Id.* at 344.
82. *Id.* at 352.

c. Motion for Advance Jury Questionnaire

Prospective jurors are examined for potential bias through the voir dire process. [83] Trial courts have broad discretion over how voir dire is conducted and how juror questionnaires will be used. [84] Jury selection processes vary widely among districts and even from judge to judge within a district. [85]

In high-stakes, white-collar cases in which the defendants often have substantial resources, the parties routinely request that prospective jurors be required to complete juror questionnaires. The Supreme Court has recognized the value of questionnaires in the voir dire process. In *Skilling v. United States*, [86] in assessing a challenge to the voir dire process, the Court discussed the role of a seventy-seven-question, fourteen-page survey that asked prospective jurors about such things as their sources of news and exposure to possibly prejudicial pretrial publicity. [87] In upholding the voir dire process, the Court observed that the questionnaire—drafted largely by the defendant—"helped to identify prospective jurors excusable for cause and served as a springboard for further questions put to remaining members of the array." [88]

Voir dire and questionnaires in cartel cases involving foreign corporations and executives normally have several questions aimed at discovering potential biases that could prevent a juror from being fair and impartial. For example, in *United States v. AU Optronics*, [89] the Antitrust Division prosecuted a Taiwanese company and Taiwanese nationals for their alleged participation in an international cartel involving TFT-LCD panels. The case involved Taiwanese and Korean companies and executives. The defendants' proposed twelve-page questionnaire contained sixty-five questions (164 questions including subparts); the government's was seven pages long and contained thirty-six questions.

Although the parties' proposed questionnaires differed widely, they both covered many of the same topics, including age, place of birth, marital status, education, employment status, employment history, children, prior jury service, lawsuit experience, experience as a witness,

---

83.   *See* FED. R. CRIM. P. 24.
84.   Skilling v. United States, 561 U.S. 358, 385-95 (2010).
85.   *See* ANTITRUST DIV. MANUAL, *supra* note 5, at IV-73.
86.   561 U.S. 358 (2010).
87.   *Skilling*, 561 U.S. at 388-95, 388 n.22.
88.   *Id.* at 388.
89.   No. 09-00110 (N.D. Cal. 2010).

and experience as a victim of serious crime.[90] The defendant's proposed questionnaire contained a number of questions that appeared to be aimed at uncovering bias directed at Asian businesses. For example: "Do you agree, or disagree with the following statement: Asian companies these days have an advantage over their American competitors?" Also, do you consider companies from Taiwan, China, Korea, and Japan to be "more, less or just as honest as American business executives?"[91]

2. Evidentiary and Discovery-Related Motions

a. Bill of Particulars

Rule 7(f) of the Federal Rule of Criminal Procedure permits a defendant to request that the court order the government to provide a bill of particulars.[92] The primary purpose of a bill of particulars is to inform the defendants of the charges against them with sufficient specificity to allow them to prepare an adequate defense, avoid prejudicial surprise at trial, and avoid double jeopardy.[93] The purpose of a bill of particulars is not "(1) to obtain discovery from the government; (2) to compel disclosure of the evidentiary proof the government plans for trial; or (3) to require the government to explain its legal theories."[94] A bill of particulars is intended to supplement the indictment,[95] not to remedy a faulty indictment.[96]

The 1966 amendment to Federal Rule of Criminal Procedure 7(f) eliminated the requirement that a defendant "show cause" for a bill of

---

90. Supplemental Joint Status Conference Statement of Defts. and the United States, United States v. AU Optronics, No. 09-00110 (N.D. Cal. Sept. 7, 2011).

91. *Id.*

92. Fed. R. Crim. P. 7(f) provides: "The court may move for a bill of particulars before or within 10 days after arraignment or at a later time if the court permits. The government may amend a bill of particulars subject to such conditions as justice requires."

93. *See ABA CRIMINAL ANTITRUST LITIGATION HANDBOOK, supra* note 15, at 100-01.

94. *Id.* at 104.

95. United States v. Inryco, Inc., 642 F.2d 290, 295 (9th Cir. 1981).

96. *ABA CRIMINAL ANTITRUST LITIGATION HANDBOOK, supra* note 15, at 101 ("The sufficiency of the indictment must be judged within the four corners of the document, without the help of a bill of particulars and regardless of whether one is requested by a defendant.").

particulars.[97] The purpose of this amendment was to "encourage a more liberalized attitude by the courts toward bills of particulars."[98] Some courts have stated that doubts as to whether particulars are necessary should be resolved in favor of a defendant.[99] But it is open to debate whether courts have followed the Advisory Committee's Note.[100]

Trial courts have broad discretion in ruling on a motion for a bill of particulars.[101] Generally, the court should grant the motion if the particulars sought are necessary to enable the defendant, with reasonably diligent efforts, to prepare a defense and to avoid prejudicial surprise at trial.[102] In addition, the court may consider the complexity of the charges, the clarity of the indictment, the potential for premature disclosure of government evidence not otherwise discoverable, the possible surprise to the defendant at trial, the degree of discovery otherwise available to a defendant, the number of defendants in the case, the geographical scope of the alleged conspiracy, and the extent of voluntary disclosure provided by the government.[103]

The Antitrust Division typically opposes requests for bills of particulars on the principal grounds that (1) the indictment adequately advises the defendant of the charges;[104] (2) the defendant is in possession

---

97. *Id.* at 100.
98. FED. R. CRIM. P. 7, advisory committee's note to 1966 amendment.
99. United States v. Rogers, 617 F. Supp. 1024, 1028 (D. Colo. 1985); United States v. Thevis, 474 F. Supp. 117, 124 (N.D. Ga. 1979), *aff'd*, 665 F.2d 616 (5th Cir. 1982); *see also* United States v. Roque, 2013 WL 2474686, at *6 (D.N.J. 2013) ("[T]he class of cases in which a bill of particulars should, or may, be granted is broader than the class of cases in which it must be granted.").
100. *ABA CRIMINAL ANTITRUST LITIGATION HANDBOOK, supra* note 15, at 100.
101. Will v. United States, 389 U.S. 90, 99 (1967); *ABA CRIMINAL ANTITRUST LITIGATION HANDBOOK, supra* note 15, at 106-09 (providing detailed examples of particulars that have been granted and denied in antitrust cases); *ANTITRUST DIV. MANUAL, supra* note 5, at IV-67-68;
102. *See* 1 CHARLES ALAN WRIGHT, FEDERAL PRACTICE AND PROCEDURE § 129 (3d ed. 1999); United States v. Rosa, 891 F.2d. 1063, 1066 (3d Cir. 1989); United States v. Greater Syracuse Bd. of Realtors, 438 F. Supp. 376, 379 (N.D.N.Y. 1977); United States v. Addonizio, 451 F.2d 49, 64 (3d Cir. 1971).
103. *See ABA CRIMINAL ANTITRUST LITIGATION HANDBOOK, supra* note 15, at 103, 110.
104. *Id.* at 111-12.

of,[105] or has access to,[106] sufficient information about the charges to prepare a defense;[107] and (3) a bill "should not be expanded into a device for circumventing the restrictions on pretrial discovery of specific evidence embodied in Federal Rule of Criminal Procedure 16."[108] Defense counsel frequently argues that the court should not allow the government to bury the critical details of its allegations against a defendant in its massive discovery productions.[109]

Some courts have denied a defendant's motion for a bill of particulars where full discovery or an "open file" is voluntarily provided by the government.[110] The government sometimes accompanies its opposition to a defendant's motion for a bill of particulars with a limited voluntary bill.[111] In *United States v. Peake*,[112] the defendant requested an extensive list of particulars, including: co-conspirators' identities, dates of alleged conspiratorial meetings, details related to the defendant's alleged entry into the conspiracy, emails that evidence defendant's knowledge of and participation in the conspiracy, and a list of customers that the defendant

---

105. *Id.* at 112 (discussing the government's argument that requested particulars are not required because a defendant has knowledge of the specific facts underlying the charges).
106. *Id.* at 113 (discussing the government's argument that a defendant has access to extensive discovery under Federal Rule of Criminal Procedure § 16, which obviates the need for particulars).
107. *Id.* at 111.
108. *Id.* at 112; *see* United States v. Rodriguez-Torres, 560 F. Supp. 2d 108, 111 (D.P.R. 2008); *ANTITRUST DIV. MANUAL, supra* note 5, at IV-67-68. To the extent the government's evidence or theory of the case is necessary for a defendant to achieve one of the three primary purposes of a bill of particulars, the court may order the bill even though it will disclose such evidence and theory. *ABA CRIMINAL ANTITRUST LITIGATION HANDBOOK, supra* note 15, at 104.
109. *ABA CRIMINAL ANTITRUST LITIGATION HANDBOOK, supra* note 15, at 113-14.
110. *See* United States v. Canino, 949 F.2d 928, 949 (7th Cir. 1991); United States v. Walker, 922 F. Supp. 732, 739 (N.D.N.Y. 1996); United States v. Esteves, 886 F. Supp. 645, 647 (N.D. Ill. 1995); United States v. Magaw, 425 F. Supp. 636, 639 (E.D. Wis. 1977).
111. *ANTITRUST DIV. MANUAL, supra* note 5, at V-67-68. For example, the government has provided a voluntary bill of particulars in response to the defendant's motion for a bill. Mot. for a Bill of Particulars, United States v. Bennett, No. 09-656 (D.N.J. June 8, 2015).
112. 878 F. Supp. 2d 346 (D.P.R. 2012).

allegedly allocated with his co-conspirators.[113] Although some of these particulars have been granted in other antitrust cases,[114] in *Peake* the court denied the request, finding that the indictment provided the defendant with sufficient information for him to prepare a defense.[115]

In *United States v. AU Optronics Corp.*,[116] the defendants sought an extensive list of particulars, including the identities of co-conspirators and meeting participants, locations of conspiratorial meetings, identification of conspiratorial acts and statements, and extensive information on customers.[117] The court denied the defendants' motion for a bill of particulars,[118] finding that the indictment adequately advised the defendants of the charges against them.[119] The court noted that "the indictment need not specify the overt acts committed in furtherance of the charged conspiracies" and that it is "unreasonable to require the government to 'state the circumstances under which, and the words or conduct by means of which' the defendants and every alleged co-conspirator entered into the alleged conspiracies."[120] The court also ruled that while the discovery was voluminous (approximately 42 million pages of material),[121] the government produced it in a way that helped the defendants prepare their defense—by providing approximately eighty-seven highly detailed interview reports, indices of hard copy and electronic documents, and electronic discovery in a searchable format.[122]

An order denying a bill of particulars is not reviewable through a writ of mandamus.[123] It "is only reviewable upon appeal from a judgment of conviction . . . for an abuse of discretion."[124] A bill of particulars, if

---

113. Mot. for a Bill of Particulars, United States v. Peake, No. 11-00512 (D.P.R. 2012).
114. *See ABA CRIMINAL ANTITRUST LITIGATION HANDBOOK*, *supra* note 15, at 106-08.
115. *Peake*, 878 F. Supp. at 350.
116. No. 09-00110 (N.D. Cal. 2010).
117. Order Denying Defts.' Mot. to Dismiss the Indictment and for a Bill of Particulars at 5, United States v. Chen, No. 09-00110 (N.D. Cal. Jan. 29, 2011).
118. *Id.*
119. *Id.* at 8 (internal citation omitted).
120. *Id.* at 10.
121. *Id.* at 5.
122. *Id.* at 8.
123. Will v. United States, 389 U.S. 90 (1967).
124. *ABA CRIMINAL ANTITRUST LITIGATION HANDBOOK*, *supra* note 15, at 115.

ordered, does not become part of the indictment or the charge to the jury,[125] but defense counsel may move for a mistrial if the government's proof at trial materially varies from the bill.[126]

b.   Motion to Suppress

The Antitrust Division has routinely used consensual monitoring and search warrants in cartel investigations for decades.[127] Although the federal wiretap statute was amended in 2005 to allow wiretaps to be used in investigating antitrust crimes,[128] they tend to be used more sparingly than other investigative techniques. In 1998, one of the first major trials involving an international cartel, *United States v. Andreas*,[129] featured many audio and video recordings of competitor meetings and conversations that a cooperating witness had taped over a two-year period. In its decision upholding the convictions, the trial court reviewed the extensive taped evidence of the conspiracy and observed that "[a] picture is worth a thousand words, but is nothing when compared to a videotape . . . ."[130] Tapes and seized documents are often critically important in criminal antitrust cases—and the defendants regularly file motions to suppress such evidence.

Defendants may file motions under Federal Rules of Criminal Procedure 12(b)(3) and 41(h) to suppress evidence obtained in an improper search. Grounds for suppression motions include claims that search warrants were not based on probable cause as the Fourth

---

125.   *Id.* at 114.
126.   *Id.* at 115.
127.   *See* United States v. Andreas, 216 F.3d 645, 655 (7th Cir. 2000) (referring to 120-30 surreptitious tapes that cooperating witness made over a two-and-one-half year period starting in November 1992); Gary R. Spratling, Deputy Assistant Att'y Gen., Antitrust Div., U.S. Dep't of Justice, Criminal Antitrust Enforcement Against International Cartels, presented at the Advanced Criminal Antitrust Workshop (Feb. 21, 1997) (discussing use of search warrants in an international cartel investigation), *available at* https://www.justice.gov/atr/speech/criminal-antitrust-enforcement-against-international-cartels.
128.   In 2005 the federal wiretapping statute was amended to add criminal antitrust offenses to the list of "predicate offenses" for which wiretaps and other electronic surveillance may be obtained. *See* Pub. L. 109-177, 120 Stat. 192, 210 (2006) (codified as amended at 18 U.S.C. § 2516(r)).
129.   39 F. Supp. 2d 1048 (N.D. Ill. 1998), *aff'd*, 216 F.3d 645 (7th Cir. 2000).
130.   *Andreas*, 39 F. Supp. 2d at 1061.

Amendment requires or that the recordings should be excluded under 18 U.S.C. § 2515, which forbids the use at trial of any illegally obtained recordings or evidence derived from such recordings.[131] The Antitrust Division has a strong record of prevailing on suppression motions.[132] Nonetheless, even if a suppression motion fails to keep evidence out, it may provide an opportunity to uncover credibility problems with cooperating witnesses or expose problems with investigative techniques that might be useful at trial.[133]

c. *Brady* Motion: Disclosure of Exculpatory Evidence

In *Brady v. Maryland*,[134] *Giglio v. United States*,[135] and their progeny,[136] the Supreme Court held that the due process clauses of the Fifth and Fourteenth Amendments of the U.S. Constitution impose an affirmative duty on prosecutors to disclose to the defense exculpatory and impeachment evidence[137] in its possession[138] where the evidence is material either to guilt or to punishment.[139] A defendant's request is not necessary to trigger this duty to disclose.[140] A failure to make the required disclosures cannot be excused by the prosecutor's good faith because "an

---

131. 18 U.S.C. § 2515; *Andreas*, 216 F.3d at 660.

132. *See, e.g., Andreas*, 216 F.3d at 678 (upholding legality of video and audio taping by cooperating witness); United States v. Peake, 804 F.3d 81, 86-92 (1st Cir. 2015) (upholding search of defendant's laptop and cellular device).

133. *See ABA Criminal Antitrust Litigation Handbook, supra* note 15, at 235-36.

134. 373 U.S. 83 (1963).

135. 405 U.S. 150 (1972).

136. Kyles v. Whitley, 514 U.S. 419 (1995); United States v. Bagley, 473 U.S. 667 (1985); United States v. Agurs, 472 U.S. 97 (1976).

137. *See ABA Criminal Antitrust Litigation Handbook, supra* note 15, at 148-49 (providing examples of impeachment evidence that have been found to be material).

138. Exculpatory or impeachment evidence in the possession of other government agencies involved in the investigation or prosecution at issue may be imputed to the prosecutor. *Id.* at 147, 157-58.

139. *See Kyles*, 514 U.S. at 432; *Bagley*, 473 U.S. at 680; *Agurs*, 472 U.S. at 107, 111-12.

140. *See ABA Criminal Antitrust Litigation Handbook, supra* note 15, at 145.

inadvertent nondisclosure has the same impact on the fairness of the proceedings as deliberate concealment."[141]

The prosecutor's duty to disclose under *Brady* and *Giglio* extends to facially exculpatory and impeachment evidence that the prosecutor thinks is false.[142] Prosecutors cannot satisfy their *Brady* and *Giglio* obligations by making some evidence available and claiming that the rest is cumulative.[143]

(1) Materiality Standard

In *United States v. Agurs* [144] and *United States v. Bagley*, [145] the Supreme Court set forth the standards of materiality applicable to *Brady* and *Giglio* violations in different contexts. In cases involving the prosecution's knowing use of, or failure to correct, perjured testimony, the Court applies a standard of materiality that is favorable to the defendant. The evidence is presumed to be material unless failure to disclose it would be "harmless beyond a reasonable doubt."[146] In other cases, exculpatory or impeachment evidence is material "if there is a reasonable probability that, had the evidence been disclosed to the defense, the result of the proceeding would have been different."[147] A reasonable probability is shown "when the government's evidentiary suppression 'undermines confidence in the outcome of the trial.'" [148] Further, the *Kyles* court emphasized that in determining when the point of "reasonable probability" of a different result has been reached, the prosecution must consider all

---

141. Strickler v. Greene, 527 U.S. 263, 288 (1999).
142. *See* United States v. Alvarez, 86 F.3d 901, 905 (9th Cir. 1996); *ABA CRIMINAL ANTITRUST LITIGATION HANDBOOK, supra* note 15, at 148.
143. *See* Benn v. Lambert, 283 F.3d 1040, 1054-56 (9th Cir. 2002); *ABA CRIMINAL ANTITRUST LITIGATION HANDBOOK, supra* note 15, at 148.
144. 427 U.S. 97 (1976). In *Agurs*, the Supreme Court set forth varying tests of materiality in three different situations: (1) knowing failure to disclose perjured testimony, (2) failure to disclose responsive specifically requested evidence, and (3) non-disclosure in response to general request for all *Brady* materials or no request. *Id.* at 103-04, 106, 112.
145. 473 U.S. 667 (1985). In *Bagley*, the Court abandoned the *Agurs* distinction between "specific request" and "general-or-no-request" cases. *Id.* at 682.
146. *Id.* at 680; *Agurs*, 427 U.S. at 103.
147. *Bagley*, 473 U.S. at 682.
148. Kyles v. Whitley, 514 U.S. 419, 434 (1995) (quoting *Bagley*, 473 U.S. at 678).

suppressed evidence collectively, not item-by-item. [149] The degree of specificity of a defendant's *Brady* motion "may have a bearing on the trial court's assessment . . . of the materiality of the nondisclosure."[150]

(2) Knowledge of Others Imputed to the Prosecution

To comply with *Brady* and *Giglio*, the prosecutor has a duty to learn of any exculpatory and impeachment evidence "known to the others acting on the government's behalf in the case,"[151] including the prosecution team [152] and other government agencies [153] that are involved in the investigation or prosecution at issue.

Defendants in international cartel cases have argued that the government must locate and produce exculpatory and impeachment material in the possession of foreign authorities cooperating with the Antitrust Division.[154] In *United States v. Nippon Paper Industries Co.*,[155] the court held that the Antitrust Division was not required to search the files of cooperating Canadian and Japanese authorities, but was required to review the same "pool of documents that was reviewed by American authorities or their Canadian agents for the purpose of culling incriminating information" for possible exculpatory information. [156] In *United States v. Appvion Inc.*,[157] the court denied the defendant's request for an order requiring the Antitrust Division to search the files of Canadian and Japanese authorities, but required the Antitrust Division to ask the

---

149. *Id.* at 436.
150. Pennsylvania v. Ritchie, 480 U.S. 39, 58 & n.15 (1987).
151. Strickler v. Greene, 527 U.S. 263, 281 (1999) (quoting *Kyles*, 514 U.S. at 437); *Kyles*, 514 U.S. at 437.
152. A "prosecution team" is defined as "the prosecutor and anyone over whom he has authority" and "includes both investigative and prosecutorial personnel." Moon v. Head, 285 F.3d 1301, 1309 (11th Cir. 2002) (quoting United States v. Meros, 866 F.2d 1304, 1309 (11th Cir. 1989)).
153. *ABA CRIMINAL ANTITRUST LITIGATION HANDBOOK, supra* note 15, at 147, 158; *see* United States v. Merlino, 349 F.3d 144, 153-54 (3d Cir. 2003); United States v. Morris, 80 F.3d 1151, 1169 (7th Cir. 1996).
154. *ABA CRIMINAL ANTITRUST LITIGATION HANDBOOK, supra* note 15, at 147.
155. No. 95-10388 (D. Mass. Mar. 17, 1998).
156. *Id.* at 4-7; *see ABA CRIMINAL ANTITRUST LITIGATION HANDBOOK, supra* note 15, at 147 n.19.
157. No. 96-83 (E.D. Wis. July 8, 1996).

Canadian and Japanese authorities to make a voluntary review of their files for exculpatory material.[158]

(3) Duty to Identify and Disclose Brady/Giglio Material in Cartel Cases

Defendants in several large cartel cases involving voluminous amounts of discovery have argued that the government has an obligation to point out the exculpatory material. A leading case on this question is *United States v. Skilling*,[159] a fraud prosecution of an executive related to the collapse of Enron. In *Skilling*, the defendant argued that the government's production of several hundred million pages of documents without identifying any *Brady* material resulted in "effective concealment" of exculpatory evidence. In ruling that the government did not violate its discovery obligations, the court identified several steps taken to make the materials accessible: the files were electronic and searchable, the government provided a set of "hot documents" that it thought were important to its case or potentially relevant to Skilling's defense, and it provided indices to the materials produced.[160] But the court recognized that *Brady* violations might arise if the government acted in bad faith—for example, if it "padded" an open file with pointless or superfluous information to frustrate a defendant's review.[161]

In *United States v. AU Optronics*,[162] the defendants argued that the government should be ordered to identify exculpatory information in the approximately 37 million of pages of discovery that the government produced.[163] The court denied defendants' motion, finding no evidence that the government had used its production as a means of concealing *Brady* material and pointing out that the defendants were well resourced and had had the benefit of years of participation in related civil cases.[164] A rare antitrust case in which the government was ordered to identify

---

158. *Id.* at 9-11; *see ABA CRIMINAL ANTITRUST LITIGATION HANDBOOK, supra* note 15, at 147 n.19.

159. 554 F.3d 529 (5th Cir. 2009), *vacated in part on other grounds*, 561 U.S. 358 (2010).

160. *Id.* at 557.

161. *Id.*

162. No. 09-00110 (N.D. Cal. 2010).

163. Deft.'s Mot. to Compel Discovery Pursuant to Local Criminal Rule 16-2, United States v. AU Optronics Corp., No. 09-00110 (N.D. Cal. Nov. 22, 2010).

164. Order Denying Defts.' Mot. to Compel Discovery, United States v. AU Optronics Corp., No. 09-00110 (N.D. Cal. Dec. 23, 2011).

Brady/*Giglio* material for the defense is *United States v. Salyer*,[165] where a magistrate judge ordered the prosecution to identify Rule 16, *Brady*, and *Giglio* as a "matter of case management and fairness."[166] *Salyer* may be of limited precedential value. It involved facts seldom found in cartel cases: the lone defendant was in jail pending trial and was represented by a relatively small defense team with assistance from a corporate defendant.[167]

Brady and *Giglio* do not impose an affirmative duty on the prosecution "to discover information that it does not possess" or "to gather information or conduct an investigation on the defendant's behalf."[168] Nonetheless, the size, scope, and complexity of cartel cases can spawn potential *Giglio* issues that can pose significant challenges for prosecution teams. Cartel investigations are extremely complex, they often last for several years, and large numbers of attorneys, paralegals, and agents staff them. Witness development often involves several rounds of attorney proffers and interviews,[169] exploring in great detail events that happened long ago. Witnesses' recollections routinely evolve as they have additional time to reflect on events and have their recollections refreshed by newly discovered documents and by prompting from prosecutors, whose understanding of the case continues to evolve. Often this process creates *Giglio* material.

Antitrust Division policy requires staff to disclose all relevant final memoranda of interviews (MOI) of testifying trial witnesses.[170] But the policy also states that staff should consider disclosing *all* relevant final MOIs of witnesses interviewed in the course of the investigation as a way of ensuring compliance with *Brady* and *Giglio*. As the policy states, this practice "eliminates the need to review [the MOIs] for *Brady* and *Giglio*, avoids inadvertent non-disclosure of material that may be pertinent to some unanticipated defense or inconsistent with evidence as it develops at trial, and preserves the option of calling the witness."[171] If relevant MOIs are not disclosed, the policy requires that the MOIs must be reviewed

---

165. 2010 WL 3036444 (E.D. Cal. 2010).
166. *Id.* at *2.
167. *Id.* at *7.
168. *ABA CRIMINAL ANTITRUST LITIGATION HANDBOOK, supra* note 15, at 158; *see* United States v. Trados, 310 F.3d 999, 1005 (7th Cir. 2003).
169. *See Antitrust Division Criminal Discovery Policy, supra* note 26, at 19 (referring to the "central importance of witness interviews to Division cases").
170. *Id.* at 13.
171. *Id.*

carefully for *Brady* and *Giglio* material and that all MOIs containing *Brady* and *Giglio* material must be fully disclosed in a letter to the defense.

In addition to interview reports, other materials generated during cartel investigations may contain *Brady* or *Giglio* materials. Notes of attorney proffers, or emails between or among attorneys and agents containing substantive case-related material, may contain exculpatory information that Antitrust Division staff are required to produce.[172] For this reason, the *Criminal Discovery Policy* advises that attorneys and agents should avoid using email to communicate substantive, case-related information whenever possible.[173]

In *United States v. Peake*,[174] the defendant argued that he was entitled to see the raw interview notes created by agents during witness interviews because of admitted discrepancies between those notes and the final interview reports that the government produced during discovery.[175] The court denied the defendant's request, finding that the government's six-page letter clarifying some thirty-nine instances of discrepancies and omissions between formal interview memoranda and raw notes was sufficient.[176]

(4) U.S. Department of Justice Policy

DOJ policy addresses what prosecutors should do to meet their constitutional and legal obligation to ensure a fair trial and disclose material exculpatory and impeachment evidence. First, recognizing that it is sometimes difficult to assess the materiality of evidence before trial, the policy provides that "prosecutors generally must take a broad view of materiality and err on the side of disclos[ure]."[177] Second, noting that "ordinarily, evidence that would not be admissible at trial need not be disclosed," the policy nevertheless "encourages prosecutors to err on the side of disclosure if admissibility is a close question."[178]

Third, the policy requires prosecutors to disclose "exculpatory and impeachment information beyond that which is constitutionally and

---

172. *Id.* at 16.
173. *Id.*
174. 878 F. Supp. 2d 346 (D.P.R. 2012).
175. Mot. to Compel Production of Notes and Incorporated Memo. of Law, United States v. Peake, No. 11-00512 (D.P.R. July 16, 2012).
176. Order, United States v. Peake, No. 11-00512 (D.P.R. Dec. 10, 2012).
177. *JUSTICE MANUAL, supra* note 4, § 9-5.001.
178. *Id.*

legally required"[179] to ensure that trials are fair. The prosecutor must disclose (1) additional exculpatory information "that is inconsistent with any element of any crime charged against the defendant or that establishes a recognized affirmative defense";[180] and (2) additional impeachment information "that either casts a substantial doubt upon the accuracy of any evidence—including but not limited to witness testimony—[that] the prosecutor intends to rely on to prove an element of any crime charged, or might have a significant bearing on the admissibility of prosecution evidence."[181]

This disclosure requirement is applicable regardless of whether such exculpatory or impeachment information is likely or whether the prosecutor believes that such information will make a difference between conviction and acquittal of the defendant for a charged crime.[182] Following *Kyles*, the policy requires the prosecutor to consider the cumulative impact of items of information in assessing whether such information meets the standards outlined in the DOJ's *Justice Manual*.[183]

DOJ policy also addresses the timing of disclosure.[184] The law requires that exculpatory and impeachment material must be disclosed "at such a time that the defense has an opportunity to use the material effectively in preparation and presentation of its case, even if pretrial disclosure is required."[185] Delayed disclosure violates *Brady* and *Giglio* if it undermines confidence in the outcome of the trial.[186] DOJ policy requires earlier disclosure. Specifically, exculpatory information that casts

---

179. *Id.* § 9-5.001(C).
180. *Id.* § 9-5.001(C)(1).
181. *Id.* § 9-5.001(C)(2).
182. *Id.* 9-5.001(C)(1)-(2).
183. *Id.* § 9-5.001(C)(4).
184. *Id.* § 9-5.001(D).
185. *ABA Criminal Antitrust Litigation Handbook, supra* note 15, at 159; *see* Leka v. Portuondo, 257 F.3d 89, 101 (2d Cir. 2003). However, *Brady* and its progeny do not create a constitutional right to pre-trial discovery. Weatherford v. Bursey, 429 U.S. 545, 559 (1977). And the focus of a timing inquiry is "not on the effect of late disclosure on the defendant's trial strategy, but on whether late disclosure undermines confidence in the outcome of the trial." *ABA Criminal Antitrust Litigation Handbook, supra* note 15, at 159-60.
186. *ABA Criminal Antitrust Litigation Handbook, supra* note 15, at 160; *see* United States v. Fallow, 348 F.3d 248, 252 (7th Cir. 2003).

doubt upon a defendant's guilt or innocence "must be disclosed reasonably promptly after it is discovered."[187]

Impeachment information that casts doubt upon a defendant's guilt or innocence should "be disclosed at a reasonable time before trial to allow the trial to proceed efficiently." [188] Exculpatory or impeachment information "that casts doubt upon the proof of an aggravating factor at sentencing, but that does not relate to proof of guilt, must be disclosed no later than the court's initial presentence investigation."[189]

d. Motion for Disclosure of All Evidence the Government Intends to Offer Pursuant to Fed. R. Evid. 404(b)

Rule 404(b) of the Federal Rules of Evidence allows evidence of other crimes, wrongs or acts to be introduced for limited purposes, such as proof of motive, opportunity, intent, preparation, plan, or knowledge.[190] Upon request by a defendant, the government must "provide reasonable notice in advance of trial, or during trial if the court excuses pretrial notice on good cause shown" of the general nature of any Rule 404(b) evidence that it intends to introduce.[191] The defense should make an early request for notice of such evidence and file a motion to exclude it, normally on the grounds that its prejudicial effect would outweigh any probative value it might have.[192]

The government relied on Rule 404(b) in *United States v. Andreas*,[193] a case involving an international cartel in lysine, an animal food and feed additive, as the basis for introducing at trial evidence that the defendants attempted to model the lysine cartel on a cartel that had been established earlier in a separate product, citric acid.[194] The Seventh Circuit ruled that the evidence of the citric acid cartel was admissible in a case alleging a cartel in a separate product (lysine) because it helped explain some of the

---

187. *JUSTICE MANUAL, supra* note 4, § 9-5.001(D)(1).
188. *Id.* § 9-5.001(D)(2).
189. *Id.* § 9-5.001(D)(3).
190. FED. R. EVID. 404(b).
191. *Id.*
192. Fed R. Evid. 403 provides that relevant evidence may be excluded if "its probative value is substantially outweighed by the danger of unfair prejudice, confusion of the issues, or misleading the jury, or by considerations of undue delay, waste of time, or needless presentation of cumulative evidence."
193. 216 F.3d 645 (7th Cir. 2000).
194. *Id.* at 664-67.

evidence in tape-recorded lysine cartel meetings, it "provided the blueprint for" and "motivating force behind the nascent lysine scheme," and it explained the involvement of one of the defendants in the lysine cartel.[195]

In international cartel cases, prosecutors are often forced to make tactical decisions in deciding when to allege that a conspiracy started. Often cartels evolve gradually and it is unclear when competitor contacts and information exchanges cross the line to become full-fledged agreements. At times, prosecutors will attempt to introduce evidence of competitor contacts that lead up to the establishment of an alleged cartel agreement as 404(b) evidence admissible to prove such things as the alleged conspirators' motive, opportunity, intent, and preparation.[196] But courts normally admit such evidence only with a limiting instruction and may even limit the admissibility of coconspirator statements related to events that predate the start of the conspiracy alleged.[197]

e.   Motions Related to Admissibility of Co-conspirator Statements

Prosecutors in cartel cases rely heavily on Rule 801(d)(2)(E) of the Federal Rule of Evidence, which provides that: "A statement is not hearsay if . . . [it] is offered against a party and is . . . a statement by a coconspirator of [that] party during the course and in furtherance of the conspiracy." The government may introduce relevant coconspirator statements if, by a preponderance of the evidence, the court finds that a conspiracy existed, that the declarant and defendant were members of the conspiracy, and that the statements were made in the course and in furtherance of the conspiracy.[198] The contents of the offered statement "shall be considered but are not alone sufficient to establish the existence of the conspiracy and the participation therein of the declarant and the party against whom the statement is offered."[199]

The admissibility of a coconspirator statement is solely a matter for the court.[200] Trial courts use various approaches for making factual determinations on the admissibility of coconspirator statements. The court can admit the statement conditionally, subject to it being "connected up"

---

195.   *Id.*
196.   *See, e.g.,* Third Addendum to Final Pre-Trial Order at 5-7, United States v. Swanson, No. 06-692 (N.D. Cal. Jan. 22, 2008).
197.   *Id.*
198.   Bourjaily v. United States, 483 U.S. 171 (1987).
199.   FED. R. EVID. 801(d)(2).
200.   *Bourjaily*, 483 U.S. at 173.

at the conclusion of the presentation of evidence.[201] Another approach is to conduct an evidentiary hearing outside of the presence of the jury at which the government would present evidence of the statement's admissibility and the court would rule on its admissibility.[202]

A third approach is to require the government to submit to the court before trial a summary of its evidence establishing the admissibility of the proffered coconspirator statements.[203] This approach was followed in *United States v. Swanson*,[204] a large, complex case involving a cartel in the dynamic random access memory (DRAM) industry. After rounds of briefing on the issue,[205] the court decided that that it could not rule on the admissibility of coconspirator statements before trial. Instead, it required the government to provide the court, no later than 4:00 p.m. on the business day before it called a witness, a list of detailed information that established the foundation for admissibility of any coconspirator statements that would be introduced through the witness.[206]

In international cartel cases, which normally involve vast amounts of evidence and significant complexity, this approach can present challenges for the government and provide valuable discovery to the defense. For example, in *United States v. Swanson*, the government's filings in response to the court's order on coconspirator statements were detailed and voluminous. They provided to the defense the day before each witness took the stand a summary of the witness's expected testimony, a copy of each email highlighting the excerpts that constituted coconspirator

---

201. *See ABA CRIMINAL ANTITRUST LITIGATION HANDBOOK, supra* note 15, at 285; 30B MICHAEL H. GRAHAM, FEDERAL PRACTICE & PROCEDURE § 7025 (2011); United States v. Mobile Materials, 881 F.2d 866, 869 (10th Cir. 1989) (per curiam) (bid-rigging case recognizing that "the trial judge has 'considerable discretion' to admit statements conditionally, subject to their later being connected up") (citations omitted).

202. *See ABA CRIMINAL ANTITRUST LITIGATION HANDBOOK, supra* note 15, at 294; 30B MICHAEL H. GRAHAM, FEDERAL PRACTICE & PROCEDURE § 7025 (2011).

203. Order Requiring Further Hearing Regarding Coconspirator Statements at 3, United States v. Swanson, No. 06-692 (N.D. Cal. Nov. 16, 2007).

204. United States v. Swanson, No. 06-692 (N.D. Cal. 2007).

205. *See* Third Addendum to Final Pre-Trial Order, United States v. Swanson, No. 06-692 (N.D. Cal. Jan. 22, 2008); Order Requiring Further Hearing Regarding Coconspirator Statements, United States v. Swanson, No. 06-692 (N.D. Cal. Nov. 16, 2007).

206. Third Addendum to Final Pre-Trial Order at 7, United States v. Swanson, No. 06-692 (N.D. Cal. Jan. 22, 2008).

statements the witness would address, and charts addressing how each statement met the requirements for admissibility.[207]

f. Motions to Dismiss

Defendants regularly file motions under Rule 12(b)(3) of the Federal Rule of Criminal Procedure to dismiss antitrust indictments on several grounds. Bases for dismissal may include any of several defects in the indictment or in the prosecution.[208] Although motions to dismiss have been granted on occasion in criminal antitrust cases, [209] dismissals are uncommon.[210] Motions to dismiss arguing that the court lacked subject matter jurisdiction or that the Sherman Act's trade and commerce element was not met have been filed in several international cartel matters. These cases have resulted in significant decisions defining the extraterritorial reach of the Sherman Act.

---

207. *See* Notice of Filing, United States v. Swanson, No. 06-0692 (N.D. Cal. Feb. 28, 2008).

208. *See* ABA CRIMINAL ANTITRUST LITIGATION HANDBOOK, *supra* note 15, at 205-29; ANTITRUST DIV. MANUAL, *supra* note 5, at IV-68.

209. *See, e.g.*, Stolt-Nielsen S.A. v. United States, 442 F.3d 177, 187 (3d Cir. 2006) (dismissing indictment because company had not violated a conditional leniency agreement); United States v. ORS, Inc., 997 F.2d 628 (9th Cir. 1993) (conclusory allegation that "[t]he business activities of the defendants ... were within the flow of, and substantially affected, interstate trade and commerce," insufficient to establish Sherman Act jurisdiction); United States v. Braniff Airways, 428 F. Supp. 579, 583-84 (W.D. Tex. 1977) (dismissing indictment in part because of improper conduct before the grand jury).

210. *See, e.g.*, United States v. Mobile Materials, 871 F.2d 902, 906 (10th Cir. 1989) (upholding denial of motion to dismiss indictment for lack of specificity), *modified per curiam*, 881 F.2d 866 (10th Cir. 1989); United States v. Evans & Assocs. Constr. Co., 839 F.2d 656, 660 (10th Cir. 1988) (dismissal inappropriate remedy for failure to comply with order requiring disclosure of grand jury testimony to defendants), *reaff'd on reh'g*, 857 F.2d 720 (10th Cir. 1988) (en banc); United States v. Sargent Elec., 785 F.2d 1123, 1126 (3d Cir. 1986) (refusing to dismiss separate indictments for bid rigging at different steel mills); United States v. Korfant, 771 F.2d 660, 662 (2d Cir. 1985) (per curiam) (rejecting argument that indictment for price fixing in one state constituted double jeopardy after indictment for price fixing in another state); United States v. Miller, 771 F.2d 1219, 1226 (9th Cir. 1985) (rejecting argument that indictment contained insufficient factual specificity).

For example, in *United States v. Nippon Paper Industries Co.*,[211] the First Circuit reversed a trial court's decision to dismiss an indictment on the grounds that the defendant's conduct was wholly foreign and outside of Sherman Act jurisdiction in a criminal case.[212] Relying on the Supreme Court's decision in *Hartford Fire Ins. Co. v. California*,[213] the First Court held that wholly foreign conduct may be prosecuted under the Sherman Act as long as the conduct was intended to have, and did have, substantial effects in the United States.[214] The First Circuit declined to base its ruling on the Foreign Trade Antitrust Improvements Act (FTAIA).[215]

In *F. Hoffmann-La Roche Ltd. v. Empagran S.A.*,[216] the Supreme Court held that the FTAIA bars foreign purchasers from bringing suit under the Sherman Act where their foreign injuries are "independent of any adverse domestic effect."[217] The Court concluded that the intent of Congress in enacting the FTAIA was to release foreign conduct from the Sherman Act, only bringing it back within the ambit of under the Sherman Act when the foreign conduct causes domestic harm.[218]

Since *Empagran*, motions to dismiss in international cartel cases based on the extraterritorial nature of the alleged conspiracy have focused on the FTAIA as well as *Hartford Fire*.[219] For example, in *United States v. Hsiung*,[220] the government argued that the defendants' conduct both constituted import trade or commerce, which was exempted from the FTAIA, and satisfied the criteria of the FTAIA to bring the conduct within

---

211.   109 F.3d 1 (1st Cir. 1997).
212.   *Id.* at 6-8.
213.   509 U.S. 764 (1993).
214.   *Nippon Paper Industries Co.*, 109 F.3d at 9.
215.   *Id.*
216.   542 U.S. 155 (2004).
217.   *Id.* at 164 (2004).
218.   *Id.* at 159-60.
219.   Courts have disagreed on whether the FTAIA addresses the subject matter jurisdiction of the district court or establishes an element of a Sherman Act claim. Following the Supreme Court's decision in *Morrison v. National Australia Bank Ltd.*, 561 U.S. 247, 253-54 (2010), holding that the extraterritorial reach of § 10(b) of the Securities Exchange Act raises a question of merits, not of subject-matter jurisdiction, most courts have adopted the latter interpretation. *See* United States v. Hsiung, 778 F.3d 738, 751-53 (9th Cir. 2015); Minn-Chem, Inc. v. Agrium, Inc., 683 F.3d 845, 851-52 (7th Cir. 2012); Animal Sci. Prods. v. China Minmetals Corp., 654 F.3d 462, 466-70 (3d Cir. 2011).
220.   778 F.3d 738 (9th Cir. 2015).

the scope of the Sherman Act.[221] Defendants moved to dismiss the indictment, arguing that the indictment failed to allege that the defendants' conduct involved import trade or commerce under the FTAIA.[222] The district court denied the motion, finding the FTAIA was inapplicable to the import activity conducted by the defendants.[223]

The Ninth Circuit affirmed the district court's decision, holding that "transactions between the foreign defendant producers of TFT-LCDs and purchasers located in the United States" fell within the plain meaning of "import trade" and found that the indictment was replete with allegations of such transactions.[224] The Ninth Circuit also rejected the argument that the indictment inadequately alleged the intent prong of the *Hartford Fire* effects test, finding that there was no way that "the defendants could have unintentionally designated or chosen the United States market as a target of the [price-fixing] conspiracy."[225] Finally, the Ninth Circuit rejected the argument that the indictment failed to sufficiently allege that the defendants' conduct had a direct, substantial, and reasonably foreseeable effect on U.S. commerce, pointing to various allegations in the indictment.[226] Accordingly, the Ninth Circuit did not disturb the district court's order denying the defendants' motion to dismiss for failure to charge an offense.

---

221. *Id.* at 748 (internal quotation omitted).
222. Mot. of Defts. to Dismiss Indictment at 16-18, United States v. AU Optronics Corp., No. 09-0110 (N.D. Cal. Mar. 25, 2011) (addressing Hartford Fire Ins. Co. v. California, 509 U.S. 764 (1993)).
223. *Hsuing*, 778 F.3d at 744.
224. *Id.* at 755.
225. *Id.* at 748-49.
226. *Id.* at 757.

CHAPTER VI

TRIALS

A corporate or individual defendant indicted for a criminal violation of the antitrust laws may choose to stand trial for the offense. This chapter addresses key procedural and substantive issues that arise in the context of a criminal antitrust trial.

A. Juries

1. Voir Dire

Voir dire enables counsel to obtain general background information about potential jurors and evaluate whether they will be fair and impartial to all parties. Because the procedure for jury selection varies among districts and among judges within each district, the parties and the judge should discuss voir dire procedure in a pretrial conference.[1] In most federal district courts, voir dire is conducted by the district judge. Counsel may file a motion in advance of trial requesting that they be allowed to participate in voir dire, but it is within the court's discretion to accept or deny such a request.[2]

Similarly, counsel may submit proposed voir dire questions to the court,[3] but the judge may exercise his or her discretion to adopt or decline them.[4] Judges often issue written questionnaires, which potential jurors complete before entering the courtroom; counsel may review the completed questionnaires and use them to formulate additional questions (when the judge permits counsel to participate in voir dire), and to evaluate potential bias or impartiality.

---

1.   ANTITRUST DIV., U.S. DEP'T OF JUSTICE, ANTITRUST DIVISION MANUAL at IV-73 (5th ed. 2012) (last updated Apr. 2018) [hereinafter *ANTITRUST DIV. MANUAL*], *available at* https://www.justice.gov/atr/file/761166/download.
2.   FED. R. CRIM. P. 24(a)(1); *see* United States v. Rodriguez, 162 F.3d 135, 148 (1st Cir. 1998).
3.   FED. R. CRIM. P. 24(a)(2)(B).
4.   *See* United States v. Kyles, 40 F.3d 519, 524 (2d Cir. 1994).

If permitted, counsel may submit questions pertinent to the parties, facts, and legal issues involved in a case, including the jurors' views on foreign entities doing business in the U.S. and the role of the U.S. government in regulating such activity. For example, in a Sherman Act case against a Japanese company, the government proposed the following voir dire question: "Do you have any problem with the federal government enforcing U.S. price-fixing laws against foreign companies that do business in the United States?"[5]

2. *For Cause and Peremptory Challenges*

a.   Challenges For Cause

One ground for excluding a person from a jury is that such person "may be unable to render impartial jury service."[6] A juror need not be completely unbiased to serve, however: "It is sufficient if the jurors can lay aside their impressions or opinions and render a verdict based on the evidence presented in court."[7] Each party may challenge an unlimited number of jurors for cause.[8] When exercising a challenge for cause, counsel should present the reasons for challenging the juror's impartiality. A judge's denial of a challenge for cause is appealable but is reviewed under the highly deferential "manifest error" standard of review.[9]

b.   Peremptory Challenges

The parties may also use peremptory challenges to exclude jurors without stating a reason for the challenge.[10] In a felony case such as a Sherman Act prosecution, the government has six peremptory challenges, and the defense (regardless of number of defendants) has ten peremptory challenges.[11] The parties and the court should discuss the court's preferred

---

5.   Proposed Voir Dire Questions of the United States, United States v. Mitsubishi Corp., Crim. No. 00-33 (E.D. Pa. Jan. 16, 2001).

6.   28 U.S.C. § 1866(c)(2).

7.   Skilling v. United States, 561 U.S. 358, 398-99 (2010) (quoting Irvin v. Dowd, 366 U.S. 717, 723 (1961)).

8.   28 U.S.C. §1866(c)(2).

9.   Mu'Min v. Virginia, 500 U.S. 415, 428 (1991).

10.   However, under the Equal Protection Clause of the Fourteenth Amendment, a peremptory challenge may not be based solely on race or gender. Batson v. Kentucky, 476 U.S. 79 (1986).

11.   FED. R. CRIM. P. 24(b)(2).

method for exercising peremptory strikes in a pretrial conference, as this procedure varies significantly among districts. If multiple defendants are on trial, the court may, in its discretion, allot additional peremptory challenges to the defense.[12] Once a party has used all of its peremptory challenges, it must show cause for any additional challenges.

3. *Jury Consultants and Research*

Jury consultants can be essential to a successful defense, especially in a complex criminal antitrust trial. These professionals, often with backgrounds in psychology or other behavioral sciences, study the decision-making patterns and motivations of individuals asked to serve on juries. With such potentially serious outcomes, criminal antitrust prosecutions frequently necessitate the retention of a jury consultant for the defendants. The Antitrust Division sometimes utilizes the services of outside professional jury consultants in particularly complex international cartel prosecutions. Professional jury consultants with experience in criminal antitrust cases can:

- help craft jury questionnaires specifically targeted to yield the ideal juror;
- assist in evaluating responses to juror questionnaires, drawing upon the burgeoning field of jury research;
- develop strategies on how to deploy your side's limited number of peremptory challenges;
- provide strategic advice about which types of witnesses, evidence, and questions are most effective based upon interviews with jurors in previous cases;
- help prepare and select witnesses for maximum effectiveness at trial;
- act as a mock jury during practice arguments and provide feedback during debriefing sessions; and
- aid in honing trial themes.[13]

---

12. FED. R. CRIM. P. 24(b).
13. For a more comprehensive review of the utility of jury consultants in antitrust cases, consult Lisa C. Wood, *Using Jury Consultants in Antitrust Cases*, 26 ANTITRUST 101 (Fall 2011).

4. *Government Proposed Jury Questionnaire*

In international cartel cases, the Antitrust Division will often propose a jury questionnaire, to be given to prospective jurors and returned to the court in time for government trial attorneys to review the contents. In addition to the typical topics the government might be interested in exploring with potential jurors in a domestic Sherman Act case—such as views about corporate executives and beliefs about the credibility of witnesses who were immunized—the government may be interested in exploring issues unique to international cases.

For example, if the case involves witnesses, victims, or defendants who are not U.S. citizens or are not native English speakers, the government will propose a questionnaire aimed at identifying any bias a potential juror may have toward individuals or companies from another country, or who speak another first language.[14] If witnesses fall into these categories, the government will hope to identify potential jurors who may be less likely to believe the testimony of a witness who must testify using an interpreter or who has challenges giving testimony in English. The government will aim to identify any stereotypes prospective jurors may have regarding individuals or companies based on their country of origin or residence.

---

14.   Jury Questionnaire at 5, United States v. AU Optronics Corp., No. 09-0110 (N.D. Cal. Sept. 5, 2013) (asking prospective jurors if they, or anyone close to them, have ever traveled to, lived in, or worked for a company based in Taiwan, China, Korea, or Japan, and if prospective jurors read, write, or speak Korean, Japanese, or Chinese); Jury Questionnaire, United States v. Il Ung Kim, No. 06-0692 (N.D. Cal. Oct. 24, 2007) (asking prospective jurors whether they have had business experiences with foreign companies); Jury Questionnaire, United States v. Nippon Paper Indus., Co., No. 95-10388 (D. Mass. June 1, 1998) (asking prospective jurors if they, or anyone close to them, have ever been stationed in or near an Asian country or visited Japan, and if prospective jurors speak a language other than English and Spanish); Jury Questionnaire, United States v. Appvion Inc., No. 96-83 (E.D. Wis. Dec. 30, 1996) (posing multiple questions about prospective jurors' views of Japanese executives and Japanese businesses in the United States, as well as any negative sentiments about Japan because of World War II).

5. Defense Proposed Jury Questionnaire

Jurors' economic, cultural, and political backgrounds may influence, and in some cases slant, their view of themes in international cartel cases. Effective questioning of potential jurors can yield the type of educated and worldly jurors a defense needs in order to best present its case. Relevant themes to consider during jury questioning (accompanied by questions designed to assist defense counsel in evaluating prospective jurors) include civic engagement, economic sophistication, bias against foreign citizens or corporations, and personal views on antitrust issues.

B. Trial Memoranda

The Antitrust Division will almost always submit a trial memorandum to the court in advance of trial, not only to provide the court with its view of the facts of the case, but also to provide case law on issues likely to become relevant during the trial.[15] In addition to topics typically covered in a domestic Sherman Act case–such as conspiracy law, the elements of the offense, and evidentiary issues–an international cartel case typically demands that unique issues be presented and analyzed.

The government's trial memorandum will typically address potential issues relating to the Sherman Act's requirement that the conspiracy involved interstate or foreign commerce.[16] In a domestic case, the government may establish this element by showing that either (1) the defendant's activities were in the flow of interstate commerce (the "flow" theory) or (2) the defendant's activities, whether local or intrastate in

---

15. *See, e.g.,* United States' Trial Memo., United States v. Leung, No. 09-0110 (N.D. Cal. Oct. 26, 2012) (providing an overview of the case and a description of the evidentiary issues); United States' Trial Brief, United States v. Hansen, No. 09-162 (W.D. Mich. Aug. 30, 2010) (providing an overview of the case and relevant statutes, elements, and evidentiary issues); United States' Trial Memo., United States v. Swanson, No. 06-0692 (N.D. Cal. Oct. 24, 2007) (providing a summary of the case and evidence against the defendant, as well as describing plea agreements of co-conspirators and applicable laws); United States' Trial Memo., United States v. Video Network Comm., No. 05-00208 (N.D. Cal. Dec. 4, 2006) (providing an overview of the case and discussing all laws applicable to each offense).

16. Section 1 of the Sherman Act requires that the charged conspiracy be "in restraint of trade among the several States, or with foreign nations . . . ." 15 U.S.C. § 1.

nature, had or were likely to have a substantial effect on interstate commerce (the "effects" theory).[17] The same is true for an international case. For example, in the *AU Optronics* case, the government filed a trial memorandum that stated simply:

> Here the price-fixing agreement involved TFT-LCDs for use in notebook computers, desktop monitors, and televisions sold in a continuous and uninterrupted flow of interstate and foreign trade and commerce to customers located in states and countries other than the state or countries in which the defendants and their coconspirators produced TFT-LCDs.[18]

In *Nippon Paper*, the government's trial memorandum outlined both "flow" and "effects" theories. The government summarized its "flow" theory as follows:

> In the present case, the evidence will show that the conspiracy was designed to directly apply to millions of dollars of fax paper being shipped from Japan to the United States and distributed to customers in dozens of different states.[19]

The government also summarized its "effects" theory:

> [T]he government need only show that the business of the defendant and its coconspirators (the manufacture and sale of fax paper throughout the world) is "so connected with interstate [or foreign] commerce that it is logical, as a matter of practical economics, to believe that the unlawful activity [namely the price fixing conspiracy] will affect interstate [or foreign] commerce."[20]

The government's trial memorandum may also address issues regarding the Foreign Trade Antitrust Improvement Act (FTAIA), which limits the extraterritorial reach of the Sherman Act with exceptions for

---

17. *See, e.g.*, United States' Trial Memo. at 13, United States v. AU Optronics Corp., No. 09-0110 (N.D. Cal. Dec. 9, 2011) (setting forth this standard); ABA SECTION OF ANTITRUST LAW, CRIMINAL ANTITRUST LITIGATION HANDBOOK 265 (2d ed. 2006).
18. United States' Trial Memo. at 13, United States v. AU Optronics Corp., No. 09-0110 (N.D. Cal. Dec. 9, 2011).
19. Trial Brief at 16, United States v. Nippon Paper Indus., Co., No. 95-10388 (D. Mass. June 2, 1998).
20. *Id.* (quoting Cordova & Simonpietri Ins. Agency v. Chase Manhattan Bank N.A., 649 F.2d 36, 45 (1st Cir. 1981)).

import commerce and conduct that has a "direct, substantial, and reasonably foreseeable effect" on domestic commerce.[21]

In addition to interstate commerce issues, government trial memoranda in international cartel cases also typically raise unique issues related to foreign witnesses and evidence. Such issues include the use of leading questions when the witness does not speak English well or when English is not the witness's first language.[22] The government may point out that, in such a situation, leading questions are permissible under Federal Rule of Evidence 611(c) "in order to avoid the danger that the witness will misunderstand the questions and therefore answer incorrectly."[23]

The government may also discuss the anticipated use of translated documentary evidence, explaining that it will introduce English translations of foreign-language documents, certified by professional translators;[24] that it is permissible to present the jury with two different translations if the parties dispute the proper translation of a foreign document;[25] and that English translations should be admitted into evidence because "the jury will have no meaningful way to consider much

---

21. *See, e.g.,* United States' Trial Memo. at 13, United States v. AU Optronics Corp., No. 09-0110 (N.D. Cal. Dec. 9, 2011); 15 U.S.C. § 6a.

22. *See, e.g.,* United States' Trial Memo. at 28-29, United States v. AU Optronics Corp., No. 09-0110 (N.D. Cal. Dec. 9, 2011); United States' Trial Brief at 28, United States v. Andreas, No. 96-762 (N.D. Ill. June 30, 1998) ("Given that [the government's foreign witnesses] will be testifying in an American courtroom in something other than their native tongue, they may be nervous or distraught, diminishing their ability to communicate. Additionally, some or all of the government's foreign witnesses may not fully understand nonleading questions, even if they testify through an interpreter. Therefore, if necessary, the government should be allowed to ask leading questions . . .").

23. United States' Trial Memo. at 2, 8, United States v. AU Optronics Corp., No. 09-0110 (N.D. Cal. Dec. 9, 2011) (stating trial court did not abuse its discretion by allowing prosecution to use leading questions with a principal witness who spoke little English and testified through an interpreter) (citing United States v. Amjal, 67 F.3d 12, 16 (2d Cir. 1995)).

24. *E.g., id.* at 31-32.

25. *E.g., id.* at 31-32; United States' Trial Brief at 53, United States v. Appvion Inc., No. 96-83 (E.D. Wis. Dec. 4, 1996) (arguing that "it is more properly [the] function of the finder-of-fact to weigh the evidence presented by the parties as to the accuracy of the proffered translation and to determine the reliability of the translation on the basis of that evidence").

of the documentary evidence during deliberations unless it is permitted to receive and consider the certified English translations . . . ."[26]

C. Exhibits and Witness Lists

The types of witnesses that the government will call in an international cartel case are largely similar to those called in a domestic Sherman Act case. These typically include co-conspirators; corporate employees who observed the collusive conduct or conduct that the government alleges constitutes implementation of the cartel; victim witnesses, federal agents, and summary witnesses; and corporate representatives who can authenticate documents as business records. In an international cartel case, this list of witnesses may feature the addition of language experts if the context or translation of particular phrasing in a document not originally written in English is critical to the case.[27] Parties sometimes seek to call a cultural expert to interpret the meaning of certain conduct in a certain culture.[28]

The exhibit list will typically include both the original of any critical document, and the English translation of any documentary exhibit that was not originally prepared in English. Sometimes such exhibits will be labeled "Government Exhibit # 1" and "Government Exhibit 1(A)."[29]

Typically, courts presiding over international cartel cases will order that the parties exchange exhibit lists and witness lists earlier than in a domestic case, as some witnesses may not be located in the U.S. and may have to travel to testify, and counsel for both sides will need time to have

---

26. United States' Trial Memo. at 32, United States v. AU Optronics Corp., No. 09-0110 (N.D. Cal. Dec. 9, 2011); *see also* United States' Trial Brief at 63-65, United States v. Nippon Paper Indus., Co., No. 95-10388 (D. Mass. June 2, 1998) (submitting that the Government intends to offer into evidence documents in a foreign language and their translations into English, explaining why admission of those documents is appropriate, and contending that the accuracy of the translations goes to the weight the jury gives to the reliability of those documents rather than to their admissibility).

27. *See* United States v. Nippon Paper Indus., Co., 17 F. Supp. 2d 38 (D. Mass. 1998); Jointly-Submitted Government and Defendant Trial Witness List at 2, United States v. Swanson, No. 06-0692 (N.D. Cal. Oct. 25, 2007).

28. *E.g.,* United States' Mot. In Limine No. 2 to Exclude Testimony, United States v. AU Optronics Corp., No. 09-0110 (N.D. Cal. Dec. 6, 2011).

29. *See* United States' Exhibit List at 4-20, United States v. Leung, No. 09-0110 (N.D. Cal. Oct. 26, 2012).

all documents on the exhibit list translated. Even if one party provides a translation, the receiving counsel will normally want some additional time for its own translator to carefully review any proposed translations for accuracy before agreeing that they are admissible to aid the jury.

There may be instances in which the government and defense prepare competing translations of a document. In those cases, the government may raise the issue prior to trial, asking the judge to allow the jury to consider both translations.[30] This issue may also be raised by either party during trial when a translated exhibit is introduced.[31]

D. Motions in Limine

Although not specifically sanctioned by the Federal Rules of Criminal Procedure, motions in limine are commonly heard and resolved by the trial court pursuant to its inherent authority to manage trials.[32] Motions in limine may be made by either party before trial and are typically used for evidentiary issues, including the admissibility of various types of evidence or the exclusion of particular types of testimony.

1. Exclude Evidence or Argument of Reasonableness

The government may invoke Federal Rules of Evidence 401 and 402 and move to preclude the defense from offering evidence that the alleged conduct at issue in a particular international cartel prosecution was reasonable under the circumstances. Because international cartel prosecutions involve per se violations, the government will seek to exclude evidence of reasonableness on the basis that it is not relevant to whether there was an agreement in violation of Section 1 of the Sherman Act.[33] The government may move on similar grounds to exclude evidence aimed

---

30. *See* United States' Trial Memo. at 27, United States v. Swanson, No. 06-0692 (N.D. Cal. Nov. 16, 2007).
31. *See* Tr. of the Evidence Day 5 at 157, United States v. Nippon Paper Indus., Co., No. 95-10388 (D. Mass. June 8, 1998).
32. Luce v. United States, 469 U.S. 38, 41 n.4 (1984).
33. *See, e.g.*, United States v. Suntar Roofing, 897 F.2d 469, 472-73 (10th Cir. 1990) (evidence of reasonableness properly excluded); United States v. Koppers Co., 652 F.2d 290, 293 (2d Cir. 1981) (question of reasonableness properly withdrawn from jury instructions); United States v. Azzarelli Constr. Co., 612 F.2d 292, 294 (7th Cir. 1979) (inquiry into reasonableness of the restraint unnecessary for per se violation).

at justifying the conduct or demonstrating the lack of an adverse effect on competition.[34]

2. Preclude Jury Nullification Arguments

The government will typically move to exclude various types of arguments by defense counsel aimed at encouraging the jury to disregard the evidence and instead rule based on sympathy for the defendant, or on issues that are not relevant to guilt or innocence. For example, in international cartel cases, the government may file motions to exclude arguments that the defendant did not understand U.S. antitrust laws and was unaware that the conduct was against the law. Because a criminal violation of the Sherman Act is a per se offense, these types of arguments are irrelevant and the government will seek to exclude them from trial.[35]

3. Admit Guilty Pleas, Leniency Agreements and Non-Prosecution Agreements

In international cartel cases, the government will often seek to admit plea agreements of testifying corporate and individual co-conspirators.[36] It may also seek to admit leniency agreements.[37] The government seeks to

---

34.   *See, e.g.*, United States v. Coop. Theatres of Ohio, 845 F.2d 1367, 1373 (6th Cir. 1988) (question of effect of per se violation properly withdrawn from jury instructions); United States v. Metro. Enters., 728 F.2d 444, 449-50 (10th Cir. 1984) (proof of intent not required).

35.   *See* United States' Mot. in Limine to Preclude Evidence and Argument Aimed at Jury Nullification, United States v. Peake, No. 11-00512 (D.P.R. Nov. 14, 2012).

36.   *See, e.g.*, United States' Mot. in Limine to Permit Evidence of or References to Plea and Non-Prosecution Agreements at 4-6, United States v. Swanson, No. 06-0692 (N.D. Cal. Oct. 24, 2007); United States' Memo. of Law in Opp. to Deft.'s Mot. in Limine at 2-8, United States v. Romer, No. 96-00350 (E.D. Va. Dec. 17, 1996) (arguing for the admissibility of witnesses' plea agreement).

37.   *See, e.g.*, Amended Tr. of Hrg. Held on July 6, 2010 at 165-66, United States v. Norris, No. 03-00632 (E.D. Pa. Aug. 16, 2010); United States' Mot. in Limine to Permit Evidence of or References to Plea and Non-Prosecution Agreements at 6-8, United States v. Swanson, No. 06-0692 (N.D. Cal. Oct. 24, 2007).

admit these documents for the purpose of explaining and placing into context the circumstances under which co-conspirators are testifying.[38]

Without the context that these documents provide, jurors may be confused as to how the government was able to compel foreign national witnesses to come to the United States to participate in the trial, and may be confused about the witnesses' motives. The plea agreement terms will typically outline the obligations of the witness to testify in any trial in the United States as requested by the Antitrust Division and clarify the obligation of the witness to testify truthfully. The plea agreement will typically provide that if the witness does not testify truthfully, he or she will be in violation of any plea agreement entered and at risk of a prosecution for obstruction of justice.[39]

4. Exclude Evidence of Argument Regarding Lack of Specific Intent to Violate Antitrust Law or Ignorance of the Law

The government will often move the court to exclude evidence that the defendant lacked specific intent to violate the law. This argument is most commonly made in international cartel cases, when defense counsel sometimes asserts that the alleged collusion is a common way of doing business in the defendant's country of origin or residence, and thus he or she could not be expected to have realized that the conduct violated U.S.

---

38. *See* United States' Mot. in Limine to Permit Evidence of or References to Plea and Non-Prosecution Agreements, United States v. Swanson, No. 06-0692 (N.D. Cal. Oct. 24, 2007) (arguing that evidence of and references to plea agreements and non-prosecution agreements are admissible to evaluate witnesses' credibility and to rebut witnesses who deny the existence of a conspiracy).

39. *See, e.g.*, Plea Agreement, United States v. Gonzalez, No. 10-20790 (S.D. Fla. Nov. 30, 2011) (requiring co-conspirator to cooperate with prosecution of case by producing all non-privileged documents, making himself available for interviews, responding fully and truthfully to government inquiries, providing all non-privileged material or information voluntarily, and testifying truthfully subject to the penalties of perjury); Plea Agreement, United States v. Archer Daniels Midland, No. 96-00640 (N.D. Ill. Oct. 15, 1996) (requiring the defendant corporation to produce non-privileged documents and other information not already produced to the government, to secure the cooperation of any directors or employees of the corporation, and to make such persons available in the United States for service of process, interviews, grand jury testimony, and trial).

antitrust law.[40] Defense counsel often raises this issue when the defendant was located abroad, but reached an agreement that affected U.S. customers.[41] The Antitrust Division will oppose use of this argument as irrelevant to the per se nature of a Sherman Act charge.[42]

Defense counsel may seek to argue ignorance of the law in an international cartel case, citing the law in the defendant's country of origin or residence and contending that the defendant was unaware that he was violating U.S. laws. This issue is typically raised when a foreign-located defendant reached an agreement that affected U.S. customers. It is also a frequent issue in cases in which the antitrust laws in the defendant's home country do not provide for individual liability.[43]

5. Bar Testimony of Experts

The government moves to bar most experts in a criminal Sherman Act case, as an expert typically cannot have any direct knowledge of the key operative facts in a cartel offense—such as whether the defendant reached an agreement to restrain trade.

Defendants sometimes seek to introduce expert testimony related to the economic effects of the conspiracy. The government routinely files motions to prevent the testimony of experts regarding such issues as irrelevant.[44] The government may move to bar expert testimony aimed at

---

40.   *See, e.g.*, Trial Tr. at 33 (Def. Opening Statement), United States v. Appvion Inc., No. 96-83 (E.D. Wis. Jan. 15, 1997).

41.   United States v. Nippon Paper Indus., Co., 109 F.3d 1, 8-9 (1st Cir. 1997) (finding that Section 1 of the Sherman Act applies to foreign conduct that has an "intended and substantial effect in the United States").

42.   *Id.* at 7 ("[D]efendants can be convicted of participation in price-fixing conspiracies without any demonstration of a specific criminal intent to violate the antitrust laws."); United States v. Koppers Co., 652 F.2d 290, 295 n.6 (2d Cir. 1981) ("Where per se conduct is found, a finding of intent to conspire to commit the offense is sufficient; a requirement that intent go further and envision actual anti-competitive results would reopen the very questions of reasonableness which the per se rule is designed to avoid.").

43.   *Nippon Paper Indus.*, 109 F.3d at 8-9 (finding that Section 1 of the Sherman Act applies to foreign conduct that has an "intended and substantial effect in the United States").

44.   *See, e.g.*, United States' Mot. in Limine to Preclude Expert Testimony and Compel Expert Disclosures, United States v. Nusbaum, No. 09-00328 (D. Md. Oct. 2, 2009).

showing that the agreement to fix prices was reasonable, fair, or economically justified.[45]

In addition, parties in an international cartel case may seek to introduce expert testimony on cultural norms or the meaning of certain conduct, practices, or terms in a particular country, culture, or language. Such testimony may be opposed on grounds that it does not relate to the elements of a Sherman Act offense,[46] or if the "expert" is not qualified to give such testimony on an element of the offense.[47]

E. Government Proof

1. Industry Background Witness

Criminal antitrust investigations have covered nearly every sector of the economy, including consumer products,[48] manufacturing components,[49] transportation,[50] and the financial industry.[51] At trial, the government will introduce evidence that helps the jury to understand the

---

45. *See* United States' Mot. in Limine to Restrict Deft.'s Use of Expert Economic Testimony at 5-6, United States v. Swanson, No. 06-0692 (N.D. Cal Oct. 24, 2007).
46. United States' Mot. In Limine No. 2 to Exclude Testimony, United States v. AU Optronics Corp., No. 09-0110 (N.D. Cal. Dec. 6, 2011).
47. *See* United States' Objection to Proposed Expert Testimony at 3-5, United States v. B&H Maint. & Constr., No. 07-00090 (D. Colo. Dec. 13, 2007).
48. *See, e.g.*, United States v. Martin News Agency, No. 00-400 (N.D. Tex. 2000) (customer and territory allocation in magazine industry); United States v. Appvion Inc., No. 96-83 (E.D. Wis. 1996) (price fixing of fax papers); United States v. Mrs. Baird's Bakeries Inc., No. 95-294 (N.D. Tex. 1995) (price fixing of bread and bread products); United States v. Louis Trauth Diary, No. 94-52 (S.D. Ohio 1994) (bid rigging of milk products for schools).
49. *See, e.g.*, United States v. Dutton, No. 02-220 (W.D.N.C. 2002) (price fixing of polyester); United States v. SKW Metals & Alloys, Inc. (W.D.N.Y. 1996) (price fixing of ferrosilicon products); United States v. Conneaut Indus., No. 93-16 (E.D. Ky. 1993) (price fixing of fiberglass yarn).
50. *See, e.g.*, United States v. Rivera-Herrera, No. 15-00361 (D.P.R. 2015) (bid rigging of school bus transportation services); United States v. Peake, No. 11-00512 (D.P.R. 2011) (price fixing of freight services); United States v. Gonzalez, No. 10-20790 (S.D. Fla. 2011) (air transportation services for cargo).
51. *See, e.g.*, United States v. Rubin/Chambers, No. 09-1058 (S.D.N.Y. 2009).

specific product, industry, and players. This evidence is the essential foundation to showing how the cartel operated and the volume of commerce affected. In presenting a case to a jury, the government typically uses witnesses from the relevant industry to provide this context and understanding. Often, the defendant's co-conspirators will serve this purpose.

2. *Electronic Evidence*

In criminal antitrust cases, the government may seek to introduce electronic evidence, most frequently in the form of emails or text messages from co-conspirators. Such evidence is often conditionally admitted as co-conspirator statements under Federal Rule of Evidence 801(d)(2)(E), pending a determination at the close of the government's evidence that the government established the existence of the conspiracy.[52]

3. *Co-Conspirator Testimony*

In antitrust cases, proving an agreement and a true meeting of the minds can be challenging—especially if documentary and other evidence provides only circumstantial proof. In these cases, the testimony of a co-conspirator is crucial. In prosecutions of individual corporate executives, co-conspirator testimony often includes testimony from other individuals employed at the defendant's current or former company, as well as executives from other companies involved in the conspiracy.[53]

4. *Admissions*

---

52.   *See, e.g.*, FED. R. EVID. 104(a); Bourjaily v. United States, 483 U.S. 171, 179-84 (1987); United States v. Kandhai, 629 F. App'x 850, 853 (11th Cir. 2015); United States v. Hough, 803 F.3d 1181, 1193 (11th Cir. 2015).

53.   *See, e.g.*, United States' Mot. Regarding Coconspirator Statements, United States v. AU Optronics Corp., No. 09-0110 (N.D. Cal. Nov. 23, 2011); Trial Memo. of the United States at 18-19, United States v. Gonzalez, No. 10-20790 (S.D. Fla. Aug. 30, 2011); Third Addendum to Final Pretrial Order, United States v. Swanson, No. 06-00692 (N.D. Cal. Jan. 22, 2008); Trial Memo. of the United States at 3, United States v. Stora Enso, No. 306-323 (D. Conn. May 7, 2007); United States' Trial Memo. at 28-30, United States v. Mitsubishi Corp., No. 00-33 (E.D. Pa. Dec. 11, 2000).

The government will routinely seek to admit the defendant's own statements as party admissions under Federal Rule of Evidence 801(d)(2)(A).[54] These admissions often come in the form of emails written by the defendant and obtained by the government either through subpoena or search warrant, and may be introduced either through the testimony of a co-conspirator witness who received the email or a summary witness. Admissions also come in the form of audio tape recordings and statements made to FBI agents during the course of the investigation.[55] Statements regarding attendance at conspiratorial meetings or acknowledging agreements can be key evidence in the government's case.[56]

5. Experts

Experts are infrequently used in criminal antitrust trials.[57] The government may seek to admit an economic expert, however, if it is seeking a criminal fine in excess of the statutory limits in Sherman Act Section 1. In *Southern Union Co. v. United States*,[58] the Supreme Court held that "any fact . . . that increases the maximum punishment authorized for a particular crime [must] be proved to a jury beyond a reasonable doubt."[59] While *Southern Union* did not specifically call for expert testimony, the government introduced for the first time expert testimony to secure a $500 million fine in *United States v. AU Optronics Corp.*[60] In that case, the expert witness testified as to the gain obtained by the

---

54.   FED. R. EVID. 801(d)(2)(A).

55.   *See, e.g.*, United States' Mot. to Admit Audio Recordings, United States v. Peake, No. 11-00512 (D.P.R. Jan. 17, 2013); United States' Mot. Regarding Admissibility of Certain Evidence, United States v. AU Optronics Corp., No. 09-0110 (N.D. Cal. Nov. 23, 2011).

56.   *See, e.g.*, United States' Mot. in Limine for an Order Permitting Conspirators to Testify About the Existence of an Agreement, United States v. Peake, No. 11-00512 (D.P.R. Nov. 14, 2012).

57.   *See* United States' Mot. in Limine to Restrict Deft.'s Use of Expert Economic Testimony, United States v. Swanson, No. 06-00692 (N.D. Cal. Oct. 24, 2007) ("[P]rice fixing is among the practices that are '*conclusively presumed to be unreasonable* and therefore illegal without elaborate inquiry as to the precise harm they have caused or the business excuse for their use.'") (emphasis in original) (quoting Northern Pacific Ry. Co. v. United States, 356 U.S. 1, 5 (1958)).

58.   567 U.S. 343 (2012).

59.   *Id.* at 346.

60.   2012 WL 2120452 (N.D. Cal. 2012).

conspirators as a whole as a result of the conspiracy to support a fine in excess of the corporate statutory limit of $100 million.[61]

6. Summary Witnesses

Because cartel cases frequently involve large amounts of data and documents, summary witnesses are used to synthesize information and present it in a digestible form for the jury. Summary witnesses may be used to testify regarding phone records, email communications, banking records, and other business records.[62] The government also frequently uses a summary agent witness who can testify about many aspects of the investigation to help paint a complete picture of the cartel for the jury.

7. Customer Victims

The government will also typically present a customer victim witness to help place into context the harm caused by an antitrust conspiracy. It is often a challenge for the government to show the jury that antitrust crimes produce tangible harm.[63] Presenting a customer victim witness can help the jury to view a cartel as a serious crime with real victims.[64]

F. Potential Defenses to Criminal Antitrust Charges

1. Factual Defenses

a. Intent Defenses

(1) No Intent by Individual to Commit Violation

Intent is a necessary element of a criminal violation of the Sherman Act.[65] Without the actual intent to join in an arrangement to fix prices,

---

61. *Id.* at *4.
62. *See* FED. R. EVID. 1006; *see, e.g.*, United States' Expert Witness Notice, United States v. Smith, No. 06-242 (D. Or. Feb. 14, 2007); United States' Trial Brief at 81, United States v. Southwest Bus Sales, No. 92-40006 (D.S.D. Sept. 16, 1992).
63. *See, e.g.*, Jury Trial Tr. Day 4 at 95-103, United States v. Peake, No. 11-00512 (D.P.R. May 5, 2014).
64. *Id.* at 106; Trial Tr. at 111-47, United States v. Appvion Inc., No. 96-83 (E.D. Wis. Jan. 15, 1997).
65. *See* United States v. U.S. Gypsum Co., 438 U.S. 422, 443 (1978).

divide markets, rig bids, or commit another antitrust crime, a conspirator cannot be convicted under the Sherman Act.[66] A defendant may assert as an affirmative defense their lack of intent to honor a purported conspiratorial agreement.[67] For example, in *U.S. v. Bestway Disposal*,[68] the government put forward evidence that rival garbage haulers had verbally agreed to divide territory, but failed to prove that the parties intended to honor that agreement.[69] To the contrary, because the defendants' actions showed that "none of them ever fully intended it," the court directed an acquittal.[70]

This does not mean that a defendant can raise as a valid defense that she did not specifically intend to violate the antitrust law. For example, to be convicted of price fixing violations under the Sherman Act, a defendant need only intend *to fix prices*, not necessarily to violate the Sherman Act.[71] This takes on increased importance in international criminal cartel cases, which often involve foreign defendants who may raise as a defense their unfamiliarity with U.S. antitrust laws.[72]

(2) No Intent by Corporation to Commit Violation

Corporate violations are effectuated by a corporation's human agents. A defendant corporation might defend itself in an antitrust prosecution by arguing that its agents were not acting on behalf of the corporation. As in

---

66. *Id.*; *see also* United States v. Andreas, 216 F.3d 645, 669 (7th Cir. 2000) ("[A] defendant's subjective intent is a required element of a criminal antitrust violation . . . [and] a defendant who pretended to agree but did not intend to honor the agreement could not be convicted of a crime.").

67. To prove a defendant actually intended to enter a conspiracy, "the government [is] required to show that [the defendant] knowingly joined or participated in the conspiracy." United States v. Rose, 449 F.3d 627, 630 (5th Cir. 2006) (citing United States v. Young Bros., 728 F.2d 682, 687 (5th Cir. 1984)).

68. 724 F. Supp. 62 (W.D.N.Y. 1988).

69. *Id.* at 67. The evidence included prima facie proof of market division, including an agreement between competitors that "I will stay out of [one geographic market] if you stay out of [a nearby geographic market]." *Id.*

70. *Id.* at 68 (course of dealing showed that "each defendant lost commercial accounts to and took commercial accounts from other of the named defendants").

71. *See, e.g.*, United States v. Nippon Paper Indus. Co., 109 F.3d 1, 7 (1st Cir. 1997); United States v. Brown, 936 F.2d 1042, 1046 (9th Cir. 1991).

72. *See, e.g.*, *Nippon Paper Indus. Co.*, 109 F.3d 1.

other corporate contexts, an agent acting beyond the scope of its actual or apparent authority will not subject the corporation to liability. [73] In addition, in order to subject a corporation to criminal liability, an employee must have been acting with the intent to benefit the corporation. [74] This is ultimately a question for the jury, and courts will not typically dismiss a claim against a corporation based upon this defense. [75]

b.   Lack of Effect on U.S. Commerce

(1) Domestic Conspiratorial Conduct

Defendants facing criminal antitrust charges for conduct that occurred in the U.S. may defend against those charges by demonstrating that their actions could not "restrain" trade. [76] To meet its burden, the government must prove that a conspiracy is, "as a matter of practical economics," capable of affecting U.S. commerce. [77] Although the Supreme Court originally required antitrust plaintiffs to show that the defendant's activity "substantially and adversely affect[ed] interstate commerce," [78] it later lowered this standard to allow the plaintiffs to show that the activities "infected by" the conspiracy [79] had a "not insubstantial effect on the

---

73. *See* United States v. Koppers Co., 652 F.2d 290, 298 (2d Cir. 1981), *cert. denied*, 454 U.S. 1083 (1981); *see also* United States v. Automated Med. Labs., 770 F.2d 399, 406 (4th Cir. 1985) (corporation "may be held criminally liable for the unlawful practices [of its agents] if its agents were acting within the scope of their employment, which includes a determination of whether the agents were acting for the benefit of the corporation").

74. *See, e.g.*, United States v. Singh, 518 F.3d 236, 249 (4th Cir. 2008).

75. *See* United States v. Fla. W. Int'l Airways, 853 F. Supp. 2d 1209, 1237 (S.D. Fla. 2012).

76. *See* 15 U.S.C. § 1 (only "conspirac[ies] ... in restraint of trade or commerce among the several States ... or with foreign nations" merit criminal antitrust prosecution).

77. *See* Summit Health, Ltd. v. Pinhas, 500 U.S. 322, 322 (1991) ("Because the essence of any § 1 violation is the illegal agreement itself, the proper analysis focuses upon the potential harm that would ensue if the conspiracy were successful, not upon actual consequences.").

78. Hospital Bldg. Co. v. Trs. of Rex Hosp., 425 U.S. 738, 743 (1976).

79. For example, a real estate auction "infected by" a bid rigging conspiracy, *see* United States v. Romer, 148 F.3d 359 (4th Cir. 1998), or a commodities

interstate commerce involved." [80] The Court further lessened the government's burden when it held the government need not prove that the conspiracy actually affected commerce; the government must show only that, were the conspiracy successful, it *could* affect commerce. [81]

Given the antitrust prosecutor's exceedingly low bar following *Summit Health*, this defense will likely fail in most circumstances in domestic conduct cases, although it might succeed in some exceedingly rare situations. [82]

(2) Foreign Conspiratorial Conduct

U.S. criminal antitrust law applies to conspiratorial conduct directly affecting U.S. commerce, regardless of where that conspiratorial conduct occurs. [83] When the alleged conspiratorial conduct occurs outside of the U.S.—which will often be the case in international criminal cartel prosecutions—the FTAIA applies. The FTAIA excludes from the reach of U.S. antitrust law "(1) export activities and (2) other commercial activities taking place abroad, *unless* those activities adversely affect domestic

---

market "infected by" a price fixing conspiracy, *see* Plea Agreement, United States v. Archer Daniels, 96-00640 (N.D. Ill. Oct. 15, 1996).

80. McLain v. Real Estate Bd. of New Orleans, 444 U.S. 232, 246 (1980).

81. *See Summit Health*, 500 U.S. at 331-32.

82. *See* United States v. Bestway Disposal Corp., 724 F. Supp. 62, 69 (W.D.N.Y. 1988) (expressing "strong doubts as to whether there was sufficient proof between the alleged 'infected' activity and its affect [*sic*] on interstate commerce to support criminal [antitrust] charges" based upon the fact that defendants purchased equipment out of state, moved garbage that originated out of state, and received payment from out of state companies). Note, however, that this dicta was penned prior to the Supreme Court's *Summit Health* decision.

83. *See, e.g.*, United States v. Aluminum Co. of America (Alcoa), 148 F.2d 416, 443-44 (2d Cir. 1945). Defense arguments that conspiratorial conduct must take place within U.S. borders have historically been unsuccessful. For example, in *United States v. Nippon Paper Industries Co.*, 944 F. Supp. 55, 66 (D. Mass. 1996), Nippon Paper was indicted for fixing the price of fax paper; the trial court held that the criminal provisions of the Sherman Act do not apply to entirely extraterritorial conduct. The First Circuit reversed, holding that the Sherman Act applies to conduct that has an "intended and substantial effect" in the United States even if all of the conspiratorial conduct took place outside the United States. United States v. Nippon Paper Industries Co., 109 F.3d 1, 9 (1st Cir. 1997).

commerce, imports to the United States, or exporting activities of one engaged in such activities within the United States."[84] The FTAIA generally bars criminal prosecution for conspiratorial activity occurring outside of the U.S., except where that activity has a "direct, substantial, and reasonably foreseeable effect" on U.S. commerce.[85]

The federal appellate circuits are split regarding the degree of directness required by the FTAIA's "direct effects" exception. Under the more restrictive approach adopted by the Ninth Circuit, foreign conduct can serve as grounds for a criminal prosecution only if the effect on U.S. commerce flowed "as an immediate consequence of the defendants' activity."[86] The Second[87] and Seventh Circuits[88] have set a lower standard. In those circuits, prosecutors need only establish a "reasonably proximate causal nexus" between the foreign conduct and domestic commerce to establish a Sherman Act violation.[89] Defense counsel should heed these differing standards during venue considerations, as prosecutors face a more stringent standard in the Ninth Circuit than in the Second or Seventh.

c.   Variance Defense

On occasion, the factual record developed at trial shows a substantial deviation from the allegations charged in the government's indictment, for example, if an indictment alleges a single conspiracy when, in fact, multiple conspiracies are later found to exist. If such a deviation prejudices a defendant, it could constitute reversible error, as it did in *Kotteakos v. United States*.[90] In that case, the government charged the defendant with

---

84.   F. Hoffmann-La Roche Ltd. v. Empagran S.A., 542 U.S. 155, 161 (2004); 15 U.S.C. § 6a.

85.   15 U.S.C. § 6a; *see* United States v. Hsuing, 778 F.3d 738, 756 (9th Cir. 2015). This analysis mirrors the analysis the Supreme Court has applied to interpret similar 'direct effects' language in the Foreign Sovereign Immunities Act (FSIA). *See* Republic of Argentina v. Weltover, Inc., 504 U.S. 607, 618 (1992) ("[A]n effect is 'direct' if it follows 'as an immediate consequence of the defendant's . . . activity.'").

86.   *See* United States v. Hsuing, 778 F.3d 758 (quoting United States v. LSL Biotechnologies, 379 F.3d at 680-81).

87.   Lotes Co. v. Hon Hai Precision Indus., 753 F.3d 395, 410-11 (2d Cir. 2014).

88.   Minn-Chem Inc. v. Agrium Inc., 683 F.3d 845, 856-57 (7th Cir. 2012).

89.   *Id.*

90.   328 U.S. 750 (1946).

participating in one conspiracy to defraud financial institutions. The facts showed, however, that "at least eight, and perhaps more, separate and independent groups" of conspirators,[91] which the Court held as sufficient grounds for reversal.[92]

In criminal antitrust prosecutions, there are three relevant factors courts use to determine whether a single conspiracy exists:[93] (1) whether there was common goal,[94] (2) the nature of scheme,[95] and (3) overlap of participants in the various dealings.[96] If multiple conspiracies do indeed exist, it could provide a defendant with a factual defense,[97] grounds to

---

91. *Id.* at 754.
92. *Id.* at 776-77. The Court held this was grounds for reversal, even in spite of the trial court's instruction to the jury to separate the conspiracies in its analysis.
93. *See* United States v. Therm-All, Inc., 373 F.3d 625, 636-37 (5th Cir. 2004) (citing United States v. Morgan, 117 F.3d 849, 858 (5th Cir. 1997)); *see also* United States v. Anderson, 326 F.3d 1319, 1327 (11th Cir. 2003) ("No material variance exists if a reasonable fact finder could have found the existence of a single conspiracy.") (citing United States v. Chastain, 198 F.3d 1338, 1349 (11th Cir. 1999)).
94. *See* United States v. Richardson, 532 F.3d 1279, 1284-85 (11th Cir. 2008) ("Courts typically define the common goal element as broadly as possible. . . . '[C]ommon' for the purposes of this test means 'similar' or 'substantially the same' rather than 'shared' or 'coordinate.'") (internal citations omitted).
95. *See* United States v. Morris, 46 F.3d 410, 415-16 (5th Cir. 1995) (The "nature of scheme" criterion means "if an agreement contemplates bringing to pass a continuous result that will not continue without the continuous cooperation of the conspirators to keep it up, then such agreement constitutes a single conspiracy. . . . [T]he existence of a single conspiracy will be inferred where the activities of one aspect of the scheme are necessary or advantageous to the success of another aspect or to the overall success of the venture, where there are several parts inherent in a larger common plan.") (citations omitted).
96. *See* United States v. Maceo, 947 F.2d 1191, 1197 (5th Cir. 1991), *cert. denied*, 503 U.S. 949 (1992) ("A single conspiracy does not require every member to participate in every transaction . . . . The fact that the participants in the various dealings overlapped to a substantial degree supports the conclusion that there was one single conspiracy.") (citations omitted).
97. *See, e.g.*, Trial Tr., United States v. Farmer, Case No. 13-00162 at 32-35 (D.P.R. May 7, 2015) (arguing in closing statement that the government alleged multiple conspiracies; jury found defendant not guilty).

dismiss an indictment, or grounds to sever the case against that individual defendant.[98]

d.   Traditional Factual Defenses to Conspiracy

Because most antitrust cartel prosecutions are premised in the prohibitions against "conspirac[ies] . . . in restraint of trade or commerce," the defendants may raise some of the traditional defenses raised by the defendants facing other criminal conspiracy charges.

(1)   "No Agreement" Is a Valid Defense

The "essence of any violation of Section 1 [of the Sherman Act] is the illegal agreement itself." [99] If the evidence does not demonstrate a "meeting of the minds," then the prosecution cannot meet its burden of proof for a criminal antitrust violation.[100] Prosecutors can establish the existence of this agreement through either direct or circumstantial evidence,[101] although a conspiracy "nearly always must be proven through inferences that may fairly be drawn from the behavior of the alleged conspirators."[102] Prosecutors also may seek to offer evidence of alleged effects of the conspiracy, such as decreased supply or increased prices. Successful defenses, therefore, will often focus on providing alternative explanations for the prosecution's circumstantial evidence that shows the conduct is as consistent with innocence as with guilt.[103] Such evidence may raise a reasonable doubt in jurors' minds that a conspiratorial agreement ever existed.

---

98.   *See* United States v. Grassi, 616 F.2d 1295, 1302 (5th Cir. 1980) (if variance will impact a "substantial right of the defendant," motion to sever may be appropriate).

99.   United States v. Apple Inc., 952 F. Supp. 2d 638, 689 (S.D.N.Y. 2013) (citing Summit Health, Ltd. v. Pinhas, 500 U.S. 322, 330 (1991)).

100. *See* Monsanto Co. v. Spray-Rite Serv. Corp., 465 U.S. 752, 764 (1984) (To prove "agreement," "[t]here must be evidence that tends to exclude the possibility that the [alleged antitrust conspirators] were acting independently.").

101. *See, e.g.*, Mayor of Baltimore v. Citigroup, Inc., 709 F.3d 129, 136 (2d Cir. 2013).

102. *Apple*, 952 F. Supp. 2d at 689 (quotation omitted).

103. *See, e.g.*, Continental Baking Co. v. United States, 281 F.2d 137, 146 (6th Cir. 1960) (defendants argued that prices were determined by external factors).

(2) "Withdrawal" Is a Valid Defense to Minimize Liability

A defendant may limit its liability for some acts of the alleged conspiracy by arguing that it affirmatively withdrew from the conspiracy.[104] To constitute an effective withdrawal, a defendant must cease illegal activities and either (1) alert the authorities or (2) communicate its withdrawal in a manner "reasonably calculated to inform" co-conspirators.[105] One circumstance that often arises in cartel cases involves the defendant who has retired or resigned from the company where the alleged collusion took place. If an individual voluntarily resigns from a company engaged in a conspiracy, the act of resigning can constitute an affirmative withdrawal.[106]

Defendants have the burden of proof in establishing withdrawal, but the potential benefits are substantial.[107] If a defendant meets the standards for withdrawal, he or she will not be liable for acts of co-conspirators made after the date of withdrawal.[108] Additionally, on the date a defendant withdraws from a conspiracy, the five-year statute of limitations for that defendant's criminal antitrust violations begins, whereas the remaining conspirators' limitations period begins anew after any conspirator acts in furtherance of that conspiracy.[109]

---

104. *See* Smith v. United States, 568 U.S. 106, 110 (2013) ("Withdrawal terminates the defendant's liability for postwithdrawal acts of his co-conspirators, but he remains guilty of conspiracy.") (citations omitted).
105. *See* United States v. U.S. Gypsum Co., 438 U.S. 422, 464-65 (1978) ("Affirmative acts inconsistent with the object of the conspiracy and communicated in a manner reasonably calculated to reach coconspirators have generally been regarded as sufficient to establish withdrawal or abandonment.").
106. *See, e.g.,* United States v. Nerlinger, 862 F.2d 967, 974 (2d Cir. 1988) (defendant "unquestionably disavowed the [mail fraud] conspiracy when he resigned from" his company). *But cf.* United States v. Lash, 937 F.2d 1077, 1083 (6th Cir. 1991) (because defendant's "termination of employment was not voluntary" departure from company did not constitute withdrawal from company's mail fraud conspiracy.).
107. *In re* TFT-LCD (Flat Panel) Antitrust Litig., 820 F. Supp. 2d 1055, 1060 (N.D. Cal. 2011) ("Withdrawal, however, is an affirmative defense, which the defendant has the burden of proving.") (citing U.S. v. Finestone, 816 F.2d 583, 589 (11th Cir. 1987)).
108. *See, e.g., Smith* 568 U.S. at 110.
109. *See* United States v. Salmonese, 352 F.3d 608, 614 (2d Cir. 2003); Grunewald v. United States, 353 U.S. 391, 396-97 (1957).

(3) "No Overt Act" Is Not a Valid Defense

The general federal conspiracy statute requires an "overt act" in furtherance of the conspiracy to subject the defendants to criminal liability.[110] Criminal conspiracies charged under Sherman Act, however, have no such requirement.[111]

2. Individual Defendant's Decision to Testify or Not Testify

As in other criminal prosecutions, a defendant facing criminal antitrust prosecution has a constitutional protection against self-incrimination.[112] An antitrust defendant—like any other defendant in federal court—cannot be forced to testify as a witness against himself in court, during sentencing,[113] or through other less direct forms of communication,[114] if he or she has a reasonable fear that the testimony he or she gives could be used in a subsequent state or federal proceeding in the United States.[115]

If a criminal antitrust defendant chooses not to testify, prosecutors are theoretically forbidden from commenting—implicitly or explicitly—about the defendant's silence.[116] Strategically, to establish several of the

---

110. 18 U.S.C. § 371 ("If two or more persons conspire . . . and one or more of such persons do any act to effect the object of the conspiracy," each is guilty of criminal conspiracy.).

111. *See* United States v. Rose, 449 F.3d 627, 630 (5th Cir. 2006) ("[C]onspiracies under the Sherman Act are not dependent on any overt act other than the act of conspiring."); United States v. Andreas, 39 F. Supp. 2d 1048, 1073 (N.D. Ill. 1998), *aff'd*, 216 F.3d 645 (7th Cir. 2000) ("Unlike standard criminal conspiracies, liability attaches under Sherman Act conspiracies based solely on the agreement . . . .").

112. U.S. CONST. amend. V.

113. *See* White v. Woodall, 572 U.S. 415, 421 (2014) ("[T]he privilege against self-incrimination applies to the penalty phase."); *see also* Mitchell v. United States, 526 U.S. 314, 323-24 (1999) ("[E]ntry of the plea petitioner would surrender the right 'at trial' to invoke the privilege. . . . [T]he warning would not have brought home to petitioner that she was also waiving the right to self-incrimination at sentencing.").

114. *See, e.g.,* Schmerber v. California, 384 U.S. 757, 764 (1966) ("It is clear that the protection of the privilege reaches an accused's communications, whatever form they might take, and the compulsion of responses which are also communications, for example, compliance with a subpoena to produce one's papers.").

115. *See, e.g.,* Kastigar v. United States, 406 U.S. 441, 444-45 (1972).

116. *See, e.g.,* Griffin v. California, 380 U.S. 609, 613-14 (1965).

defenses detailed in this chapter (intent defenses, defense of withdrawal, etc.), a cartel defendant's own testimony could be an invaluable asset, if not the only source of relevant evidence. The choice to testify, though, carries with it inherent and important risks. For example, when a defendant chooses to testify, she waives her Fifth Amendment protections, at least as far as the scope of relevant subjects of cross-examination.[117]

3. Legal Defenses

a.   Statute of Limitations

(1) Standard Five-Year Statute of Limitations

The government cannot prosecute an alleged criminal antitrust violation more than "five years . . . after such offense shall have been committed."[118] An antitrust conspiracy is deemed to have been committed on the date on which either (1) the purposes of the conspiracy have been achieved or (2) the conspiracy has been abandoned.[119] Under traditional conspiracy principles, co-conspirators remain liable for co-conspirators' acts in furtherance of the conspiracy,[120] and the limitations period can begin anew for all co-conspirators as a result of a single co-conspirator continuing to act.[121] In a number of cases, defendants have been successful in arguing a statute of limitations defense to dispose of federal conspiracy charges.[122]

---

117.   *See* Brown v. United States, 356 U.S. 148, 154 (1958).
118.   18 U.S.C. § 3282(a).
119.   *See* United States v. Kissel, 218 U.S. 601, 608 (1910) ("If [conspirators] do continue such efforts in the pursuance of the plan the conspiracy continues up to the time of abandonment or success."); *see also* United States v. Inryco, Inc., 642 F.2d 290, 293 (9th Cir. 1981) ("While a Sherman Act conspiracy is technically ripe when the agreement to restrain competition is formed, it remains actionable until its purpose has been achieved or abandoned . . . .").
120.   *See, e.g.*, Pinkerton v. United States, 328 U.S. 640, 647-48 (1946); United States v. Spotted Elk, 548 F.3d 641, 672-73 (8th Cir. 2008).
121.   *See, e.g.*, United States v. Anderson, 326 F.3d 1319, 1328 (11th Cir. 2003) (statute of limitations started to run after one conspirator's receipt of final payment under anticompetitive contract).
122.   *See, e.g.*, United States v. Grimm, 738 F.3d 498, 503 (2d Cir. 2013) (reversing convictions where government failed to prove any conspiratorial activity within the five-year limitations period).

(2) Tolling

In international cartel cases, federal law provides that a prosecutor can extend the limitations period relatively easily by formally requesting evidence located in a foreign country. Often, much of the evidence of the alleged criminal conduct in international cartel cases may be located overseas. Federal law permits prosecutors to toll the Sherman Act's five-year statute of limitations for up to three additional years if the prosecution can show the court that (1) evidence is located in a foreign country and (2) prosecutors have made an official request for that evidence.[123]

It is an unsettled question of law whether prosecutors are required to make this showing prior to the expiration of the Sherman Act's five-year limitations period, or whether such a request can have retroactive effect if made after the five-year period expires.[124] Federal law does not require prosecutors to make these requests publicly, so the subject(s) of these investigations may have no notice that their statute-of-limitations period has been constructively extended by such a request until after an indictment is issued and the defense moves to dismiss on statute of limitation grounds.[125]

---

123. 18 U.S.C. § 3292; *see also* United States v. Lyttle, 667 F.3d 220, 224-25 (2d Cir. 2012) (upholding suspension of limitations period where district court was provided with a copy of the government's official request, a transcript of grand jury testimony, and a sworn affidavit from a government investigator); United States v. Ratti, 365 F. Supp. 2d 649, 657-58 (D. Md. 2005) (upholding suspension of limitations period where district court was provided with copy of request to Italian government under Multilateral Assistance Treaty).

124. *See, e.g.,* United States v. Bischel, 61 F.3d 1429, 1434-35 (9th Cir. 1995) (holding that court can retroactively suspend running of a statute of limitations even if application made after original period had passed). *But see* United States v. Kozeny, 541 F.3d 166, 176 (2d Cir. 2008) (rejecting "an interpretation of section 3292 that permits an application to be filed after the statute of limitations has run . . . ."); United States v. Brody, 621 F. Supp. 2d 1196, 1202 (D. Utah 2009) ("[Section] 3292 requires the application before the statute has run.").

125. *See* United States v. Lyttle, 667 F.3d 220, 225 (2d Cir. 2012) ("[T]here is nothing improper about ex parte proceedings to determine whether to issue [Section] 3292 orders."); *see also* United States v. Torres, 318 F.3d 1058, 1061 (11th Cir. 2003) ("Under [Section] 3292, the government may apply, ex parte, for suspension of the statute of limitations when it seeks evidence located in a foreign country.").

In addition, as is the case in other federal statutes of limitations, the period is tolled while a defendant is "fleeing from justice."[126] Therefore, while a foreign defendant may escape the personal jurisdiction of U.S. federal courts by remaining in her home country, during that period, federal law tolls her limitations period.

b. Double Jeopardy

The U.S. Constitution prohibits trying a defendant twice for the same offense.[127] A defendant charged a second time for an additional antitrust conspiracy may raise an affirmative defense rooted in double jeopardy principles by arguing that the two conspiracies are not two distinct conspiracies but instead one larger conspiracy that the government is precluded from prosecuting anew.[128] Once a defendant raises this defense by providing "a non-frivolous or prima facie showing of a single conspiracy," the government must then prove by a preponderance of the evidence that it has charged the defendant with two distinct antitrust conspiracies.[129]

c. Jurisdiction-Based Defenses

(1) Personal Jurisdiction

The jurisdictional requirements of the U.S. federal courts apply in equal force to criminal antitrust prosecutions. Thus, a defendant may argue in a pretrial motion that a federal court's exercise of personal jurisdiction

---

126. 18 U.S.C. § 3290; *see also In re* Extradition of Handanovic, 829 F. Supp. 2d 979, 992 (D. Or. 2011) ("To meet this burden, the government must show that the defendant knew that [she] was wanted by the police and [she] failed to submit to arrest.") (quotation omitted).
127. U.S. CONST. amend. V.
128. *See* United States v. Beachner Const. Co., 729 F.2d 1278, 1279 (10th Cir. 1984) (upholding district court's holding that two "alleged bid-rigging schemes . . . were each part of a single, continuing conspiracy . . . .").
129. *See In re* Grand Jury Proceedings, 797 F.2d 1377, 1380 (6th Cir. 1986); *see also* United States v. McGowan, 854 F. Supp. 176, 180 (E.D.N.Y. 1994), *aff'd*, 58 F.3d 8 (2d Cir. 1995) ("[T]he moving defendant bears the initial burden of demonstrating that the two charged conspiracies were in fact the same. If a defendant makes a sufficient showing of overlap, the burden shifts to the government 'to rebut the inference of unity.'").

violates principles of due process,[130] that he lacks "minimum contacts" with the U.S.,[131] or that he has not "purposefully availed" himself of the privilege of conducting business in the U.S.[132]

Under federal criminal procedure rules, a defendant must be present—at least in an initial appearance—to stand trial.[133] As a practical matter, foreign antitrust defendants have evaded criminal antitrust prosecution simply by remaining outside of the U.S. In 2014, however, the Antitrust Division secured the first extradition of a foreign national to face criminal charges for a violation of the U.S. antitrust laws.[134] The Antitrust Division has signaled it plans to continue this aggressive international criminal enforcement, so antitrust prosecution will likely become increasingly difficult to evade.[135]

(2) Venue

While not a "defense" per se, an international cartel defendant could move to transfer criminal antitrust charges against him if those charges were not brought in a proper venue.[136] Venue is proper for most individual

---

130. *See* Glencore Grain Rotterdam B.V. v. Shivnath Rai Harnarain Co., 284 F.3d 1114, 1121 (9th Cir. 2002) ("The personal jurisdiction requirement, by contrast, 'flows . . . from the Due Process Clause . . . [and] represents a restriction on judicial power not as a matter of sovereignty, but as a matter of individual liberty.'") (citing Ins. Corp. of Ir. v. Compagnie des Bauxites de Guinee, 456 U.S. 694, 701 (1982)).

131. Int'l Shoe Co. v. Washington, 326 U.S. 310, 316 (1945).

132. Daimler AG v. Bauman, 571 U.S. 117, 135 n.13 (2014) ("[A] corporation can purposefully avail itself of a forum by directing its agents or distributors to take action there."); Burger King Corp. v. Rudzewicz, 471 U.S. 462, 472-73 (1985).

133. FED. R. CRIM. P. 43(a).

134. *See* Press Release, U.S. Dep't of Justice, Office of Public Affairs, First Ever Extradition on Antitrust Charges (Apr. 4, 2014), *available at* https://www.justice.gov/opa/pr/first-ever-extradition-antitrust-charge.

135. *See* Brent Snyder, Deputy Ass't Att'y Gen., Antitrust Div., U.S. Dep't of Justice, Individual Accountability for Antitrust Crimes, Remarks at the Yale Global Antitrust Enforcement Conference (Feb. 19, 2016), *available at* https://www.justice.gov/opa/file/826721/download ("The Antitrust Division is committed to ensuring that culpable foreign nationals, just like U.S. co-conspirators, serve significant prison sentences for violating the antitrust laws of the United States.").

136. *See* FED. R. CRIM. P. 18, 21(a).

criminal antitrust defendants in any district where their crimes were "begun, continued, or completed."[137] For cartel conduct that occurred entirely outside of the U.S., venue is proper in the district where the first conspirator is "arrested or is first brought."[138] Venue is proper for corporate defendants (1) in the judicial district in which the corporation "is an inhabitant" and (2) in any district in which the corporation "may be found or transacts business."[139] In addition, high-profile cases, a foreign defendant may have a strong case for a venue change, given that if a court finds an "unacceptable level of prejudice" resulting from a trial in a given venue, the Federal Rules of Criminal Procedure *mandate* a change in venue.[140]

(3) Subject Matter Jurisdiction

Federal law grants all federal courts explicit subject matter jurisdiction over criminal antitrust cases.[141] Thus, unless facing an action in a state court, no subject matter jurisdiction defenses are available to international cartel defendants.

4. International Cartel Defenses

Most defenses to domestic antitrust cartel charges apply with equal force when defending against international cartel charges, including those "Factual Defenses" and "Legal Defenses." Three of these defenses take on special significance in international cartel cases.

a. The Foreign Trade Antitrust Improvement Act (FTAIA)

International cartel defendants may have a stronger "affecting-commerce" defense than that available to domestic cartel defendants. Especially in courts in the Ninth Circuit, a foreign defendant can argue

---

137. 18 U.S.C. § 3237.
138. 18 U.S.C. § 3238. If no offender has yet been "arrested or brought into any district," venue is proper in the district containing the "last known residence of the offender" or of any of the co-conspirators. *Id.*
139. 15 U.S.C. § 22.
140. FED. R. CRIM. P. 21(a); *see* United States v. Walker, 665 F.3d 212, 223 (1st Cir. 2011) (court must change venue if "pervasive pretrial publicity has inflamed passions in the host community past the breaking point").
141. 15 U.S.C. § 4 ("The several district courts of the United States are invested with jurisdiction to prevent and restrain violations of [the Sherman Act]").

that the anticompetitive effect on U.S. commerce was not an "immediate consequence" of his conspiratorial acts.[142] In such a situation, the FTAIA would inoculate that foreign defendant from criminal prosecution.[143]

b. Tolling

Criminal charges under the Sherman Act are subject to a five-year statute of limitations period.[144] As noted above, when significant evidence of an antitrust cartel's activities exists in a foreign country, prosecutors can toll that limitations period by up to three years by filing an "official request" seeking that evidence.

c. Venue

Although not technically a "defense," an international cartel defendant can seek a change of venue if she can prove an "unacceptable level of prejudice" will occur in a given geographic forum.[145] Due to overarching due process concerns, federal courts may be especially sensitive to the potential prejudice against a foreign cartel defendant in an American courtroom.[146]

G. Jury Instructions

1. *2009 ABA Model Jury Instructions in Criminal Antitrust Cases*

In 2009, the American Bar Association (ABA) published Model Jury Instructions in Criminal Antitrust Cases, an update to a work originally published in 1984.[147] This publication provides model jury instructions specific to criminal antitrust trials, with explanatory commentary

---

142. *See* United States v. Hsuing, 758 F.3d 1074, 1094 (9th Cir. 2014) (quoting United States v. LSL Biotechnologies, 379 F.3d 672, 680-81 (9th Cir. 2004)).

143. 15 U.S.C. § 6a.

144. 18 U.S.C. § 3282(a).

145. FED. R. CRIM. P. 21(a).

146. *See, e.g.*, United States v. Walker, 665 F.3d 212, 223 (1st Cir. 2011) (court must change venue if "pervasive pretrial publicity has inflamed passions in the host community past the breaking point").

147. ABA SECTION OF ANTITRUST LAW, MODEL JURY INSTRUCTIONS IN CRIMINAL ANTITRUST CASES (2009) [hereinafter *ABA MODEL JURY INSTRUCTIONS*].

referencing pertinent case law and the practices of various federal circuits. Defense counsel should reference these model instructions as a starting point and tailor them to the case being tried.

2. Government Criminal Antitrust Instructions

In international cartel cases, the government may propose instructions that address special issues, such as foreign-located evidence, foreign-language evidence, the interstate commerce element, venue, and antidumping laws.

a. Foreign-Located Evidence

The government may seek an instruction cautioning the jury that witnesses located outside of the U.S. cannot be compelled to testify at trial. In *Nippon Paper*, for example, the court instructed the jury that:

> Neither the government nor the defense has the ability to compel the attendance of this trial of a witness from outside the United States. The subpoena power of this Court does not extend beyond the borders of the United States.[148]

b. Foreign-Language Evidence

The government may seek an instruction that cautions the jury to consider only English-language evidence. In *United States v. AU Optronics Corp.*,[149] the defendants were charged with participating in an international conspiracy to fix prices for TFT-LCD panels that were incorporated into finished products, such as computers or television sets sold in or delivered to the United States. Some of the evidence was in Chinese or Korean. The jury was instructed to consider only evidence provided through official court interpreters and translators:[150]

---

148. Tr. of the Evidence Day 20 at 2138, United States v. Nippon Paper Indus., Co., No. 95-10388 (D. Mass. July 1, 1998).

149. United States v. AU Optronics Corp., No. 09-00110 (N.D. Cal. 2013).

150. Jury Instructions at 5, United States v. AU Optronics Corp., No. 09-00110 (N.D. Cal. Oct. 9, 2013).

c. Interstate Commerce

In Section 1 cases, a basic instruction on interstate commerce—the third element—is vital. Cases involving foreign or import commerce may invite or require more detailed instructions on this element.

For example, in *United States v. AU Optronics*, the court instructed jurors that the Sherman Act applies to "conspiracies that occur, at least in part, within the United States" as well as to "conspiracies that occur entirely outside the United States if they have a substantial and intended effect in the United States."[151] The government was thus required to prove either that at least one conspirator took an action in furtherance of the conspiracy within the United States, or that the conspiracy had a substantial and intended effect in the United States, or both.[152] To determine whether the conspiracy had such an effect, the jury was permitted to consider the total amount of trade or commerce of the products delivered or sold in the United States, but the government did not need to quantify the value of the effect.[153]

Finally, in determining the gross gain from the conspiracy, the jury was instructed to consider the gross gain from affected sales of the price-fixed product manufactured abroad and sold in the United States. The jury was further instructed that the gain should not be reduced by any taxes or costs associated with the sales of the products.[154]

d. Venue

When the government has alleged a conspiracy with international reach, it may propose an instruction clarifying the legal standard for venue. Although such an instruction is not unique to international cases, it arises more frequently in this context because of the increased likelihood that the defense will challenge venue. To satisfy venue, the government need only establish that "an act," such as a phone call or fax, in furtherance of the conspiracy occurred within the district.[155] Because venue is not an element

---

151. *Id.* at 10.
152. *Id.*
153. *Id.* at 11.
154. *Id.* at 16.
155. *See* ABA SECTION OF ANTITRUST LAW, CRIMINAL ANTITRUST LITIGATION HANDBOOK 413 (2d ed. 2006) [hereinafter *ABA CRIMINAL ANTITRUST LITIGATION HANDBOOK*] ("Unlike its findings on the essential elements of the offense, the jury needs only find by a preponderance of the evidence

of the offense, [156] the standard is preponderance of the evidence; circumstantial evidence is sufficient to prove the point. [157]

e. Antidumping Laws

In *United States v. Nippon Paper*, the defendant was charged with joining an unlawful conspiracy to fix prices in the international thermal fax paper market. The court noted in its jury instructions that it is a violation of U.S. antidumping laws for a foreign manufacturer to sell a product in the United States at a price below that of its home country, or at a price below its costs to manufacture the good. [158] It is not, however, illegal for a manufacturer to set prices in its home at a level below the cost to manufacture the goods in its own country. [159] It is similarly not unlawful for "competitors to meet and agree that they will take steps to not violate the U.S. antidumping laws, provided that they do not agree to fix prices." [160]

The instructions in *United States v. Appvion Inc.*, a case stemming from the same international conspiracy to fix prices of thermal fax paper, stated that a defendant may lawfully prepare an antidumping petition. [161] A defendant may also, in advance of the actual filing, threaten or warn that the filing of such a petition is anticipated, or meet with domestic competitors in order to discuss pricing and cost information necessary to pursue an antidumping petition. [162]

---

that the alleged conduct was committed in the judicial district where the court sits.").

156. *See ABA CRIMINAL ANTITRUST LITIGATION HANDBOOK, supra* note 155, at 413 n.59 (citing United States v. Chen, 378 F.3d 151, 159 (2d Cir. 2004)) (noting that "venue is not an element of the crime; the government therefore bears the burden of proving venue only by a preponderance of the evidence").

157. Tr. of the Evidence Day 20 at 2140, United States v. Nippon Paper Indus., Co., No. 95-10388 (D. Mass. July 1, 1998).

158. *Id.* at 2148.

159. *Id.*

160. *Id.* at 2135.

161. Jury Instructions at 20, United States v. Appvion Inc., No. 96-83 (E.D. Wis. Jan. 13, 1997).

162. *Id.*

3. Common Defense Instructions

The parties are entitled to file proposed jury instructions, and the court must inform the parties how it intends to rule on those instructions before closing arguments.[163] The defense should prepare its proposed instructions well in advance of trial and use them to frame its themes and presentation of evidence throughout the trial.

a. Preliminary Instruction: Indictment

The defense should request an instruction explaining that the indictment is merely an accusation and is not evidence of the defendant's guilt. For example, the ABA suggests the following instruction: "The indictment in this case is the formal method of accusing a defendant of a crime and placing the defendant on trial. It is a document that sets forth the offense(s) charged. It is not evidence against the defendant and does not create any inference of guilt. The indictment in this case charges the defendant with a violation of Section 1 of the Sherman Act. [Court reads indictment or parts thereof.] The defendant denies that [he] [she] [it] is guilt of the charge."[164]

Defense counsel should also advocate that the judge read only the crime charged, as opposed to the entire indictment, which, if extensive, may unduly bias the jury against the defendant before it has heard any evidence.

b. Final Instructions

(1) Standard Final Instructions

In any criminal case, the jury should be instructed that the defendant is presumed innocent and that if the prosecution fails to prove each element of the offense beyond a reasonable doubt, the jury must acquit.[165]

In some criminal antitrust prosecutions, multiple defendants will be tried jointly. In this scenario, the jury should be instructed that it is to consider each defendant separately, not considering for one defendant evidence admitted against another, and that it should apply the law to each

---

163. FED. R. CRIM. P. 30(a).
164. *ABA MODEL JURY INSTRUCTIONS, supra* note 147, at 1.
165. *Id.* at 20; *see id.* at 47 (providing model jury instructions for a Sherman Act Section I violation).

defendant as if she were being tried alone.[166] If the defendants cooperate in their defense, the jury should also be instructed that their cooperation does not constitute evidence of a conspiracy.[167]

In the event that the defendant is charged with multiple offenses, the jury should be instructed to consider each count separately and that its decision on one count should not influence its decision on any other count.[168]

If the defendant elects not to testify, the jury should be instructed as follows: "A defendant in a criminal case is never required to testify. No inference of guilt or any other inference may be drawn from the failure of a defendant to testify. Furthermore, a defendant is never required to call any witness or produce any evidence. [She] has a perfect right to rely upon the government's obligation to prove the charges against [her] beyond a reasonable doubt."[169]

(2) Instructions Pertinent to Sherman Act Prosecutions

The government or court will submit jury instructions explaining the elements of a Section 1 violation. To prove a violation of Section 1 of the Sherman Act, the government must establish three elements: (1) that the charged conspiracy was knowingly formed and was in existence at or about the time alleged; (2) that the defendant knowingly joined the charged conspiracy; and (3) that the charged conspiracy either substantially affected interstate commerce or occurred within the flow of interstate or foreign commerce.[170] The defense should ensure that the instructions on the elements of the offense do not understate the government's burden or the elements necessary for a conviction. It is also critical to submit "failure of proof" instructions regarding elements that the government may not have proven beyond a reasonable doubt. For example, in *United States v. Farmer*,[171] the defense submitted the following instruction on the element of conspiracy:

---

166. *Id.* at 36.
167. *Id.* at 38.
168. *Id.* at 39.
169. *Id.* at 137.
170. U.S. DEP'T OF JUSTICE, JUSTICE MANUAL, ANTITRUST RESOURCE MANUAL § 1 (2018), *available at* https://www.justice.gov/jm/antitrust-resource-manual-1-attorney-generals-policy-statement.
171. United States v. Farmer, No. 13-00162 (D.P.R. May 7, 2015).

If you conclude in this case that Thomas Farmer was not a member of a conspiracy to fix prices of both barge and vessel rates of Crowley, Horizon, and Sea Star spanning all four maritime routes between Puerto Rico and the continental United States [i]ncluding both Southbound and Northbound maritime freight, you must return a verdict of not guilty.[172]

(3) Existence of a Conspiracy

In a price-fixing prosecution, mere parallel conduct does not constitute a conspiracy. The defense should therefore seek an instruction explaining that such parallel conduct alone is not illegal and "may be consistent with ordinary and proper competitive behavior in a free and open market."[173] If there is evidence that the defendant may have joined a conspiracy other than the one charged, defense counsel should submit an instruction that the defendant is on trial only for the conspiracy charged, and that participation in any other conspiracy is not grounds for a guilty verdict.[174] If pertinent, defense counsel should also submit an instruction explaining that buying and selling transactions among competitors do no constitute price fixing. One such instruction explained: "It is lawful for buyers of goods or services to discuss and decide on prices of those goods or services with the sellers of the goods or services, even if the buyers and sellers are otherwise competitors."[175]

(4) Knowledge of the Conspiracy

Defense counsel should ensure that the instruction regarding the element of knowledge explains the following: (1) that knowledge requires

---

172. Defense Theory Instruction #1, United States v. Farmer, No. 13-00162 (D.P.R. May 7, 2015).

173. *ABA MODEL JURY INSTRUCTIONS, supra* note 147, at 58; *see also* Trial Tr. at 2222-23, United States v. Taubman, No. 01-429 (S.D.N.Y. Dec. 4, 2001) (explaining that "a business may adopt policies and prices identical to those of its competitors as long as such actions are the result of an independent business decision and not the result of an agreement or understanding among competitors").

174. *See, e.g.,* Trial Tr. at 2193, United States v. Taubman, No. 01-429 (S.D.N.Y. Dec. 4, 2001).

175. Jury Instructions at 15, United States v. AU Optronics Corp., No. 09-00110 (N.D. Cal. Oct. 9, 2013), *available at* http://www.americanbar.org/content/dam/aba/publications/antitrust_law/at325050_tft_lcd_final_jury_instructions.authcheckdam.pdf.

that the defendant "acted voluntarily and intentionally, and not because of a mistake, accident, or other innocent reason"; (2) that the defendant must have joined the conspiracy "with the intent to aid or advance the object or purpose of the conspiracy"; (3) that "mere knowledge of a conspiracy without participation in the conspiracy is also insufficient to make a person a member of the conspiracy"; (4) that the jury's determination of knowledge "must be based solely on the actions of the defendant as established by the evidence"; and (5) that the jury "should not consider what others may have said or done to join the conspiracy" and "[m]embership of the defendant in this conspiracy must be established by evidence of [her] own conduct — by what [she] said or did."[176]

(5) Joining the Conspiracy

Mere knowledge of a conspiracy is insufficient to establish a defendant's guilt; she must also join the conspiracy. Defense counsel should consider submitting the following instruction, which emphasizes this important point: "[A] person who has no knowledge of a conspiracy but who happens to act in a way which furthers some object or purpose of the conspiracy does not thereby become a member of the conspiracy. Similarly, mere knowledge of a conspiracy without participation in the conspiracy is also insufficient to make a person a member of the conspiracy."[177]

(6) Interstate Commerce

Parties often stipulate the element of interstate commerce prior to trial. However, in some cases, the defense may consider proposing an instruction regarding the FTAIA that excludes from U.S. antitrust enforcement "(1) export activities and (2) other commercial activities taking place abroad, unless those activities adversely affect domestic commerce, imports to the United States, or exporting activities of one engaged in such activities within the United States."[178]

(7) Co-conspirator Testimony

Antitrust prosecutions often rely heavily on the testimony of co-conspirators with plea agreements or immunity. To ensure that the jury

---

176. *ABA MODEL JURY INSTRUCTIONS, supra* note 147, at 71-72.
177. *Id.* at 71.
178. F. Hoffmann-La Roche Ltd. v. Empagran S.A., 542 U.S. 155, 161 (2004).

considers the high potential for bias of such testimony, it should be instructed that a co-conspirator's testimony "should always be received with caution and considered with great care" and that the co-conspirator's testimony, if unsupported by other evidence, should only form the basis of a conviction if the jury believes it beyond a reasonable doubt.[179] Moreover, the jury should also be instructed that a co-conspirator's guilty plea should not be considered as evidence of the defendant's guilt.[180]

(8) Corporate Officer Liability

If the defendant is a corporate officer who oversaw potential members of a conspiracy, the jury should be reminded that the officer must have knowingly joined the conspiracy, and that "a person is not responsible for the conduct of others performed on behalf of a corporation merely because that person is an officer, employee or other agent of the corporation."[181]

c. Affirmative Defenses

(1) Withdrawal

If the defendant has raised the affirmative defense of withdrawal, consider submitting this ABA model instruction:

> If you find the defendant to have been a member of the conspiracy charged, the defendant is presumed to have remained a member of the conspiracy and is liable for all actions taken during and in furtherance of the conspiracy until it is shown that the conspiracy has been completed or abandoned, or that the defendant withdrew from the conspiracy.
>
> The defendant has the burden of coming forward with a preponderance of evidence that [he] [she] [it] withdrew from the conspiracy. To prove something by a preponderance of the evidence is to prove that it is more likely true than not true. This is a lesser standard than "beyond a reasonable doubt." If you find that the defendant has met the burden of coming forward with a preponderance of evidence that [he] [she] [it] withdrew from the conspiracy, then the government must prove beyond a reasonable doubt that the defendant did not withdraw from the

---

179. *ABA MODEL JURY INSTRUCTIONS*, *supra* note 147, at 116.
180. *See, e.g.*, Jury Instructions at Wilson Instruction No. 20, United States v. Andreas, No. 96-762 (N.D. Ill. Sept. 2, 1998).
181. *ABA MODEL JURY INSTRUCTIONS*, *supra* note 147, at 101.

conspiracy or did not withdraw from it before [insert date five years before the return of the incident].

In order for you to find that the defendant withdrew from the conspiracy, the evidence must show that (he) (she) (it) did some affirmative act inconsistent with the object of the conspiracy and communicated in a manner reasonably calculated to reach its co-conspirators. Mere inactivity is not proof of withdrawal. Furthermore, even if a defendant tells others of [his] [her] [its] intent to withdraw, [he] [she] [it] has not legally withdrawn if [he] [she] [it] continued to act knowingly to further the object of the conspiracy.

[Evidence that the defendant initiated competition with others has been admitted to assist you in deciding whether the defendant has withdrawn from the alleged conspiracy.]

Although a defendant who was a member of the conspiracy may withdraw from the conspiracy, the defendant is still responsible with all other co-conspirators for the illegal acts, if any, committed by that defendant or by any other co-conspirator while the defendant was a member of the conspiracy, up until the time of the defendant's withdrawal. If you should find in this case that the defendant withdrew from the conspiracy, and that the defendant's withdrawal from the conspiracy took place before (the date five years before the return of the indictment), and that the defendant did not later re-enter the conspiracy, you must find the defendant not guilty of the offense charge.

[If there was a withdrawal before [the date five years before the return of the indictment], then, for you to return a guilty verdict, the government must prove beyond a reasonable doubt that there was re-entry into the conspiracy by the defendant and that the re-entry either took place after [the date five years before the return of the indictment] or that it took place before that date and that the defendant remained as a member of the conspiracy after that date.][182]

(2) Statute of Limitations

Section 1 of the Sherman Act is subject to a five-year statute of limitations.[183] The defense should therefore propose a jury instruction

---

182.   *ABA MODEL JURY INSTRUCTIONS, supra* note 147, at 78.
183.   18 U.S.C. § 3282(a).

explaining that the defendant is not guilty if her conduct occurred prior to the limitations period.[184]

(3) Venue

If in dispute, the jury should be instructed that it must find by a preponderance of the evidence that the conspiracy or some act in furtherance of the conspiracy occurred in the federal district forming the basis for the trial's venue.

4. Theory of Defense Instructions

Generally, the defense is entitled to an instruction on a particular defense if there is any evidentiary support for the defense.[185] Theory of defense instructions should be tailored to the particular defense theory being asserted.[186] In deciding whether to instruct the jury on a theory of defense, the court views the facts in the light most favorable to the defense, without regard to the strength or credibility of the evidentiary support for the theory.[187] It is a reversible error in a criminal case not to give an adequate presentation of a theory of defense, but a court's refusal to deliver a requested instruction is only reversible if that instruction "(1) [is] a correct statement of the law, (2) [is] not substantially covered by the charge actually delivered to the jury, and (3) concerns a point so important in the trial that the failure to give it substantially impairs the defendant's defense."[188]

5. Post-trial Motions

Post-trial motions are governed by the Federal Rules of Criminal Procedure and most commonly include the defense's motion for a

---

184. *See ABA MODEL JURY INSTRUCTIONS, supra* note 147, at 89, for a model instruction on the statute of limitations.
185. *See* United States v. Davis, 183 F.3d 231, 250 (3d Cir. 1999); Beardslee v. Woodford, 358 F.3d 560, 577 (9th Cir. 2004); United States v. Boucher, 796 F.2d 972, 975 (7th Cir. 1986); United States v. Mercer, 853 F.2d 630, 633 (8th Cir. 1998); United States v. All Star Indus., 962 F.2d 465, 473 (5th Cir. 1992).
186. *ABA MODEL JURY INSTRUCTIONS, supra* note 147, at 101.
187. United States v. Frost, 125 F.3d 346, 372 (6th Cir. 1997); United States v. Sanchez-Lima, 161 F.3d 545, 549 (9th Cir. 1998).
188. Frost, 125 F.3d at 372.

judgment of acquittal pursuant to Federal Rule of Criminal Procedure 29 and motion for a new trial pursuant to Federal Rule of Criminal Procedure 33.

A motion for a judgment of acquittal will be granted if the evidence presented at trial is insufficient to support a conviction as a matter of law.[189] The trial court will assess whether, in the light most favorable to the defendant, a jury could infer guilt beyond a reasonable doubt.[190] Some courts have applied a higher standard to antitrust prosecutions, requiring that a reasonable jury *must* infer guilt, and holding that circumstantial evidence is insufficient to sustain a conviction if the evidence is equally consistent with both innocence and guilt.[191] Defense counsel need not wait until the conclusion of the trial to move for a judgment of acquittal. In a jury trial, motions can be made at the close of the government's case and/or at the close of all evidence, but in any event should be made post-trial or at the close of evidence to preserve the issue for appeal.

Defense counsel also may move for a new trial pursuant to Federal Rule of Criminal Procedure 33. Trial courts have broad discretion to grant motions for a new trial when in the "interest of justice,"[192] but the motions are rarely successful. Most often, motions for a new trial are made on the grounds of newly discovered evidence. Other grounds for a new trial are recognized, however, including prosecutorial misconduct including failure to disclose exculpatory evidence, [193] and errors including juror misconduct[194] or ineffective assistance of counsel.[195]

Motions for a new trial based on newly discovered evidence must satisfy the following requirements: (1) the evidence must be newly discovered since trial; (2) the evidence must not be that which could have been discovered with due diligence before or during trial; (3) the evidence

---

189. FED R. CRIM. P. 29; *see* United States v. Turner, 490 F. Supp. 583, 589-91 (E.D. Mich. 1979), *aff'd*, 633 F.3d 219 (6th Cir. 1980).
190. *See* United States v. Collins, 340 F.3d 672 (8th Cir. 2003).
191. United States v. Gen. Elec. Co., 869 F. Supp. 1285, 1290 (S.D. Ohio 1994).
192. FED. R. CRIM. P. 33(a).
193. Kyles v. Whitley, 514 U.S. 419, 421-22 (1995); Giglio v. United States, 405 U.S. 150, 153 (1972); Brady v. Maryland, 373 U.S. 83, 87 (1963); United States v. Colon-Munoz, 318 F.3d 348, 358 (1st Cir. 2003).
194. *See, e.g.*, United States v. Moten, 582 F.2d 654 (2d Cir. 1978).
195. *See, e.g.*, United States v. Villalpando, 259 F.3d 934 (8th Cir. 2001).

must be material and non-cumulative; and (4) the evidence must be of a type that likely would have resulted in acquittal if introduced at trial.[196]

H. Significant International Cartel Trials

1. *United States v. Northcutt and Scaglia*[197]

a. Government

In 2007, the Antitrust Division brought charges against Val Northcutt and Francesco Scaglia for their participation in a global conspiracy to fix prices, rig bids, and allocate the market for marine hose, which is used to transfer oil between tankers and storage facilities.[198] Northcutt was a regional sales manager, and Scaglia was the deputy manager of Manuli's Oil & Marine Division.

The investigation into the marine hose industry went public in 2007, when the FBI arrested more than half a dozen executives from around the globe who had gathered in Houston to attend an industry conference. The Antitrust Division alleged that from 1986 through 2007, the conspirator companies allocated marine hose business among themselves using a price list and refraining from competing by either not bidding or submitting intentionally high bids.[199] The conspiracy was carried out, in part, through Peter Whittle, the cartel coordinator who acted as a clearinghouse for sharing information among competitors. In addition, conspirators met in person to discuss anticompetitive agreements, including one meeting covertly recorded by law enforcement. The cartel allegedly affected prices for the sale of marine hose and related products worldwide, including products sold to the Department of Defense.[200]

196. *See, e.g.*, United States v. McRae, 795 F.3d 471, 478 (5th Cir. 2015); United States v. Harrington, 410 F.3d 598, 601 (9th Cir. 2005); United States v. Willis, 257 F.3d 636, 642 (6th Cir. 2001).
197. 2008 WL 162753 (S.D. Fla. 2008).
198. An indictment against a third individual was unsealed on December 20, 2007. Order to Unseal Indictment, United States v. Bangert, No. 07-60183 (S.D. Fla. Dec. 20, 2007).
199. *Northcutt*, 2008 WL 162753, at *3.
200. *Id.*

b. Defense

By the time of trial, nine executives had pleaded guilty for their direct participation in the conspiracy, as had five international marine hose companies: Bridgestone Corporation of Japan, Dunlop Oil & Marine Ltd. of the United Kingdom, Manuli SpA of Italy, Parker ITR SrL of Italy, and Trelleborg of France.[201]

At trial, Northcutt and Scaglia argued that they were relatively low-level employees, significantly less culpable than other co-conspirators. Scaglia argued that, although he attended a price-fixing meeting, he had been unaware of the purpose of the meeting in advance, and did not say anything during the meeting.[202] The defendants' primary arguments focused on relative culpability and witness credibility. Defense counsel cross-examined Peter Whittle, the cartel coordinator, on prior inconsistent statements, the several million dollars he personally received as a result of the conspiracy, and other crimes he committed outside of the United States' jurisdiction. Both defendants testified at trial, disavowing knowledge of the conspiracy and denying having significant involvement in pricing decisions. Both defendants were acquitted.[203]

c. Extradition

In addition to the individuals publicly indicted, Romano Pisciotti, an Italian national and former executive of Parker ITR Srl, was indicted under seal in March 2011. In June 2013, Pisciotti was arrested in Germany, where he landed on a layover at the Frankfurt airport when returning to Italy from a trip in Nigeria. Pisciotti was held in prison in Germany for two months, while the German court determined whether extradition was appropriate. Pursuant to its 1978 extradition treaty with the United States, Germany—which imposes individual criminal liability for antitrust

---

201. Pls.' Am. Mot. for Preliminary Approval of Proposed Settlements at 5, *In re* Marine Hose Antitrust Litig., No. 08-1888 (S.D. Fla. Dec. 22, 2008).
202. *Cf.* Deft's Mot. to Dismiss and Supporting Memo. of Law at 16, *In re* Marine Hose Antitrust Litig., No. 08-01888 (Apr. 23, 2008) ("Plaintiffs' allegations that the 'defendants' generally 'discussed improving communications' and 'rules for implementing' an anti-competitive plan . . . do not even begin to show that Mr. Scaglia reached an agreement with anyone else or conspired with anyone else.") (citations omitted).
203. Criminal Minutes, United States v. Northcutt, No. 07-60220 (S.D. Fla. Nov. 10, 2008).

violations—extradited Pisciotti to the United States in April 2014. Very shortly after his extradition, Pisciotti pleaded guilty to one count of conspiracy and was sentenced to two years in prison and a $50,000 fine.[204] Pisciotti's extradition and sentence were milestones in the Antitrust Division's efforts to hold foreign nationals accountable for criminal antitrust violations.

2. *United States v. Andreas et al.*[205]

a. Government

In 1998, the Antitrust Division brought a case against three executives from Archer Daniels Midland (ADM) for their participation in a price-fixing conspiracy to raise the price of lysine, an animal feed additive.[206] The basic allegations were that in early 1992, Michael Wilson met with representatives from two other lysine companies in Mexico City to discuss price agreements and allocate sales volumes among the market participants.[207] In Mexico City, the competitors reached pricing agreements. Then, in October 1993, Terrance Andreas met with competitors and reached a volume allocation agreement to support the previously negotiated price agreement. The lysine price-fixing conspiracy continued until June 1995, when the FBI raided ADM's offices.[208]

The government's investigation relied on Mark Whitacre, an ADM executive who began cooperating with the FBI in an undercover investigation of the conspiracy in October 1992. As evidence at trial revealed, from October 1992 through June 1995, the FBI and Whitacre audiotaped or videotaped many of the cartel's meetings in cities including Tokyo, Paris, Mexico City, and Hong Kong. Those tapes became key trial evidence.[209] Whitacre himself was ultimately prosecuted, after it was

---

204.   Judgment in a Criminal Case, United States v. Pisciotti, No. 10-60232 (S.D. Fla. Apr. 24, 2014).

205.   39 F. Supp. 2d 1048 (N.D. Ill. 1998), *aff'd*, 216 F.3d 645 (7th Cir. 2000).

206.   *Id.* at 1054.

207.   Information at 1, United States v. Archer Daniels Midland Co., No. 96-00640 (N.D. Ill. Oct. 15, 1996). The motion picture, "The Informant" (2009) is loosely based on the facts of this investigation and litigation.

208.   United States v. Andreas, 39 F. Supp. 2d at 1055, *aff'd*, 216 F.3d 645 (7th Cir. 2000).

209.   *See* United States v. Andreas, 1998 WL 42261, at *1 (N.D. Ill. 1998), *aff'd*, 216 F.3d 645 (7th Cir. 2000).

learned that he had been embezzling money from ADM during the period of his cooperation with the FBI.[210]

b. Defense

At trial, the defendants Andreas and Wilson challenged the government's use of tapes as evidence, arguing that admitting the tapes would violate their due process rights because Whitacre engaged in "selective" taping and the FBI instructed Whitacre to destroy exculpatory tapes.[211] According to the defendants, the FBI's failure to adequately supervise Whitacre, in addition to the allegations of selective taping and destruction of evidence, rendered the tapes so unreliable as to make them "constitutionally defective."[212] Following a six-day evidentiary hearing, the court found that the defendants' argument was grounded in a dispute of facts to be resolved by the jury and determined that the defendants would had ample opportunity to impeach Whitacre's credibility and the reliability of the tapes during trial.[213]

Another key defense at trial was that the defendants attended meetings with competitors for various legitimate reasons, including to gather market information, exchange sales data, share technology, and discuss environmental concerns.[214] With only five market participants and no trade associations, the defense argued that ADM and its competitors needed to communicate with one another to understand the market for lysine. The defendants insisted that they fended off any attempts at price discussions at those meetings and spoke only about general business strategies.

Finally, the defense highlighted instances of "cheating" on the allegedly fixed price, and emphasized the fact that prices were at their lowest during the conspiracy period.[215] The defense introduced exhibits and testimony that tended to show that prices were low and competition was intense after ADM entered the market, including charts to show how prices fell and never returned to the pre-ADM level.[216]

---

210. *Id.*
211. *Id.*
212. *Id.* at *5.
213. *Id.* at *6.
214. *See* United States v. Andreas, 39 F. Supp. 2d 1048, 1057 (N.D. Ill. 1998).
215. *See* United States v. Andreas, 1999 WL 515484, at *5 (N.D. Ill. 1999), *aff'd and remanded*, 216 F.3d 645 (7th Cir. 2000).
216. *Id.*

c.   Trial Outcome and Appeal

After a ten-week trial, the jury convicted all three ADM executives. Andreas and Wilson were sentenced to twenty-four months in prison and $350,000 in criminal fines. Whitacre was sentenced to thirty months in prison. Antitrust Division prosecutors argued at sentencing that Wilson and Andreas were the conspiracy's masterminds. The court, however, did not find that either had controlling roles.[217]

Both the government and defense appealed.[218] The government argued in its appeal that Andreas and Wilson should have received longer sentences because of their leadership and managerial roles in the conspiracy. The defense argued that: (1) the evidence was insufficient to support Andreas's conviction; (2) the agreement to allocate sales volumes was not per se unlawful; (3) the government conferred benefits on the defendants by granting formal immunity to an ADM representative; (4) the Whitacre tapes should not have been admitted; (5) the trial court's jury instructions were improper; (6) the government's closing argument was improper; and (7) the district court incorrectly calculated the volume of commerce affected by the violation.[219]

In a published opinion, the Seventh Circuit affirmed the convictions, but agreed with the government that Andreas and Wilson should have received longer sentences for their leadership roles in the conspiracy. The Seventh Circuit vacated the defendants' sentences and remanded the case for a recalculation.[220] On remand, the district court increased Andreas's prison term to thirty-six months and Wilson's to thirty-three months.

3.   United States v. AU Optronics[221]

a.   Government

In 2010, the Antitrust Division brought Sherman Act charges against AU Optronics (AUO), its U.S. subsidiary AU Optronics Corporation America, and current and former AUO executives Hsuan Bin Chen, Hui Hsiung, Lai-Juh Chen, Shiu Lung Leung, and Tsannrong Lee for their participation in a conspiracy to suppress and eliminate competition by fixing prices of standard-sized thin-film transistor liquid crystal display

---

217.   *See Andreas*, 216 F.3d at 679-80.
218.   *Id.* at 650.
219.   *Id.* at 658.
220.   *Id.* at 680.
221.   2011 WL 2020716 (N.D. Cal. 2011).

panels (TFT-LCDs).[222] The indictment alleged that executives from AUO and other leading TFT-LCD producers participated in more than sixty regularly scheduled group meetings in Taiwan, referred to as "Crystal Meetings," as well as bilateral meetings among the competitors for LCD panels.[223] In the Crystal Meetings, held at the headquarters of various co-conspirator companies, the competitors reached agreements to fix and stabilize prices of TFT-LCDs used in notebook computers, desktop computer monitors, and televisions.[224] The competitors reached additional agreements on pricing at the bilateral meetings, and used those meetings to monitor each other's compliance with price agreements.[225] The TFT-LCD price-fixing conspiracy continued until at least December 2006, when the government's investigation became public.[226]

At trial, the government presented evidence to show that the individual defendants attended, to varying degrees, both the Crystal Meetings and the bilateral meetings. This evidence included, among other things, witness testimony from co-conspirators, written internal AUO reports of Crystal Meetings in Taiwan, and documents prepared by employees of AUO in preparation for those meetings.[227]

The AUO trial was unique in that it represented the first time the Antitrust Division sought a criminal fine in litigation under the alternative fine provision of the Sentencing Reform Act, which allows a maximum fine of twice the gross gain or twice the gross loss resulting from the charged offense.[228] The district court held that, in order to obtain a penalty beyond the Sherman Act's $100 million statutory maximum, the government must prove any sentence-increasing fact beyond a reasonable doubt. [229] The government introduced economic expert testimony

---

222. *Id.*; Superseding Indictment ¶¶ 1-2, United States v. AU Optronics Corp., 2010 WL 5641429 (N.D. Cal. 2010).
223. Superseding Indictment ¶ 17, United States v. AU Optronics Corp., 2010 WL 5641429 (N.D. Cal. 2010).
224. *Id.* ¶¶ 3, 17(a).
225. *Id.* ¶ 17(e).
226. *Id.*
227. United States v. Hsiung, 778 F.3d 738, 744 (9th Cir. 2014).
228. 18 U.S.C. § 3571(d).
229. Order Denying United States' Mot. for Order Regarding Fact Finding for Sentencing Under 18 U.S.C. § 3571(d), United States v. AU Optronics Corp., 2011 WL 2837418 at *4 (N.D. Cal. 2011) (citing Apprendi v. New Jersey, 530 U.S. 466 (2000)). In *Apprendi*, the Supreme Court held that "any fact that increases the penalty for a crime beyond the prescribed

concerning the pecuniary gain as a result of the conspiracy; most of this testimony centered on the government's theory that the Crystal Meetings resulted in higher prices than would have existed otherwise, which the government argued evidenced the baseline from which the jury could calculate the economic gain. The jury found that the government proved the overcharges beyond a reasonable doubt, and that the conspirators obtained over $500 million in ill-gotten gains. Due to an earlier court ruling,[230] the jury could consider the gains representing the profits of all of the conspiracy participants—not just AUO.

b.   Defense

Before trial, the AUO defendants moved to dismiss the indictment based on jurisdictional grounds under the Foreign Trade Antitrust Improvement Act (FTAIA).[231] The defense argued that the charges related to "wholly foreign conduct," which is barred from prosecution under the FTAIA.[232] The district court disagreed, finding that the alleged conduct— specifically, instructions to contact competitors and form pricing agreements from the foreign parent company to employees of its U.S. subsidiary—met the FTAIA standard.[233]

At trial, AUO argued that it did not obtain any gains from the conspiracy. Specifically, AUO contended that it had merely been bluffing its competitors at the Crystal Meetings and that, rather than fixing and aligning its prices with its competitors as alleged by the government, AUO used the Crystal Meetings to obtain a competitive advantage over its competitors and undercut them on price.[234] Additionally, AUO's economic expert testified that AUO did not realize any pecuniary gain

---

statutory maximum must be submitted to a jury, and proved beyond a reasonable doubt." 530 U.S. at 490.

230.   Order on Preliminary Jury Instructions, United States v. AU Optronics Corp., No. 09-00110 (N.D. Cal. Dec. 23, 2011).

231.   15 U.S.C. § 6a.

232.   *In re* TFT-LCD (Flat Panel) Antitrust Litig., 2011 WL 1464858, at *2 (N.D. Cal. 2011); *see* United States v. AU Optronics Corp., 2012 WL 2120452, at *3-*4 (N.D. Cal. 2012).

233.   *In re TFT-LCD (Flat Panel) Antitrust Litig.*, 2011 WL 1464858, at *5.

234.   Trial Tr. Vol. 7 at 183-84, United States v. Bai, No. 09-00110 (N.D. Cal. Sept. 23, 2013).

resulting from its participation in the Crystal Meetings, and offered no opinion about gains realized by any other member of the conspiracy.[235]

c. Trial Outcome and Appeal

Following an eight-week trial, AUO, its U.S. subsidiary, and former executives Hsuan Bin Chen and Hui Hsiung were convicted. The district court imposed a $500 million criminal fine on AUO, and thirty-six-month prison sentences and $200,000 criminal fines on each individual executive.[236] The jury found executives L.J. Chen and Hubert Lee not guilty, and a mistrial was declared as to the last employee, Steven Leung.[237]

The defendants appealed their convictions, arguing that (1) their conspiracy was beyond the reach of the Sherman Act, as amended by the FTAIA; (2) the Sherman Act does not apply extraterritorially to the conspiracy; (3) a rule of reason, rather than a per se, analysis was appropriate; and (4) venue was improper.[238] AUO also argued that the $500 million fine exceeded the maximum allowed by law.[239]

The FTAIA aspect of the appeal focused on the definition of conduct that has a "direct" effect on domestic commerce. In a published opinion, the Ninth Circuit ruled that the FTAIA did not apply because the government sufficiently proved at trial that the defendants engaged in import trade to the United States. The panel affirmed the judgments of conviction and the $500 million criminal fine.[240]

---

235. United States v. AU Optronics Corp., 2012 WL 2120452, at *4-5 (N.D. Cal. 2012).

236. United States v. Hsiung, 778 F.3d 738, 745 (9th Cir. 2014).

237. Leung was later convicted on retrial. *See* Verdict Form, United States v. Leung, No. 09-00110 (N.D. Cal. Dec. 19, 2012).

238. *Hsiung*, 778 F.3d at 742.

239. *Id.* at 745.

240. *Id.* at 761.

CHAPTER VII

PLEA NEGOTIATIONS AND SENTENCING

Once a defendant is convicted of a criminal antitrust offense, either following a guilty verdict in a jury trial or upon acceptance by the court of a guilty plea, the court must impose a sentence. Individual defendants convicted of an antitrust offense may face imprisonment, criminal fines, an obligation to pay restitution, and other financial penalties. Corporate defendants also face criminal fines and an obligation to pay restitution. In addition, corporate defendants can face ongoing monitoring and other obligations to the government after sentencing. This chapter addresses plea negotiations and sentencing in international cartel cases.

A. Trends in U.S. Cartel Sentencing

In the past three decades, there has been significant increase in the size of the corporate criminal fines imposed in criminal antitrust cases in the United States. In the 1980s, fines totaling $188 million were imposed in cases brought by the Antitrust Division of the U.S. Department of Justice (DOJ).[1] In the 1990s, that total rose to $1.6 billion, and the first decade of this century saw the total jump to $4.75 billion.[2] In FY 2014 and FY 2015,

---

1. *See* Scott D. Hammond, Deputy Assistant Att'y Gen., Antitrust Div., U.S. Dep't of Justice, The Evolution of Criminal Antitrust Enforcement Over The Last Two Decades, presented to the ABA Criminal Justice Section, National Institute On White Collar Crime at 5 (Feb. 25, 2010), *available at* https://www.justice.gov/atr/file/518241/download.

2. *Id*; *see also* Carl Shapiro, Deputy Assistant Att'y Gen., Antitrust Div., U.S. Dep't of Justice, Update From The Antitrust Division, presented at the ABA Section of Antitrust Law Fall Forum 1-2 (Nov. 18, 2010), *available at* http://www.justice.gov/atr/public/speeches/264295.pdf (discussing increase in the amount obtained from criminal antitrust fines between 2006 and 2010).

$1.3 billion and $3.6 billion in fines were imposed in Antitrust Division cases each year.[3]

A number of factors account for this increase in the size of corporate fines in antitrust criminal cases, including the Antitrust Division's focus on investigating and prosecuting large international cartels, its increased cooperation with foreign competition law enforcement agencies, and the adoption of the 1993 Corporate Leniency Policy. The Antitrust Criminal Penalty Enhancement and Reform Act of 2004 (ACPERA),[4] the *U.S. Sentencing Guidelines,* and the Alternative Fine Statute[5] also play a significant role in bringing about the recent trend of increasing fines obtained by the Antitrust Division.

There has also be an upward trend in sentencing of individual defendants, with the average jail sentence increasing from eight months in the 1990s to twenty-four months during the period from 2010-2015.[6] There are several factors that may account for this increase in average jail sentence, including that the maximum sentence for an antitrust offense was increased to ten years under ACPERA.[7] The higher levels of commerce involved in global investigations has also led to larger fines.[8] In addition, the number of defendants sentenced in criminal antitrust cases steadily rose in the late 1990s through the 2000s, to eighty-two individual cases charged in 2011.[9] The longest sentence imposed in connection with a criminal antitrust charge to date is five years.[10]

---

3.   Antitrust Div., U.S. Dep't of Justice, Criminal Enforcement Trends Charts Through Fiscal Year 2017 (updated Mar. 12, 2018), *available at* https://www.justice.gov/atr/criminal-enforcement-fine-and-jail-charts.

4.   Antitrust Criminal Penalty Enhancement and Reform Act of 2004, Pub. L. No. 108-237, § 215(a), 118 Stat. 661, 668 (2004).

5.   18 U.S.C. § 3571(d).

6.   Antitrust Div., U.S. Dep't of Justice, Criminal Enforcement Trends Charts Through Fiscal Year 2017 (updated Mar. 12, 2018), *available at* https://www.justice.gov/atr/criminal-enforcement-fine-and-jail-charts.

7.   118 Stat. at 668.

8.   *See* Antitrust Div., U.S. Dep't of Justice, Sherman Act Violations Yielding a Corporate Fine of $10 Million or More (2018), *available at* https://www.justice.gov/atr/sherman-act-violations-yielding-corporate-fine-10-million-or-more.

9.   *See* Antitrust Div., U.S. Dep't of Justice, Antitrust Division Workload Statistics FY 2007-2016, *available at* e file/788426/download.

10.   *See* Press Release, U.S. Dep't of Justice, Office of Public Affairs, Former Sea Star Line President Sentenced to Serve Five Years in Prison for Role in Price-Fixing Conspiracy Involving Coastal Freight Services Between

A final recent trend is that the Antitrust Division may seek forward-looking relief, for example corporate monitors or compliance programs, in cases in which the corporate defendant's conduct is deemed particularly egregious. Historically, the DOJ has sought such provisions in other federal criminal cases, but corporate monitors or compliance programs have not been typical in criminal antitrust cases.

B. U.S. Sentencing Guidelines

1. U.S. Sentencing Guidelines—Overview

Any discussion of plea negotiations and sentencing in a criminal antitrust case begins with the potential criminal fine range and length of incarceration for any individual defendant. The *U.S. Sentencing Guidelines* promulgated by the U.S. Sentencing Commission are the starting point for U.S. courts to assess appropriate sentences in federal criminal cases. The *Sentencing Guidelines* identify specific and detailed factors that a court can consider in establishing ranges for the purposes of imposing periods of imprisonment and criminal fines.

The legislative background to the Sentencing Reform Act of 1984 reflects several objectives that led to the development of the *Sentencing Guidelines*:

- to enhance the ability of the criminal justice system to combat crime through an effective, fair sentencing system;
- to achieve reasonable uniformity in sentencing by narrowing the wide disparity in sentences imposed for similar criminal offenses committed by similar offenders; and
- to seek proportionality in sentencing through a system that imposes appropriately different sentences for criminal conduct of differing severity.[11]

---

  the Continental United States and Puerto Rico (Dec. 3, 2013), *available at* https://www.justice.gov/opa/pr/former-sea-star-line-president-sentenced-serve-five-years-prison-role-price-fixing-conspiracy.

11. *See* U.S. SENTENCING COMM'N, SENTENCING GUIDELINES MANUAL ch. 1 (2016) [hereinafter *SENTENCING GUIDELINES*].

The Supreme Court held in *United States v. Booker* [12] that the *Sentencing Guidelines* are not mandatory.[13] While the sentencing ranges the *Sentencing Guidelines* establish are no longer mandatory, they remain one of the factors—if not the most important factor—a judge must consider in establishing the appropriate fine in a criminal antitrust case. In fact, the Supreme Court has described the now-advisory *Sentencing Guidelines* as the "starting point and the initial benchmark" for the sentencing court.[14] Federal prosecutors and defense counsel also use the *Sentencing Guidelines* in their negotiation of guilty pleas prior to any sentencing. The *Sentencing Guidelines* include specific considerations, including the nature of the offense with which a corporate or individual defendant has been charged, the level of participation in the offense, mitigating and aggravating circumstances, and losses or harm to any victims.

2. Statutory Provisions and Sentencing Guidelines Regarding Criminal Antitrust Offenses

a.   Maximum Fines and Penalties under ACPERA

ACPERA increased the maximum fines for corporations and individuals convicted of antitrust offenses. [15] Under ACPERA, the maximum criminal fine for a corporation is $100 million, and the maximum criminal fine for an individual is $1 million.[16] An individual

---

12.   543 U.S. 220 (2005).
13.   *Id.* at 767-68 (invalidating on Sixth Amendment right to jury trial grounds the mandatory operation of the Guidelines).
14.   Gall v. United States, 552 U.S. 38, 49 (2007).
15.   Antitrust Criminal Penalty Enhancement and Reform Act of 2004, Pub. L. No. 108-237, § 215(a), 118 Stat. 661, 668 (2004).
16.   ACPERA provides additional incentives for companies and individuals to apply for leniency by limiting civil damages in antitrust cases. Corporations that provide "satisfactory cooperation" to civil claimants can benefit by avoiding treble damages and avoiding joint and several liability. In the United States, civil suits that parallel criminal investigations and federal prosecutions have become the norm, and the detrebling of damages and decoupling of joint and several liability for cooperating defendants under ACPERA sets the floor for civil damages for antitrust violations.

defendant convicted of a criminal violation of Section 1 of the Sherman Act may be imprisoned for up to ten years.[17]

Although the maximum fine under ACPERA is $100 million, the government may seek a greater fine under a provision of the Comprehensive Crime Control Act and the Criminal Fine Improvements Act, which is often referred to as the "Alternative Fine Statute."[18] If ACPERA sets the floor of a corporation or individual's liability, then the Alternative Fine Statute sets the ceiling.[19] This alternative fine provision has the effect of increasing the statutory $100 million maximum fine under the Sherman Act to twice the gain received by the defendant or twice or loss suffered by the victims of the cartel conduct.[20] The Antitrust Division has obtained many fines through plea agreements (and one through litigation) greatly exceeding the statutory maximum fine of $100 million through this alternative fine provision.[21]

b. Sentencing Guidelines for Criminal Antitrust Cases

After the Supreme Court's decision in *Booker*, the Antitrust Division announced that the Antitrust Division would continue to rely on the *Sentencing Guidelines* as establishing the appropriate sentences in its cases.[22] It is the Antitrust Division's policy to continue to insist on sentences that are called for by the *Sentencing Guidelines* and to oppose

---

17. 15 U.S.C. § 1, as amended by Antitrust Criminal Penalty Enhancement and Reform Act of 2004, Pub. L. No. 108-237, § 215(a), 118 Stat. 661, 668.

18. 18 U.S.C. § 3571(d).

19. 18 U.S.C. § 3571(d).

20. *See id.*

21. *See* Antitrust Div., U.S. Dep't of Justice, Sherman Act Violations Yielding Corporate Fine of $10 Million or More (2018), *available at* https://www.justice.gov/atr/sherman-act-violations-yielding-corporate-fine-10-million-or-more; *see also* United States v. Hsiung, 778 F.3d 738, 760-61 (9th Cir. 2014) (affirming $500 billion corporate criminal fine calculated based on "gross gains" to the defendants pursuant to section 3571(d)).

22. *See* Scott D. Hammond, Deputy Ass't Att'y Gen., Antitrust Div., U.S. Dep't of Justice, Antitrust Sentencing in the Post-Booker Era: Risks Remain High for Non-Cooperating Defendants, presented at the ABA Section of Antitrust Law's Spring Meeting (Mar. 30, 2005), *available at* http://www.justice.gov/atr/public/speeches/208354.htm.

any departures not supported by the relevant facts or law.[23] Because more than 90 percent of the corporate defendants charged with an antitrust offense in the United States enter negotiated plea agreements with the Antitrust Division calling for an agreed-upon joint sentencing recommendation to the court,[24] lawyers in the United States should have a thorough understanding of the operation of the *Sentencing Guidelines.*

The *Sentencing Guidelines* provision that most directly apply to antitrust offenses are U.S.S.G. 2R1.1 (Antitrust Offenses: Bid-Rigging, Price-Fixing or Market-Allocation Agreements Among Competitors) and 8C2.4-5 (Sentencing of Organizations: Determining Fines—Other Organizations). These provisions provide guidance for how to calculate a numerical "offense level" for a particular corporate or individual defendant that is then used to determine fines and incarceration. Basic offense levels can be subject to enhancements based on the defendant's conduct.

(1) Sentencing Guidelines 2R.1.1 and 8C2.4-5

Chapter 2 of the *Sentencing Guidelines* addresses offense levels for specific federal criminal offenses, including antitrust offenses. Section 2R1.1, first adopted in 1991, is the primary provision that applies to criminal convictions for antitrust offenses.[25] Section 2R1.1 provides several factors to be considered in establishing an offense level for individual and corporate defendants convicted of an antitrust offense.

Under Section 2R1.1, from a base offense level specified in guideline (12), there are two potential enhancements to increase the base level: (1) if the conduct involved bid rigging and the defendant participated in an agreement to submit non-competitive bids; and (2) if the "volume of commerce attributable to the defendant" exceeds $1,000,000. The "volume of commerce"[26] enhancement is a critical factor in antitrust

---

23.	*See* Hammond, Evolution of Criminal Antitrust Enforcement, *supra* note 1, at 7.

24.	*See* Scott D. Hammond, Deputy Assistant Att'y Gen., Antitrust Div., U.S. Dep't of Justice, The U.S. Model of Negotiated Plea Agreements: A Good Deal with Benefits for All, presented to the OECD Competition Committee Working Party No. 3 (Oct. 17, 2006), *available at* http://www.justice.gov/atr/public/speeches/ 219332.htm.

25.	*See SENTENCING GUIDELINES, supra* note 11, ch. 8.

26.	This chapter discusses volume of commerce in more detail in the context of plea negotiations. Volume of commerce can be calculated by sales, revenue, or by another metric that relates to the product or service involved

sentencing because it provides for an increase of points at certain levels of commerce above $1 million up to $1.6 billion. This enhancement can result in increasing a defendant's base offense level, which can be more than doubled if the amount attributable to a defendant exceeds $1 billion. As a practical matter, most global cartel investigations will involve a volume of commerce that greatly exceeds $1,000,000 and therefore triggers sentencing enhancements.

The term "volume of commerce" is not defined in the *Sentencing Guidelines* or the comments to Section 2R1.1. The Antitrust Division typically evaluates sales or revenue relating to the goods or services that were affected by the violation, or the contract value in bid-rigging settings.[27] As is discussed later in this chapter, evaluating the affected volume of commerce in cases involving an alleged global conspiracy can be complex and is a critical aspect of plea negotiations with the Antitrust Division and any subsequent sentencing.

(2) Corporate Defendants

For any corporate defendant in a federal criminal case, Chapter 8 of the *Sentencing Guidelines* sets forth guidelines for calculating fine levels. For a corporate antitrust defendant, the base offense level is often set upon consideration of volume of commerce.[28] Under Section 2R1.1, in lieu of a calculation based on pecuniary loss, twenty percent of the volume of affected commerce is used in determining the base fine.

Section 8C2.5 sets forth several considerations for calculating a "Culpability Score," which is then used to determine the level of a criminal

---

in the antitrust offense. In global cartel cases, the volume of commerce attributable to the defendant is often the most significant area of negotiation with government prosecutors in determining whether to enter into a guilty plea to an antitrust offense.

27. *See* Antitrust Div., U.S. Dep't of Justice, Model Annotated Corporate Plea Agreement ¶ 4(b) (last updated Aug. 29, 2016), *available at* https://www.justice.gov/atr/file/889021/download [hereinafter *Model Corporate Plea Agreement*].

28. SENTENCING GUIDELINES, *supra* note 11, § 8C2.4 provides for several ways in which a base fine for a corporate defendant can be established. One of those ways is if chapter 2 of the Guidelines provides for organizational fines. As 2R1.1 specifically addresses corporate defendants in antitrust cases, under 8C2.4, the volume of commerce calculation typically applies in cartel cases.

fine from the initial base fine level. Among the factors that are considered in calculating the Culpability Score for a corporate defendant are:

- the number of employees and whether high-level personnel in the company participated in, condoned, or were willfully ignorant of the offense;
- whether the conduct was pervasive throughout the company;
- any prior history of misconduct by the company;
- any violation by the company of an existing judicial order or condition;
- any acts of the company to obstruct justice during the government's investigation, prosecution, or sentencing;
- the existence of an effective compliance program; and
- self-reporting and acceptance of responsibility by the company.

These factors apply to antitrust and other criminal offenses, and can result in adding or subtracting points to the calculation of a company's score.

The Antitrust Division has not historically recommended that a corporate defendant receive any credit for the mitigating factor of an effective compliance program. [29] This may be for several reasons, including: (1) it is common in antitrust cases for there to be a high-level executive involved in the violation, in which case a company may not receive credit for a compliance program; [30] and (2) it may be perceived as

---

29.   While the sentencing guidelines provide for up to a three point reduction in the culpability score for a company compliance program, the Antitrust Division did not ask for such reductions. *See SENTENCING GUIDELINES*, note 11, § 8C2.5(f)(3)(C); Brent Snyder, Deputy Assistant Att'y Gen., Antitrust Div., U.S. Dep't of Justice, Deputy Assistant Attorney General Brent Snyder Delivers Remarks at the Sixth Annual Chicago Forum on International Antitrust (June 8, 2015), *available at* http://www.justice.gov/opa/speech/deputy-assistant-attorney-general-brent-snyder-delivers-remarks-sixth-annual-chicago; Brent Snyder, Deputy Assistant Att'y Gen., Antitrust Div., U.S. Dep't of Justice, Compliance Is a Culture, Not Just a Policy, Remarks as Prepared for the International Chamber of Commerce/United States Council of International Business Joint Antitrust Compliance Workshop, at 8 (Sept. 9, 2014) ("[T]he Division . . . almost never recommends that companies receive credit at sentencing for a preexisting compliance program"), *available at* http://www.justice.gov/atr/file/517796/download.

30.   There is a rebuttable presumption that the compliance program was not effective if an employee with substantial authority participated in,

undermining the Leniency Program to give sentencing credit for a compliance program if an entity was not the first to report violations (even if it made efforts to detect or deter such violations through a compliance program).[31]

Included here is a sample sentencing calculation, which has been simplified to show certain key factors in a *Sentencing Guidelines* analysis:

Base Fine	20 percent of volume of affected commerce (§§ 2R1.1(d)(1) & 8C2.4(b))	$30 million (20 percent of $150 million U.S. revenue, not limited to bid-rigging events charged for trial)
Culpability Score		
Base Offense Level	(§ 8C2.5(a))	5 (add 5 points to start)
Involvement in or Tolerance of Criminal Activity	(§ 8C2.5(b)(1)) – number of employees at the company or per unit, and whether high-level employee was involved	4 (add 4 points if unit had 1,000 employees and high-level executive was involved)
Prior History	(§ 8C2.5(c)) – none	0 (no past enforcement history)
Violation of Order	(§ 8C2.5(d)) – none	0 (no prior judicial order)

---

condoned, or was willfully ignorant of the offense; the majority of cartel cases investigated by the Antitrust Division involve company employees who are viewed by the Division as having a sufficiently high level of authority that credit will not be given under §§ 8C2.5(f)(3)(B)(i)-(ii) of the *Sentencing Guidelines.*

31.   If the company did not come forth as an amnesty applicant, the company cannot use § 8C2.5(f)(3)(C) of the *Sentencing Guidelines* to avoid the rebuttable presumption; specifically, the program does not meet the requirement that "the compliance and ethics program detected the offense before discovery outside of the organization or before such discovery was reasonably likely."

Obstruction of Justice	(§ 8C2.5(e)) – none	0 (no efforts to impede or obstruct investigation or prosecution)
Effective Program to Prevent and Detect Violations	(§ 8C2.5(f))	0 (compliance program – Antitrust Division has not historically given points for a compliance program)
Acceptance of Responsibility	(§ 8C2.5(g))	-2 (company cooperated and accepted responsibility, but did so after the government was already investigating)
Total Culpability Score		7
Minimum and Maximum Multipliers	(§ 8C2.6) Range for culpability score governed by 8C2.6, but floor is 0.75 for antitrust offenses	1.4 to 2.8
Minimum and Maximum Fine Range		**$42 million–$84 million**

(3) Individual Defendants and Other Adjustments to Sentencing Guidelines

Section 2R.1.1 provides that for individual defendants in antitrust cases, the guideline fine range shall be from 1 to 5 percent of the volume of commerce, but not less than $20,000.

An individual's offense level under Section 2R1.1 is also the foundation to establishing a range for possible incarceration. As previously noted, for antitrust offenses, ACPERA increased the maximum sentence to ten years. The *Sentencing Guidelines* provide factors to be considered in determining what sentence up to ten years may be appropriate given the defendant's conduct. The *Sentencing Guidelines* strongly favor incarceration for individuals who violate the antitrust laws.[32] It is unlikely that the defendants can avoid a *Sentencing Guidelines* sentence recommending imprisonment unless they provide the government with "substantial assistance" by cooperating with the government's ongoing investigation. In practice, the Antitrust Division seeks incarceration for virtually all individual defendants, even those who plead guilty and provide substantial cooperation.[33] The expectation is that most defendants will be incarcerated for some period of time.[34] In general, the *Sentencing Guidelines* do not allow probation as an alternative to imprisonment for an offense level of nine or higher.[35]

Once a base offense level is established for an individual under Section 2R1.1, Chapter 3 of the *Sentencing Guidelines* provides for adjustments to be made to the offense level based on:

- any victim-related enhancements, including if the defendant abused a position of trust;
- the defendant's role in the offense, including if he or she was a leader or organizer of the criminal activity;[36]
- whether the defendant obstructed the government's investigation;[37]
- whether and to what extent the defendant cooperated with the government's investigation and prosecution;[38] and
- whether the defendant accepted responsibility for the illegal conduct.[39]

Once any adjustments have been applied to the offense level, Chapter 5 of the *Sentencing Guidelines* sets forth a table that provides for a sentencing range based on that level and the defendant's criminal history, if any. For example, for a defendant whose offense level is sixteen (just three points above the base offense level for an antitrust offense) with no criminal history, the *Sentencing Guidelines* range is twenty-one to twenty-

---

32. *See* SENTENCING GUIDELINES, *supra* note 11, § 2R1.1 cmt.
33. *See* Hammond, *supra* note 1, at 7 ("The Division will not agree to a 'no-jail' sentence for any defendant, and our practice is not to remain silent at sentencing if a defendant argues for a no-jail sentence").
34. *Id.*
35. *See* SENTENCING GUIDELINES, *supra* note 11, § 5B1.1.
36. *Id.* §§ 3B1.1, 3B1.2, 8C2.8(a)(2) & cmt n.1.
37. *Id.* §§ 3C1.1, 8C2.5(e).
38. *Id.* §§ 3E1.1, 5K1.1, 8C2.5(g), 8C4.1.
39. *Id.* §§ 3E1.1, 8C2.5(g).

seven months. A defendant who has enhancements based on volume of commerce or other negative factors may face a *Sentencing Guidelines* range of several years.[40]

Included here is a sample sentencing calculation, which has been simplified to show certain key factors in a *Sentencing Guidelines* analysis:

Base Offense Level for an Antitrust Offense	12 (§ 2R1.1)	12
Volume of Commerce	+6 (More than $40,000,000 affected volume of commerce (§ 2R1.1(b)(2))	18
Participation in an Agreement to Submit Non-Competitive Bids (Bid-Rigging)	+1 (§ 2R.1.1(b)(1))	19
Aggravating Role	+3 Defendant was a manager or supervisor (§ 3B.1.1)	22
Obstruction of Justice	+2 Defendant destroyed documents after receiving a grand jury subpoena. (§ 3C.1.1)	24
Acceptance of Responsibility	+2 Defendant pleaded guilty and accepted responsibility, but did so late in the investigation. (§ 3E1.1)	-2
Total Offense Level		22

---

40.   *Id.* ch. 5 pt. A.

Guidelines Range for a Defendant with No Criminal History	Zone C and Criminal History Category I	41-51 months
Guidelines Fine Range	1-5 percent of the affected volume of commerce, but not less than $20,000 (§ 2R1.1(c))	**$400,000-$2 million**

These calculations are a key factor in estimating the potential criminal fines and/or incarceration for companies and individuals in cartel investigations, but they are not the only factor. From the *Sentencing Guidelines* range of fines and length of incarceration, the government and defense counsel often negotiate the volume of affected commerce and other elements based on legal or factual arguments that could result in a different level. At sentencing, the Antitrust Division can seek upward or downward adjustments. The most common adjustment, which is a downward departure, is recommended where a company or individual cooperates with the government's investigation by providing "substantial assistance" that results in a reduction of a fine or the length of recommended incarceration.[41] Companies and individuals can also seek fine reductions based on an inability to pay the fine indicated by the *Sentencing Guidelines* if they can demonstrate significant, concrete financial hardship.[42]

---

41. *See, e.g.*, Brent Snyder, Deputy Assistant Att'y General, Antitrust Div., U.S. Dep't of Justice, Individual Accountability for Antitrust Crimes, Remarks as Prepared for the Yale School of Management Global Antitrust Enforcement Conference, at 11 (Feb. 19, 2016), *available at* https://www.justice.gov/opa/file/826721/download ("As in any other criminal prosecution, the *United States Sentencing Guidelines* provide for a substantial assistance departure to account for the cooperation that a defendant—corporate or individual—provides"); *see* Antitrust Div., U.S. Dep't of Justice, Model Corporate Plea Agreement ¶ 10 (stating that "the United States agrees that it will make a motion, pursuant to U.S.S.G. § 8C4.1,19 for a downward departure from the Guidelines fine range in this case" upon truthful and "substantial assistance"), *available at* https://www.justice.gov/atr/file/889021/download.

42. *SENTENCING GUIDELINES, supra* note 11, §§ 8C4.1-11, 8C3.3.

C. Plea Negotiations

1. Plea Negotiations—Overview

It is common in criminal antitrust investigations for prosecutors and counsel to discuss the potential for a plea agreement with the government to resolve charges. There is no constitutional right in the United States to plea bargain, and therefore it is at the government's discretion to negotiate a guilty plea with any particular defendant.[43] Plea agreements can be reached prior to the filing of criminal charges or after a defendant has been indicted. As a practical matter, however, historically the majority of corporate defendants convicted of an antitrust offense by the Antitrust Division have pleaded guilty prior to the filing of any criminal charges, rather than litigating charges through trial. Indeed, in the past decade, of the 630 criminal cases charged by the Antitrust Division from 2005 to 2015,[44] there was only one completed jury trial of a corporate defendant on antitrust charges.[45]

For criminal antitrust cases, there are several rules and resources that are useful to practitioners, including (1) the Federal Rules of Criminal Procedure, which govern federal court practice in criminal cases; (2) the *Justice Manual*,[46] which addresses some broader DOJ policies that apply to all criminal pleas; (3) the Antitrust Division's Model Corporate and Individual Plea Agreements;[47] and (4) the form of charges in criminal antitrust cases, including criminal informations and indictments, including

---

43.   *See* Weatherford v. Bursey, 429 U.S. 545, 561 (1977) ("[T]here is no constitutional right to plea bargain; the prosecutor need not do so if he prefers to go to trial.").

44.   Antitrust Div., U.S. Dep't of Justice, Antitrust Division Workload Statistics FY 2007-FY 2016, *available at* https://www.justice.gov/atr/file/788426/download; Antitrust Div., U.S. Dep't of Justice, Criminal Enforcement Trends Charts Through Fiscal Year 2017 (updated Mar. 12, 2018), *available at* https://www.justice.gov/ atr/criminal-enforcement-fine-and-jail-charts.

45.   *See* United States v. AU Optronics, No. 09-0110 (N.D. Cal. 2012).

46.   *See* U.S. DEP'T OF JUSTICE, JUSTICE MANUAL (2018), *available at* https://www.justice.gov/jm/justice-manual [hereinafter *JUSTICE MANUAL*].

47.   *See Model Corporate Plea Agreement, supra* note 27; Antitrust Div., U.S. Dep't of Justice, Model Annotated Individual Plea Agreement (last updated Aug. 29, 2016), *available at* https://www.justice.gov/atr/file/888481/download [hereinafter *Model Individual Plea Agreement*].

the nature of factual allegations to which pleading defendants must admit (or "allocute").

The implications of pleading guilty to criminal antitrust charges include admitting to wrongdoing that constitutes a felony in the United States and agreeing to pay a crime fine and, for individuals, potential incarceration. Guilty pleas involve a written agreement that is public and is the subject of an open hearing that victims and other parties can attend. There are also collateral consequences that may flow from the admission of wrongdoing, including regulatory and other debarment, disclosure requirements for regulated and public entities, exposure to private damage litigation, and other impairment of rights for individuals.[48]

With these implications, companies and individuals nevertheless weigh with their counsel the likelihood that criminal fines may be reduced and that potential length of incarceration may be shortened by negotiating a consensual resolution of criminal charges. Substantial cooperation with the government's ongoing investigation is often the most effective way to reduce a fine and the length of any sentence of incarceration. Beyond the chance to reduce fines and any incarceration, entering into a plea agreement achieves certainty as to some, even if not all, factors that would be determined by a jury and court in a criminal trial. Such certainty is often of great importance to corporate and individual defendants who have been subject to government investigation, which often has significant adverse impacts on ongoing business and personal interests.

2. *U.S. Department of Justice Policies and Strategy*

The DOJ's *Justice Manual* sets forth some general policies that relate to plea negotiations in federal criminal investigations, including antitrust investigations. Section 9-27.420 of the *Justice Manual* specifically identifies some of the relevant factors that federal prosecutors can consider in exercising the discretion to negotiate a plea agreement with a particular

---

48. *See Model Individual Plea Agreement, supra* note 47, ¶ 17 ("The defendant understands that, upon sentencing, the Antitrust Division will report his conviction to the Department of Justice's Bureau of Justice Assistance pursuant to 10 U.S.C. § 2408 for inclusion in the Defense Procurement Fraud Debarment Clearinghouse database and the System for Award Management"); U.S. Gen. Servs. Admin., Frequently Asked Questions: Suspension & Debarment, *available at* http://www.gsa.gov/portal/content/ 192903 (summarizing U.S. federal regulations and policies requiring debarment of contractors and other parties convicted of antitrust and fraud offenses) (citing FAR 9.405-2(b) and 41 C.F.R. § 105-68).

defendant, rather than pursue charges through a jury trial. Those factors include:

- the defendant's willingness to cooperate in the investigation or prosecution of others;
- the defendant's history with respect to criminal activity;
- the nature and seriousness of the offense or offenses charged;
- the defendant's remorse or contrition and his/her willingness to assume responsibility for his/her conduct;
- the desirability of prompt and certain disposition of the case;
- the likelihood of obtaining a conviction at trial;
- the probable effect on witnesses;
- the probable sentence or other consequences if the defendant is convicted;
- the public interest in having the case tried rather than disposed of by a guilty plea;
- the expense of trial and appeal;
- the need to avoid delay in the disposition of other pending cases; and
- the effect upon the victim's right to restitution.

In addition, there are other department-wide policies that limit federal prosecutors' discretion to forgo charges in plea agreements, which seek to ensure that guilty pleas still reflect and address serious conduct.[49]

There are also specific practices and considerations that apply to plea negotiations by the Antitrust Division, including the following:

- Leniency Program: There is only one company—the successful amnesty applicant—that can meet program requirements in order to avoid a criminal charge. After that company is accepted into the Leniency Program, no other company can negotiate that same resolution. Accordingly, other companies that are viewed by the

---

49. For example, there is a policy within the DOJ that is often referred to as the "Ashcroft Memo," under which prosecutors must seek a plea to the most "serious, readily provable offense" to be charged. Memo. from John Ashcroft, Att'y Gen., U.S. Dep't of Justice, Department Policy Concerning Charging Criminal Offenses, Disposition of Charges, and Sentencing (Sept. 22, 2003), *available at* https://www.justice.gov/archive/opa/pr/2003/September/03_ag_516.htm.

Antitrust Division as culpable for a criminal violation will likely have to negotiate a plea agreement and admit to the offense.[50]

- Early Cooperation: Companies and individuals that seek to negotiate plea agreements earlier in an investigation may have a greater ability to seek credit for cooperating that will reduce a fine and sentence. Indeed, most plea agreements negotiated by the Antitrust Division occur after it has initiated an investigation, but prior to any indictment. The reason is that the Antitrust Division often already has a cooperating company—a leniency applicant— that has provided substantial cooperation to the Antitrust Division in the form of information, documents, and witnesses who have knowledge of the antitrust violation that implicates other companies and their employees. The more companies that have already agreed to cooperate, the more difficult it is to provide unique and useful information to Division prosecutors.

- Treatment of Employees in Corporate Pleas: The Antitrust Division has its own policies and practices with regard to the inclusion or exclusion of individual employees in corporate plea agreements. Under the Corporate Leniency Program, current employees who cooperate with an ongoing investigation in which their employer company is the leniency applicant will be included in the "non-prosecution" coverage under the program. However, the Antitrust Division does not guarantee any employee—current or former—coverage under a corporate plea agreement. The Antitrust Division's 2013 revised "carve out" policy provides that employees whose conduct warrants prosecution will be "carved out" and not included in any non-prosecution coverage if the company pleads guilty to an antitrust offense.[51] Under the Antitrust Division's historical practice, prosecutors may exercise

---

50. In a few limited circumstances, the Antitrust Division has agreed to other resolutions of an antitrust criminal investigation (*e.g.*, deferred prosecution agreements or non-prosecution agreements). These agreements are not common and in most global cartel investigations are not likely to be considered as alternatives to a guilty plea by Division prosecutors. *See* U.S. Dep't of Justice, Antitrust Division, Municipal Bonds Investigation 2014 Case Filings, *available at* https://www.justice.gov/atr/division-update/2014/municipal-bonds-investigation.

51. Antitrust Div., U.S. Dep't of Justice, Statement on Carve-Out Policy (2013) [hereinafter *Statement on Carve-Out Policy*], *available at* https://www.justice.gov/opa/pr/statement-assistant-attorney-general-bill-baer-changes-antitrust-division-s-carve-out.

discretion on an employee-by-employee basis as to whether some employees will be given non-prosecution coverage in the company's plea agreement. In the future, it may be that such coverage is limited in light of more recent broader DOJ policies[52] that encourage prosecutors to seek individual accountability by bringing charges against individual defendants involved in corporate wrongdoing.

- Leniency Plus Fine Reductions: Companies generally can seek cooperation credit for cooperating with the government, but there are ways to seek a reduction of a criminal fine that are unique to Antitrust Division cases. For example, there may be fine discounts that may be gained for "Leniency Plus," which a company may seek if it is the successful amnesty applicant for the purpose of an antitrust violation in one market, but was not able to secure leniency for another product market and faces potential criminal exposure for a second violation.[53]

- Restitution Requirement—Pending Private Litigation: As criminal antitrust cases frequently involve significant criminal fines for corporate defendants and private class actions seeking damages for the antitrust violation may follow a guilty plea, the Antitrust Division may not seek a restitution order if private litigation has already been filed seeking the same recovery for victims. Restitution is otherwise typically required at criminal sentencing.

- Ability to Pay Assessment: The Antitrust Division will consider "ability to pay" concerns during plea negotiations, and in the past has permitted corporate and individual defendants to submit financial information that enables prosecutors and investigators to assess whether the defendant is financially unable to make immediate payment or if such payment would be unduly

---

52. *See* Memo. from Sally Q. Yates, Deputy Att'y Gen., U.S. Dep't of Justice, Individual Accountability for Corporate Wrongdoing (Sept. 9, 2015), *available at* www.justice.gov/dag/file/769036/download.

53. The size of the Amnesty Plus discount depends on a number of factors, including: (1) the strength of the evidence provided by the cooperating company in the leniency product; (2) the potential significance of the violation reported in the leniency application, measured in such terms as the volume of commerce involved, the geographic scope, and the number of co-conspirator companies and individuals; and (3) the likelihood that the Division would have uncovered the additional violation absent the self-reporting. Of these three factors, the first two are given the most weight.

burdensome.[54] In such circumstances, the Antitrust Division may determine in its discretion to allow payment in installments and waive interest.

3. Defense Considerations for Companies and Individuals

Key considerations for defense counsel in assessing a potential plea agreement and preparing for meetings with government prosecutors include: (1) form of the plea; (2) scope of charges and conduct to be included in the plea; (3) the *Sentencing Guidelines* "volume of commerce" calculation; (4) credit and obligations of substantial assistance to the government; (5) collateral consequences for parallel investigations and private antitrust litigation; (6) treatment of employees; (7) any additional penalties or relief the government may seek after a successful trial; and (8) concerns for individual defendants, including location of incarceration, immigration issues, and indemnification.

a. Form of the Plea

Federal Rule of Criminal Procedure 11, which applies to all federal criminal cases in the United States, sets forth the procedures for entering into guilty pleas.

The Antitrust Division frequently seeks to negotiate corporate pleas in which the government and defendant agree to a *Sentencing Guidelines* range and fine level, rather than present a government recommendation to the federal court (which the defendant does not oppose). Federal Rule of Criminal Procedure 11 governs the types of plea agreements that may be entered in federal cases. Sections 11(C)(1)(B) and 11(C)(1)(c) provide for two variations of a plea agreement:

- Section B Plea: The DOJ will "recommend, or agree not to oppose the defendant's request, that a particular sentence or sentencing range is appropriate or that a particular provision of the Sentencing Guidelines, or policy statement, or sentencing factor does or does not apply (such a recommendation or request does not bind the court)"; or

---

54. *See Model Corporate Plea Agreement, supra* note 27, ¶ 9 n.11 (providing that, if the defendant requests and the staff agrees, the fine may be paid in installments, payable over a period not exceeding five years, and interest may be waived).

- Section C Plea: The DOJ and defense "agree that a specific sentence or sentencing range is the appropriate disposition of the case, or that a particular provision of the Sentencing Guidelines, or policy statement, or sentencing factor does or does not apply (such a recommendation or request binds the court once the court accepts the plea agreement)."

Defense counsel may favor a Section C Plea that allows a defendant some level of certainty in the sentence or sentencing range. Whether the Antitrust Division will seek a Section B or C Plea may depend, however, on the federal district in which the case will be filed and other case-specific factors. Local practice in the federal district in which the case is filed may disfavor pleas in which the court does not have the discretion to alter the terms at sentencing.

b.   Scope of Charges and Conduct to Be Included in the Plea

Federal Rule of Criminal Procedure 11(b)(2)-(3) requires a federal court confirm that a plea is voluntary and that it has a "factual basis" for the defendant to enter a plea of guilty to a criminal offense. These requirements mean that a defendant typically needs to confirm and admit to the prosecutor's statement of facts that is set forth in the charges and also orally in court. For this reason, prior to any plea negotiation, defense counsel must evaluate the following key elements of a potential plea agreement and related charge and determine if any points are disputed:

- the time frame for the conduct (including if statute of limitations would bar a charge);
- all products or services that would be covered;
- the object of the agreement/conspiracy;
- the geographic scope of the conduct and commerce;
- the affected volume of commerce;
- the participants in the agreement/conspiracy; and
- other non-antitrust charges that could be brought.[55]

---

55.   *See* ANTITRUST DIV., U.S. DEP'T OF JUSTICE, AN ANTITRUST PRIMER FOR FEDERAL LAW ENFORCEMENT PERSONNEL § I (Sept. 2018), *available at* https://www.justice.gov/atr/page/file/1091651/download (describing "companion violations," including mail and wire fraud, that are prosecuted in antitrust cases); ANTITRUST DIV., U.S. DEP'T OF JUSTICE, ANTITRUST

Any of these areas could be the subject of discussion with the prosecutors and might be material in shaping the outcome.

c. Guidelines Volume of Commerce Calculation

Of all of the points for discussion in a plea negotiation, one of the most critical is the affected volume of commerce (VOC) that will be used to calculate the *Sentencing Guidelines* fine range for a company or an individual. The Antitrust Division and other global competition agencies may be able to take the legal position that the commerce of all alleged co-conspirators can be used to calculate a cartel fine. As a practical matter, however, in U.S. plea negotiations, the volume of commerce attributable to a particular defendant is the starting point.[56] That limitation does not necessarily end the inquiry, and the following questions should be asked in preparing for plea negotiations:

- Which products or services are being included in a VOC calculation?
- If there is extraterritorial conduct involved in the case, is the VOC calculated based not only on U.S. sales, but also overseas sales that are "foreign commerce" not properly considered for the purpose of a U.S. plea?
- Is the relevant product or service a component of a larger assembly or suite of services, and therefore should the VOC be calculated from that component only?

DIVISION MANUAL at II-7 (5th ed. 2012) (last updated Apr. 2018), *available at* https://www.justice.gov/atr/file/761166/download.

56. Although it is well established that revenue and sales of a defendant contribute to a sentencing calculation, as the term "volume of commerce" is not defined, courts have engaged in an analysis of which sales should be included in any particular case. *Compare* United States v. SKW Metals & Alloys, Inc., 195 F.3d 83, 91 (2d Cir. 1999) (if conspiracy was a "non-starter" or there were sales during ineffective periods of a conspiracy are not 'affected by' the illegal agreement, such commerce should be excluded), *with* United States v. Hayter Oil Co., 51 F.3d 1265, 1273 (6th Cir. 1995) (all sales made by defendants during conspiracy are "affected" by the conspiracy, and not limited to sales that were made at or above the target price), *and* United States v. Andreas, 216 F.3d 645, 678 (7th Cir. 2000) ("[T]he presumption must be that all sales during the period of the conspiracy have been affected by the illegal agreement," which can be rebutted by proof that consumers were not harmed.).

- If there is a statute of limitations defense, should certain years of sales or revenue be excluded?
- Even within a particular time period, were there specific customer contracts or sales that were not impacted by the conduct under investigation?
- In a bid-rigging case, is the VOC being calculated based on the contracts that were impacted (versus all contracts in the time period)?
- What cooperation, Leniency Plus, or other discounts are likely to be applied once the VOC is negotiated?

Statute of limitations defenses and challenges to subject matter jurisdiction over conduct and commerce under the Foreign Trade Antitrust Improvement Act (FTAIA)[57] have been the subject of particular attention in litigated cases. FTAIA litigation (in both civil and criminal antitrust cases) has focused on whether in international cartel cases, which often involve overseas conduct, sales are "foreign commerce" that cannot be included in a VOC calculation for a U.S. case.[58] There is little dispute that the Antitrust Division can charge cases involving defendants located overseas who sell directly to consumers in the United States. But where the sales impacted by the antitrust violation are *not* made directly to U.S. consumers and could be framed as foreign commerce, the Antitrust Division may need to demonstrate that the foreign commerce had a direct, substantial, and reasonably foreseeable impact on the United States.[59] The fact pattern in which this concern has most often arisen is where an overseas defendant sells components outside of the United States that are ultimately included in a product for sale into the United States. Exclusion of overseas sales that are not deemed sufficiently direct may have a material effect on the *Sentencing Guidelines* calculation in certain international cases.[60]

---

57.   15 U.S.C. § 6a.

58.   *See, e.g.*, United States v. Hsiung, 778 F.3d 738, 751 (9th Cir. 2014); Animal Sci. Prods., v. China Minmetals Corp., 654 F.3d 462, 465 (3d Cir. 2011).

59.   *See* Hartford Fire Ins. v. California, 509 U.S. 764, 796 (1993) ("[I]t is well established by now that the Sherman Act applies to foreign conduct that was meant to produce and did in fact produce some substantial effect in the United States.").

60.   *See, e.g.*, Plea Agreement, United States v. Solvay S.A., No. 06-0159 (N.D. Cal. Apr. 20, 2006), *available at* https://www.justice.gov/atr/case-document/plea-agreement-381; Plea Agreement, United States v. Hynix

Two cases illustrate how courts may evaluate overseas sales to the United States. In *United States v. Hsiung*,[61] the Ninth Circuit evaluated two fact patterns, finding that the government had proven both "import commerce" (i.e., direct sales), and also sufficient facts to demonstrate direct, substantial and reasonably foreseeable impact on the United States for indirect sales.[62] The indictment charged defendants with: (i) fixing the price of products targeted by defendants to be sold in the United States or for delivery to the United States; or (ii) fixing the price of components that were incorporated into finished products "destined" for delivery to the United States.[63]

In contrast, in a civil case, *Lotes Co. v. Hon Hai Precision Industry Co.*,[64] the Second Circuit affirmed dismissal of antitrust claims where the complaint alleged collusion by overseas defendants in failing to license patents to the plaintiff, which allegedly excluded the overseas plaintiff from the market for USB connectors, resulting in higher prices for U.S. consumers.[65] The allegations did not involve collusion in connection with any direct sales to the United States, and the court found that even there was a "direct, substantial, and reasonably foreseeable effect" in the United States, the conduct alleged in the case—a failure to license—did not cause the plaintiff's injury.[66] In contrast with *Hsiung*, *Lotes* illustrates that, beyond direct sales or sales of components into products destined for U.S. consumers, other overseas conduct and commerce may fall outside the scope of U.S. enforcement.

d.   Credit and Obligations of Substantial Assistance

One of the most significant ways in which a company or individual can seek a reduction in a criminal fine or the potential length of incarceration is to provide "substantial assistance" to the government in its ongoing investigation. If a defendant provides substantial assistance, a prosecutor may seek a "downward departure" (i.e., a reduction in sentence from the *Sentencing Guidelines* range that would otherwise apply).

Semiconductor Inc., No. 05-249 (N.D. Cal. May 11, 2005), *available at* https://www.justice.gov/atr/case-document/plea-agreement-181.
61.   778 F.3d 738 (9th Cir. 2014).
62.   *See id.* at 748, 754-60.
63.   *Id.* at 757.
64.   53 F.3d 395 (2d Cir. 2014).
65.   *Id.* at 415.
66.   *See id.*

Sections 5K1.1 and 8C4.1 provide for a downward departure in both corporate and individual cases.

Substantial cooperation is demanding, however, and may require a company or individual to provide extensive information and devote significant time to assisting government prosecutors in their continuing investigation. For corporate defendants, cooperation will likely involve agreeing to provide document productions (of U.S. and overseas material) as the government's investigation continues, and making current and former employees available for interviews and potential testimony.[67] For individual defendants, substantial cooperation may mean meeting with the government to provide information and identifying documents, and agreeing to testify at any trial of other defendants.[68]

The extent of a company's or individual's cooperation is the subject of an Antitrust Division recommendation at sentencing, which is a factor that the court will consider in determining any fine and/or length of incarceration.

e.　Collateral Consequences—Parallel Investigations and Litigation

A guilty plea in a U.S. case involves a public admission of wrongdoing and the filing of a written charge and plea agreement. For this reason, the impact on other related investigations and private litigation is critical. A guilty plea may be used as evidence in a U.S. civil antitrust case for damages, and may also be considered evidence in a parallel cartel investigation by another competition authority. For example, Section 5(a) of the Clayton Act provides that a civil or criminal judgment obtained by the government is admissible as prima facie evidence in a treble damages action.[69] The specific facts admitted by a company or individual in the course of pleading guilty—the timeframe for participation in a cartel, the products involved, the volume of commerce, the location of events—may be alleged in other cases in a manner that cannot be contested.

67.　*See Model Corporate Plea Agreement, supra* note 27, ¶¶ 13-14.

68.　The Antitrust Division's plea agreements with individual defendants include provisions that expressly provide for cooperation in the form of interviews, testimony, and other means of providing information in furtherance of an ongoing investigation. *See, e.g.,* Plea Agreement, United States v. Zarefsky, No. 09-01058 (S.D.N.Y. Jan. 12, 2012), *available at* https://www.justice.gov/atr/case-document/file/509106/download (plea agreement of individual defendant who testified at trial).

69.　*See* 15 U.S.C. § 16(a).

Beyond other cartel investigations and antitrust litigation, federal antitrust offenses are felonies in the United States and may trigger regulatory and disclosure requirements for both companies and individuals. It is therefore important for counsel to assess what, if any, impact the scope of a plea agreement and charge will have on other matters.[70] As a related matter, counsel may need to assess which corporate entities or affiliates would be the pleading entity if there is more than one corporate entity that the Antitrust Division views to be involved.[71] Whether the pleading entity is a U.S. or overseas entity (or an unregulated subsidiary) may make a significant difference in the collateral consequences that flow from a criminal conviction.

f.   Treatment of Employees in a Corporate Plea Agreement

There are several ways employees may become relevant in the negotiation of a corporate plea agreement. First, the government may seek to "carve out" certain employees whom it may seek to investigate further and potentially charge at a later point.[72] Second, prosecutors may seek the company's cooperation through interviews and information from specific current and former employees. The United States is a jurisdiction in which in-person and live testimony is expected in the course of investigations and any trials. There are therefore significant implications for companies, in particular if a company may need to provide cooperation *against* its current employees or if employees (even if not culpable for any conduct) are not willing to cooperate with the government.

---

70.   Collateral consequences such as exposure to other investigations and litigation are relevant in evaluating terms in plea negotiations that could aggravate and increase exposure, but have not historically been an effective ground to avoid prosecution for antitrust offenses. These and other collateral consequences are addressed in the *Justice Manual* in section 9-28, which discusses factors to be considered in exercising prosecutorial discretion in investigations involving business organizations. However, it is expressly stated that some of the considerations may not be appropriate when considering antitrust offenses. The section states that certain considerations "would not necessarily be appropriate in an antitrust investigation, in which antitrust violations, by definition, go to the heart of the corporation's business." *JUSTICE MANUAL, supra* note 46, § 9-28.400.

71.   *See Model Corporate Plea Agreement, supra* note 27, ¶ 13 n.23.

72.   *See Statement on Carve-Out Policy, supra* note 51.

g.   Additional Penalties or Relief after Litigated Jury Trial

Prior to any plea negotiation, counsel need to assess with a corporate or individual client whether it is likely that a consensual resolution of a criminal investigation will yield a more favorable outcome than a litigated trial. In cases in which counsel assesses that the government has substantial evidence of an antitrust violation, and the issues to be disputed focus primarily on the extent of any fine or length of incarceration, a plea may enable the company or individual to secure a resolution and avoid:

- the maximum criminal fine based on the government's calculation of volume of commerce;
- the maximum length of incarceration under the *Sentencing Guidelines* and any upward departure the government might seek at sentencing;
- corporate probation, a corporate monitor, and any required reporting to the government that may be sought in sentencing;
- cost of litigation through trial; and
- enhanced exposure to parallel investigations and civil litigation based on the facts and findings of a public jury trial and sentencing.

The potential full exposure of a trial and contested sentencing can be seen in the one corporate criminal antitrust trial in the past decade, *United States v. AU Optronics,*[73] in which the Antitrust Division sought $1 billion in criminal fines and the company argued at sentencing that even if the conviction stood, it should only pay a $285 million fine.[74] The district court sentenced the company to a $500 million fine and significant post-sentencing obligations, including implementing an antitrust compliance program, submitting to an independent corporate monitor at its own expense, and acknowledging publicly in trade press that it had engaged in wrongdoing.[75] The government argued that AU Optronics should be sentenced at a significant level because of its lack of cooperation and failure to acknowledge its wrongdoing in a case that the government

---

73.   United States v. AU Optronics, No. 09-110 (N.D. Cal. Oct. 2, 2012).
74.   Deft.'s Sentencing Memo., Part One; Scope and Application of 18 U.S.C. Section 3571 at 2, United States v. AU Optronics, No. 09-110 (N.D. Cal. Sept. 11, 2012).
75.   *See* Judgment in a Criminal Case, United States v. AU Optronics, No. 09-110 (N.D. Cal. Oct. 2, 2012).

argued was egregious. None of the post-sentencing remedies in *AU Optronics* are common in plea agreements in U.S. cases.

h. Individual Defendant Considerations

There are other significant considerations for individuals in plea negotiations. In recent years, it has been increasingly likely that even individuals who cooperate with the government will be sentenced to some period of incarceration, so there is no guarantee that a plea will avoid time in prison. U.S. defendants serve time in U.S. prison and are not often transferred to home jurisdictions if they are foreign nationals. As a result, prior to engaging in plea negotiations for an individual, there are several issues to consider:

- Fugitive Status: Foreign nationals who do not plead and are indicted may have a restricted ability to travel globally when they are pending trial. The Antitrust Division utilizes Interpol Red Notices and other enforcement tools to track fugitive individuals and may have the ability to seek arrest and extradition from other countries.[76]
- Extradition: Even in jurisdictions that have an extradition treaty with the United States, extradition proceedings may take significant time when the defendants do not voluntarily submit to U.S. jurisdiction. In anticipation of a reduced sentence, some individuals will decide after careful consideration to submit voluntarily to U.S. jurisdiction.
- Immigration Status: Non-U.S. citizens who reside in the United States may lose their immigration status upon a felony conviction. The Antitrust Division may agree to make a recommendation to the U.S. Department of Homeland Security in favor of the defendant as part of a plea agreement that involves cooperation with the government.

---

76. In *United States v. Pisciotti*, an Italian national defendant was indicted, arrested in Germany, and extradited to the United States to face price-fixing charges. *See* Press Release, U.S. Dep't of Justice, Office of Public Affairs, First Ever Extradition on Antitrust Charge (Apr. 4, 2014), *available at* https://www.justice.gov/opa/pr/first-ever-extradition-antitrust-charge. The defendant pleaded guilty and agreed to cooperate with the Antitrust Division. *See* Plea Agreement, United States v. Pisciotti, No. 10-60232 (S.D. Fla. Apr. 24, 2014) *available at* https://www.justice.gov/atr/case-document/file/507541/download.

- Cooperation and Testimony against Other Individuals: Individuals who seek to reduce the length of potential incarceration by cooperating often need to assess whether they will be able to provide cooperation with regard to former colleagues and other individuals. This cooperation could include public testimony about former colleagues and other individuals.
- Ability to Request Self-Surrender and Location for Incarceration: In plea negotiations, individuals may be able to seek the Antitrust Division's agreement to recommend to the Bureau of Prisons that consideration be given to specific locations near the individual's family or home. In addition, individuals may be able to request to self-surrender for any sentence after a short period of time that allows for affairs to be put into order and other arrangements to be made. These accommodations are not guaranteed in a contested sentencing.
- Future Employment and Rights: It is important for individuals to be advised by their counsel and assess what implications a guilty plea will have for their ability to seek employment, their right to vote, and other practical aspects of their day-to-day lives that will be impaired by a felony conviction.
- Indemnification: Individual defendants may seek to have their current or former employer indemnify them for any criminal fines and attorney's fees incurred in the Antitrust Division's investigation. The extent to which any fine or fees can be indemnified depends on any contractual provision and applicable state law.[77] It may make a difference if the employee admits that he had reasonable ability to know the conduct was unlawful and pleads to the offense.

4. Confidentiality of Plea Negotiations

Corporate and individual considerations are typically the subject of detailed discussions with the Antitrust Division. Negotiation may include: (1) counsel meetings with prosecutors to discuss facts and legal arguments; (2) presentation by the government of examples of its evidence

---

77. 18 U.S.C. § 3572(f) ("If such an obligation is imposed on a director, officer, shareholder, employee, or agent of an organization, payments may not be made, directly or indirectly, from assets of the organization, unless the court finds that such payment is expressly permissible under applicable State law.").

(referred to as a "reverse proffer") or by defense counsel if procedural protections are given; (3) a detailed understanding of what the government's charges will be; and (4) drafts of a plea agreement that will be signed by counsel and the defendant or corporate representative.

Rule 11(c)(1) of the Federal Rules of Criminal Procedure provides that federal courts are not permitted to be involved in the plea negotiation between the government and a defendant. Indeed, plea negotiations are not admissible in any civil or criminal case if the negotiations did not result in a guilty plea or if the guilty plea was ultimately withdrawn.[78] Nevertheless, as a guilty plea and any admissions or statements by the defendant may be admissible in other circumstances, counsel must take great care during negotiations with the government. With individuals, counsel must make sure to avoid any inadvertent waiver of the individual's Fifth Amendment rights against self-incrimination with factual admissions, should the individual decide not to plead guilty.

5. Rule 11 Hearing: Entry of a Guilty Plea

A plea of guilty to a criminal charge must be presented and accepted by a federal court to be valid and enforceable. Companies and individuals may enter a plea of guilty to an indictment or an information, which is the charging document used when a defendant pleads to a criminal charge prior to an indictment being returned by a grand jury.

a.   Criminal Informations and Indictments

Criminal indictments and informations are both written, formal criminal charges on which an individual or corporation accused of antitrust violations is brought to trial.[79] Each indictment or information should "set forth the facts evidencing the elements of the offense sought to be charged," although each will require a varying amount of factual detail.[80] As an antitrust violation is a federal felony punishable by a maximum of ten years imprisonment, the crime must be prosecuted by indictment, unless the defendant has waived indictment after being advised of the nature of the charge and of his rights.[81]

A criminal information is a charge drafted by the prosecutor that includes, just as an indictment, the facts and law supporting the charge. An

---

78.   *See* FED. R. EVID. 410.
79.   *See* U.S. DEP'T OF JUSTICE, GRAND JURY MANUAL (1st ed. 1991).
80.   *See id.* at VII-3.
81.   *Id.*

information, however, need not contain a signature line for the grand jury foreperson. [82] Moreover, a plea agreement will often accompany an information and be presented to the court at the time the information is presented. [83] A defendant pleading to an information will thus have an opportunity to review the information before prosecutors present it to the court. [84] Within certain constraints, the parties may negotiate the description of the information, but like the indictment, the contours of an information remain exclusively within the discretion of the prosecutor.[85]

b.　Plea of Guilty, Plea of Nolo Contendere, and Alternative Agreements

In a criminal prosecution, a defendant generally either pleads guilty and accepts responsibility for the facts, or pleads not guilty and contests the matter at trial.[86] Under Rule 11 of the Federal Rules of Criminal Procedure, the court must determine the factual basis for the plea, which typically involves the defendant's admission to the facts.[87] Rule 11 also provides, however, that a defendant may also enter a nolo contendere plea, in which the defendant does not expressly admit guilt but nonetheless waives the right to a trial and enters a plea and is sentenced based on the charges.[88]

Rule 11 permits a court to accept a nolo contendere plea only with its consent after it gives due consideration to the parties' views and the public interest in the effective administration of justice.[89] Thus, a defendant has

---

82.　*Id.*

83.　*Id.*

84.　*Id.*

85.　*Id.*

86.　The DOJ has entered into alternative agreements with corporate defendants known as Deferred Prosecution Agreements that involve defendant's agreement to acknowledge a law violation. Although such agreements are often filed with a U.S. federal court, they do not involve a guilty plea by the defendant. Such agreements therefore are not convictions that trigger sentencing unless the defendant is subsequently determined to have violated the provisions of the agreement. Under such circumstances, the DOJ may seek to charge and convict the defendant.

87.　FED. R. CRIM. P. 11(b)(3).

88.　FED. R. CRIM. P. 11(a)(3).

89.　FED. R. CRIM. P. 11(a)(3). In considering the "public interest," courts consider, among other things, the following factors: nature of the offense; duration of the violations; size of the defendants; impact on the economy;

no absolute right to enter such a plea.[90] For purposes of sentencing, a court considers the very same factors upon a guilty plea or plea of nolo contendere.[91] Furthermore, a guilty plea is often admissible in subsequent civil litigation against the defendant, whereas a nolo contendere plea is likely not.[92]

The DOJ has discouraged the disposition of criminal cases by means of nolo contendere pleas. The *Justice Manual* directs prosecutors to oppose the acceptance of nolo contendere pleas unless the Assistant Attorney General with supervisory responsibility over the subject matter "concludes that the circumstances of the case are so unusual that acceptance of such a plea would be in the public interest."[93] Nolo contendere pleas are therefore very rare in criminal antitrust cases. Within the last twenty-five years, there have only been two cases in which the courts accepted a nolo plea over the objections of the Antitrust Division.[94]

The DOJ has also entered into alternative agreements with corporate defendants known as Deferred Prosecution Agreements, which involve defendant's agreement to acknowledge a law violation. Although such agreements are often filed with a federal court, they do not involve a guilty plea by the defendant. Such agreements therefore are not convictions that trigger sentencing unless the defendant is subsequently determined to have violated the provisions of the agreement. Under such circumstances, the DOJ may seek to charge and convict the defendant. Alternative resolutions to criminal antitrust charges have been rare in light of the Corporate Leniency Program, which has aimed to incentivize early cooperation by

---

deterrent effect; views of the government; cost-benefit of certain collateral consequences; and potential conservation of judicial resources.

90.   *See JUSTICE MANUAL, supra* note 46, § 9-27.500.

91.   *See* FED. R. CRIM. P. 11(b)(1)(A-O).

92.   North Carolina v. Alford, 400 U.S. 25, 35-36, n.8 (1970); FED. R. CRIM. P. 11(e); U.S. DEP'T OF JUSTICE, CRIMINAL RESOURCE MANUAL § 627, *available at* https://www.justice.gov/jm/criminal-resource-manual-627-inadmissibility-pleas-federal-rule-criminal-procedure-11e6.

93.   *See JUSTICE MANUAL, supra* note 46, § 9-27.500; *see also id.* § 9-16.010 (describing the approval requirement for consent to nolo contendere pleas).

94.   *See* United States v. Fla. W. Int'l Airways, 282 F.R.D. 695 (S.D. Fla. 2012) (granting consent to enter a nolo contendere plea due to extraordinary circumstances, where the majority of defendant corporation's liability for participation in a price-fixing conspiracy with other air cargo carriers was attributable to its highest-ranking commercial officer, who was "immune from prosecution because he was a secret executive of another company"); United States v. Alaska Brokerage Int'l, No. 06-11 (W.D. Wa. 2006).

companies and individuals by making clear that those failing to self-report conduct first will be forced to plead guilty.[95]

c.   Rule 11 Plea Colloquy

At the plea hearing, once a defendant has expressed his decision to plead guilty to a criminal charge, the court places the defendant under oath and addresses the defendant personally in open court.[96] A plea to a federal felony results in the waiver of several constitutional and legal rights that the defendant would have to contest the charges. Accordingly, during this open address, the court must inform the defendant of, and determine that the defendant understands, the following:

- the government's right, in a prosecution for perjury or false statement, to use against the defendant any statement that the defendant gives under oath;
- the right to plead not guilty or, having already so pleaded, to persist in that plea;
- the right to a jury trial;
- the right to be represented by counsel—and if necessary have the court appoint counsel—at trial and at every other stage of the proceeding;
- the right at trial to confront and cross-examine adverse witnesses, to be protected from compelled self-incrimination, to testify and present evidence, and to compel the attendance of witnesses;
- the defendant's waiver of these trial rights if the court accepts a plea of guilty or nolo contendere;
- the nature of each charge to which the defendant is pleading;
- any maximum possible penalty, including imprisonment, fine, and term of supervised release;
- any mandatory minimum penalty;
- any applicable forfeiture;
- the court's authority to order restitution;

---

95.   *See, e.g.,* Scott D. Hammond, Deputy Assistant Att'y General, Antitrust Div., U.S. Dep't of Justice, Cornerstones of Effective Leniency, Presented Before the ICN Workshop on Leniency Programs (Nov. 22-23, 2004), *available at* https://www.justice.gov/atr/speech/cornerstones-effective-leniency-program (describing the "threat of severe sanctions" as a key facet of an effective cartel enforcement program).
96.   FED. R. CRIM. P. 11(b)(1).

- the court's obligation to impose a special assessment;
- in determining a sentence, the court's obligation to calculate the applicable sentencing-guideline range and to consider that range, possible departures under the *Sentencing Guidelines*, and other sentencing factors under 18 U.S.C. § 3553(a);
- the terms of any plea-agreement provision waiving the right to appeal or to collaterally attack the sentence; and
- that, if convicted, a defendant who is not a U.S. citizen may be removed from the United States, denied citizenship, and denied admission to the United States in the future.[97]

The court must then determine that the plea is voluntary and did not result from force, threats, or promises external to those in a plea agreement.[98] For guilty pleas, the court must determine that there is a factual basis for the plea.[99]

The parties must disclose the plea agreement in open court when the plea is offered, unless the court for good cause allows the parties to disclose the plea agreement in camera.[100] If the court accepts such a plea agreement, it must inform the defendant that the agreed disposition will be included in the judgment.[101] By contrast, if the court rejects a plea agreement, the defendant must be advised of the consequences of the rejection, including that the court may dispose of the case less favorably than the plea agreement contemplated.[102]

A defendant may withdraw a plea of guilty before the court accepts the plea, for any reason or no reason. After the court accepts the plea (but before sentencing), however, a defendant may only withdraw a plea if the court rejects a plea agreement or the defendant can show a fair and just reason for requesting withdrawal.[103] After a court imposes sentence, the defendant may not withdraw a guilty plea, and the plea may only be set aside on direct appeal or collateral attack (e.g., a federal habeas petition).[104]

---

97. *Id.*
98. *Id.* § (b)(2).
99. *Id.*
100. *Id.* § 11(c)(2).
101. *Id.* § 11(c)(4).
102. *Id.* § 11(c)(5).
103. *Id.* § 11(d).
104. *Id.* § 11(e).

D. Sentencing Procedures

Rule 32 of the Federal Rules of Criminal Procedure governs sentencing and judgment in federal criminal cases and sets forth the timing of submissions prior to a sentencing hearing. Corporate defendants may seek an expedited sentencing in which the defendant pleads guilty and is sentenced in one hearing, but otherwise a sentencing hearing typically is a separate proceeding that follows a presentence investigation by the court's office and submissions by the government and defense counsel.

1. Presentence Submissions

Prior to sentencing, Rule 32 provides that the federal court's Probation Office prepare a Presentence Report (PSR) based on an interview of the defendant and an evaluation of the offense and the defendant's background.[105] The assigned probation officer, who frequently handles a variety of federal criminal cases (not exclusively antitrust), prepares a PSR containing information about the offense, the defendant, and the statutory range of punishment and a calculation of the relevant sentencing guidelines.[106]

As the PSR also addresses any grounds for imposition of a sentence outside of the *Sentencing Guidelines* range, both the government and defense counsel often submit substantial information regarding aggravating and mitigating factors. The defense and the Antitrust Division must be provided a copy of the PSR at least thirty-five days before sentencing, and must submit any written objections within fourteen days of the sentencing hearing and otherwise may respond to the PSR (e.g., in the form of a sentencing memorandum).[107] The PSR is a confidential document that may not be disclosed to the public and must be filed under seal. With the PSR, the probation officer also submits a confidential sentencing recommendation, which can be disclosed to the parties if the court allows.

The Antitrust Division's sentencing memoranda may include the following types of information:

- a summary of key evidence underlying the antitrust offenses committed by the defendant;

---

105. *See id.* § 32.
106. *See SENTENCING GUIDELINES, supra* note 11, § 6A1.1.
107. *See* FED. R. CRIM. P. 32.

- aggravating circumstances, including egregiousness of the conduct, lack of cooperation, and obstruction;
- information about victims and harm caused by the defendant;
- evidence regarding additional relevant conduct not charged at trial that can be considered for sentencing;
- calculations to support volume of commerce, including sales and revenue information and expert reports;
- *Sentencing Guidelines* calculation and any basis for departure; and/or
- requests for post-sentencing reporting, monitoring, and compliance programs.

2. Sentencing Hearing

Although not as formal as trial proceedings, federal sentencing hearings can be contested proceedings. At sentencing, the court considers not only the *Sentencing Guidelines* range, but also evidence and the presentencing submissions that relate to the factors set forth under 18 U.S.C. § 3553. The Section 3553 factors govern the imposition of a federal criminal sentence and include, among others:

- the nature and circumstances of the offense and the history and characteristics of the defendant;
- the need for the sentence imposed to reflect the seriousness of the offense, to promote respect for the law, and to provide just punishment for the offense; to afford adequate deterrence to criminal conduct; and to protect the public from further crimes of the defendant;
- the need to provide the defendant with needed educational or vocational training, medical care, or other correctional treatment in the most effective manner;
- the kinds of sentences available;
- the kinds of sentences and the sentencing range established by the *Sentencing Guidelines*;
- pertinent policy statements of the Sentencing Commission;
- the need to avoid unwarranted sentence disparities among defendants with similar records who have been found guilty of similar conduct; and

- the need to provide restitution to any victims of the offense.[108]

A federal court must allow the defendant and counsel for both parties—and, in appropriate cases, victims—to provide input before a sentence is imposed. The court may allow the parties to call witnesses and present evidence about mitigating or aggravating factors. It is common, in particular, in individual cases for the defendants to call witnesses that can attest to character, community service, and other mitigating factors. The government may also seek to call victim witnesses. Neither the Federal Rules of Evidence nor constitutional provisions related to evidentiary matters apply at sentencing, and the court may consider hearsay and other evidence that would not be admissible at any jury trial. The standard of proof suggested in the *Sentencing Guidelines* is a preponderance of evidence standard.[109]

For a sentence to be sustained on appeal, the court must outline on the record its findings with regard to the appropriate *Sentencing Guidelines* range and any basis for upward or downward departures from the *Sentencing Guidelines* range. Federal Rule of Criminal Procedure 32 also requires that the court make findings on the record as to any matters in dispute at the time of sentencing. Although presentence notice is not required, if the court sentences the defendant within the *Sentencing Guidelines* range, sufficient presentence notice is required to be given to the parties in the event of a departure that is outside of the *Sentencing Guidelines* range. For prosecutors and defense counsel, it is useful to prepare a checklist for sentencing that allows the parties to perceive if any required element of the sentencing has not been stated on the record.

3. Procedures for Release Pending Appeal

For individuals, it is typical that a defendant will be remanded into custody of the Bureau of Prisons at the time of sentencing, unless the defendant has been granted release status pending any appeal of the conviction. Under the Bail Reform Act of 1984,[110] a defendant who has been sentenced and awaits a determination on his appeal may be released if a court finds:

---

108. *See id.*
109. *SENTENCING GUIDELINES, supra* note 11, § 6A1.3 cmt.
110. *See* 18 U.S.C § 3143(b)(1).

(A) by clear and convincing evidence that the person is not likely to flee or pose a danger to the safety of any other person or the community if released under section 3142(b) or (c) of this title; and

(B) that the appeal is not for the purpose of delay and raises a substantial question of law or fact likely to result in—

(i) reversal,

(ii) an order for a new trial,

(iii) a sentence that does not include a term of imprisonment, or

(iv) a reduced sentence to a term of imprisonment less than the total of the time already served plus the expected duration of the appeal process.

The Antitrust Division is not required to consent to a motion seeking release pending appeal and has tended to oppose such motions in the absence of unique circumstances.

CHAPTER VIII

COMPLIANCE

A. Introduction

Antitrust compliance has become increasingly important as the risks of cartel conduct, including the punishments doled out by authorities both in the United States and in an increasing number of jurisdictions abroad, have never been higher. A truly effective compliance program should not only prevent cartels to begin with, but it should also limit conduct, which, even if not illegal, may expose a company to suspicion of cartel behavior, which itself comes at a significant cost. This chapter discusses ways in which companies can avoid or limit antitrust liability through effective corporate compliance programs and policies.

B. Compliance Programs

Companies involved in cartel activity must move quickly to assess their antitrust compliance programs in order to avoid the potential consequences of having poor programs. Companies that undertake extraordinary efforts to implement new, or strengthen existing, compliance programs after coming under investigation may qualify for reduced fines in the United States and elsewhere.[1] The U.S. Department

---

1. *See, e.g.*, U.S. Sentencing Memo. & Mot. for a Downward Departure at 8, United States v. Kayaba Indus. Co., LTD d/b/a KYB Corp., No. 15-00098 (S.D. Ohio Oct. 5, 2015), ECF No. 21 (recommending a 40 percent downward departure from the Guidelines fine range in part because the company had developed and implemented a "comprehensive and innovative compliance policy"); Plea Agreement ¶ 13, United States v. Barclays PLC, No. 15-00077 (D. Conn. May 20, 2015), ECF No. 6. Other jurisdictions offering fine reductions for compliance efforts include the United Kingdom, France, Canada, and Brazil. *See* OFFICE OF FAIR TRADING, OFT'S GUIDANCE AS TO THE APPROPRIATE AMOUNT OF A PENALTY (Sept. 2012), *available at* www.gov.uk/government/uploads/system/uploads/attachment_data/file/2 84393/oft423.pdf; Autorité de la Concurrence, Framework Document of

of Justice (DOJ) will recommend a sentencing reduction where a company demonstrates its extraordinary efforts to bring about a top-to-bottom change in the corporate culture that allowed the cartel offense to occur.[2] In addition, a company that strengthens an ineffective program can avoid a sentence of probation and monitorship. Compliance programs that merely exist on paper are not sufficient.

Certain industries can be considered "high risk" for cartel behavior and are thus more likely to be subject to antitrust scrutiny. Industries in which there are few market players, high barriers to entry, a declining market, and standardized products are more prone to cartel activity.[3] Industries in which enforcers have focused in recent years—such as the banking sector—are also likely to see continued investigations. Organizations operating in these industries should consider affirmatively evaluating their antitrust compliance programs to determine whether they require updating. Similarly, companies that have previously been involved in cartel activity may face an increased chance of further investigation.

---

10 February 2012 on Antitrust Compliance Programmes, *available at* www.autoritedelaconcurrence.fr/ doc/framework_document_compliance_10february2012.pdf; Competition Bureau, Corporate Compliance Programs (June 3, 2015), *available at* www.competitionbureau.gc.ca/eic/site/cb-bc.nsf/vwapj/cb-bulletin-corp-compliance-e.pdf/$FILE/cb-bulletin-corp-compliance-e.pdf; ADMIN. COUNCIL FOR ECON. DEF., GUIDELINES FOR COMPETITION COMPLIANCE PROGRAMS (2016), *available at* http://en.cade.gov.br/topics/publications/guidelines/compliance-guidelines-final-version.pdf.

2. Although the U.S. Sentencing Guidelines provide that a company with an "effective" compliance program can receive a lower culpability score and accompanying reduction in its fine, historically in cartel situations, the DOJ has not recommended any sentencing credit for pre-existing compliance programs. *See* U.S. SENTENCING GUIDELINES MANUAL § 8B2.1 (U.S. SENTENCING COMM'N 2018) [hereinafter *SENTENCING GUIDELINES*]. In practice, the relatively high rank of employees typically engaged in or willfully ignorant of "cartel" conduct precludes companies from qualifying for sentencing credit for existing compliance programs. Indeed, if a compliance program is truly effective, then no cartel conduct should have occurred in the first place.

3. *See, e.g.,* U.S. DEP'T OF JUSTICE, ANTITRUST DIV., PRICE FIXING, BID RIGGING, AND MARKET ALLOCATION SCHEMES: WHAT THEY ARE AND WHAT TO LOOK FOR (June 25, 2015), *available at* www.justice.gov/atr/price-fixing-bid-rigging-and-market-allocation-schemes.

Other high risk factors include regular trade association meetings, industry events, or joint ventures and similar arrangements that provide opportunities for competitors to meet, so companies that participate in such events regularly should be especially vigilant.[4] Antitrust compliance programs should be re-evaluated and reinvigorated on a regular basis, and especially if they have been operating for some time without direct involvement or review by senior management or the board of directors.

1. Key Components of Effective Antitrust Compliance Programs

There is no one-size-fits-all compliance program. To design an effective program, a company should tailor a program's features to its specific circumstances and antitrust risks after reviewing its own business practices and considering the market(s) in which it operates. Nonetheless, certain standards are widely recognized as best practices of effective antitrust compliance programs.[5] These include:

- Top-down commitment shown through active involvement of senior officials;
- Robust training for employees;
- Regular monitoring and auditing;
- Opportunities for anonymous reporting and protection for whistleblowers; and

---

4. *See, e.g.*, Matthew J. Bester & Creighton J. Macy, *Keys to Compliance—Practical Antitrust Issues Involving Trade Associations*, AM. ASS'N (Nov. 5, 2015), *available at* http://apps.americanbar.org/litigation/committees/corporate/articles/fall2015-1115-keys-compliance-practical-antitrust-issues-involving-trade-associations.html.

5. *See, e.g.*, ABA SECTION OF ANTITRUST LAW, ANTITRUST COMPLIANCE: PERSPECTIVES AND RESOURCES FOR CORPORATE COUNSELORS 161-171 (2d ed. 2010) [hereinafter RESOURCES FOR CORPORATE COUNSELORS]. *See also, e.g.*, SENTENCING GUIDELINES, *supra* note 2, § 8B21(b); U.S. DEP'T OF JUSTICE, JUSTICE MANUAL § 9-28.800 (2018), *available at* https://www.justice.gov/jm/jm-9-28000-principles-federal-prosecution-business-organizations#9-28.800; U.S. Sentencing Memo. & Mot. for a Downward Departure at 7, United States v. Kayaba Indus. Co., LTD d/b/a KYB Corp., No. 15-00098 (S.D. Ohio Oct. 5, 2015), ECF No. 21; INT'L CHAMBER OF COMMERCE, THE ICC ANTITRUST COMPLIANCE TOOLKIT (2013) [hereinafter ICC COMPLIANCE TOOLKIT], *available at* https://cdn.iccwbo.org/content/uploads/sites/3/2013/04/ICC-Antitrust-Compliance-Toolkit-ENGLISH.pdf.

- Discipline of employees who violate law or policy, and incentives for employees to comply.

a.   Top-down Commitment to Compliance

A successful antitrust compliance program requires participation and oversight from senior officials. To be truly effective, compliance should be part of a corporation's culture, and a culture of compliance is much more likely to permeate an organization if a company's top leadership demonstrates its commitment to antitrust compliance.[6]

Executives and the board of directors should support compliance efforts and fully engage with the program. This requires that the corporate board be knowledgeable about the program, its implementation and effectiveness. Senior management should also be completely knowledgeable about the program and should be given the necessary resources, including enough support staff, to monitor the program actively. Moreover, senior management should themselves adopt a culture of compliance in specific business divisions and should actively foster a commitment to compliance.

One way in which a company can demonstrate its "top down" dedication to antitrust compliance is by assigning responsibility for and oversight of its antitrust compliance program to a high-level executive who is both highly visible and respected throughout the organization. This individual should be empowered to act independently and granted the authority and resources necessary to implement and enforce a program throughout the company. He or she should regularly report on compliance matters to the board of directors and should also participate in senior management decisions potentially implicating antitrust compliance.

b.   Training and Education for Employees

All executives and managers of custodians, as well as most employees, should receive education in antitrust compliance to educate individuals about the line between permissible and prohibited conduct. Companies should provide antitrust compliance training for subsidiaries, distributors, agents, and contractors worldwide as well. New employees should receive

---

6.   *See* Brent Snyder, Compliance is a Culture, Not Just a Policy, Remarks Before the International Chamber of Commerce/United States Council of International Business Joint Antitrust Compliance Workshop (Sept. 9, 2014) [hereinafter Snyder, Compliance is a Culture], *available at* www.justice.gov/atr/file/517796/download.

antitrust training as part of their orientation, and sessions should be conducted and materials presented in the languages that the employees speak.

Ideally, the first training an employee receives will be conducted in-person (i.e., in a classroom setting) and thereafter annual reminders can be done individually through e-learning courses.[7] A company can measure the effectiveness of the training by testing employees' knowledge of the relevant law and policy both before and after training sessions. Employees should be required to successfully paraphrase content to demonstrate their understanding of the material presented.

Sessions should be specific to the industry and jurisdiction and tailored to the situations that employees are most likely to encounter. Training should identify examples of prohibited and permitted practices through case studies and should make use of role play to enable employees to practice responding to various risky situations. Training is particularly important for employees in positions that entail a higher risk of antitrust violations, including those with responsibility for sales or pricing and those who attend trade or industry association meetings or have other opportunities to communicate with competitors. A company may consider implementing one-on-one training for these high-risk personnel.[8]

Training should be conducted by or with the participation of local in-house counsel. Senior personnel should participate in training sessions for lower-level staff in order to demonstrate the importance of the training and the company's commitment to the compliance program.

c.   Proactive Monitoring and Regular Internal Audits

Risky activities must be regularly monitored and audited. Companies may require that certain high-risk employees fill out questionnaires regarding their contacts with competitors or attend brief interviews with in-house or outside counsel regarding potential antitrust risks. In addition, the company should review business practices that may unwittingly foster anti-competitive behavior by tying revenue or compensation to results that the company would have difficulty achieving unilaterally, or that reward improper coordination with competitors. Employees working in performance-driven corporate cultures may be more susceptible to

---

7.   For a discussion regarding best practices in training, see RESOURCES FOR CORPORATE COUNSELORS, *supra* note 5, at 79-86, 89-113.

8.   *See, e.g.,* U.S. Sentencing Memo. & Mot. for a Downward Departure at 7, United States v. Kayaba Indus. Co., LTD d/b/a KYB Corp., No. 15-00098 (S.D. Ohio Oct. 5, 2015), ECF No. 21.

collusion, where, for example, promotions or bonuses are based on relative performance but demand is declining. Similarly, a message from senior management that targets must be met by any means possible may incentivize anti-competitive conduct.

In addition to prohibitions, it is helpful for global antitrust compliance policies to contain affirmative mandates for independent decision-making. For example, policies may require that salespeople certify that prices were independently determined and that they did not exchange information with competitors when deciding prices.[9]

Some companies have also implemented systems whereby employees who will be in contact with competitors must first seek and obtain approval from the legal department. For example, prior approval may be a prerequisite to attend trade shows or industry meetings, vendor conferences, social events, or meetings to discuss joint ventures. Where contact with competitors has been authorized, or competitive information has been collected regarding competitors (e.g., from trade associations), and the contacts are not memorialized in formal minutes, a brief report should be made regarding such contacts, including the time, place, parties involved, and information collected. Such records serve to confirm that any such contacts and information were authorized and conducted pursuant to antitrust compliance guidelines. Both the prior approval requests and the reports of competitor meetings should be regularly audited by in-house counsel.

A necessary part of an effective compliance program includes regular internal audits.[10] There are two types of audits—program audits and substantive legal assessments. A compliance program audit examines whether an organization has implemented best practices or procedures to monitor actual or potential compliance violations and take action should any violation be identified. Reports by a company's internal or external auditors may be useful sources of information about the operation of the company's antitrust compliance program.

The goal of a substantive legal assessment is to determine whether any violation has, in fact, occurred. A company may choose to take a "deep dive" into the most potentially problematic areas, such as sales, marketing, or business planning. The focus should be on the highest risk businesses and regions.

There are various options for proactively detecting potential violations of antitrust law. Generally speaking, audits should not be pre-announced.

---

9. *Id.*
10. *See, e.g.,* ICC COMPLIANCE TOOLKIT, *supra note 5,* at 52.

They may be conducted as mock dawn raids. They should include document reviews of both paper and electronic files, as well as interviews. Audits should be conducted by in-house or outside counsel, as opposed to an internal or external auditor, in such a way as to protect legal privilege to the greatest extent possible.[11] Note that exact approaches may vary depending on the applicable privacy or privilege laws, so companies operating in counties outside the U.S. should pay particular attention to those local rules.[12]

d.   Anonymous Reporting and Protection for Whistleblowers

Companies should implement anonymous—or at least confidential—reporting mechanisms to allow employees to register complaints or report on conduct that may violate the corporate antitrust compliance policy. This is particularly important so that lower-level employees who may feel they have been ordered by a superior to engage in risky behavior, or have witnessed such behavior by a superior, have a safe outlet for reporting it. For example, a larger company may choose to create an anonymous hotline for employees to call if they suspect a violation has occurred.[13] While hotlines may not be practical for smaller organizations, all companies should have internal systems in place for employees to seek confidential guidance about potential criminal behavior or to report misconduct without fear of reprisal.

These types of programs encourage employees to take ownership of the company's compliance and ethics by self-monitoring and reporting. They also incentivize compliance at all levels of an organization because every employee becomes a potential whistleblower.

Companies should also consider implementing appropriate non-retaliation protections for whistleblowers who report potential violations. Some jurisdictions have passed specific legislation protecting antitrust whistleblowers from retaliation. For example, the Canadian Competition

---

11.   For a discussion of global privilege concerns in internal audits, *see* RESOURCES FOR CORPORATE COUNSELORS, *supra* note 5, at 170.

12.   In Europe, for example, certain data privacy and labor laws impose limitations on companies' abilities to search their employees' documents. *See* RESOURCES FOR CORPORATE COUNSELORS, *supra* note 5, at 171.

13.   Note that certain European privacy protection laws may be implicated by anonymous reporting programs, thus any such programs that will operate in Europe will need to be carefully designed to avoid running afoul of these regimes. *See* RESOURCES FOR CORPORATE COUNSELORS, *supra* note 5, at 168-69.

Act prohibits dismissal, suspension or other types of discipline against employees for their disclosure of antitrust misconduct or their refusal to engage in prohibited conduct. [14] The United Kingdom has similar whistleblower legislation.[15] In the United States, a bill to offer antitrust whistleblower protection nationally has passed the U.S. Senate by unanimous consent and has been received in the House of Representatives. [16] Companies can encourage employees to report potential misconduct without fear of reprisal by implementing similar protections and explaining to employees that they will not be disciplined for coming forward.

However, there may be situations where truly culpable employees who willfully violate company policy or antitrust law then seek to avoid discipline by disclosing their wrongdoing. For example, whistleblower protections may not apply to employees who initiated the conduct they then later disclose.[17] Such employees should not be punished for reporting the behavior that violated the company's compliance policy, but they may be punished for the behavior itself.

e.   Discipline for Employees Who Violate Company Policy or Law and Incentives to Comply

The DOJ Antitrust Division (Antitrust Division) has not as a matter of departmental policy inserted itself into the personnel decisions of companies by requiring that culpable employees be dismissed. However, the Antitrust Division has publicly advocated for disciplinary action against employees who have personally violated U.S. antitrust laws.[18] In particular, if a company is unwilling to remove culpable employees from

---

14.   Competition Act, R.S.C. 1985, c. C-34, s. 66.2 (Can.).

15.   Public Interest Disclosure Act 1998, c. 23, § 2 (Eng.).

16.   Criminal Antitrust Anti-Retaliation Act of 2017, S. 807, 115th Cong. (2017).

17.   *Id.* § 216(a)(2)(A).

18.   *See, e.g.*, William Baer, Prosecuting Antitrust Crimes, Remarks Before the Georgetown University Law Center Global Antitrust Enforcement Symposium 8 (Sept. 10, 2014) [hereinafter Baer, Prosecuting Antitrust Crimes], *available at* www.justice.gov/atr/file/517741/download ("It is hard to imagine how companies can foster a corporate culture of compliance if they still employ individuals in positions with senior management and pricing responsibilities who have refused to accept responsibility for their crimes and who the companies know to be culpable.").

positions of authority where they may be able to influence subordinates who might be called to testify against them or from positions, such as sales positions, where they can continue to engage in suspect conduct, the DOJ may view that as a sign that the company is not truly committed to antitrust compliance.[19] Discipline of culpable individuals is increasingly important as the DOJ continues to intensify its focus on individual accountability for antitrust crimes.[20]

Accordingly, penalties should be implemented for non-compliance with the company's policy. Willful non-compliance should result in a strong penalty such as compensation reduction, loss of opportunity for promotion, or even suspension or dismissal where appropriate. Senior employees must be held accountable for the actions of their subordinates.

In addition, compliance should be incentivized, and managers and employees who comply with the company's antitrust policy appropriately rewarded. Legal compliance should be an element of the evaluation process for advancement within the company.

The need for confidentiality must be properly balanced against the need to fully document disciplinary actions and procedures. In-house or outside counsel should be involved in any decisions about whom to discipline as well as all communications with employees regarding disciplinary action. Moreover, as documentation regarding discipline may ultimately be discoverable in civil actions, such documentation should refer to disciplinary action taken for violations of company policy, as opposed to violations of antitrust law.

2. Written Elements of a Corporate Antitrust Compliance Program

A corporate antitrust compliance program typically consists of a code of conduct, policy manual, and easy-to-follow guidelines. A code of conduct should articulate an organization's values and principles, and act as a tool to encourage discussion of ethics and compliance and assist employees in dealing with ethical dilemmas they may face.[21] The code of

---

19. *Id.*; Snyder, Compliance is a Culture, *supra* note 6, at 7.
20. *See* Brent Snyder, Individual Accountability for Antitrust Crimes, Remarks Before the Yale School of Management Global Antitrust Enforcement Conference 2-4 (Feb. 19, 2016), *available at* www.justice.gov/opa/file/826721/download; Memorandum from Sally Quillian Yates, Deputy Att'y Gen., U.S. Dep't of Justice, to Assistant Att'y Gen., Antitrust Div., et al. (Sept. 9, 2015), *available at* www.justice.gov/dag/file/769036/download.
21. For a model code of conduct, *see* RESOURCES FOR CORPORATE COUNSELORS, *supra* note 5, at 269.

conduct should include antitrust principles, and employees should be required to affirmatively certify their compliance with the code of conduct, including the antitrust provisions.

Companies should also implement a standalone antitrust policy which lists the key rules to follow and the key requirements of the antitrust compliance program. [22] Any global antitrust compliance policy should articulate a zero-tolerance approach to conduct that violates the antitrust laws of any country in which the company does business. It should also prohibit both express and tacit agreements, understandings, or arrangements with competitors concerning prices or other matters of competitive significance unless expressly addressed in the policy or approved by the legal department and any necessary authorities. For companies operating in jurisdictions where even information exchanges with competitors are illegal (e.g., in Europe), those types of exchanges should also be prohibited. Companies should also consider prohibiting conduct which could give rise to the appearance of an antitrust violation even if such conduct is not clearly unlawful.

Any antitrust policy should explain the processes to follow to ensure that any legitimate competitor contacts are clearly evidenced as such. It should also describe the steps to take when seeking guidance as to whether particular conduct raises potential antitrust concerns. Finally, companies should provide an antitrust compliance manual which presents user-friendly guidelines for employees to reference for advice about how to handle specific situations and what to do in other situations not specifically addressed in the manual. [23]

3. *Privilege*

Preserving the attorney-client privilege with respect to compliance materials is important and requires taking certain proactive steps. [24] Different jurisdictions have different laws regarding attorney-client privilege and the degree to which it applies to communications between a

---

22. For a model policy, *see id.* at 257.
23. For a model manual, *see id.* at 235.
24. For strategies on protecting in-house confidential communications from disclosure, *see* RESOURCES FOR CORPORATE COUNSELORS, *supra* note 5, at 121 (discussing developing preambles; ensuring knowledge of privilege rules in each jurisdiction; avoiding mixed business and legal advice; hiring local outside counsel in foreign jurisdictions; and avoiding blanket privilege legends).

corporation and its in-house legal staff. Thus, companies need to consider privilege rules on a jurisdiction-specific basis.

Under U.S. law, unless accompanied by a fact-based discussion, privilege will generally not attach to a company's antitrust compliance policy—or to mere recitations of antitrust law.[25] Indeed, some companies choose to publish their compliance policy online to show their commitment to compliance. U.S. courts are more likely to consider antitrust compliance policy and training materials to be protected from discovery by the attorney-client privilege, however, if they apply antitrust law to the client's specific business circumstances or practices.[26] Distribution of otherwise privileged materials to corporate employees does not necessarily undermine privilege, but the dissemination of materials to many hundreds of employees may make it more difficult to assert privilege.[27]

---

25. *See In re* Domestic Drywall Antitrust Litig., 2014 WL 5090032, at *1 (E.D. Pa. 2014); *see also* Hartford Life Ins. Co. v. Bank of Am. Corp., 2007 WL 2398824, at *6 (S.D.N.Y. 2007) (finding company's compliance training slide show was not privileged as it "contain[ed] only generic descriptions of the law" and did not "apply any of these generalized legal principals to specific factual situations").

26. *Compare In re* Brand Name Prescription Drugs Antitrust Litig., 1996 WL 5180, at *2 (N.D. Ill. 1996) (holding attorney-client privilege extended to company's antitrust compliance presentation prepared by in-house counsel where it "describ[ed] the application of the antitrust laws to specific aspects of [defendant]'s business . . . provide[d] legal advice and reveal[ed] client confidences regarding certain of [defendant]'s business practices") *with In re* Sulfuric Acid Antitrust Litig., 432 F. Supp. 2d 794, 796-97 (N.D. Ill. 2006) (finding that a series of hypothetical questions and "Quick Reference Guidelines" contained in antitrust compliance materials distributed to sales employees were not protected by attorney-client privilege because manuals were "instructional devices, not responses to requests for legal advice").

27. *See, e.g., In re* Currency Conversion, 2010 WL 4365548, at *4 (S.D.N.Y. 2010) (holding that otherwise privileged communication will "not lose [its] privileged status when shared among corporate employees who share responsibility for the subject matter of the communication"). *But see In re* Domestic Drywall Antitrust Litig., 2014 WL 5090032, at *1 (E.D. Pa. 2014) (declining to extend privilege to policy that company distributed "widely within its organization, including to more than 120 employees who attended a training session").

Companies should consider implementing practices to protect compliance-related communications from discovery by regulators and private litigants under the attorney-client privilege, including:

- Requests for advice about the compliance policy or reports pursuant to anonymous hotlines or similar programs for whistleblowers should be made to in-house lawyers;
- Compliance-related documents should be properly labeled as confidential and privileged as appropriate, but blanket privilege labels should be avoided;
- In-house lawyers and/or outside counsel should be involved in training sessions that discuss company-specific scenarios;
- The involvement of business people in conducting internal audits should be limited to simple fact-gathering as necessary;
- Outside counsel should be consulted when potentially questionable conduct is discovered;
- In-house lawyers and/or outside counsel should be involved in all discussions and decisions regarding employee discipline (i.e., such decisions and their implementation should not be left to human resources departments to handle alone); and
- Jurisdiction-specific privilege rules should be reviewed and conduct tailored accordingly depending on the areas of operations.

4. Importance of an Effective Antitrust Compliance Program

Creating or enhancing an existing antitrust compliance program will require resources—both money and time. But the need to have an effective antitrust compliance policy is particularly clear against the backdrop of record fines and prison sentences. For example, in fiscal year 2015, the Antitrust Division opened sixty criminal cases and obtained $3.6 billion in criminal fines relating to criminal antitrust conduct.[28] The average prison term for individuals convicted in the United States was nineteen months between fiscal year 2010 and fiscal year 2018.[29] While there are up-front costs to planning and implementing the program, the rewards (and potential savings) of doing so cannot be overstated. Indeed, an effective program can go a long way to preventing, or at least mitigating, the severe

---

28. *See* U.S. Dep't of Justice, Antitrust Div., Criminal Enforcement Trends Charts Through Fiscal Year 2018 (Jan. 28, 2019), *available at* www.justice.gov/atr/criminal-enforcement-fine-and-jail-charts.
29. *Id.*

financial penalties and reputational harm that may arise from violations of antitrust law. Companies that fail to take steps to create or improve their antitrust compliance programs may find themselves faced with an independent corporate monitor tasked with improving, creating, and/or implementing a program for them.

C. Antitrust Corporate Monitorships

When a company has been convicted of a criminal antitrust offense, courts are authorized to impose a term of probation between one to five years in addition to monetary fines or restitution.[30] The *U.S. Sentencing Guidelines* requires that a term of probation be imposed if, among other circumstances, (1) an organization "has 50 or more employees, or was . . . was otherwise required under law to have an effective compliance and ethics program; and . . . does not have such a program" or (2) probation "is necessary to ensure that changes are made within the organization to reduce the likelihood of future criminal conduct."[31] As part of probation, a court may require a company to hire, at its own expense, an independent monitor to review the company's compliance program and to ensure that an effective compliance program is developed and implemented.

Similarly, pursuant to their inherent authority and Rule 53 of the Federal Rules of Civil Procedure, courts in civil cases may, as part of a remedial order requiring the adoption of an effective antitrust compliance policy, appoint an external monitor to review and evaluate changes to the policy and training programs to ensure compliance and prevent future antitrust violations.[32]

---

30. 18 U.S.C. § 3561(c).
31. *SENTENCING GUIDELINES*, *supra* note 2, § 8D1.1(a)(3), (6).
32. *In re* Peterson, 253 U.S. 300, 312 (1920) ("Courts have . . . inherent power to provide themselves with appropriate instruments required for the performance of their duties" including the "authority to appoint persons unconnected with the court to aid judges in the performance of specific judicial duties."); Powell v. Ward, 487 F. Supp. 917, 935 (S.D.N.Y. 1980), *aff'd and modified*, 643 F.2d 924 (2d Cir. 1981) ("Courts have inherent authority to appoint nonjudicial officers to aid in carrying out their judicial functions. In addition, Rule 53 . . . establishes a statutory basis for the appointment of a master."); United States v. Apple, Inc., 2013 WL 4774755, at *6 (S.D.N.Y. 2013), *aff'd*, 791 F.3d 290 (2d Cir. 2015) (injunction requiring Apple to adopt policies and training to promote compliance with the antitrust laws and appointing monitor "to review and evaluate" Apple's adoption of the required policies and training).

In the context of criminal antitrust prosecutions, the Antitrust Division generally has not sought to appoint a monitor as part of a convicted company's probation. However, in policy speeches by former Antitrust Division officials, the Government has stated that it will seek the appointment of compliance monitors in "the most egregious cases" where a convicted company does not have an effective internal compliance program.[33] Specifically, the Government has explained that a company's compliance culture may be deemed lacking if the company continues to employ culpable individuals "in positions of substantial authority; or in positions where they can continue to engage directly or indirectly in collusive conduct; or in positions where they supervise the company's compliance and remediation programs; or in positions where they supervise individuals who would be witnesses against them."[34] In these situations, the Antitrust Division may "insist on probation, including the use of monitors, if doing so is necessary to ensure an effective compliance program and to prevent recidivism."[35]

1. Purpose of Corporate Monitorships

The Antitrust Division has explained that court-supervised probation, including the use of corporate monitors, is a "means of assuring that [a] company devises and implements an effective compliance program."[36]

In *United States v. AU Optronics Corp.*, which is discussed in more detail below, the Government recommended that the defendant be required to hire a compliance monitor, explaining that the monitor's primary purpose was "to review [the defendant's] current compliance program and to ensure that [the defendant] develops a program containing the recommend elements" of an effective compliance program.[37] The court agreed with the Government's recommendation and appointed a monitor

---

33.   Snyder, Compliance is a Culture, *supra* note 6, at 9 ("[A]ctive refusal to accept responsibility, including resisting effective compliance, will result in probation and independent monitors." *Id.* at 11.); Baer, Prosecuting Antitrust Crimes, *supra* note 18, at 8.

34.   Baer, Prosecuting Antitrust Crimes, *supra* note 18, at 8.

35.   *Id.*

36.   *Id.*

37.   United States' Sentencing Memorandum at 54, United States v. AU Optronics Corp., No. 09-00110 SI (N.D. Cal. Sept. 11, 2012), ECF No. 948.

to provide quarterly reports regarding the defendant's antitrust compliance.[38]

Although in the civil context, an external compliance monitor also was appointed in *United States v. Apple, Inc.*, and the explanations in that case are instructive.[39] As part of an injunction issued after finding Apple in violation of Section 1, the court ordered Apple to adopt antitrust policies and training programs to promote compliance with the laws and appointed a monitor for two years to "to review and evaluate" Apple's adoption of the required policies and training.[40] In his initial report, the monitor further explained that his role was to provide an "assessment of Apple's internal compliance policies, procedures, and training and, if appropriate, mak[e] recommendations reasonably designed to improve Apple's policies, procedures, and training for ensuring antitrust compliance."[41] However, commentators have also noted that monitors must "balance efforts to prevent the repeat of corporate crime in a way that does not prevent pro-competitive corporate behavior."[42]

2. United States v. AU Optronics Corp.

The only criminal case to date in which the Antitrust Division has sought the appointment of a compliance monitor was in connection with its prosecution of AU Optronics Corp. (AUO). In *United States v. AU Optronics Corp.*, after an eight-week trial, AUO, its subsidiary, and several executives were found guilty of conspiring to fix prices for thin-film transistor liquid crystal display panels.[43] At sentencing, in addition to

---

38. Judgment in a Criminal Case at 3, United States v. AU Optronics Corp., No. 09-00110 SI (N.D. Cal. Oct. 1, 2012), ECF No. 976.

39. Final Judgment and Order Entering Permanent Injunction at 10-14, United States v. Apple, Inc., No. 12-2826 (S.D.N.Y. Sept. 5, 2013), ECF No. 374. *See also* United States v. Apple Inc., 992 F. Supp. 2d 263, 280-81 (S.D.N.Y. 2014) (holding that the appointment of an external compliance monitor was a "permissible exercise of judicial power"), *aff'd*, 787 F.3d 131 (2d Cir. 2015).

40. Final Judgment and Order Entering Permanent Injunction, supra note 39, at 11.

41. Report of the External Compliance Monitor at i, United States v. Apple, Inc., No. 12- 2826 (S.D.N.Y. Apr. 14, 2014), ECF No. 462.

42. D. Daniel Sokol, *Policing the Firm*, 89 NOTRE DAME L. REV. 785, 843 (2013).

43. *See* Special Verdict Form, United States v. AU Optronics Corp., No. 09-00110 SI (N.D. Cal. Mar. 13, 2012), ECF No. 851; Press Release, U.S.

a $500 million fine, the court ordered a three-year probation term.[44] As part of its probation, AUO was required to (1) "develop, adopt, and implement an effective compliance and ethics program;" (2) publicly "acknowledge the fact of conviction, the nature of the punishment imposed, and the steps that will be taken to prevent the recurrence of similar offenses" in major trade publications; and (3) "hire, at [its] own expense, an independent monitor" within 60 days of sentencing.[45]

The two primary reasons the Antitrust Division used to justify its request for the appointment of a monitor were that: (1) "[w]hile all of AUO's corporate co-conspirators recognized that their conspiracy was illegal and accepted responsibility for their participation in that scheme, AUO refused even to acknowledge that its participation in the same agreement was, or should be considered, illegal;" and (2) "AUO continued to employ convicted price fixers and indicted fugitives."[46] Accordingly, at sentencing, the Antitrust Division argued that there was "no reason to assume that its conviction and the imposition of a criminal fine, alone, [would] cause AUO to cease engaging in collusive practices."[47] Under these circumstances, the Antitrust Division argued that because "AUO cannot be expected to develop and implement and effective compliance program" on its own, it was necessary for the court to appoint a compliance monitor to ensure that AUO did so.[48]

In connection with its request for a monitor, the Antitrust Division provided some specific guidance for the company and the monitor as to the minimum elements that would be required of AUO's antitrust

---

Dep't of Justice, Taiwan-Based AU Optronics Corporation, Its Houston-Based Subsidiary and Former Top Executives Convicted for Role in LCD Price-Fixing Conspiracy (Mar. 13, 2012), *available at* www.justice.gov/opa/pr/ taiwan-based-au-optronics-corporation-its-houston-based-subsidiary-and-former-top-executives.

44. Judgment in a Criminal Case at 2, 4, United States v. AU Optronics Corp., No. 09-00110 SI (N.D. Cal. Oct. 1, 2012), ECF No. 976; Press Release, U.S. Dep't of Justice, Taiwan-Based AU Optronics Corporation Sentenced to Pay $500 Million Criminal Fine for Role in LCD Price-Fixing Conspiracy (Sept. 20, 2012), *available at* https://www.justice.gov/opa/pr/taiwan-based-au-optronics-corporation-sentenced-pay-500-million-criminal-fine-role-lcd-price.

45. Judgment in a Criminal Case, supra note 44, at 3.

46. Baer, Prosecuting Antitrust Crimes, *supra* note 18, at 8-9.

47. United States' Sentencing Memorandum at 53, United States v. AU Optronics, No. 09-00110 SI (N.D. Cal. Sept. 11, 2012), ECF No. 948.

48. *Id.* at 54.

compliance program for the Government to consider it effective. Specifically, the Antitrust Division proposed requiring the following measures:

- The assignment of one or more senior corporate officials . . . report[ing] directly to the Audit Committee of the AUO Board of Directors, with responsibility for the implementation and oversight of compliance with policies and procedures established in accordance with the antitrust compliance program;
- [P]eriodic communications by senior management . . . that provide strong, explicit, and visible support and commitment to its corporate policy against violations of the antitrust laws and in support of its antitrust compliance program; and
- A reporting system administered by the senior corporate official(s) . . ., including an anonymous "Helpline" for directors, officers, employees, agents, and business partners to confidentially report suspected violations of the antitrust laws and/or the [company's] antitrust compliance code, and a procedure for investigating such reports.[49]

In addition, as part of its judgment, the court detailed the process by which the monitor would be selected. Within 30 days of sentencing, AUO was required to recommend to the U.S. Probation Office and the Antitrust Division "a pool of three qualified monitor candidates and . . . a description of each candidate's qualifications and credentials."[50] After consulting with the Antitrust Division, the Probation Office had "sole discretion" to select one of the candidates proposed by AUO, select a candidate of its own choosing, or instruct AUO to provide three additional candidates for consideration.[51] Once selected the monitor would provide

---

49. Declaration of Heather S. Tewksbury in Support of United States' Sentencing Memorandum, Ex. C at 2-3, United States v. AU Optronics Corp., No. 09-00110 SI (N.D. Cal. Sept. 11, 2012), ECF No. 948-3.

50. Judgment in a Criminal Case, supra note 44, at 3. The Office of Probation and Pretrial Services is part of the Administrative Office of the United States Courts and the Probation Offices in individual district courts administer probation and supervised release as provided under federal law. *See* 18 U.S.C. §§ 3601-03.

51. Judgment, United States v. AU Optronics Corp., No. 09-00110 (N.D. Cal. Oct. 1, 2012). The Judgment also provided that monitor would be an employee of AUO, but could not hold any prior interest or relationship with AUO. *Id.*

quarterly reports to the Probation Office.[52] *AU Optronics* is the only example to date of the Antitrust Division requesting a monitor in the criminal context.[53]

3.   *Corporate Monitors in FCPA Prosecutions*

While monitors have been rare in the antitrust context, the DOJ Criminal Division's use of corporate monitors is increasingly common in prosecutions of other white-collar crimes, including violations of the Foreign Corrupt Practices Act (FCPA).[54]

The FCPA prohibits bribery of foreign officials and requires that publicly traded companies maintain accurate accounting controls to facilitate detection of potentially illegal payments.[55] As the Criminal Division has stepped-up its enforcement of the FCPA over the past 10 years, it has "increased the use of corporate monitors as a remedy in FCPA cases."[56] The increased use of monitors also corresponds to the broader trend of resolving FCPA violations through non-prosecution and deferred prosecution agreements.[57]

The DOJ Criminal Division has provided some guidance with respect to the use of monitors in connection with FCPA settlements that may be instructive in the criminal cartel context. Specifically, in 2012 the Criminal Division published *A Resource Guide to the U.S. Foreign Corrupt Practices Act*, which explains that "[a]ppointment of a monitor is not appropriate in all circumstances, but it may be appropriate, for example, where a company does not already have an effective internal compliance program or needs to establish necessary internal controls."[58] The guide

---

52.   *Id.*
53.   Snyder, Compliance is a Culture, *supra* note 6, at 10.
54.   Sokol, *supra* note 42, at 823.
55.   15 U.S.C. §§ 78dd-1.
56.   Sokol, *supra* note 42, at 825.
57.   Angela Xenakis, Aaron Johansen & Jeffrey Morrow, *The Future of FCPA Hybrid Monitorships*, LAW360 (May 15, 2014), www.law360.com/articles/538246 ("Over the last decade, the number of corporate DOJ investigations resolved through deferred prosecution agreements and nonprosecution agreements has increased from a mere two or three per year in the early 2000s to approximately 30 or more each year.").
58.   U.S. DEP'T OF JUSTICE & SEC. & EXCH. COMM'N, A RESOURCE GUIDE TO THE U.S. FOREIGN CORRUPT PRACTICES ACT 71 (Nov. 14, 2012), *available*

also provides a list specific of factors used to determine whether to appoint a corporate monitor:

- Seriousness of the offense;
- Duration of the misconduct;
- Pervasiveness of the misconduct, including whether the conduct cuts across geographic and/ or product lines;
- Nature and size of the company;
- Quality of the company's compliance program at the time of the misconduct; and
- Subsequent remediation efforts.[59]

Generally, where a monitor provision is included, FCPA agreements have required an appointment for at least three years. In recent years, however, it has become increasingly common for FCPA agreements to include a provision for so-called "hybrid" monitorships where the Criminal Division "requires at least 18 months of oversight from an independent monitor," and following that period, "the corporation's compliance requirements shift to self-monitoring and reporting."[60]

Through recent settlements, the Criminal Division has also provided some indication as to where it will require full-scale monitorships, hybrid monitorships, or no monitoring requirements in connection with respect to FCPA agreements. Specifically, the Criminal Division has required full-scale monitorships where the FCPA violation was relatively severe and there is no indication that a company has been cooperative or taken steps to remediate the conduct.[61] However, where the companies provide substantial cooperation, but their conduct was severe or the cooperation was delayed or otherwise problematic, settlements have included provisions for hybrid monitorships.[62] Finally, where there are extensive

at   www.justice.gov/sites/default/files/criminal-fraud/legacy/2015/01/16/guide.pdf.
59. *Id.*
60. Xenakis, *supra* note 57. In 2013, four of the Criminal Division's FCPA settlement agreements required independent compliance monitors and three of the four agreements provided for "hybrid" monitorships. *Id.*
61. *See, e.g.*, Deferred Prosecution Agreement, United States v. Total, SA, No. 13-00239 (E.D. Va. May 23, 2013), ECF No. 2.
62. *See, e.g.*, Deferred Prosecution Agreement, United States v. Bilfinger SE, No. 4:13-00745 (S.D Tex. Dec. 9, 2013), ECF No. 3 (cooperation came "at a late date"); Deferred Prosecution Agreement, United States of America v. Diebold, Inc., No. 5:13-00464 (N. D. Ohio Oct. 22, 2013), ECF No. 1-1

cooperation and remediation efforts by the company, and the FCPA violations are relatively minor, it is less likely there will be a need for an independent monitor.[63]

4. Corporate Monitor Grades

In rendering their reports, monitors may issue letter grades (e.g., A, B, C, D, F) for the various aspects of the compliance program the monitor has been appointed to address—such as written policy, compliance training, reporting, disciplinary actions, and executive leadership.[64] The meaning of letter grades is generally understood by those within the business, by the court, the Government, and elsewhere. Without clear grading, "there is a risk that the company and its officers may read what they want to read" in a monitor's report and "see only the positive and miss criticism and unsatisfactory progress."[65] In addition, grades assist with quickly identifying problematic areas and prioritizing the issues that need to be addressed.

(remediation efforts were "not sufficient to address and reduce the risk of recurrence"); Deferred Prosecution Agreement, United States v. Weatherford Int'l Ltd., No. 4:13-00733 (S.D. Tex. Nov. 26, 2013), ECF No. 4 (requiring monitor to ensure continued compliance with remediation efforts and cooperation with the DOJ).

63. *See, e.g.*, Letter from Eugene Miller, Assistant U.S. Att'y, & Daniel S. Kim, Trial Att'y, U.S. Dep't of Justice, to William J. Bachman & Jon R. Fetterolf, Williams & Connolly LLP (Dec. 20, 2013) *available at* https://www.justice.gov/sites/default/files/criminal-fraud/legacy/2014/01/03/adm-npa.pdf (Archer Daniels Midland Co. Non-Prosecution Agreement); Deferred Prosecution Agreement, United States v. Parker Drilling Co., No. 1:13-00176 (E.D. Va. Apr. 16, 2013), ECF No. 2; Letter from Sarah Coyne, Chief, Bus. & Sec. Fraud Section, U.S. Att'y, & Daniel S. Kim, Trial Att'y, U.S. Dep't of Justice, to Thomas A. Hanusik, Crowell & Moring LLP (Apr. 22, 2013), *available at* www.justice.gov/sites/default/files/criminal-fraud/legacy/2013/04/23/Ralph-Lauren.-NPA-Executed.pdf (Ralph Lauren Corp. Non-Prosecution Agreement).

64. Robert W. Tarun, Alternative Remedies: Corporate Monitors and U.S. Antitrust Enforcement, Remarks Before the 2014 ICN Cartel Workshop 13 (Oct. 3, 2014), *available at* http://www.ftc.gov.tw/icncartel2014/pdf/2014.10.03.%20BOS%2014%20%20%20Robert%20Tarun.pdf.

65. *Id.*

5. *Economic Impact*

A common criticism of the use of corporate monitors concerns the significant costs that are associated with the monitor's efforts.[66] The costs—in fees charged by the monitor and costs to the company in improving its company's compliance program—may add up into the tens of millions of dollars and could be even more depending on the size of a company.[67] A monitor's work will likely include a comprehensive review of the organization, interviews with employees, and an extensive review of internal and external documents and correspondence.[68]

In addition, there are costs associated with transferring certain business decisions from company officers to an independent monitor, as well as costs associated with the disruption of regular business activities as the monitor does the work required. Most monitors are former prosecutors, former judges, or current practitioners who may have limited business experience. As a result, these monitors "may not know what programs are effective to implement and may undertake compliance work that does not improve actual compliance but rather increases costs in a way that does not maximize shareholder value of the firm."[69]

The use of compliance monitors to ensure that cartel conduct is not repeated emphasizes the importance of antitrust compliance programs. Companies that fail to implement a truly effective compliance program remain exposed to the risks associated with cartel conduct and may ultimately be compelled to adopt such a program under the supervision of an independent corporate monitor.

---

66. *See, e.g.*, Steven Davidoff Solomon, *In Corporate Monitor, a Well-Paying Job But Unknown Results*, NY TIMES (Apr. 15, 2014), https://dealbook.nytimes.com/2014/04/15/in-corporate-monitor-a-well-paying-job-but-unknown-results/.
67. Sokol, *supra* note 42, at 828.
68. *Id.*
69. *Id.* at 829-30.

CHAPTER IX

CARTEL CASES UNDER NON-U.S. COMPETITION LAWS

A. Brazil

1. Competition law

a. Overview

There are several laws and regulations that address anticompetitive practices in Brazil. The main law is the Brazilian Antitrust Law,[1] which deals with antitrust violations at the administrative level in Brazil. Other laws are the Brazilian Economic Crimes Law,[2] the Brazilian Public Bidding Law,[3] and the Brazilian Clean Company Law.[4]

Article 36 of the Brazilian Antitrust Law provides that any conduct that has the potential to restrain, distort or in any way harm competition shall constitute an antitrust violation, even if any such effects are not achieved and regardless of the subjective intention of the wrongdoer. Listed among the conduct that may constitute antitrust violations are explicit or tacit agreements between competitors to fix prices or allocate markets.

b. Exemptions/Immunities

The Brazilian Antitrust Law does not provide any exemption to particular sectors or entities. To the contrary, Article 31 expressly provides that the statute "applies to individuals or legal entities of public or private law, as well as to any associations of entities or individuals, whether de facto or de jure, even temporarily, incorporated or unincorporated, even if engaged in business under the legal monopoly system."

---

1. Law No. 12,529/2011.
2. Law No. 8,137/1990.
3. Law No. 8,666/1993.
4. Law No. 12,846/2013.

c. Standard of Proof

Under the Brazilian Antitrust Law, the finding of an antitrust violation does not require evidence that the conduct at issue effectively produced negative effects in regards to competition. It is sufficient to show that the conduct has the potential of harming competition by way of, for example, excluding competitors from the market or allowing competitors to charge supracompetitive prices for their products or services. Potential effects may be shown based on the analysis of factors such as the structure of the relevant market, the market power of the alleged wrongdoers, barriers to entry, the characteristics of the product or service concerned, and price elasticity of demand, among others.

In cartel cases, it is not necessary to conduct a detailed market analysis in order to show that the conduct at issue has the potential to harm competition. This is because the harmful effects of cartels are so clear that it should not be necessary for the competition authorities to expend resources on an exhaustive inquiry into them. Cartels may be presumed to produce negative market effects, and it is up to the companies involved in the alleged practice to prove otherwise.

The Brazilian Antitrust Law does not expressly set forth the types of evidence that may be relied on to demonstrate an antitrust violation at the administrative level. This matter is governed by Law No. 13,105, dated March 16, 2015 (Brazilian Civil Procedural Code), which applies to administrative proceedings pursuant to Article 115 of the Brazilian Antitrust Law. However, precedents by the Brazilian Antitrust Authority (CADE) establish that an antitrust violation may be supported by either direct or indirect evidence, including emails, letters, minutes of meetings, depositions of witnesses, or telephone tapping. [5] Direct evidence encompasses materials that establish facts particular to the conduct under investigation, while indirect evidence means evidence of other facts from which it is possible to infer the conduct under investigation. Penalties may

---

5. *See* Administrative Proceeding No. 08012.002299/2000-18, where the convicted individuals discussed the cartel scheme over the telephone; Administrative Proceeding No. 08012.007602/2003-11 and Administrative Proceeding No. 08012.002493/2005-16, where the convicted individuals attended meetings with the purpose of fixing prices; Administrative Proceeding No. 08012.001826/2003-10, where the individuals exchanged e-mails and discussed the cartel scheme over the telephone; and Administrative Proceeding No. 08012.006019/2002-11, where the convicted individuals exchanged letters, attended meetings and discussed the cartel scheme over the telephone.

be based solely on indirect evidence where CADE deems it sufficient to establish the existence of unlawful conduct.

Considering the punitive nature of CADE's actions and its implications to businesses and individuals, a violation must be proved based on a preponderance of evidence. This standard requires that the party bearing the burden of proof shows that it is more probable than not that is has met the standard of proof it bears. The burden of proof in a proceeding that investigates the existence of a cartel agreement lies with CADE. However, if there is evidence of undue contacts between competitors, the burden of proof will be reversed, and the defendants will be charged with proving the absence of illegality in such contacts.

d.   Whether Information Exchange Is Violative

Exchange of competitively sensitive information is also potentially illicit. In practice, however, separating the exchange of sensitive information from other conduct—such as price fixing—is not an easy task, and CADE has usually found that competitors shared information in order to agree on a given course of action. For this reason, in most cases CADE analyzes information exchange in conjunction with other conduct.

e.   Whether Enforced Civilly or Criminally

(1) Civil Enforcement

Companies and individuals involved in anticompetitive practices are also subject to litigation prosecution in Brazil. The affected entities or individuals may recover losses they sustained as a result of a violation, apart from obtaining an order to cease the illegal conduct. State and Federal Prosecutors' Offices may also file a lawsuit on behalf of consumers that may have experienced damages arising from the anticompetitive or corrupt practices. In both cases, the plaintiffs may seek compensation for pecuniary damages and moral damages.

(2) Criminal Enforcement

There are no criminal sanctions for companies in connection with antitrust investigations in Brazil. Only individuals may face criminal charges.

The Brazilian Economic Crimes Law provides that cartels are a criminal offense and that individuals involved in cartels may be subject to two types of penalties: (i) fine and (ii) imprisonment from two to five years. The sanctions vary according to the economic gains obtained by the wrongdoer and his/her financial status.

Bid rigging is also a criminal offense. Article 90 of the Brazilian Public Bidding Law provides that the commission of fraud in a bidding proceeding by any means (including cartels) is a criminal offense punishable by imprisonment from two to four years, and a fine.

f.   Extraterritorial Application of Competition Law

Pursuant to Article 2 of the Brazilian Antitrust Law, CADE will have jurisdiction (i) over acts entirely or partially performed within the Brazilian territory, and (ii) over those acts that when performed abroad had or could have had effects in Brazil.

Effects arising from a domestic cartel are presumed. With respect to international cartels, CADE has confirmed its stance that the mere possibility of the cartel producing effects in Brazil would be enough to confirm its jurisdiction, even if no conduct was carried out in the Brazilian territory.

Since the early 2000s, when cartel investigations became a priority for CADE, the assessment of effects generated in Brazil by international cartels has remained a controversial topic. But certain of CADE's rulings in 2016 set out the following criteria for determining whether an alleged violation had effects in the Brazilian market: (i) evidence that Brazil (or Latin or South America) was an explicit target of the alleged cartel; (ii) evidence that the alleged cartel had a worldwide scope, thus including Brazil; (iii) whether the allegedly cartelized products were exported to Brazil; and/or (iv) whether the allegedly cartelized products were used as input for finished products exported to Brazil.[6]

In cases where the alleged cartel had a clear regional scope and did not include Brazil, the fact that the cartel members exported to Brazil did not lead CADE to rule against the companies under investigation. For instance, in the investigation concerning an alleged cartel in the plastic products market, CADE concluded that there was no evidence of potential effects in Brazil as there was no indication in the case files that the cartel

---

6.   These cases concern the markets for certain electronic components (Administrative Proceeding No. 08012.005255/2010-11), for glass components for cathode ray tubes (Administrative Proceeding No. 08012.005930/2009-79), for plastic products (Administrative Proceeding No. 08012.000774/2011-74 and 08700.009161/2014-97), and for thermoplastic elastomers (Administrative Proceeding No. 08012.000773/2011-20).

included Brazil in its scope, or that the products covered in the cartel agreements were exported to Brazil or used for the production of goods exported to Brazil. The simple fact that the companies had exported the relevant products to Brazil was not sufficient to establish a violation of Brazilian law. A similar approach was followed in the investigation concerning the market for thermoplastic elastomers.

On the other hand, in cases where the cartel was allegedly global in its geographic scope, CADE inferred that there were effects in the Brazilian territory notwithstanding the fact that sales to Brazil were minimal or even non-existent in the case of some defendants. This was CADE's position in the electronic components and the glass components for cathode ray tubes cases. In the investigation concerning the market for cathode ray tubes glass, former Commissioner Gilvandro Araujo stated that in order for CADE to be responsible for investigating an international cartel, its potential effects in Brazil have to be concrete and able to materialize. In order to analyze the materiality of the effects, CADE examined the volume of the exports of the allegedly cartelized products to Brazil and their importance as inputs for other finished products exported to Brazil.

2. Enforcement Authority and Actions

a. Name/Description of Authority

CADE is divided in two departments: the General Superintendence and the Administrative Tribunal.

(1) General Superintendence

The General Superintendence is responsible for initiating and conducting investigations related to infringements, adopting preventive measures intended to cease anticompetitive practices, negotiating and entering into leniency agreements, and otherwise preventing and prosecuting antitrust infringements. After concluding its investigation, the General Superintendence will issue a non-binding opinion with its findings on the alleged antitrust violation and a recommendation to CADE's Tribunal, which should be either to dismiss the case, or to impose penalties for breach of the law.

(2) Tribunal

The Administrative Tribunal is composed of seven members, whose responsibilities are to issue rulings on anticompetitive conduct cases and to review mergers and other cases of economic concentration. At CADE's Tribunal, a Reporting Commissioner will be appointed to issue a report and a vote on the case after hearing CADE's Attorney General, who will issue a non-binding opinion. The Reporting Commissioner may seek an opinion on the case from the Public Prosecutor's Office, and usually does so in cartel investigations. Once the Reporting Commissioner has concluded her investigations, the case will be brought to judgment before CADE's Tribunal at a public meeting. CADE's Tribunal may decide to dismiss the case if it finds no clear evidence of cartel activity; or to impose penalties and order the defendants to cease the antitrust violation.

b.   Whether Investigation on Prosecution Are Bifurcated

CADE is the agency responsible for investigating, prosecuting and ruling on antitrust infringements.

c.   Investigation Techniques

Evidence of an antitrust violation can be collected by the different investigative tools available to CADE, or by a leniency agreement or settlement agreements executed between the authority and individuals or companies involved in the antitrust violation.

During its investigation, the General Superintendence has broad powers, including the power to search companies' premises and to seize documents and/or other materials. For instance, if it believes that additional information is needed before the formal investigation is launched, the General Superintendence can take steps to collect such information by means of information requests to the leniency applicants, dawn raids at premises of the companies allegedly involved in the reported conduct, etc.

The General Superintendence can conduct dawn raids without prior notice, provided a court order is granted defining its scope. CADE has carried out 40 dawn raids since 2000. The raids are carried out by the federal and/or civil police, public prosecutors, competition authorities, and/or court officials. Without a court order, CADE may carry out inspections at a company's offices, facilities and headquarters as long as the company under investigation is notified in advance of the place, date, and the purpose of the inspection.

CADE also has authority to request documents and/or information from the defendants and third parties, and to impose fines if a party fails to comply with CADE's request. Depending on the nature of the information requested, the defendant may have grounds to refrain from presenting it to CADE (for example, documents protected by legal privilege). The consequences of not providing a particular piece of information to CADE will depend upon the nature of such information.

It is noteworthy that Brazil does not have a compulsory disclosure rule similar to the discovery process in the U.S. According to due process rules in Brazil, the defendants are allowed to produce all the evidence that they deem appropriate to defend the case, including providing documents, expert reports, studies, as well as producing witnesses or requesting the deposition of other defendants or third parties. As mentioned above, CADE does have general authority to request information and documents from both the defendants and third parties, but the defendants are not required to produce evidence that might incriminate them.

In addition, CADE's cooperation with foreign antitrust authorities in cartel cases is increasing. CADE has executed cooperation agreements with several foreign competition authorities, including authorities in Argentina, Canada, Chile, China, Ecuador, the European Union, France, Peru, Portugal, Russia, and the United States.

d. Sanctions/Penalties

In Brazil, corporate defendants are subject to fines for anticompetitive behavior ranging from 0.1 percent to 20 percent of the gross revenues registered by the company, group, or conglomerate in the fiscal year prior to the launching of the investigation in the line of business in which the infringement occurred.

A regulation issued in 2012 set out a list of lines of business to guide the authorities when imposing fines for antitrust infringements, but the lines of business listed in the regulation are often broader than the traditional concept of relevant market. For this reason, in November 2016, CADE issued a resolution allowing the specificities of the conduct to be taken into account in the definition of markets as the basis of calculation of the fine whenever the "line of business" established by the regulation is clearly disproportionate

CADE has not yet clarified under which circumstances it may go beyond the revenues of the defendant to assess fines on the basis of the defendant's entire group or conglomerate revenues. There was only one case (industrial gases) under the previous Brazilian Antitrust Law in which CADE decided that the fines should be based on the total revenues of the defendant's group in Brazil.[7] The decision in that case was mainly driven by the fact that the cartel arguably benefited entities of the defendant's group in Brazil other than just the investigated entity.

Directors and officers are subject to fines from 1 to 20 percent of the fine imposed on the company; other individuals may be liable for fines ranging from R$50,000 to R$2 billion. Companies are jointly and strictly liable for the involvement of their employees and executives in a cartel.

In addition to pecuniary fines, the company and/or individuals may be subject to the following administrative sanctions, among others: (i) debarment from participating in public procurement procedures and obtaining tax benefits and funds from public financial institutions up to five years; (ii) inclusion of the company's name in the Brazilian Consumer Protection List; (iii) publication of the decision in a major newspaper or on the company's website; (iv) corporate spin-off, transfer of control, sale of assets or partial interruption of the company's activities; (v) mandatory license of IP rights to third parties; and (vi) prohibition of individuals from exercising market activities or representing companies.

The level of fines imposed takes into account the factors listed under Article 45 of the Brazilian Antitrust Law: (i) the gravity of the violation; (ii) whether the party under investigation has acted in good faith; (iii) the economic benefits the party under investigation aimed to achieve by means of the anticompetitive conduct; (iv) whether or not the party has successfully achieved its goal; (v) the extension of actual or potential harm to competition, the Brazilian economy, consumers, and/or third parties; (vi) the negative impacts of the conduct on the market; (vii) the economic condition of the party under investigation; and (viii) recidivism (in which case the fine is doubled).

CADE makes a distinction between "hardcore cartels" and "soft cartels" when determining the level of the applicable fines. "Hardcore cartels" include to agreements to fix price, allocate markets, or rig public bids, and are punished by higher fines.[8] The term "soft cartels" usually refers to the exchange of sensitive information and the standardization of business practices among competitors.

Precedents involving hardcore cartels provide that corporate defendants may be subject to fines ranging from 15 to 19 percent of their gross revenue in the line of business in which the infringement occurred.[9] Fines levied in hardcore cartels under the previous regime, Law No. 8,884,

---

7.   Administrative Proceeding No. 08012.009888/2003-70.
8.   Administrative Proceeding No. 08012.002127/2002-14.
9.   Administrative Proceeding No. 08012.004472/2000-12.

ranged from 15 to 20 percent of the companies' annual gross revenue. CADE has not yet ruled on any "soft cartels" under the Brazilian Antitrust Law. Under Law No. 8,884, CADE typically imposed fines below 10 percent in such cases.

3. Leniency Program and Settlements

The Brazilian Antitrust Law allows for leniency and settlement agreements to be executed by companies and individuals involved in antitrust violations.

a. Requirements

(1) Leniency

Brazilian authorities will agree to sign a leniency agreement when the following requirements are met:

(i) the party applying for leniency is the first to report the conduct;

(ii) the applicant admits having participated in the conduct and agrees to describe it in a history of conduct statement;

(iii) the applicant agrees to collaborate with CADE's investigation;

(iv) the collaboration results in the identification of other members of the cartel, and in obtaining evidence of the antitrust violation;

(v) the applicant ceases its involvement in the alleged conduct; and

(vi) at the time the applicant comes forward, CADE's General Superintendence has not received sufficient information about the alleged conduct to ensure the conviction of the applicant.

(2) Settlements

Parties applying for a settlement in a cartel case are required to cooperate with the investigation and to acknowledge their involvement in the conduct. The acknowledgement is made by means of a statement in which the party describes its individual role in the conduct, along with supporting documents. The negotiation process is typically kept confidential.

b. Immunity vs Reduction in Fines

(1) Leniency

In Brazil, companies and individuals may receive immunity against administrative and criminal sanctions by signing a leniency agreement with CADE. Once a leniency agreement is reached, the applicant may be granted full or partial immunity from administrative penalties. Full immunity is only granted to applicants who reach the authorities before they had any knowledge about the conduct. Otherwise the applicant would only be granted partial immunity, and the applicable penalty could be reduced by one to two-thirds.

In the event directors and employees involved in the cartel execute the leniency agreement together with the applicant, the Public Prosecutors' Office and the General Superintendence, leniency shelters these individuals from criminal suits and sanctions under the Brazilian Economic Crimes Law, the Brazilian Public Bidding Law and the Criminal Code. In such cases, the limitation period is suspended and the Public Prosecutors' Office cannot file a criminal suit against such individuals. Notwithstanding this, leniency does not grant immunity against damage claims or against claims from other enforcement authorities, such as the Brazilian anticorruption, securities, and financial authorities.

(2) Settlements

Parties applying for settlement in a cartel case are required to cooperate with the investigation and to acknowledge their involvement in the conduct under investigation (i.e., to plead guilty).

Settling the defendants are required to pay a fine that is no lower than the minimum applicable fine. Thus, the fine must never be below 0.1 percent of the gross revenues registered by the company. Also, it must never be lower than the economic benefit obtained by the defendant through the conduct, provided that such a benefit can be estimated. There is no record of any cases in which CADE has used such a standard, however. This is probably due to the fact that the authorities find it very difficult to estimate the referred benefit.

The most important advantage in settling an investigation is reduction of the applicable fine. Article 187 of CADE's Resolution No. 1 establishes a predetermined level of discounts depending on when the defendant comes forward and the degree of cooperation expected. If the investigation is still being conducted by the General Superintendence, settling parties may be granted reductions ranging from 25 percent to 50 percent of the applicable fine, depending on the order in which they enter into the agreements. If the General Superintendence has already finished its investigation and the case is before CADE's Tribunal, the reduction may not exceed 15 percent of the fine that would likely be imposed.

c. Procedure

(1) Leniency

CADE's leniency negotiation process encompasses three phases: (i) securing a marker, (ii) leniency negotiation, and (iii) execution of the leniency agreement. The leniency application begins with the request for a marker, which allows the applicant to complete its internal investigation without the risk that a third party obtains leniency for the same conduct. To be eligible to secure a marker, the applicant must meet with the General Superintendent or the chief of staff of the General Superintendence, and provide general information on the parties to the alleged cartel, the conduct and the affected market, the affected territory and the estimated duration of the alleged cartel. The marker will be granted 3 days from the date of the meeting.

Once a marker is granted, the applicant has 30 days to complete its internal investigation and present a formal leniency proposal, providing CADE with additional information on the alleged conduct. In practice, this 30-day period is frequently extended, so that leniency agreements are usually signed between six and twelve months after the marker is granted. The negotiation period is limited to six months when there is a second applicant in line for leniency.

The leniency proposal can be presented either in written or oral form. The formal proposal must contain the above-mentioned information (i.e., the who, what, where and when of the cartel conduct) and also a description of all information and documents that will be provided to support the leniency agreement. If the applicant is also applying for leniency in connection with the reported conduct in other jurisdictions, the leniency proposal must contain information on the status of the other leniency applications. The applicant will be waived from the having to provide such information whenever a foreign antitrust authority prohibits the applicant from providing any information on the leniency application.

Based on the information and documents provided by the applicant, CADE drafts a history of conduct statement, which contains a detailed account of the facts discovered in the applicant's internal investigation. This statement and documents provided by the applicant will be used by CADE to draft an opening note, which contains objections raised against the targets of the investigation and supports CADE's decision to formally open an investigation.

The leniency agreement is not subject to the review or approval of CADE's Tribunal. However, CADE's Tribunal must verify whether the applicant has fully complied with its duties under the agreement, and either (i) determine full immunity from administrative sanctions if the applicant provided information about a previously unknown anticompetitive practice; or (ii) reduce the applicable sanctions by one to two thirds if the applicant provided information about an already known anticompetitive practice (and depending on the extent of collaboration of the applicant with the investigations).

CADE has been increasingly relying on leniency agreements for launching investigations. The table below shows the number and types of leniencies executed by CADE from 2012 to 2018.

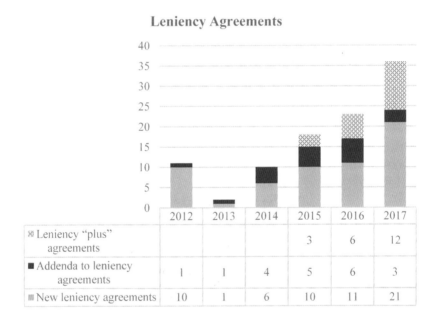

Leniency Agreements

	2012	2013	2014	2015	2016	2017
✳ Leniency "plus" agreements				3	6	12
■ Addenda to leniency agreements	1	1	4	5	6	3
▥ New leniency agreements	10	1	6	10	11	21

(2) Settlement

The Brazilian Antitrust Law allows the defendants to settle a case with CADE at any time during the investigation before CADE's Tribunal issues its final decision on the matter. The settlement negotiation can be initiated either by means of a proposal presented by the defendant or a proposal addressed by the General Superintendence to the defendant. A defendant can approach CADE with a proposal to settle the investigation as soon as the General Superintendence releases the technical note that launches the formal investigation; there is no need to wait until the defense deadline starts to run.

Settlement in Brazil is a one shot game; if the proposal presented by the defendant is not accepted by either the General Superintendence or the Tribunal, the defendant does not have the right to present a new settlement proposal to CADE. Following submission of the proposal, a commission formed by CADE's officials will be assigned to negotiate the terms of the settlement. Once the negotiations are concluded, the defendant is required to present a final proposal based on the terms and conditions agreed upon with the General Superintendence, which will then submit the final settlement proposal for final approval by CADE's Tribunal.

The settlement negotiation may take approximately six months, given that both the General Superintendence and the Tribunal have the ability to suspend the formal deadlines if additional investigation is required before they conclude the negotiations. Both the settlement proposal and the negotiation may be kept confidential if so requested by the parties and agreed to by CADE. However, once the Tribunal reaches a final decision accepting the final settlement proposal presented by the defendant, the settlement becomes public and a non-confidential version of the settlement agreement is made available on CADE's website.

The timing of the settlement negotiation impacts the level of discount that the party may get from CADE. If the investigation is still being conducted at the level of the General Superintendence, the first defendant to settle may be granted a discount of 30 percent to 50 percent of the applicable fine. The second defendant to settle may be granted a discount of 25 percent to 40 percent of the applicable fine. In subsequent settlements, a discount of up to 25 percent of the expected fine may be granted. If the General Superintendence has already finished its investigation and the case has already been passed on to CADE's Tribunal, the discount for a settlement cannot exceed 15 percent of the likely fine.

Since the enactment of the Brazilian Antitrust Law, the number of settlements negotiated by CADE has been rapidly increasing, as demonstrated in the table below. This movement indicates a growing improvement in CADE's settlement program.

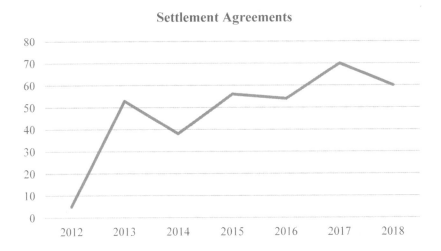

Settlement Agreements

4. Conclusion

CADE's activities in cartel prosecution show not only that this enforcement is a top priority in Brazil, but also that the leniency and settlement processes have evolved and improved over the years. The development of cartel-prosecution strategies has allowed CADE to build stronger and more compelling cases, while also providing increasing certainty and transparency to the defendants and companies seeking agreements with the authority.

B. Canada

1. Competition Law

a. Overview

Hardcore cartel offenses, such as price fixing, market allocation, and bid rigging, are criminal offenses in Canada. Canada's Competition Act[10] prohibits such conduct as per se criminal, meaning that the conduct's anticompetitive effects are presumed and need not be proven. The conduct considered per se criminal will be familiar to American attorneys as it is

---

10.   R.S.C. 1985, c. C-34.

broadly similar to that identified in jurisprudence under section 1 of the Sherman Act.[11]

Three per se criminal offenses are most relevant for international cartel enforcement. First, subsection 45(1) of the Competition Act prohibits agreements or arrangements between or among competitors to fix prices, allocate markets, or restrict output.[12] The Competition Act defines "competitor" to include a potential competitor.[13]

Second, subsection 46(1) of the Competition Act prohibits the implementation in Canada of a directive to give effect to a foreign conspiracy.[14] Third, subsection 47(2) of the Competition Act prohibits bid rigging.[15]

b.　Any Major Exemptions/Immunities

There are four statutory defenses and exceptions to a charge under Section 45. First, subsection 45(4) provides a defense for agreements that would otherwise violate subsection 45(1) but are ancillary to and necessary for a broader agreement which, considered alone, does not violate subsection 45(1).[16] Second, subsection 45(5) provides a defense for

---

11.　15 U.S. § 1.
12.　R.S.C. 1985, c. C-34 § 45(1).
13.　*Id.* § 45(8).
14.　R.S.C. 1985, c. C-34 § 46(1).
15.　R.S.C. 1985, c. C-34 § 47. Subsections 47(1) defines bid rigging to mean either "an agreement or arrangement between or among two or more persons whereby one or more of those persons agrees or undertakes not to submit a bid or tender in response to a call or request for bids or tenders, or agrees or undertakes to withdraw a bid or tender submitted in response to such a call or request" or "the submission . . . of bids or tenders that are arrived at by agreement or arrangement between or among two or more bidders or tenderers, where the agreement or arrangement is not made known to the person calling for or requesting the bids . . . ."
16.　Subsection 45(4) reads:
No person shall be convicted of an offense under subsection (1) in respect of a conspiracy, agreement or arrangement that would otherwise contravene that subsection if
(a) that person establishes, on a balance of probabilities, that
　(i) it is ancillary to a broader or separate agreement or arrangement that includes the same parties, and

agreements related only to the export of goods from Canada (subject to limited exceptions). Third, subsection 45(6) exempts agreements between affiliates and those between federal financial institutions. [17] Finally, subsection 45(7) provides a defense for conduct authorized or required by law. [18]   Like subsection 45(6), subsection 47(3) exempts agreements between affiliated companies from the bid-rigging prohibition in section 47.

c. Standard of Proof

To convict an accused criminal, the prosecution must prove all elements of the offenses in sections 45, 46, and 47 beyond a reasonable doubt. In civil cases, discussed below, the plaintiff must prove all elements of the offenses on a balance of probabilities, although lower courts have suggested that the trial judge is justified in scrutinizing the evidence with greater care owing to the serious nature of the allegations. [19]

d. Whether Information Exchange is Violative

Sharing competitively sensitive information with a competitor, without more, is not an offense in Canada. Rather, the competitors must form an agreement or arrangement before facing liability. Although not itself an offense, an exchange of competitively sensitive information can be problematic because it can be evidence of an underlying agreement, or can assist the formation of an agreement. For this reason, the Competition Bureau discourages exchanges of competitively sensitive information. Its *Competitor Collaboration Guidelines* describe some best practices with

---

      (ii) it is directly related to, and reasonably necessary for giving effect to, the objective of that broader or separate agreement or arrangement; and

    (b) the broader or separate agreement or arrangement, considered alone, does not contravene that subsection.

    Id. § 45(4).

17.   Section 49 of R.S.C. 1985, c. C-34, contains a specific offense related to certain agreements between federal financial institutions.

18.   The CCB has issued a bulletin on the application of the Competition Act to such conduct: COMPETITION BUREAU, "REGULATED" CONDUCT (Sept. 27, 2010), *available at* http://www.competitionbureau.gc.ca/eic/site/cb-bc.nsf/eng/03273.html.

19.   Pharmacy Ltd. et al v. Blue Cross of Canada, 2003 NSSC 179 (Can.).

respect to sharing information between competitors.[20] Generally speaking, the older and more aggregated the information, the less problematic the exchange.

e.   Whether Enforced Civilly or Criminally

Canada's cartel laws are enforced by the government through criminal prosecutions and by private plaintiffs through civil actions. Sections 45, 46, and 47 are criminal offenses enforced by the Canadian government. Canadian criminal procedure is broadly similar to its U.S. counterpart:

- the process is adversarial before an independent trier of fact;
- the accused is presumed innocent until proven guilty;
- all elements of the offense must be proven beyond a reasonable doubt; and
- the Constitution protects against unreasonable search and seizures, unreasonable detention, and conviction arising from unlawfully obtained evidence.[21]

Section 67 sets out the procedure for prosecuting the Competition Act's criminal offenses.[22] Under subsection 67(3), only the provincial superior courts have jurisdiction to try certain offenses,[23] including conspiracy (section 45) and bid rigging (section 47).[24] An exception to this exists under section 73, where the federal Attorney General may initiate criminal proceedings in the Federal Court for charges laid under Part VI of the Competition Act if the accused consents to the Federal Court's jurisdiction.[25]

---

20.   COMPETITION BUREAU, COMPETITOR COLLABORATION GUIDELINES, *available at* http://www.competitionbureau.gc.ca/eic/site/cb-bc.nsf/eng //03177.html, s. 3.7.
21.   Evidence obtained unconstitutionally may be excluded if its admission would bring the administration of justice into disrepute.
22.   R.S.C. 1985, c. C-34 § 67.
23.   While under Canada's Constitution criminal law is an area of federal jurisdiction, the administration of justice falls under provincial jurisdiction, meaning that almost all criminal offenses are tried in a provincial superior court. By contrast, Canada's Federal Court has a more limited jurisdiction.
24.   *Id.* § 67(3).
25.   *Id.* § 73.

An accused individual may elect to be tried by a judge and jury, or by a judge sitting alone.[26] An accused corporation does not have this option and must be tried without a jury.[27] If an individual consents to be tried in the Federal Court under section 73, the trial will take place without a jury.[28]

The cartel offenses prohibited by sections 45, 46, and 47 of the Competition Act are indictable offenses that proceed by way of indictment in a provincial superior court. The indictment contains a written accusation and lists the charges laid against the accused. Once an agent of the Attorney General drafts and signs this charging document, it is filed with the court.

While there is no statute of limitation for these indictable offenses, the Canadian Constitution gives any person charged with an offense the right to be tried without unreasonable delay.[29] A delay in bringing charges will rarely be relevant to an accused's right to be tried within a reasonable time, but once the Crown lays charges, it engages the accused's constitutional right. When determining whether charges should be stayed for unreasonable delay, a court will consider the length of the delay, any waiver of time periods, the reasons for the delay, and prejudice to the accused.[30]

When prosecuting an indictable offense, the Supreme Court of Canada has imposed a duty of disclosure on the Crown.[31] The Crown must disclose to the accused "all information in its possession, whether exculpatory or inculpatory, unless the information is 'clearly irrelevant' or is protected from disclosure by privilege."[32] The issue of privilege is particularly relevant when the Commissioner commences criminal proceedings after receiving information through the CCB's immunity and leniency programs. In these circumstances, the Ontario Superior Court of Justice recently found that the Crown cannot invoke settlement privilege to deny

---

26.   *Id.* § 67(1).
27.   *Id.* § 67(4).
28.   *Id.* § 73(2).
29.   Canadian Charter of Rights and Freedoms § 11(b), Part I of the Constitution Act, 1982, *being* Schedule B to the Canada Act, 1982, c. 11 (U.K.).
30.   *See* R. v. Morin, (1992) 1 S.C.R. 771 (Can.); R. v. Jordan, (2016) 1 S.C.R. 631 (Can.), where the Supreme Court of Canada established presumptive maximum periods of delay after which charges will be stayed.
31.   *See* R. v. Stinchcome, (1991) 3 S.C.R. 326 (Can.).
32.   R. v. Nestlé Canada Inc., 2015 ONSC 810 (Can. Ont. Sup. Ct.).

disclosure when the person providing the information does so knowing that the Crown intends to rely on it to bring criminal charges.[33]

With respect to civil enforcement, like the United States, Canada has a sophisticated and active class action plaintiffs' bar. Plaintiffs typically advance civil antitrust claims as class actions under three heads of liability.[34] First, section 36 of the Competition Act provides a statutory cause of action permitting the plaintiffs to recover damages for harm caused by conduct contrary to Part VI of the Competition Act, which includes sections 45 (conspiracy) and 47 (bid rigging).[35] Second, the plaintiffs advance common law tort claims, most often unlawful means conspiracy. Finally, the plaintiffs advance claims in restitution.

f.   Extraterritorial Application of Competition Law

Canadian criminal courts require subject-matter jurisdiction over the offense and personal jurisdiction over the accused to render judgment.

As to subject-matter jurisdiction, the Criminal Code provides that no person shall be convicted of an offense committed outside of Canada.[36] The Criminal Code, however, does not explain what is required for an offense to have been committed *in* Canada. This presents challenges where elements of an offense may occur in multiple jurisdictions, including Canada.

The Supreme Court of Canada has held that a Canadian court has jurisdiction over an offense when there is a "real and substantial link" between the offense and Canada.[37] It defined a "real and substantial link" as a "significant portion of the activities constituting [the] offense" having taken place in Canada.[38] Applied to subsection 6(2) of the Criminal Code, the "real and substantial link" test indicates that an offense is committed in Canada where a significant portion of the activities constituting the offense took place in Canada.

---

33.   *Id.*, ¶ 68.

34.   Note that this refers to common law provinces, not Quebec.

35.   Notably, Part VI does not include an offense of monopolization, thus there is no statutory cause of civil action available to the plaintiffs in Canada for monopolization. Monopolization-type cases are reviewable by the Competition Tribunal on application by the CCB under section 79 of the Competition Act.

36.   R.S.C. 1985, c. C-46 § 6(2).

37.   Libman v. The Queen, (1985) 2 S.C.R. 178 (Can.).

38.   *Id.*, ¶ 74.

The "real and substantial link" test has not been applied in a contested criminal trial of a Competition Act offense. This lack of jurisprudence can make it difficult for foreign individuals to determine whether or not conduct engaged outside of Canada is an offense in Canada.

The CCB has not provided formal guidance on when it considers a Competition Act offense to have been committed in Canada under the "real and substantial link" test. The CCB's Immunity and Leniency Bulletin, however, implies that the CCB considers an offense to have occurred in Canada where it is included in the scope of the parties' agreement, regardless of where the parties formed that agreement.[39]

It is not obvious that an agreement that did not extend to Canada but had indirect effects in Canada would qualify under the "real and substantial link" test. For example, an agreement to fix the price of widgets sold in the United States may cause the price of goods containing widgets to rise in Canada. Civil plaintiffs rely on such "passing on" arguments to seek compensation for the amount of the "illegal overcharge" passed on to indirect purchasers (i.e., those who bought products containing widgets). The Supreme Court of Canada's comment in *Libman v. The Queen*[40] that the protection of the public is a legitimate purpose of the criminal law could support an argument that indirect effects in Canada are enough for foreign conduct to be considered criminal in Canada. Still, to date, it remains unclear whether or not wholly foreign conduct that has only indirect effects constitutes a Competition Act offense in Canada.

Personal jurisdiction is established by the physical presence of the accused before the court or the proper service on the accused of a summons to appear. With respect to foreign individuals, physical attendance can be achieved via extradition, if possible under Canada's treaties with foreign nations. Foreign corporations cannot be extradited, so obtaining personal

---

39. COMPETITION BUREAU, IMMUNITY AND LENIENCY PROGRAMS UNDER THE COMPETITION ACT, *available at* http://www.competitionbureau.gc.ca/eic/site/cb-bc.nsf/eng/04391.html, ¶18.. ("The [Competition] Act may be violated whether or not the applicant supplies products directly or indirectly in, from or into Canada. A party should seek immunity regardless of whether it supplies products directly or indirectly into Canada. Further, a party that does not sell products into Canada as part of a market allocation agreement, contrary to section 45 of the [Competition] Act, or a party that agrees not to submit a bid in response to a call or request for bids or tenders contrary to section 47 of the [Competition] Act may also seek immunity.").

40. *Libman*, 2 S.C.R. 178 ¶ 67.

jurisdiction requires service of a summons.[41] But under the Criminal Code, a summons may only be served in Canada.[42] Thus, in the case of a foreign corporation, so long as its senior officers remain outside of Canada, a summons cannot be served on it. In such circumstances, a Canadian court cannot obtain personal jurisdiction over a foreign corporation unless that corporation voluntarily submits to the jurisdiction of the Canadian court. Many foreign corporations have done so to take advantage of the CCB's Immunity and Leniency Programs and the accompanying certainty for themselves, their Canadian subsidiaries, and their officers and employees.

Given the practical difficulties of obtaining personal jurisdiction over foreign corporations, section 46 of the Competition Act is a powerful tool for the CCB because it permits prosecution of a Canadian subsidiary that unknowingly implements a foreign conspiracy in Canada. Although a Canadian court may lack personal jurisdiction over the foreign parent, it can readily obtain jurisdiction over the Canadian subsidiary.

Where there is no Canadian subsidiary or the subsidiary was not involved in the sale of the price-fixed product, there may not be any reasonable prospect of convicting a foreign corporation, owing to an inability to obtain personal jurisdiction over it.

2. *Enforcement Authority and Actions*

a.   Name/Description of Authority

The Commissioner of Competition (Commissioner) is the public official appointed under subsection 7(1) of the Competition Act with responsibility for the administration and enforcement of the Competition Act, the Consumer Packaging and Labeling Act, the Precious Metals Marking Act, and the Textile Labelling Act. The Commissioner heads the Canadian Competition Bureau (CCB), which is an independent law enforcement agency that investigates conduct for the purposes of the administration and enforcement of the legislation under the Commissioner's mandate.

---

41.   CRIMINAL CODE, R.S.C. 1985, c. C-46 § 703.2.
42.   *Id.* § 703.1; Re: Shulman and The Queen (1975), 23 C.C.C. (2d) (Can. B.C. C.A.); R. v. R.J. Reynolds Tobacco Co. (Delaware), 2007 ONCA 749 (Can.); Alassia Newships Management Inc. v. British Columbia (Provincial Court), (2018) B.C.C.A. 92 (Can. B.C.C.A.).

b. Bifurcated Investigation and Prosecution: Prosecution by the Public Prosecution Service of Canada

The Commissioner and CCB investigate but do not prosecute criminal conduct under the Competition Act. Instead, once satisfied of the commission of a criminal offense, the CCB will refer the matter to the Public Prosecution Service of Canada (PPSC) for prosecution.[43] The PPSC, on behalf of the Director of Public Prosecutions (DPP), retains an independent discretion regarding whether or not to proceed with charges against the accused.

c. Whether Investigation and Prosecution are Bifurcated

The Competition Act grants significant investigatory powers to the Commissioner to carry out his mandate of administration and enforcement. Under section 11, the Commissioner may apply to a court for an order requiring a party to produce certain records or attend a sworn examination.[44] Section 15 gives the Commissioner the power to make ex parte applications to a judge for search and seizure warrants. This search and seizure power is in addition to the provisions available under Canada's Criminal Code, which provide for warrants when there are reasonable grounds to believe that an offense "has been or is suspected to have been committed."[45]

The Competition Act's investigatory powers become available to the Commissioner only after he has initiated a formal inquiry under section 10. Section 10 provides that the Commissioner shall commence an inquiry when he has reason to believe that:

- a person has committed or is about to commit a criminal offense under Part VI or Part VII;[46]
- a person has contravened an order made pursuant to certain provisions of the Competition Act;[47] or
- grounds exist for an order under the Competition Act's civil reviewable practice provisions.[48]

---

43. The PPSC is headed by the Director of Public Prosecutions (DPP).
44. R.S.C. 1985, c. C-34 § 11.
45. R.S.C. 1985, c. C-46 § 487(1)(a).
46. R.S.C. 1985, c. C-34 § 10(1)(b)(iii).
47. *Id.* § 10(1)(b)(i).
48. *Id.* § 10(1)(b)(ii).

Section 10 also requires an inquiry when the Minister of Industry directs the Commissioner to investigate possible violations of the Competition Act's criminal or civil provisions, [49] or when six adult Canadian residents apply to the Commissioner for an inquiry. [50] The Commissioner conducts all inquiries under section 10 privately. [51]

d. Investigation Techniques

(1) Warrants, Wiretaps, etc.

After the Commissioner has commenced an inquiry, he may apply with a sworn information to a county, superior, or federal court judge for a search and seizure warrant under section 15. [52] The court may issue the warrant if it is satisfied that there are reasonable grounds to believe that a person has contravened an order made pursuant to certain of the Competition Act's provisions, that grounds exist for an order under its civil reviewable practice provisions, or that a person has committed or is about to commit an offense under Part VI or Part VII. [53] The Commissioner must also present reasonable grounds to believe that there is evidence of these circumstances on the premises. [54] If the court is satisfied that these circumstances exist, it may authorize the Commissioner to enter and search the premises specified in the warrant and allow the Commissioner to seize or copy any record. [55] These procedures must be followed unless "exigent circumstances" exist, such as circumstances where getting a warrant would result in the loss or destruction of the evidence. [56]

Under section 16, a person authorized by a warrant may "use or cause to be used any computer system on the premises to search any data

---

49.   *Id.* § 10(1)(c).
50.   *Id.* §§ 9, 10(1)(a).
51.   *Id.* § 10(3). For the CCB's interpretation of this provision, *see* COMPETITION BUREAU, INFORMATION BULLETIN ON THE COMMUNICATION OF CONFIDENTIAL INFORMATION UNDER THE COMPETITION ACT (Sept. 30, 2013), *available at* http://www.competitionbureau.gc.ca/eic/site/cb-bc.nsf/vwapj/cb-bulletin-confidential-info-2013-e.pdf/$file/cb-bulletin-confidential-info-2013-e.pdf.
52.   *Id.* § 15.
53.   *Id.* § 15(1)(a).
54.   *Id.* § 15(1)(b).
55.   *Id.* §§ 15(1)(c)-(d).
56.   *Id.* §§ 15(7)-(8).

contained in or available to the computer system."[57] The power to search and seize "any data contained in or available to the computer" is also found in the Criminal Code.[58] The plain language of these legislative regimes suggests that any record contained on servers located offsite would come under the scope of the warrant, provided the information was accessible to the computer being searched. The CCB endorsed this interpretation in a 2008 Information Bulletin, stating that "data that are accessible via [a] computer system can be searched even if the data are not located on the premises."[59]

The Federal Court of Appeal has accepted that this language gives government agencies the authority to search and seize records physically contained on offshore servers. In a 2008 tax case, the Court of Appeal upheld the trial judge's analysis:

> [W]hen information, though stored electronically outside Canada, is available to and used by those in Canada, [the law] must be approached from the point of view of the realities of today's world. Such information cannot truly be said to "reside" only in one place or be "owned" by only one person. The reality is that the information is readily and instantaneously available . . . . It is irrelevant where the electronically-stored information is located.[60]

The trial and appellate decisions in that case focused on the company's actual use in Canada of the data stored offshore, finding that "[t]he most important issue . . . is the ability of [the Canadian company], to access and use the information."[61] To the Court of Appeal, documents stored outside Canada were as "easily accessible as documents in their filing cabinets in their Canadian offices."[62]

While both levels of the Federal Court in that case found that information stored offshore can fall within the reach of a Canadian search warrant, they limited this scope to information that is available to and *used*

57. *Id.* § 16(1).
58. R.S.C. 1985, c. C-46 § 487(2.1).
59. COMPETITION BUREAU, INFORMATION BULLETIN ON SECTIONS 15 & 16 OF THE COMPETITION ACT 7 (Apr. 25, 2008), *available at* http://www.competitionbureau.gc.ca/eic/site/cb-bc.nsf/vwapj/Section-1516-final-e.pdf/$FILE/Section-1516-final-e.pdf.
60. eBay Canada Limited v. Canada (National Revenue), 2007 FC 930, ¶ 23 (Can.).
61. *Id.*, ¶ 12.
62. eBay Canada Ltd. v. M.N.R., 2008 FCA 348, ¶ 20 (Can.).

by those in Canada. This suggests that, if a Canadian company has access to data held offshore by a foreign affiliate, the information may remain out of reach of Canadian officials exercising a search warrant if it is not regularly accessed by Canadian employees. This approach is also consistent with jurisprudence from the Supreme Court of Canada on the law relating to computer searches more generally.[63]

(2) Section 11 Orders

Like search warrants available under section 15, once the Commissioner commences a formal inquiry, the Commissioner can apply to the court under section 11 for an order requiring a party to produce certain records, make a written return under oath or affirmation, or attend for a sworn examination. [64] While both procedures require judicial authorization, the test for obtaining a warrant is much stricter than that followed for a section 11 order. To obtain a section 11 order, the Commissioner must only show that he has commenced a formal inquiry and that the party subject to the order "is likely to have information that is relevant to the inquiry."[65]

This lower standard has allowed the Commissioner to obtain production and testimonial orders with relative ease.[66] The lower standard is indicative of the investigative rather than adjudicative nature of section 11 proceedings, and of the fact that information obtained through these orders is used for inquiry purposes, not for the prosecution of criminal offenses.[67] In fact, subsection 11(3)[68] protects individuals compelled to give evidence from having their testimony used against them in any criminal proceedings, conforming with the Canadian Constitution's

---

63.   For a more detailed discussion on the scope of search warrants related to antitrust matters in Canada, *see* Casey W. Halladay & Joshua Chad, *A Database Too Far? Interpreting the Competition Bureau's Search Powers*, 27 CANADA COMPETITION L. REV. 453 (2014).

64.   R.S.C. 1985, c. C-34 § 11.

65.   *Id.* § 11(1).

66.   *See* Michelle Lally & Kaeleigh Kuzma, *Powers of Investigation*, *in* FUNDAMENTALS OF CANADIAN COMPETITION LAW (James B. Musgrove, ed., 3rd ed. 2015) 397, 401.

67.   *Id.* at 402.

68.   R.S.C. 1985, c. C-34 § 11(3) (with the exception of prosecution for perjury or giving contradictory evidence).

protection against self-incrimination.[69] Potentially significant, however, is the fact that this protection does not explicitly extend to records produced by an individual subject to an order.

The Commissioner has been advised against seeking section 11 orders when he already suspects that a person is involved in criminal activity.[70] If a court determines that the inquiry was predominately criminal in nature, the Commissioner risks having evidence produced pursuant to a section 11 order excluded as an unlawful search and seizure.[71] In these circumstances, the Commissioner is well advised to avail himself of the more stringent procedures required to obtain a search warrant.

e. Sanctions/Penalties

Canadian courts have imposed significant fines on domestic and foreign corporations convicted of Competition Act offenses. Conviction under section 45 (conspiracy) carries a maximum penalty of fourteen years in prison, a $25 million fine, or both. The offense in section 46 applies only to corporations and, consequently, a fine in the discretion of the court is the only penalty available. Conviction under section 47 (bid rigging) carries a maximum penalty of fourteen years in prison, a fine in the discretion of the court, or both.

Despite the fourteen-year prison terms contemplated by the Competition Act, however, non-monetary sentences for Competition Act offenses have been modest relative to the jail terms imposed in the United States. No non-Canadian natural person has been indicted for participating in an international cartel. The majority of Canadians sentenced for Competition Act offenses have received conditional sentences to be served under house arrest. Changes in 2012 to the sentencing provisions in the Canadian Criminal Code removed the availability of conditional sentences for offenses carrying a maximum sentence of fourteen years, meaning that conditional sentences, which can be served under house arrest, are no

---

69. Canadian Charter of Rights and Freedoms § 13, Part I of the Constitution Act, 1982, *being* Schedule B to the Canada Act, 1982, c. 11 (U.K.).

70. Brian Gover, *Review of section 11 of the Competition Act* (Aug. 12, 2008) *available at* http://www.competitionbureau.gc.ca/eic/site/cb-bc.nsf/eng/02709.html.

71. *See* R. v. Jarvis, (2002) 3 S.C.R. 757 (Can.). The Supreme Court of Canada held that when a tax audit turned into a criminal investigation, constitutional protections were invoked, and tax officials could no longer use the federal Income Tax Act's less stringent inspection and production powers.

longer available for violations of sections 45 (conspiracy) or 47 (bid rigging).[72]

In addition to the penal consequences, individuals and corporations convicted of offenses under the Competition Act will be disqualified from doing business with the Government of Canada for ten years (and may be disqualified from doing business with provincial or municipal governments as well).[73] Affiliates of the convicted corporation may also be disqualified if they participated in the offenses that led to the conviction.

As a member of INTERPOL, Canadian officials can respond to red notices issued by the U.S. Department of Justice (DOJ) or other enforcement agencies. These officials have the ability to coordinate and provide assistance to locate, deport, or extradite foreign fugitives on Canadian soil.

Unlike German officials,[74] Canadian officials have not stopped, held, and extradited a non-Canadian individual based on a red notice for antitrust offenses, but a Canadian national has been extradited to the United States to face such charges.[75] Under the U.S.-Canada extradition treaty, "[e]xtradition shall be granted for conduct which constitutes an offense punishable by the laws of both Contracting Parties by imprisonment or other form of detention for a term exceeding one year or any greater punishment."[76] For the first time relating to antitrust charges, the United States successfully invoked the treaty in 2014 to extradite a Canadian to the United States to face bid-rigging, fraud, and conspiracy charges.[77] The authors are not aware of Canadian officials issuing red notices for Competition Act offenses.

---

72. Safe Streets and Communities Act, S.C. 2012, c. 1 (Can.).
73. PUBLIC WORKS AND GOVERNMENT SERVICES CANADA, GOVERNMENT OF CANADA'S INTEGRITY REGIME, *available at* http://www.tpsgc-pwgsc.gc.ca/ci-if/ci-if-eng.html.
74. For a discussion of the extradition from Germany of Italian executive Romano Pisciotti, *see id.* at 3-4.
75. *See* Mark L. Krotoski, *Extradition in International Antitrust Enforcement Cases*, ANTITRUST SOURCE, Apr. 2015, *available at* http://www.americanbar.org/content/dam/aba/. . ./antitrust_source/apr15_krotoski_4_22f.pdf.
76. Protocol Amending the Treaty on Extradition Between Canada and the United States of America, art. 1, Can.-U.S., Jan. 11, 1988, 1853 U.N.T.S. 407.
77. United States v. Bennett, 2014 BCCA 145 (Can. B.C.).

3. Leniency Program

a. Requirements

The CCB has two "leniency" programs.[78] The Immunity Program promises immunity from prosecution (i.e., amnesty) to the first person to report an offense under the Competition Act where the CCB is either unaware of the offense or, if it is already aware, lacks sufficient information to refer the matter to the prosecutor.

In addition to being the first to report the conduct to the CCB, the immunity applicant must:

- terminate its participation in the illegal activity;
- not have coerced others to be a party to the illegal activity;
- not have been the only party involved in the offense; and
- provide complete, timely, and ongoing cooperation throughout the course of the CCB's investigation and subsequent prosecution(s), including disclosure of any and all conduct of which the applicant is aware that may constitute an offense under the Competition Act and in which it may have been involved.

In the case of corporate applicants, current directors, officers, and employees will also receive immunity from prosecution provided they cooperate with the investigation.

Full immunity is only available to the first to report the conduct. Later applicants may take advantage of the CCB's Leniency Program, which promises lenient treatment to subsequent cooperating parties. The CCB will recommend lenient treatment where the applicant:

- has terminated its participation in the activity;
- agrees to cooperate fully and in a timely manner, at its own expense, with the CCB's investigation and any subsequent prosecution; and
- agrees to plead guilty.

---

78. The CCB does not itself have the authority to grant immunity or leniency. Rather, for those qualifying participants, the CCB will recommend immunity or leniency in accordance with its programs to the PPSC. Although the PPSC must make an independent assessment, the CCB recommendation has in practice always been adopted.

On September 27, 2018, the CCB issued a revised Immunity and Leniency Programs under the Competition Act for public consultation.[79] The revised Programs include several changes such as a return to interim or conditional immunity pending complete cooperation and the availability of up to a 50 percent fine reduction for all leniency applicants depending on the value of their cooperation.

b.   Immunity vs. Reduction in Fines

Lenient treatment refers principally to a recommended fine discount, which until September 2018 depended almost entirely on the order in which the applicant requested a leniency marker. To calculate its fine recommendation, the CCB generally uses a proxy of 20 percent of the applicant's affected volume of commerce in Canada. It then applies a cooperation discount. As of September 2018, every leniency applicant can receive a cooperation discount of up to 50 percent. Previously, a 50 percent discount was available only to the first-in leniency applicant.[80] The CCB will determine the cooperation discount based on the value of the leniency applicant's cooperation. Timeliness of cooperation remains an important factor, so earlier applicants will likely still receive larger discounts than later applicants will. In addition to the cooperation discount, the first-in leniency applicant secures immunity for its current directors, officers and employees, provided they cooperate.

The CCB also offers "Immunity Plus" to leniency applicants who are the first to disclose information regarding another offense. In those circumstances, the applicant will receive immunity for the new offense and the CCB will recommend an additional 5 to 10 percent reduction in the applicant's fine for the original offense.

c.   Procedure (Marker, Cooperation)

The procedure for obtaining immunity and leniency in Canada will be familiar to U.S. attorneys, as it largely follows the process developed by the DOJ Antitrust Division.

The process begins with the applicant, usually through counsel, communicating with the Senior Deputy Commissioner, Cartels and

---

79.   COMPETITION BUREAU, IMMUNITY AND LENIENCY PROGRAMS UNDER THE COMPETITION   ACT,   *available*   *at* http://www.competitionbureau.gc.ca/eic/site/cb-bc.nsf/eng/04391.html.

80.   Second-in overall, behind the immunity applicant.

Deceptive Marketing Practices Branch of the CCB on a no-names basis. Counsel may inquire about the availability of immunity or leniency. At this stage, counsel need not disclose the client's name, but will need to provide sufficient information, such as the product, conduct, and time period, so that the CCB can determine whether an immunity or leniency position is available and, if so, which one. If an immunity or leniency position is available, the CCB will invite counsel to accept a marker for the position on behalf of the client. If counsel accepts the marker, the client's identity must be revealed.

In international cartel investigations where an applicant is cooperating with antitrust enforcement agencies in other countries, the CCB expects a waiver to permit it to discuss its investigation with those other authorities, although this requirement may change under the revised programs. The applicant can provide the waiver orally, consistent with the generally paperless immunity or leniency process the CCB accepts.

The CCB's Immunity and Leniency Programs require a proffer from the applicant within thirty days of obtaining a marker. Absent a marker extension, failure to proffer within this time period may result in the applicant's marker lapsing and it losing its immunity or leniency position to the next applicant in line (if there is one). While the Programs insist on an initial proffer within thirty days, in practice, the CCB recognizes that circumstances may require or weigh in favor of an extension of the thirty-day period. The CCB will also extend markers where an applicant's internal investigation continues and it intends to continue to proffer information to the CCB. In each case, the CCB's decision to extend an applicant's marker is discretionary and the applicant's failure to request a marker extension may cost it its immunity or leniency position. Applicants have a positive obligation to update their proffers as they become aware of new or corrected information.

The CCB's *Immunity and Leniency Programs under the Competition Act* sets out in significant detail the information the CCB expects to receive at the proffer stage. It includes information about the parties, the product, the industry, the specific market, the conduct, the impact of the conduct, and the witnesses and documents available from the applicant to prove the offense.

Typically, an applicant's counsel proffers the information to the CCB. The proffer may occur on a hypothetical basis. In other words, counsel may present information that the applicant could hypothetically provide were it to receive immunity or leniency and cooperate with the investigation. The CCB also accepts proffers on a "without prejudice" basis, meaning that if the applicant does not receive immunity or leniency, the information proffered will not be used against the applicant in a future criminal prosecution.

The proffer process is complete when the CCB has received sufficient information from the applicant to make an immunity or leniency recommendation to the PPSC. The PPSC considers the CCB's recommendation and has independent authority to determine whether to enter into an immunity or plea agreement with the applicant. If it agrees with the recommendation, the PPSC will negotiate an (interim) immunity agreement or plea agreement with the applicant.

Following execution of the applicable agreement, an applicant must continue to cooperate with the CCB's investigation and any subsequent prosecution of the offense by the PPSC. This will often include providing documents and making employees available to be interviewed (if neither have occurred already during the proffer process). If the matter goes to a contested trial, employees will be required to testify against their former coconspirators.

To qualify for leniency, an applicant must agree to plead guilty. That agreement is formalized by the execution of a plea agreement negotiated between the applicant and the PPSC. The PPSC maintains a template corporate plea agreement.[81]

Unlike in the United States, the plea agreement is confidential and is not filed with the court. Several other plea-related documents, however, are filed with the court and are made publicly available after the conviction. These documents typically include more detail about the anticompetitive conduct than do U.S. plea agreements. For example, the prosecutor and the accused will sign a Statement of Admissions that provides the evidentiary foundation for the guilty plea and jointly recommended sentence. The Statement of Admissions will include a description of the anticompetitive conduct, the time period involved, and the affected volume of commerce, among other details. It may include information that the CCB has gathered from third parties and that the accused has no knowledge of but does not dispute for the purposes of the plea. The prosecutor will also file a written submission in support of the jointly recommended sentence.

The sentencing judge can only depart from the jointly recommended sentence if the sentence would bring the administration of justice into

---

81. PUBLIC PROSECUTION SERVICE OF CANADA, ORGANIZATION IMMUNITY AGREEMENT TEMPLATE, *available at* http://www.ppsc.gc.ca/ eng/pub/fpsd-sfpg/fps-sfp/tpd/p5/ch02.html#section_9.

disrepute.[82] As a practical matter, the authors are not aware of any judge having rejected a jointly recommended sentence in the context of a Competition Act offense.

An important distinction between the U.S. and Canadian processes is that Canadian courts do not require the attendance of a senior officer as representative of the accused pleading guilty. Counsel may appear for the corporate accused; however, it is prudent to have available the board resolution confirming the corporation's decision to plead guilty.

Accused who plead guilty can expect widespread disclosure of the guilty plea and conviction. The CCB issues a press release, usually the same day as the accused is convicted and sentenced. Competition reporters and sometimes other media outlets republish the news. Invariably, the plea and sentence come to the attention of the plaintiffs' class action firms in the United States and Canada.

C. European Commission

1. Competition Law

a.   Article 101 of the TFEU

(1) Elements of the Offense

Article 101 of the Treaty on the Functioning of the European Union[83] is the EU's counterpart to Section 1 of the Sherman Act. Article 101(1) of the TFEU prohibits agreements between companies, decisions by associations of companies, and concerted practices which may affect trade between Member States and which have as their object or effect the prevention, restriction, or distortion of competition within the internal market.[84] While Article 101(1) of the TFEU generally captures conduct similar to that of Section 1 of the Sherman Act, certain elements of Article 101(1) of the TFEU are unique.

---

82.   R. v. Anthony-Cook, [2016] 2 S.C.R. 204 (Can.).
83.   Consolidated Version of the Treaty on the Functioning of the European Union Art. 101, Oct. 26, 2012, 2012 O.J. (C 326) 47 [hereinafter TFEU]. As of December 1, 2009, the Treaty of Lisbon became effective and introduced a renumbering of the articles in the Treaty Establishing the European Community.
84.   *Id.* Art. 101(1) of the TFEU.

Article 101(1) of the TFEU covers anticompetitive agreements and concerted practices. [85] "Concerted practices" refer to "coordination between [companies] by which [ ] practical cooperation between them is knowingly substituted for the risks of competition."[86] This includes the exchange of "sensitive business information," or all information that increases a company's ability to predict its competitors' market behavior and thus undermines the uncertainty inherent to functioning competition. The exchange or even one-sided disclosure of information relating to a company's *future* conduct tends to be particularly sensitive. Concerted practices require (1) concerting amongst participating companies, (2) subsequent conduct on the market, and (3) a causal link between the two. That causal link is presumed, provided that the participating companies remain active on the market.[87] The concept of concerted practices means that the Commission does not have to establish the existence of an agreement.

A series of acts or continuous conduct may qualify as a single, complex and continuous infringement. This applies even if one or several elements of that series of acts or continuous conduct could constitute in themselves an infringement of Article 101(1) of the TFEU.[88] A single, complex and continuous infringement can be established where the alleged conduct (1) involves a series of acts that form part of an "overall plan," (2) displays a continuity of certain practices and patterns, and (3) has an identical object that distorts competition within the internal market.

A single and continuous infringement can exist even if there are intermittent periods of no cartel activity, as long as the objective of the anti-competitive practices remains the same throughout the entire time period.[89] However, if the conduct before and after a period of no cartel

---

85. *Id.* Art. 101(1) of the TFEU.
86. Case C-8/08, T-Mobile Netherlands BV v. Raad van bestuur van de Nederlandse Mededingingsautoriteit, 2009 E.C.R. I-04529, ¶ 26 (Eur. Ct. Justice).
87. *Id.* ¶ 51.
88. Case C-204/00 P, Aalborg Portland v. Commission, 2004 E.C.R. I-00123, ¶ 258 (Eur. Ct. Justice); Case C-49/92 P, Commission v. Anic Partecipazioni S.p.A, 1999 E.C.R. I-04125, ¶ 81 (Eur. Ct. Justice); Case COMP/40.055 – Parking Heaters (June 17, 2015) (summary at 2015 O.J. (C 425) 9), *available at* http://ec.europa.eu/competition/antitrust/cases/dec_docs/40055/40055_713_11.pdf.
89. Case T-377/06, Comap SA v. Commission, 2011 E.C.R. II-01115, ¶ 85 (Gen. Ct.).

activity can be clearly distinguished, each period of conduct may qualify as a separate infringement.

It is irrelevant whether a company directly participated in only one or some of the constituent elements of the cartel, provided that it (1) intended to contribute to the overall plan, (2) could have at least reasonably foreseen the actual conduct by the other cartel participants, and (3) was prepared to take the risk.[90] The company's specific contribution to the cartel may be reflected in the fine imposed on it, but not in assessing the existence of its involvement or the cartel.[91] It is a company's burden to prove that its participation in any anticompetitive meetings was without any anticompetitive intent. To avoid liability, the company must firmly and unambiguously distance itself from the illegal conduct in the meeting itself or report the initiative to the administrative authorities.[92]

Article 101(1) of the TFEU distinguishes between "restrictions by object" and "restrictions by effect." An agreement or concerted practice that has as its object the prevention, restriction, or distortion of competition is regarded as being injurious to the proper functioning of competition by its very nature. For that reason, there is no need to take into account the actual effects of an agreement or concerted practice once its anticompetitive object is established. To constitute a restriction by object, it is sufficient that conduct has the potential of having a negative impact on competition.[93]

To determine whether an agreement involves a restriction by object, numerous factors are considered, such as its provisions, its objectives, and the economic and legal context of which it forms a part. Attention should also be paid to the nature of the goods or services affected, the real conditions of the functioning, and the structure of the market.[94] The Commission may also take into account the parties' intentions.[95] Conduct

---

90. *Anic Partecipazioni*, C-49/92 P, ¶ 87; Case T-384/06, IBP Ltd & Int'l Bldg. Prods. France SA v. Commission, 2011 E.C.R. II-01177, ¶ 56 (Gen. Ct.).

91. *Anic Partecipazioni*, C-49/92 P, ¶ 90 .

92. Case C-68/12, Protimonopolný úrad Slovenskej republiky v. Slovenská sporitel' ňa a.s., http://eur-lex.europa.eu/legal-content/EN/TXT/?uri=CELEX:62011CJ0226, ¶ 27 (Eur. Ct. Justice), cited in 2013 O.J. (C 114) 19.

93. Case C-226/11, Expedia Inc. v. Autorité de la concurrence, http://eur-lex.europa.eu/legal-content/EN/ALL/?uri=CELEX:62011CJ0226, ¶¶ 35-37 (Eur. Ct. Justice), cited in 2013 O.J. (C 38) 6.

94. *Id.*, ¶ 21.

95. *T-Mobile Netherlands BV*, C-8/08, ¶ 24 .

that gives rise to cartel cases will usually be considered as a restriction by object.

Article 101(1) of the TFEU only applies to agreements that restrict competition in an *appreciable* manner. According to the Commission, agreements between or concerted practices involving actual or potential competitors generally do not appreciably affect competition if the market share of the parties does not exceed 10 percent.[96] However, this safe harbor does not apply to agreements or concerted practices whose object are to restrict competition because they, by their very nature, are deemed to have an appreciable effect on competition.[97]

(2) Exemptions

Article 101(3) of the TFEU provides an exemption for certain agreements and concerted practices that may fall under Article 101(1) of the TFEU. Article 101(3) of the TFEU is based on the belief that some restrictive agreements may generate objective economic benefits that outweigh their negative effects.[98] Thus, Article 101(1) of the TFEU does not apply to agreements and concerted practices which (1) contribute to improving the production or distribution of goods, promote technical or economic progress, (2) while allowing consumers a fair share of the resulting benefit, (3) do not impose restrictions that are indispensable to the attainment of these objectives, and (4) do not substantially eliminate competition with respect to the relevant products.

The provision is applicable to individual agreements and categories of agreements by way of "block exemptions."[99] Whereas the party or authority alleging infringement of Article 101(1) of the TFEU must prove the infringement, the company claiming an Article 101(3) of the TFEU exemption bears the burden of proving that the conditions of that article are fulfilled.[100] Generally, typical cartel conduct will not create economic

---

96. Commission Notice on agreements of minor importance which do not appreciably restrict competition under Article 101(1) of the Treaty on the Functioning of the European Union (De Minimis Notice), 2014 O.J. (C 291) 1.
97. *Expedia*, C-226/11, ¶ 37.
98. *See* Commission Notice on Guidelines on the Application of Article 81 (3) of the Treaty, 2004 O.J. (C 101) 97, ¶¶ 32-37.
99. *See* Council Regulation (EC) No 1/2003, art. 1(2), 2003 O.J. (L 1) 1 (explaining the implementation of the rules on competition in Articles 81 and 82 of the Treaty) [hereinafter Regulation 1/2003].
100. *See* Regulation 1/2003, art. 2.

efficiencies nor benefit consumers, and thus will fail to qualify for an exemption.[101]

b. Principles of Corporate Liability

(1) No Criminal Liability

Fines imposed by the Commission for infringements of Article 101 of the TFEU are administrative in nature. The Commission does not have the power to impose criminal fines. However, certain Member States provide for criminal sanctions for specific forms of cartel conduct or infringements of Article 101 of the TFEU generally.

(2) Individual, Corporate and Parental Liability

The Commission's power to impose fines for infringements of Article 101 of the TFEU is limited to companies and does not extend to individuals. In the EU, a company is liable for any and all natural persons who are entitled to act on its behalf. There is no requirement that the individuals were authorized to participate in the specific anticompetitive conduct, and the company may be held liable even if the individuals acted in violation of the company's compliance policy. Moreover, for Article 101 of the TFEU to apply, no action by or knowledge on the part of the partners or top managers of the company is necessary. [102]

The term "company" must be understood broadly as designating an economic unit which may consist of several persons, natural or legal.[103] A parent company and its subsidiary form an economic unit if the subsidiary does not independently decide upon its conduct on the market but carries out, in all material respects, the instructions given to it by the parent company. To attribute the conduct of a subsidiary to its parent company, the Commission must prove that the parent company could and did in fact exercise decisive influence over the subsidiary. All economic, organizational, and legal relations between both companies must be taken into account. A rebuttable presumption that a parent company did, in fact, exercise decisive influence arises where the parent owns all or almost all shares of the subsidiary. To rebut the presumption, the parent company

---

101. *See* Commission Notice on Guidelines on the application of Article 81 (3) of the Treaty, 2004 O.J. (C 101) 97, ¶ 46 and case law cited.

102. *Protimonopolný úrad Slovenskej republiky*, C-68/12 ¶¶ 25-28.

103. *See* Case C-97/08 P, Akzo Nobel v. Commission, 2009 E.C.R. I-08237,¶¶ 55-59 (Eur. Ct. Justice).

must prove that the subsidiary determined its conduct on the market autonomously.[104]

Generally, the conduct of any direct and indirect affiliate can be attributed to the ultimate parent company of the group. Financial investors may also be held liable for the conduct of their portfolio companies.[105] Parent companies may have to answer for infringements by joint ventures, provided that they together exercised a decisive influence on the joint venture.[106] Generally, no attribution of liability occurs between sister companies. The conduct of a parent company is generally not attributed to its subsidiary.

In practice, the Commission addresses its decisions to the companies that were directly involved in the infringement and their ultimate parent entity. These companies will be held jointly and severally liable for the payment of the fine imposed on them.

(3) Liability and M&A Transactions

Specific rules apply if the business involved in cartel activity is transferred. The seller and the target will be jointly and severally liable for the target's infringement up until the time title to the target's business passes to the buyer (closing). As a general rule, the buyer is not liable for the target's conduct prior to closing. If the target continues to be involved in cartel activity after closing, however, the buyer will be jointly and severally liable with the target from the closing date, even in cases where the buyer has no knowledge of the cartel. Only in exceptional cases may the buyer be liable for the target's conduct prior to closing, notably if the target ceases to exist as a result of the transaction or if the transaction occurs exclusively within one and the same corporate group.

For the seller, the limitation period starts to run at closing, while the limitation periods for the target and, if the conduct continues after closing, for the buyer does not start to run until the conduct ends. Often, the Commission's investigation will initially focus on the target and the

---

104. *Akzo Nobel*, C-97/08 P,¶¶ 60 to 62.
105. Case AT.39610 – Power Cables, Comm'n Decision (April 2, 2014 (summary at 2014 O.J. (C 319) 10).
106. Case C-179/12 P, The Dow Chemical Co. v. Commission, ¶ 56, http://eur-lex.europa.eu/legal-content/EN/TXT/?uri=CELEX:62012CJ0179 (Eur. Ct. Justice), cited in 2013 O.J. (C 344) 28; case T-543/08, RWE v. Commission, http://eur-lex.europa.eu/legal-content/EN/TXT/?uri=CELEX:62008TJ0543, ¶¶ 99-130 (Ct. First Instance), cited in 2014 O.J. (C 292) 25.

current owner, while the previous owner may not learn about the investigation until a much later stage. However, the Commission's investigation against the target company, the buyer, or any other company involved in the alleged cartel will also interrupt the limitation period towards the seller even if the seller is not aware of the investigation.[107] Moreover, the seller, although liable for the target's conduct, will not benefit from any immunity or leniency reduction for which the target and the buyer may qualify.

c.   Statute of Limitations

The limitation period for the imposition of fines is five years. In principle, the limitation period begins to run on the day on which the infringement is committed.[108] In the event of continuing or repeated infringements, however, the limitation period begins to run the day the infringement ceases.[109] The limitation period is interrupted by any action by the Commission or the competition authority of a Member State taken for the purpose of an investigation or proceedings.[110] This interruption applies to all companies or associations of companies that participated in the infringement.[111] In case of an interruption, the limitation period of five years starts to run afresh.[112] At the latest, however, the limitation period expires when a ten-year-period has elapsed without the Commission having imposed a fine or a periodic penalty payment.[113]

d.   International Scope of Article 101 of the TFEU

The scope of Article 101 of the TFEU is not limited to companies located within the EU, and applies to agreements and practices that cover countries outside the EU, provided that they are capable of affecting trade between Member States.[114] While the Commission consistently applies the effects doctrine, the CJEU formally adheres to the territoriality principle. The practical differences are rather limited, however, as the CJEU does

---

107.   *See* Regulation 1/2003, art. 25(4).
108.   *Id.*, art. 25(1)(b), 25(2).
109.   *Id.*, art. 24(2).
110.   *Id.*, art. 25(1).
111.   *Id.*, art. 25(4).
112.   *Id.*, art. 25(5).
113.   *Id.*
114.   Commission Notice on Guidelines on the effect on trade concept contained in Articles 81 and 82 of the Treaty, 2004 O.J. (C 101) 81, ¶ 100.

not focus on where the agreement is concluded, but rather on where the agreement is executed (the "implementation doctrine").[115]

The Commission has jurisdiction if a cartel is implemented in the EEA. For an agreement to be implemented in the EEA, it is sufficient that the cartelized product is sold in the EEA, irrespective of where the sources of supply or production facilities are located.[116] Under the implementation doctrine, Article 101 of the TFEU also applies where a vertically integrated company incorporates cartelized goods into finished products in production facilities outside the EU and sells the finished products in the EU to independent third parties, even if the market for the finished products constitutes a separate market from that concerned by the infringement.[117]

2. Enforcement Authority and Actions

a.   European Commission and European Competition Network

(1) Enforcement Authority

Ultimate responsibility for the efficient and consistent enforcement of the antitrust rules lies with the Commission. Pursuant to Article 16 of Regulation 1/2003, however, national competition authorities (NCAs) share responsibility for the effective application of European antitrust law. To ensure effective enforcement of EU competition rules, the Commission and the NCAs have established the European Competition Network (ECN).[118]

---

115.   Joined Cases 89, 104, 114, 116, 117, 125 & 129/85, Ahlström Osakeythtiö v. Commission, 1999 E.C.R. I-00099 (Eur. Ct. Justice).

116.   Case T-91/11 Innolux v. Commission, http://eur-lex.europa.eu/legal-content/EN/TXT/?uri=CELEX:62011TJ0091, ¶ 63 (Ct. First Instance), cited in 2014 O.J. (C 112) 27.

117.   Case   T-104/13   Toshiba   Corp.   v.   Commission,   http://eur-lex.europa.eu/legal-content/EN/TXT/?uri=CELEX:62013TJ0104,   ¶ 161 (Ct. First Instance), cited in 2015 O.J. (C 346) 21.

118.   Rules applying within the ECN are set out in Regulation 1/2003 and the Joint Statement of the Council and the Commission on the Functioning of the Network of Competition Authorities (Dec. 10, 2002), *available at* http://ec.europa.eu/competition/ecn/joint_statement_en.pdf (described in more detail Commission Notice on Cooperation within the Network of Competition Authorities, 2004 O.J. (C 101) 43).

(2) Cooperation and Exchange of Information

According to Article 11(1) of Regulation 1/2003, the Commission and the NCAs are to apply EU competition rules in close cooperation. Article 12(1) of Regulation 1/2003 provides the Commission and NCAs with the power to share and use in evidence any matter of fact or law, including confidential information. However, information exchanged shall only be used in evidence for the purpose of applying Articles 101 or 102 of the TFEU and with respect to the subject matter for which it was collected by the transmitting authority.[119]

To avoid discouraging applicants from voluntarily reporting cartel activity, the Commission has created safeguards for information contained in leniency applications and all information that has been collected following any fact-finding measures that could not have been carried out but for a leniency application. [120] If an NCA receives a leniency application, it must inform all other members.[121] Other members are not be allowed to use that information to start their own investigations, however. Moreover, information which has been provided by a leniency applicant may only be exchanged between two competition authorities if: (1) the leniency applicant agrees to the exchange; (2) the leniency applicant has applied for leniency with both authorities in the same case; or (3) the receiving competition authority provides a written commitment not to use the information submitted or any information it may obtain after the date of the transmission to impose sanctions on the applicant or its subsidiaries or employees. The same rules apply to information which a competition authority has collected during an inspection or has received in response to a request for information which it could not have conducted or issued but for the leniency application.

NCAs are entitled to carry out inspections in their own territories for other NCAs in order to establish an infringement of EU competition law. Moreover, at the request of the Commission, NCAs shall undertake inspections that the Commission considers to be necessary or has ordered by decision.

---

119. Regulation 1/2003, art. 12(2).
120. *See* Commission Notice on Cooperation within the Network of Competition Authorities, 2004 O.J. (C 101) 43, ¶¶ 39-41.
121. Regulation 1/2003 art. 11.

b. European Commission Investigative Tactics and Procedures

(1) Preliminary Investigation Stage, Investigative Powers

The Commission's investigation usually consists of two different phases: (1) the preliminary investigation stage and (2) the inter partes stage. These phases are separated by the Commission's formal decision to initiate proceedings[122] and the statement of objections, which sets out in detail the Commission's competition concerns.

In order to investigate potential cartel infringements, the Commission has the power to carry out on-site inspections of companies' premises[123] and of private homes.[124] The Commission's power to request information from companies and associations of companies also plays a significant role.[125] Further, although the Commission has no compulsory power to order depositions, it has the right to interview any natural or legal person if such person consents to the interview.[126] The Commission enjoys broad discretion to determine the investigative measures it employs, subject to the principle of proportionality.[127]

(2) Inter Partes Stage

The official statement of objections concludes the investigation phase and leads to the formal inter partes stage. The statement of objections affects the rights of defense for the parties involved. The parties are granted access to all non-confidential documents in the Commission's file and are entitled to reply to the statement in writing. The parties may also request an oral hearing to defend their case, which is conducted by an independent Hearing Officer.

If the Commission's initial concerns are addressed, the Commission may abandon its objections and decide to close the case. Otherwise, the Commission may draft a decision prohibiting the identified breaches of

---

122. Commission Regulation (EC) No 773/2004 relating to the conduct of proceedings by the Commission pursuant to Articles 81 and 82 of the EC Treaty, 2004 O.J. (L 123) 18.
123. Regulation 1/2003, art. 20.
124. Regulation 1/2003, art. 21.
125. Regulation 1/2003, art. 18.
126. Regulation 1/2003, art. 19.
127. Case T-39/90, Samenwerkende Elektriciteits-Produktiebedrijven NV v. Comm'n of the European Communities, 1991 E.C.R. II-01497, ¶¶ 51-52 (Ct. First Instance).

antitrust law. The draft decision will subsequently be submitted to the NCAs' advisory committee and, finally, to the college of commissioners to adopt the decision.

(3) Settlement Procedure

In 2008, the Commission introduced a settlement procedure for cartels, enabling it to settle cartel cases through a simplified procedure where the parties acknowledge their involvement in and liability for the cartel.[128] In return, the parties can receive a 10 percent fine reduction. The settlement process entails certain additional practical benefits for companies. In order to achieve a settlement, the Commission may accept to limit its charges to certain time periods, products or aspects of the cartel. Settlement decisions are also relatively short, which means they tend to be less useful to the plaintiffs in follow-on litigation. The settlement procedure is not to be confused with the Commission's leniency program. Where a company agrees to settle a case and qualifies for leniency, the settlement reduction will be applied on top of the leniency bonus. The Commission has a broad discretion to determine which cases may be suitable for a settlement procedure. Although parties can indicate their interest in settlement discussions, they have neither the right nor duty to settle.

The settlement process is organized around three settlement meetings with intermittent phases of advocacy. In the first settlement meeting, the Commission will set out the facts and evidence with which it intends to charge the companies. The companies will then get access to that evidence, including any leniency materials. At this stage, the Commission will seek to reach an agreement with the companies about the facts and the value of sales affected by the alleged infringement. The companies are asked to formally confirm their agreement during the second settlement meeting. The companies may then assert arguments relevant to the level of potential fine, such as the gravity of the infringement, any mitigating factors, and the scope and value of their cooperation with the Commission. During the third settlement meeting, the Commission will communicate to the parties the fine range that it intends to impose in a settlement decision. If the

---

128. *See* Commission Regulation (EC) No 622/2008, 2008 O.J. (L 171), 2008 O.J. (L 171) 3 (amending Regulation (EC) No 773/2004, as regards settlement procedures in cartel cases); Commission Notice on the conduct of settlement procedures in view of the adoption of decisions pursuant to Article 7 and Article 23 of Council Regulation (EC) No 1/2003 in cartel cases, 2008 O.J. (C 167) 1.

company wishes to proceed with the settlement process, it must submit a settlement submission providing:

- an acknowledgement of its liability for the infringement, as previously agreed with the Commission;
- an indication of the maximum fine the company foresees being imposed by the Commission, reflecting the amount previously communicated by the Commission;
- the company's confirmation that it has been informed of the Commission's objections in a satisfactory manner and that it has been given the opportunity to be heard;
- its confirmation that it will request neither access to the file nor a formal oral hearing; and
- its agreement to receive the statement of objections and final decision of the Commission in a given EU language (typically English).

On that basis, the Commission will issue a statement of objections and, if the companies confirm that the statement of objections reflects their respective settlement submissions, eventually adopt a final decision.

The Commission may revert to the standard procedure at any time until the final decision, particularly if not all companies agree to settle. Similarly, the parties may decide to discontinue settlement discussions at any time until they have formally introduced a settlement submission, which cannot be unilaterally revoked unless not fully reflected in the Commission's statement of objections and final decision. However, if a company discontinues the settlement process, the Commission must determine the company's liability irrespective of any views exchanged during the settlement discussions. As the General Court held in *Timab v. Commission*, a company will not be able to argue a breach of legitimate expectations if the Commission ultimately choses to impose a fine which is higher than the range discussed during settlement discussions.[129]

---

129. Case T-456/10, Timab Indus. & CFPR v. Commission, http://eur-lex.europa.eu/legal-content/EN/TXT/?uri=CELEX:62010TJ0456, ¶¶ 75-107 (Gen. Ct.), cited in 2015 O.J. (C 221) 6.

c. Decision-making Powers

(1) Administrative Fines

The Commission is empowered to impose severe fines on companies and associations of companies that intentionally or negligently infringe European antitrust law.[130] The fine can be up to 10 percent of the total annual turnover of the entire group that the company forms a part of.

The Commission has issued guidelines for setting fines[131] and uses a two-step methodology when setting a fine. To determine the basic amount of the fine, the Commission uses as a starting point the value of the company's sales of goods or services to which the infringement directly or indirectly relates in the relevant geographic area. In a global cartel case, the Commission will primarily focus on sales made to customers located in the EEA ("direct sales"). Direct sales are distinguished from indirect sales. Indirect sales occur where (1) cartelized goods are sold to a third party outside the EEA, (2) that third party incorporates these cartelized goods into its products outside the EEA, and (3) the third party subsequently sells its downstream products to customers located in the EEA. The Commission has the authority to include indirect sales, in particular if a fine based on only direct sales would not be sufficiently severe to deter future infringements. To date, the Commission has not taken into account indirect sales for fine calculation purposes.[132] However, the Commission does take into account sales of "transformed products." Transformed product sales are captive sales of cartelized products and occur where (1) a member of the cartel incorporates goods into its own products and (2) subsequently sells these downstream products to customers located in the EEA.[133]

---

130. Regulation 1/2003, art. 23(2)(a).
131. Commission Guidelines on the method of setting fines imposed pursuant to Article 23(2)(a) of Regulation No 1/2003, 2006 O.J. (C 210) 2.
132. *See, e.g.,* Case COMP/39.209 -LCD (Liquid Crystal Displays), Comm'n Decision, ¶¶ 380, 381 (December 8, 2010) (summary at 2011 O.J. (C 295) 8), *available at* http://ec.europa.eu/competition/antitrust/ cases/dec_docs/ 39309/39309_3643_4.pdf and Case AT.39437 – TV and Computer Monitor Tubes, Comm'n Decision, ¶¶ 1020, 1021 (December 5, 2012) (summary at 2013 O.J. (C 303) 13), *available at* http://ec.europa.eu/ competition/antitrust/cases/dec_docs/39437/39437_6784_3.pdf.
133. This applies irrespective of whether cartelized goods are processed by the entity involved in the cartel or sold by that entity to another entity which belongs to the same corporate group, be it in or outside of the EEA *cf.* Case

The Commission will apply a percentage of the company's value of affected sales. Depending on the gravity of the infringement ("gravity factor"), that percentage can be up to 30 percent. Other factors are taken into account, such as the nature of the infringement, the combined market share of all the companies involved, the geographic scope of the infringement, and whether or not the infringement was implemented. In cases involving horizontal price fixing, market sharing, and output limitations, the percentage applied will generally be in the range of 15 to 20 percent. The resulting amount will be multiplied by the number of years and months of the company's participation in the infringement. Irrespective of the duration of the infringement, the Commission will add a sum of between 15 and 25 percent of the value of sales to deter companies from entering into illegal cartels ("entry fee").

Thereafter, the Commission will adjust the basic amount for aggravating and mitigating circumstances. Aggravating circumstances include recidivism and a company's refusal to cooperate with the Commission in its investigation. A refusal to cooperate may be found if a company prevents Commission officials from entering the premises, serving the inspection decision, or talking to its management staff.[134] The fine may also be increased if the company instigated or had the leading role in the infringement. The Commission may also increase the fine on companies with a particularly large turnover beyond the sales of goods or services to which the infringement relates to ensure the fines have a sufficiently deterrent effect ("deterrent multiplier").

On the other hand, the basic amount may be reduced if the company concerned provides evidence that it immediately terminated the infringement after the Commission's intervention and/or cooperated effectively with the Commission outside the scope of the Leniency Notice and beyond its legal obligation to do so. Furthermore, the amount may be reduced if the company's conduct was a result of negligence or was authorized or encouraged by public authority or by legislation.

The final fine must not exceed 10 percent of the total turnover in the preceding business year of the relevant company. However, this 10 percent cap applies *per infringement*. Hence, where a company has committed multiple infringements, the total amount of fines can exceed 10 percent of

---

C-231/14 P – Innolux v. Commission, http://eur-lex.europa.eu/legal-content/EN/TXT/?uri=CELEX:62014CJ0231, ¶¶ 44-51 (Eur. Ct. Justice), cited in 2015 O.J. (C 294) 12.

134. Case COMP/F/38.456, Bitumen Nederland, Comm'n Decision, 2007 O.J. (L 196) 40, ¶ 340.

total sales, even if the several infringements are addressed in the same decision. The fine will be reduced in case of a successful immunity application (by 100 percent), leniency application (by up to 50 percent) and/or settlement (by 10 percent).

(2) Cooperation with other Antitrust Regulators

The Commission actively cooperates with antitrust enforcement agencies around the world and, to that end, has entered into numerous bilateral cooperation agreements. For example, in 1991, the Commission signed its first cooperation agreement with the U.S. [135] The agreement includes provisions regarding notification and coordination of enforcement activities and exchanges of information. Subsequently, the EU and the U.S. entered into the Positive Comity Agreement (1998)[136] and the Administrative Arrangement on Attendance. [137] Comparable cooperation agreements have also been signed with several other non-EU countries.[138] These agreements, including the agreements with the U.S., generally do not allow the Commission to share confidential information and evidence obtained under its leniency program. The Commission will therefore often ask leniency applicants to provide waivers which authorize such an exchange.

---

135. Agreement between the Government of the United States of America and the Commission of the European Communities regarding the application of their competition laws, 1995 O.J. (L 95) 47.
136. Agreement between the European Communities and the Government of the United States of America on the application of positive comity principles in the enforcement of their competition laws, 1998 O.J. (L 173) 28.
137. Report from the Commission to the Council and the European Parliament on the application of the Agreement between the European Communities and the Government of the United States of America regarding the application of their competition laws, COM(2000) 618 final, *available at* http://eur-lex.europa.eu/legal-content/EN/TXT/PDF/?uri=CELEX:52000DC0618.
138. Overview of the Commission's cooperation engagement on competition matters with non-EU countries, *available at* http://ec.europa.eu/competition/international/bilateral/index.html.

d. Responding to Cartel Investigations in the EU

(1) Requests for Information

Requests for information are one of the Commission's most important investigative tools. Requests for information may take the form of either a simple request or a decision. A simple request is not binding for the addressee and the company has no obligation to respond. Sanctions apply only if the company submits incorrect or misleading information.[139] If the Commission requests information by decision, the company is obliged to respond, and sanctions can be imposed if the information is not supplied within the required time limit.[140] The Commission may issue a request for information if there is suspicion of a specific cartel infringement. The Commission needs to disclose, clearly and unequivocally, the suspicions which justify the request for information so the addressee can assess whether the requested information is necessary for the purposes of the investigation.[141] "Fishing expeditions" are not permitted. Moreover, the request for information must be necessary and proportionate to the purpose of the investigation.

(2) Inspections

The Commission may enter the premises of companies, examine and take copies of business records, seal the business premises and records during an inspection, ask questions, and record the answers. The Commission may also raid other premises (including private homes of directors, managers and staff members) if there is a reasonable suspicion that information related to the business and the subject matter of the inspection, which may be relevant to prove a serious infringement of Article 101 of the TFEU, is kept on these premises. If an inspection is ordered by a formal Commission decision, the relevant company is obliged to cooperate in the investigation (subject to legal privilege and the right against self-incrimination). Failure to produce required books or other business records in complete form, to answer questions, or to submit to the inspection can be sanctioned. The Commission may only search for documents which are related to the subject-matter of the inspection, and

139. Regulation 1/2003, art. 23(1)(a).
140. *Id.*, art. 23(1)(b).
141. Case C ‑ 247/14 P, HeidelbergCement v. Commission, http://eur-lex.europa.eu/legal-content/EN/TXT/?uri=CELEX:62014CJ0247, ¶ 27 (Eur. Ct. Justice).

information obtained during an inspection must not be used for any purposes other than those specified in the inspection decision. The Commission may, however, initiate a new investigation to verify or supplement information obtained "by chance" in a previous inspection if that information indicates an infringement of the EU competition rules.[142]

(3) European Commission's Powers to Investigate outside the EEA

Outside the EEA, the Commission's ability to investigate is limited by the principles of international law. Therefore, the Commission may not conduct on-site inspections outside the EEA. However, if the Commission raids a company located in the EEA and that company has access to information located outside the EEA (e.g., to data saved on a server abroad), the Commission will be able to access and take copies of that information.

The Commission may not issue formal decisions to companies located outside the EEA that order the production of documents. The Commission may send informal requests for information to companies located abroad. However, the Commission has no power to sanction such companies for non-compliance. Therefore, if the company under investigation is located abroad but has a subsidiary in the EEA, the Commission will usually issue a formal request for information to the EEA subsidiary. The Commission may order the production of any and all documents which are in the possession of the subsidiary or any entity which belongs to the same corporate group, provided the addressee of the decision has effective control over the documents. The subsidiary's obligation to produce documents applies irrespective of whether the documents are located in the EEA or abroad.[143]

3. Leniency Program

The Commission has established a leniency program which rewards cooperation by companies involved in a cartel.

---

142. Case C-583/13P – Deutsche Bahn v. Commission, http://eur-lex.europa.eu/legal-content/EN/TXT/?uri=CELEX:62013CJ0583, ¶¶ 57-59 (Eur. Ct. Justice), cited in 2015 O.J. (C 279) 6.

143. Useful practical information about the Commission's investigate powers abroad can be found in the Commission's Antitrust Manual of Procedures (March 2012), *available at* http://ec.europa.eu/competition/antitrust/anti-trust_manproc_3_2012_en.pdf.

a. Commission's Leniency Notice

In its Leniency Notice from December 2006,[144] the Commission set out the framework for rewarding investigatory cooperation by companies which are or have been party to secret cartels affecting the EU.

Under the Leniency Notice, companies may obtain full immunity from fines or a fine reduction of up to 20 to 50 percent, mainly depending on the time the Commission is contacted and on the quality of the evidence provided. Immunity from any fines will only be granted to the company that is first to submit information and evidence to the Commission. The immunity applicant, but not subsequent leniency applicants, is entitled to additional benefits in case of follow-on damage claims. While cartel offenders, as a general matter, are jointly and severally liable for the entire harm caused by the cartel and thus have to respond to damage claims brought by all customers, including those who purchased the cartelized products from other cartel members or third parties ("umbrella damages"), the immunity applicant's liability is generally limited to harm directly related to its own sales.[145]

Immunity from fines will be granted to a company involved in a secret cartel if that company is the first to submit information and evidence that enables the Commission to either carry out a targeted inspection in connection with the alleged cartel or to establish an infringement of Article 101 of the TFEU.

The company must provide the Commission with a written or oral corporate statement, which includes a detailed description of the alleged cartel arrangement and the names of all other companies that participated in the alleged cartel.

To gain immunity, the company also must fully cooperate throughout the Commission's administrative procedure and immediately end its involvement in the alleged cartel. No immunity will be granted if the company, while contemplating an application, has destroyed, falsified or concealed evidence of the alleged cartel, or at any time took steps to coerce other companies to join or remain in the cartel, or if the company has disclosed the fact or contents of its contemplated or pending application (except to other competition authorities).

---

144. Commission Notice on Immunity from fines and reduction of fines in cartel cases, 2006 O.J. (C 298) 17.
145. Directive 2014/104/EU of the European Parliament and of the Council of 26 November 2014 on certain rules governing actions for damages under national law for infringements of the competition law provisions of the Member States and of the European Union, art. 11, 2014 O.J. (L 349) 1.

Once the Commission has received the information set out above and has verified that the company meets the conditions for immunity, it will grant the company conditional immunity in writing. A final decision on immunity will be taken only in the Commission's infringement decision.

Where the conditions for immunity are not met, a company disclosing its participation in an alleged cartel may at least be eligible for a reduction of the fine that would otherwise have been imposed.

A fine reduction requires the company to provide the Commission with evidence of the infringement that represents significant added value as compared to the evidence already in the Commission's possession. In addition, the company must fully cooperate with the Commission and end its involvement in the alleged cartel following its application. Moreover, the company must keep its cooperation with the Commission strictly confidential. Depending on the chronological order of the added value provided, the Commission will consider a reduction of the fine of:

- 30 to 50 percent for the first company to provide significant added value;
- 20 to 30 percent for the second company to provide significant added value; and
- Up to 20 percent for all subsequent companies that provide significant added value.

Within each of these bands, the Commission will determine the specific percentage to be granted to a company based on the value of the evidence provided and the time it was submitted.

In determining the level of added value submitted, the Commission will consider the extent to which the evidence provided strengthens the Commission's ability to prove the alleged cartel. For instance, incriminating evidence directly related to the facts in question ("stand-alone evidence") will generally be considered to have greater value than evidence with only contextual relevance. Particularly high value will be afforded to written, contemporaneous evidence of cartel conduct.

Once the Commission has examined the formal application and the evidence presented, it will inform the company, in writing, of its preliminary intention to either grant a fine reduction within a specified band or to reject the application. In practice, the Commission will usually issue such a letter at the same time it opens proceedings and/or adopts a statement of objections. At the end of the administrative procedure, the Commission will then adopt its final decision and, in case it grants a fine reduction, determine the exact level of reduction the company will benefit from.

A company which intends to seek immunity can initially apply for a marker. The marker serves to protect the applicant's place in the queue of leniency applications for a certain period to allow for gathering the necessary information and evidence. Usually, the period for obtaining a marker is no longer than four weeks.

b.   Applying for Leniency within the ECN

A leniency application with the Commission will not secure a company's leniency position with any NCA, and vice versa. To alleviate the burden associated with handling multiple applications, the ECN Model Leniency Programme[146] has introduced a model for a uniform system of summary applications for cases in which the Commission is particularly well placed to decide. If a company has filed or is in the process of filing a leniency application for immunity or a fine reduction with the Commission, it may submit summary applications with any and all NCAs which it believes might also be well placed to investigate the conduct. Should an NCA decide to pursue the case, it will determine a period of time within which the applicant must make a full submission, including all relevant evidence and information required to qualify for leniency. If the applicant submits such information within that time period, the information provided will be deemed to have been submitted on the date the summary application was made. Summary applications should each have an identical substantive scope to the respective application with the Commission. Additionally, the applicant must comply with all specific information requests of the NCAs, or risk losing the benefits of the summary application.

The ECN Model Leniency Programme has no binding effect on the courts and tribunals of the Member States.[147] However, most Member States have publicly communicated that they will accept summary leniency applications in line with the ECN Model Leniency Programme.[148]

---

146.   The ECN Model Leniency Programme was adopted in 2006 and revised in November 2012. It is available online at http://ec.europa.eu/ competition/ecn/model_leniency_en.pdf.

147.   *See* Cases C-360/09, Pfleiderer AG v. Bundeskartellamt, 2011 E.C.R. I-05161, ¶ 22 (Ct. Eur. Justice); *see also DHL Express (Italy) Srl*, C-428/14, ¶¶ 42-44.

148.   As of October 2015, 23 Member States had adopted leniency programmes in line with the ECN Model Leniency Programme; *see* MEMO/09/456,

D. Korea

1. Competition Law

The Monopoly Regulation and Fair Trade Act (MRFTA) is the primary Korean competition statute, effective April 1, 1981, The MRFTA prohibits conduct similar to what is generally prohibited in other countries, including cartel activities, abuse of dominance, and anticompetitive mergers and acquisitions, as well as unfair trade practices that may fall short of cartels or monopolizations. The Enforcement Decree of the MRFTA (Enforcement Decree) is a presidential decree setting forth specific standards and procedures to enforce the MRFTA.

The Korea Fair Trade Commission (KFTC), established pursuant to Article 35 of the MRFTA, is the primary competition enforcement agency in Korea. Cartel enforcement has been one of the KFTC's enforcement priorities since its establishment in 1981. Article 19 of the MRFTA prohibits businesses and individuals from agreeing with one another unfairly to restrain competition or from requiring others to engage in such collusion, expressly prohibiting nine types of concerted conduct:

1. price-fixing agreements;
2. agreements on trade conditions or terms, credit or payment terms;
3. output restriction agreements;
4. market allocation agreements;
5. agreements that restrain or interfere with the establishment of facilities or equipment used to produce goods or to provide services;
6. agreements that restrict types or specifications of goods or services to manufacture or sell;
7. the establishment of a company to carry out concerted sales practices;
8. bid-rigging agreements; and
9. other agreements that restrain or interfere with competitive business practices.

---

available at http://europa.eu/rapid/press-release_MEMO-09-456_en.htm?locale=en.

To date, the KFTC has issued six notifications regarding concerted activities. The most important are the Concerted Activity Review Guidelines and the Notification on Implementation of a Leniency Program, which establish the general principles and procedures concerning the evaluation of concerted activities and the treatment of leniency applicants.

2. Enforcement Authority and Actions

a. The KFTC and Administrative Enforcement Actions

The KFTC possesses quasi-judicial as well as investigative authority, similar to the U.S. Federal Trade Commission. As such, it investigates alleged violations of the MRFTA and imposes sanctions, including fines and corrective orders, on violators. The KFTC also exercises quasi-legislative authority by issuing notifications and guidelines. While the KFTC does not have the authority to impose criminal sanctions, it may refer cases to the Prosecutor's Office for criminal proceedings. The KFTC's adjudicative decisions are binding on respondents unless and until overturned by the court. The Seoul High Court has exclusive jurisdiction to hear appeals of KFTC decisions. The losing party may appeal the matter to the Korean Supreme Court.

The KFTC has gradually expanded the scope and degree of its cartel regulation and demonstrated its intent to expand criminal enforcement of the MRFTA for cartel activities. For example, in 2014, it identified 76 cartels and imposed approximately KRW 364.7 billion in administrative fines. While the KFTC referred only two cases to the Prosecutor's Office in 2012, it referred 36 cartel cases for criminal proceedings in 2014.

In 2014 and 2015, the KFTC has suffered a number of high-profile courtroom losses in which large administrative fines were vacated due to procedural or evidentiary issues reflecting deficient investigative procedures. For example, in August 2014, the Korean Supreme Court vacated sanctions imposed by the KFTC on Korean life insurance companies for alleged price fixing, affirming the Seoul High Court's decisions that the law requires not just an exchange of price information but an "agreement" to fix, maintain or change prices. Notably, this decision clarifies two principles of Korean antitrust law: that information exchange does not, in and of itself, amount to an illegal cartel agreement, and the heavy burden of proof that the KFTC must satisfy to show a "meeting of the minds." In 2015, the Korean Supreme Court similarly affirmed a decision vacating KFTC sanctions exceeding KRW 430 billion for failure to prove the presence of the alleged agreement.[149]

Recognizing that the absence of fair investigative procedures and due process hurt the KFTC's ability to carry out efficiently and effectively its enforcement mission and undermined the public's trust in the KFTC's legitimate law enforcement, the KFTC announced a comprehensive "Enforcement Process 3.0 Reform Initiative" and Investigative Procedural Rules that became effective in 2016.

b. The Prosecutor's Office and Criminal Enforcement Actions

The KFTC must refer a matter to the Prosecutor's Office to seek criminal sanctions. The KFTC is not the only government agency that can trigger a criminal cartel investigation, however. January 2014 amendments to the MRFTA require the KFTC to refer a matter to the Prosecutor's Office when requested by the Chief Prosecutor, the Chair of the Board of Audit and Inspection, the Chair of the Public Procurement Service or the Chair of the Small and Medium-Sized Business Administration. The KFTC has since displayed a tendency to utilize the criminal referral authority more aggressively against individuals as well as businesses. The Chair of the Public Procurement Service and the Chair of the Small and Medium-Sized Business Administration have started to exercise their newly gained powers to make binding requests. Further, the KFTC has stated that it would adopt a more aggressive stance in referring international cartel cases to the Prosecutor's Office.

c. Cooperation with Other Jurisdictions

Article 36-2 of the MRFTA provides the statutory basis for cooperation between Korea and other countries for competition law enforcement. Under Article 36-2(1), the Korean government may enter into an agreement with another country for the purpose of enforcing the MRFTA, so long as the agreement does not contravene the laws or interests of Korea. Under Article 36-2(2), the KFTC may assist the counterparty government's enforcement of its laws. Furthermore, Article 36-2(3) provides that even absent a formal agreement, the KFTC may assist a foreign government, upon its request, in enforcing its laws if it guarantees reciprocal assistance in identical or similar matters.

---

149. Supreme Court [S. Ct], 2013Da19387, Feb. 12, 2015 (S. Kor).

Moreover, the Korean government has made efforts to enhance cooperation with competition authorities of other jurisdictions. In recent years, the KFTC has held bilateral conferences with the competition authorities of the United States, the European Union, Japan, Russia and China. In 2009, Korea entered into an agreement concerning cooperation on anticompetitive activities with the European Union, the first of its kind between Korea and a foreign country. As of 2015, Korea had entered into a memorandum of understanding with 15 foreign countries, including the U.S. DOJ and Federal Trade Commission.

The KFTC's first successful cooperation with foreign competition authorities occurred in the 2010 international Air Cargo cartel, where 21 carriers from 16 countries colluded on air cargo rates between 1999 and 2007. The KFTC planned and conducted a dawn raid in coordination with the DOJ and the European Commission.

In Korea, there is no mechanism that allows foreign competition authorities to request confidential information obtained by the KFTC through, for instance, its leniency program. Nor is there a U.S.-style discovery system that provides access to other parties' information. Indeed, Article 22-2(2) enables the KFTC to refuse to comply with other jurisdictions' requests for information. Article 22-2(2) prohibits disclosure of information obtained by the KFTC from leniency applicants or investigation targets cooperating with the KFTC, except where the initial information provider has consented to disclosure or the information is needed for related litigation as properly determined by the court.

On the other hand, Korean law provides for the extradition of criminal offenders either through individual treaties with foreign countries or through the Extradition Act. Where an extradition treaty is in effect, it supersedes the Extradition Act. Absent an applicable extradition treaty, the Extradition Act applies, irrespective of whether the Korean government is making an extradition request of a foreign government, or vice versa. However, this statute only applies where the underlying crime is punishable by life imprisonment or imprisonment for more than one year under the laws of Korea and the other jurisdiction at issue.[150] Further, extradition is limited to those offenders who have been found guilty, are under investigation or on trial in the jurisdiction requesting extradition. The Ministry of Justice and the Prosecutor's Office may request the Seoul High Court to review and approve extradition requests.

---

150. Under Article 66(1)(9) of the MRFTA, a participant in an improper concerted activity is punishable by a term of imprisonment not exceeding three years and/or a criminal fine not exceeding KRW 200 million.

d.   Extraterritorial Jurisdiction and Reach of the MRFTA

Under Article 2-2, the MRFTA applies to all conduct that has an effect on the Korean market. Thus, when a foreign entity's conduct affects the Korean market, the MRFTA applies even when the foreign entity has no presence in Korea or the conduct at issue did not take place in Korea. Prior to the 2004 enactment of Article 2-2, the KFTC followed the international trend of extraterritorial application of competition law, demonstrated in cases like the Graphite Electrodes cartel[151] and the Vitamins cartel.[152]

A participant in an overseas cartel may advance an affirmative defense that the relevant overseas conduct had no effect on the Korean market. However, there is no Korean Supreme Court decision that provides a bright-line test for evaluating effects on the Korean market. An analysis of the KFTC's various international cartel cases reveals that an international cartel is deemed to have had an effect on the Korean market where there was a specific pricing agreement regarding the Korean market and the agreement was implemented by, for instance, selling the products or services at issue at the agreed-upon price in the Korean market. In particular, the higher Korean customers' dependence on the imported products or services at issue, the greater the likelihood of finding an effect on the Korean market. In the 2014 Air Cargo cartel decision, the Korean Supreme Court construed "effect on the Korean market" to require a "direct, substantial and reasonably foreseeable effect" on the Korean market.[153]

Under Article 19(2), certain types of potentially anticompetitive concerted activities are permitted if they promote economic or industrial policies, meet special requirements set forth in the Enforcement Decree, and receive advance approval by the KFTC at the parties' request.

Under Article 58 of the MRFTA, legitimate business activities conducted pursuant to laws or orders issued pursuant to laws are exempt from sanctions otherwise provided for under the MRFTA. Where cartel participants assert that their conduct followed a supervisory agency's administrative guidance, the KFTC grants exemptions only where the administrative guidance at issue is based on express statutory provisions.

---

151.   Korea Fair Trade Commission, 2002-077, April 4, 2002 (KFTC).
152.   Korea Fair Trade Commission, 2003-098, April 29, 2003 (KFTC).
153.   Supreme Court [S. Ct.], 2012Da13665, May 16, 2014 (S. Kor.).

e. Sanctions/Penalties

The MRFTA provides for corrective orders, administrative fines and criminal sanctions.

(1) Corrective Orders

Under Article 21 of the MRFTA, the KFTC may order cartel participants to terminate their participation in the cartel at issue, to publish such order and to implement other necessary measures, including rescission of the illegal agreements. Pursuant to its Corrective Measure Guidelines, the KFTC may issue orders prohibiting certain conduct and to perform certain remedial actions, including modification or deletion of a contractual provision and rescission of agreement.

(2) Administrative Fines

The KFTC may impose an administrative fine not exceeding 10 percent of the relevant sales turnover as determined pursuant to the Enforcement Decree. However, if no relevant sales revenue was generated, or if it is difficult to calculate the relevant sales revenue, the KFTC may issue an administrative fine not exceeding KRW 2 billion. Under Article 9(1) of the Enforcement Decree, relevant sales revenue refers to the amount of sales that the offender generated in a certain transaction area by selling the relevant products or services during the cartel period; the purchase price of the products or services at issue, if the cartel activities were carried out in relation to the purchase of products or services; or the contract price in cases of bid rigging or similar conduct.

An administrative fine is calculated in two steps. First, the base fine amount is determined by multiplying the relevant sales revenue by a multiplier that can be up to 10 percent but varies depending on the gravity of the violation. Second, the base fine amount is then adjusted in consideration of various factors, including the duration and frequency of the violation, and aggravating or mitigating circumstances.

Aggravating circumstances may include whether:

1. The offender was the leader or instigator of the cartel;
2. The offender took retaliatory measures against another entity that did not participate in the cartel;
3. The offender or its employees obstructed or refused to cooperate with the KFTC investigation into the cartel;

4. A high-level executive of the offender was involved in the cartel; and

5. The offender participated in the instant cartel within three years after it was sanctioned by the KFTC for participation in another previous cartel.

Mitigating circumstances may include the following:

1. Non-performance of the cartel agreement;
2. Insignificant role in the cartel (e.g., participation in the cartel as a result of another's suggestion or deception);
3. Full cooperation with the KFTC investigation into the cartel;
4. Remedial measures voluntarily undertaken; and
5. Entering into the cartel agreement through negligence in the ordinary course of business or notwithstanding substantial compliance efforts by the entity at issue.

(3) Criminal Sanctions

Under Article 66(1)(9) of the MRFTA, a cartel participant can be punished with imprisonment for a term not exceeding three years or a criminal fine not exceeding KRW 200 million. Under Article 70, criminal sanctions may also be imposed on a representative, agent, employee or other member of the corporation that has participated in a cartel.

(4) Consent Decrees

Although the MRFTA was amended in December 2011 to provide for consent decrees for certain types of competition law cases, they are not available for cartel activities. Therefore, under the MRFTA, there are no early resolutions or settlement procedures for cartel activities.

f. Leniency Program

The Korean leniency program has been in effect since April 1997. Article 35(1) of the Enforcement Decree provides specific criteria governing sanction exemptions and reductions. The KFTC has also issued a notification regarding the leniency program (the Leniency Notification) to establish specific program procedures.

To benefit from the leniency program, an applicant must satisfy the following requirements under Article 35(1) of the Enforcement Decree:

1. At the time the applicant reports the cartel activity at issue, the KFTC has not received any information about the cartel activity or has not obtained sufficient evidence to prove it;
2. The applicant reports the cartel activity and cooperates fully with the KFTC by submitting relevant information throughout the investigation; and
3. The applicant has ceased its involvement in the cartel.

The applicant that reports its cartel activity before the commencement of the KFTC's investigation and that is the first to provide sufficient evidence of that cartel will be granted an exemption from administrative sanctions as well as exemption from referral to the Prosecutor's Office. Even when the KFTC has already begun its investigation, the first applicant to present sufficient evidence of the cartel before the KFTC has collected sufficient evidence of the cartel, and to cooperate fully with the KFTC's investigation, will be granted the exemptions. The second-in-line applicant to present sufficient evidence of the cartel and fully cooperate with the KFTC will be granted a 50 percent reduction of any administrative fine and also exemption from criminal referral.[154]

However, these leniency benefits are further subject to the following restrictions under Article 35(1)(6) of the Enforcement Decree:

1. In a two-party cartel, while the first leniency applicant is eligible for a full exemption from sanctions, the second leniency applicant is not automatically eligible for any reduced sanctions; and
2. Once two years have passed since a member of a particular cartel filed the first leniency application with the KFTC or began to cooperate with the KFTC as the first party providing cooperation with respect to that particular cartel, the other cartel members are no longer eligible for reduced sanctions. In other words, a late

---

154. While only the first two leniency applicants regarding a particular improper concerted activity are eligible for exemption from or reduction of administrative fine under the formal leniency program, as the case may be, late applicants or non-applicant parties may also be eligible for a maximum 30 per cent discretionary reduction of administrative fine for cooperation with the KFTC under the KFTC's Administrative Fine Notification.

leniency applicant cannot expect to receive full leniency benefits.[155]

Moreover, on January 2, 2015, the KFTC revised the Leniency Notification, which eliminated the KFTC Secretariat's practice of issuing preliminary or provisional markers for leniency standing. As revised, the only available markers are permanent markers issued by the KFTC full commission after its formal deliberations.

In 2016, the KFTC further revised the Leniency Notification to:

1. Require each leniency applicant to appear before the KFTC's full Commission during a separate leniency application status hearing so that the Commissioners may verify the credibility of the leniency applicant and substance of the leniency application; and

2. Deny leniency benefits to applicants that, without the KFTC's prior consent, disclose the fact of its leniency filing to a third party including any other participants in the cartel activity at issue.

In addition, the "Leniency Plus" program in Article 35(1)(4) of the Enforcement Decree allows mitigation of a corrective order and an additional reduction of up to 20 percent of administrative fines for cartel activity to a party in one cartel that qualifies as the first or second party to report another, smaller cartel to the KFTC or cooperates with the KFTC's investigation of that second cartel. Under Article 13 of the Leniency Notification, however, if the magnitude of the second cartel activity is greater than the first, then, depending on how much larger the second cartel is, the party may be eligible for a 30, 50 or even 100 percent reduction of administrative fine for the first cartel.[156]

A party that meets the requirements for the leniency program or the Leniency Plus program will lose such status if it has forced another party to participate or to continue to participate in the cartel activity, or such party has been a repeat offender of Article 19(1) of the MRFTA within the past five years.[157]

---

155. As noted above, however, even late-filing applicants may still receive discretionary cooperation credit in some situations.

156. The scale of an improper concerted activity is determined on the basis of relevant sales.

157. Article 35(1)(5) of the Enforcement Decree; Article 6-3 of the Leniency Notification.

In 2002, the KFTC introduced a whistle-blower program offering a monetary reward to the first informant who presents sufficient evidence of a cartel. In an effort to further promote the whistle-blower program, the KFTC increased the maximum monetary reward from KRW 2 billion to KRW 3 billion in 2012. From 2002 to 2014, the KFTC awarded a total of approximately KRW 1 billion to whistle-blowers in 45 cases.

E. Japan

Article 3 of the Act on Prohibition of Private Monopolization and Maintenance of Fair Trade (Law No. 54 of 1947, the AMA)[158] prohibits "unreasonable restraint[s] of trade," which includes cartel conduct and bid-rigging. The AMA is enforced by the Japan Fair Trade Commission (JFTC).

1. Unreasonable Restraint of Trade

a. Constituent Elements of the Violation

AMA Article 2(6) defines "unreasonable restraint of trade" as conduct:

- by any enterprise,
- in concert with other enterprises,
- mutually restricting or conducting their business,
- contrary to the public interest,
- thereby causing a substantial restraint of competition in any particular field of trade.

These elements are addressed in turn below.

b. Explanation of the Elements

(1) "In Concert with Other Enterprises"

To meet this requirement, "communication of minds," or an agreement between enterprises, must be proved. In the context of a price-fixing cartel, the Tokyo High Court stated that "communication of minds"

---

158. For English translation, *see* http://www.jftc.go.jp/en/legislation_gls/amended_ama09/index.html.

means "mutually recognizing or anticipating that the same or a similar price increase will be conducted, and that multiple enterprises intend to keep in step with each other. While one party's recognition of another party's price increase is not sufficient, it need not be an explicit agreement to restrict each other. Mutual recognition and implicit admission of other's price hike is sufficient."[159] The Tokyo High Court also indicated that when the JFTC proves prior contact and communication among competitors followed by unnatural concerted conduct by those competitors, then "meeting of minds" can be inferred unless extraordinary circumstances are found.[160] Accordingly, an information exchange between competitors alone does not meet this requirement. Nevertheless, exchanges of sensitive information are often made in the context of concerted conduct, and thus the JFTC and courts can rely on evidence of information exchange even in the absence of an admission of an agreement or "communication of minds."

(2) "Mutually Restrict or Conduct their Business"

There needs to be a competitive relationship between enterprises in order to meet this requirement.[161] Thus, a vertical restraint is not regarded as an "unreasonable restraint of trade." This does not mean that mutual restriction of trade cannot be committed by enterprises in different distribution levels. For example, in the *Seal Bid-Rigging Criminal Case*, a distributor controlling its manufacturing subsidiary was found guilty of bid-rigging among manufacturers, even though the distributor itself was not eligible to bid, because there was a substantial competitive relationship between the enterprises.[162]

In some cases, although there facially seemed to be only unilateral restriction of trade, the JFTC has found mutual restriction of trade among competitors. For example, in the *Shikoku Road Service (SRS) Bid-Rigging Case*, SRS and three competitors agreed that SRS would win bids to build highways in the Shikoku area, which was not typically serviced by the

---

159. Tokyo High Court Judgement, Sept. 25, 1995, *Toshiba Chemical Case*.
160. *Id.*
161. *See, e.g.*, Tokyo High Court Judgement, Mar. 9, 1953, *Newspapers Distribution Arrangement Case* (denying mutual restrictions of trade between newspaper publishers and their distributors when they agreed to allocate the markets for distributors).
162. Tokyo High Court Judgement, Dec. 14, 1993, *Seal Bid-Rigging Criminal Case*.

three competitors.[163] The JFTC found this to be a mutual restriction of trade, because even though the competitors would not normally have bid in the Shikoku area anyway, they expected that, if they agreed not to win the bids in Shikoku, then SRS would in turn not participate in bids in their operating area.[164]

(3) "Contrary to the Public Interest"

The JFTC seems to interpret "contrary to the public interest" to mean violating the economic order of free competition. From this standpoint, whenever a "substantial restraint of competition" takes place, "public interest" would almost always be harmed. Thus, this requirement is considered to be almost meaningless at present. In some cases, the defendants try to justify their conduct on the basis of safety or environmental reasons. However, the JFTC does not consider these arguments when evaluating whether conduct is "contrary to the public interest." Rather, such arguments are taken into account when determining whether there was a "substantial restraint of competition."[165]

(A) "CAUSING A SUBSTANTIAL RESTRAINT OF COMPETITION"

The Tokyo High Court explained this requirement as "causing the situation where competition itself reduces, and thus particular enterprises or a group of enterprises can control a market in some degree by changing prices, quality, volume or other conditions at their own will." [166] The degree or extent of controlling the market need not rise to the level of eliminating competition, or fully controlling prices or other conditions.[167] Accordingly, "a substantial restraint of competition" could be found even if some customers did not accept the prices increased by the conspiracy, or if some outsider enterprises not involved in the bid-rigging won bids.

The "substantial restraint of competition" requirement is fulfilled once the situation arises, or will arise, where particular enterprises can control a market to some degree. Thus, an "unreasonable restraint of trade" can be found when a cartel agreement is made, but before it has been put into effect. In the *Modifier Cartel Case*, for example, the court found it was

---

163. The JFTC Recommendation Decision, Dec. 4. 2002, *Shikoku Road Service Bid-Rigging Case.*

164. *Id.*

165. *See* 1.b(4)(A).

166. Tokyo High Court Judgement, Sept.19,1951, *Toho Subaru Case.*

167. Tokyo High Court Judgement, Dec.10,2010, *Modifier Cartel Case.*

sufficient that particular enterprises could control the market, even though economic analysis showed only a small nexus between price hike activity and actual prices.[168] Theoretically speaking, a cartel is not per se illegal in Japan. However, as the *Modifier Cartel Case* shows, it is difficult in practice to rebut cartel allegations by claiming that cartel activity has not substantially restrained competition. The JFTC tends to think that competitors do not engage in meaningless activities, so if there is an agreement among competitors, there must also be "a substantial restraint of competition."

(B) "PARTICULAR FIELD OF TRADE"

A "particular field of trade" consists of particular suppliers and users, where suppliers compete for users. "Particular fields of trade" can be defined in a multi-layered way. Accordingly, a certain definition of a "particular field of trade" does not foreclose other definitions. In cartel cases, in contrast with merger control cases, it is usually sufficient for the JFTC to define a "particular field of trade" in accordance with the extent covered by the cartel agreement. One "unreasonable restraint of trade" can be committed per "particular field of trade." For example, in the *Wire Harness Cartel Cases* in Japan, the JFTC defined five fields of trade with respect to each OEM (Toyota, Nissan, Honda, Fuji Heavy Industry, and Daihatsu) and found five different cartels.[169] Accordingly, the JFTC granted leniencies with respect to each cartel separately.

c.   Major Exemptions/Immunities

(1) Acts of a Certain Partnership

The AMA does not apply to acts of a partnership (including a federation of partnerships) that satisfy the following requirements. (i) the purpose of the partnership is to provide mutual support to small-scale enterprises or consumers; (ii) the partnership is voluntarily formed, and the partners may voluntarily participate in and withdraw from it; (iii) each partner possesses equal voting rights; and (iv) if a distribution of profits among partners is contemplated, the limits of the distributions are prescribed by laws and regulations or in the articles of partnership.[170]

---

168.   *Id.*
169.   The JFTC Cease and Desist Orders and Surcharge Payment Orders, Jan. 19, 2012.
170.   AMA Art. 22

Typically, joint sales or joint procurements of such partnerships are exempt from the AMA. However, this exemption does not apply if an unfair trade practice is employed,[171] or if the conduct causes a substantial restraint of competition in any particular field of trade leading to unjust price increases.

(2) Exemptions by Other Laws

Due to certain government policy considerations, some cartel-type arrangements meeting certain requirements are exempted from the AMA by other laws. Those cartels arrangements shall must be approved beforehand by the competent relevant government officials, ministers, who shall give notice to, get approval from, or consult with the JFTC about those arrangements. The laws exempting the cartels require them not to exceed necessary degree or extent, and not to be unjustly discriminatory. In addition, these laws provide that, if an unfair trade practice is employed, or a substantial restraint of competition in any particular field of trade is results from the relevant conduct, the exemption does not apply.

For instance, Insurance Business Act exempts from AMA insurance companies' cooperative acts regarding aviation insurance businesses, nuclear energy insurance businesses, automotive liability insurance businesses, or earthquake insurance businesses, or other insurances that typically joint reinsurance, when the cooperative acts meet certain requirements. The Maritime Transportation Act exempts from AMA ship operators' agreement meeting particular requirements with regard to the fares, fees, other transportation conditions, routes, allocation of vessels or sharing of shipping on routes between Japanese and foreign ports.[172] The Civil Aeronautics Act exempts from AMA domestic air carriers' agreement meeting certain requirements on joint carriage, fare agreements and other agreements relating to transportation between air carriers on routes between domestic and foreign locations, or between two foreign locations.

---

171. "Unfair trade practices" are provided by AMA Art. 2(9) and prohibited by AMA Art. 19.

172. The JFTC issued cease and desist orders and surcharge payment orders against shipping companies with respect to the automobiles international ocean shipping service cartel on March 18, 2014. Although they had notified the Minister of Land, Infrastructure, Transport and Tourism of agreements with respect to fares and allocation of vessels beforehand, the conspiracy was made outside the notification.

2. *Sanctions/Penalties*

a.   Applicable Sanctions

Sanctions for enterprises that committed an "unreasonable restraint of trade," including participation in a cartel or bid-rigging, are administrative orders and criminal penalties, and the sanctions for individuals are criminal penalties. Criminal penalties are not applied very often (less than once a year on average). Criminal penalties and administrative orders can be applied cumulatively, though there are adjustment rules to mitigate sanctions for enterprises that receive both criminal penalties and administrative orders for the same infringement.

b.   Criminal Sanctions

Criminal penalties can only be imposed on individuals and enterprises after prosecution before a court by a public prosecutor, based on the JFTC's accusation. A public prosecutor's office cannot prosecute anybody for "unreasonable restraint of trade" without the JFTC's accusation,[173] and the JFTC is the sole entity that can file such an accusation. The JFTC files an accusation with the Public Prosecutor General when it is convinced, after an investigation, that a criminal offence has taken place.[174] The JFTC's policy statement says that it will file an accusation against vicious and serious violations, including cartels or bid-rigging, that have widespread influence on people's lives, or that involve repeat offenders or offenders refusing to abide by the JFTC's administrative orders.[175]

When criminally prosecuted, an enterprise faces a maximum fine of JPY 500 million, and an individual faces a maximum 5-year jail term and a JPY 5 million fine under the AMA.[176] However, sentences of jail terms of 3 years or less can be suspended by judgement under Japanese criminal law.[177] So far, all individuals sentenced to jail terms under the AMA were provided with suspended sentences.

---

173.   AMA Art. 96.
174.   AMA Art. 74(1).
175.   The JFTC's Policy on Criminal Accusation and Compulsory Investigation of Criminal Cases Regarding the Antimonopoly Law, (rev. Oct. 3, 2009), *available*   *at* http://www.jftc.go.jp/en/legislation_gls/antimonopoly_rules.files/legislati on_guidelinesamapdfpolicy_on_criminalaccusation.pdf.
176.   AMA Arts. 89(1), 95(1)(i), 95(2)(i).
177.   Penal Code Art. 25(1)

The representatives of enterprises who either (1) knew of a planned violation but failed to take necessary measures to prevent it, or (2) failed to take necessary measures to rectify a known violation, shall also be punished by a maximum fine of JPY 5 million.[178] This is a special penalty for representatives, which has not yet actually been applied to any cases. When both a criminal fine and a surcharge are imposed on an enterprise for the same conduct, half of the criminal fine will be deducted from the amount of the surcharge.

c. Administrative Sanctions-Cease and Desist Orders and Surcharge Payment Orders

When the JFTC finds an "unreasonable restraint of trade," it issues a cease and desist order and a surcharge payment order. A cease and desist order is an order to take measures necessary to eliminate the violation.[179] If an employee, officer, or director of an enterprise that received a final and binding cease and desist order does not obey the order, the individual faces a maximum 2-year jail term and a JPY 3 million fine.[180] Although the JFTC can issue cease and desist orders even after an enterprise has already ceased its violation, the JFTC cannot issue the order if five years have passed since the enterprise ceased the violation.[181]

The methodology for calculating a surcharge is prescribed by Article 7-2 of the AMA, and the JFTC does not have any discretion in determining the amount of surcharge. The surcharge amount is calculated by multiplying the amount of affected sales during the violation period by the surcharge calculation rate described in the following table. If the violation period is longer than three years, to the surcharge is calculated based only on the most recent three years.[182]

	Original rate	Repeat (within 10 years)	Major Role	Repeat & Major Role	Less than 2 years
Other than Retailer or Wholesaler	10% (4%)	15% (6%)	15% (6%)	20% (8%)	8% (3.2%)

---

178. AMA Art. 95-2.
179. AMA Art. 7.
180. AMA Art. 90(iii).
181. AMA Art.7(2).
182. AMA Art. 7-2(1).

	Original rate	Repeat (within 10 years)	Major Role	Repeat & Major Role	Less than 2 years
Retailer	3% (1.2%)	4.5% (1.8%)	4.5% (1.8%)	6% (2.4%)	2.4% (1%)
Wholesaler	2% (1%)	3% (1.5%)	3% (1.5%)	4% (2%)	1.6% (0.8%)

Note: The numbers in parentheses are the rates for small or medium enterprises.[183]

The increased "Repeat" rate applies if an enterprise received another final and binding surcharge payment order within the past 10 years before the JFTC formally commenced its investigation.[184] If an enterprise played a "major role" in an unreasonable restraint of trade, the surcharge calculation rate shall also be increased by a factor of 1.5. An enterprise playing a "major role" means (i) an enterprise that planned to engage in a violation and required other enterprises to engage in, or to not discontinue, a violation; (ii) an enterprise that has continuously designated to other enterprises a price, supply volume, purchase volume, market share or transaction counterparty in relation to the goods or services involved in the violation; or (iii) an enterprise that has materially facilitated a violation by (a) requiring other enterprises to engage in, or to not discontinue a violation, or (b) designating to other enterprises a price, supply volume, purchase volume, market share or transaction counterparty in relation to the goods or services involved in the violation.[185]

If an enterprise falls under both of the above cases, the surcharge calculation rate shall double ("Repeat & Major Role"). As to "Less than 2 years," if the enterprise ceases the violation at least one month before the JFTC starts its investigation, the violation period is less than two years, and none of the above factors that will increase the surcharge apply, and the surcharge shall be reduced by 20 percent.

The surcharge calculation rate for wholesalers and retailers is set lower than the original rate, because their operation profit ratio is considered to be smaller than other business types such as manufacturers. This difference in the surcharge calculation rate sometimes causes disputes between the JFTC and the subjects of the orders, because an enterprise purchasing and selling products manufactured by another is not

---

183. Small or medium enterprises are defined in Article 7-2(5) of the AMA.
184. AMA Art. 7-2(7)(i).
185. AMA Art.7-2(8).

necessarily considered a retailer or a wholesaler. When there is a special relationship between the manufacturers and the violators—such as a capital relationship, technological assistance or raw material supply—the manufacturer may be viewed as a manufacturing division of the violator, and thus the lower wholesaler or retailer rate does not apply.[186] However, a study group organized by the JFTC to examine potential revisions of the AMA advocates in its report[187] issued in April 25, 2017 that the reduction rates for the "Less than 2 years" and different rates for business types should be abolished.

3. Leniency[188]

Up to five enterprises (or groups of enterprises)[189] can be granted immunity, or a reduction of surcharges, under a leniency program.[190] The immunity or reduction rate is based on a first-come basis. The first-in applicant before the JFTC formally commences investigation by onsite-inspection ("dawn-raid") is granted full immunity. The second-in applicant before a dawn-raid is granted a 50 percent surcharge reduction. The third, fourth and fifth-in applicants are granted a 30 percent reduction. Even after a dawn-raid, if the five slots for leniency applicants have not been filled, up to three enterprises can apply for leniency for a 30 percent reduction of the surcharge within 20 business days after a dawn-raid. The reduction rate is in accordance with the order in which enterprises apply for leniency, and the number of leniency slots available is prescribed in the AMA. Thus, the JFTC has no discretion. The fourth-in and fifth-in applicants before a dawn-raid and applicants after a dawn-raid must report and submit evidence of facts that the JFTC has not already ascertained, though this requirement is not as strict as the European Commission's "significant added value" threshold.

When an enterprise finds that it is involved in a cartel or bid-rigging through an internal investigation before a dawn-raid, it can anonymously

---

186. Tokyo High Court Judgement, June 9, 2014, *Fujikura case;* Tokyo High Court Judgement, Feb. 24, 2006, *Jet fuel Bid-Rigging Case*, JFTC Decision After Hearing Procedures, July 8, 1999, *Kinmon-Seisakusho Case.*
187. JFTC Study Group on the Antimonopoly Act Released Report (rev. Apr. 25, 2017), *available at* http://www.jftc.go.jp/en/pressreleases/yearly-2017/April/170425.html.
188. AMA Art. 7-2(10)-(18)
189. "Group of enterprises" is defined in AMA Art. 7-2(13).
190. Leniency slots were increased from three to five by the amendment of AMA in 2011.

call a leniency officer and ask whether leniency is still available. The officer will inform the enterprise whether leniency is available for the case, and the enterprise's ranking as a leniency applicant if it applied for leniency at that time. For enterprises that consult with the officer after a dawn-raid, the officer will inform them only whether leniency is still available. In order to obtain this information, an enterprise must identify the product or service related to the conspiracy, the time frame of the violation, and the type of illegal activity (bid-rigging, price-fixing, market allocation, etc.).

The leniency program pertains only to surcharges under the AMA. Nevertheless, in relation to criminal procedures, the JFTC announced that it will not file an accusation against the first-in applicant before a dawn-raid (or its officers and employees) who cooperate with the JFTC's investigation. As to cease and desist orders, usually the JFTC does not issue such an order to enterprises that sought leniency before a dawn-raid, though such treatment is not prescribed in law or regulation. Accordingly, the JFTC can issue the order to even first-in applicants before a dawn-raid when necessary.[191]

An applicant seeking leniency before a dawn-raid shall fax a leniency application form called "Form 1" to the JFTC as a first step. This form requires leniency applicants to provide information about the cartel to the JFTC, including the product or service subject to the violation, type of violation (bid-rigging, price-fixing cartel, market allocation, or other), and time period of the violation. This report functions as a leniency marker. The applicant shall then submit a more detailed report called "Form 2," which includes information about other participants in the cartel or bid-rigging, as well as other evidence including statements of officers or employees involved in the violation. Form 2 must be submitted within the deadline set by the JFTC, which is normally 10 business days after submission of Form 1.

In order to apply for leniency after a dawn-raid, a company must fax to the JFTC a prescribed form called "Form 3." As with Form 2, Form 3 requires detailed information and evidence. Once a dawn-raid is conducted, however, the raided companies often rush to get one of the remaining leniency slots. As the JFTC lets the leniency applicant who filed Form 3 to supplement it with more detailed information and evidence within 20 business days after a dawn-raid, it is advisable to report information just

---

191. For instance, though Sanki Engineering was granted immunity from a surcharge and criminal penalty, it received a cease and desist order (the JFTC Surcharge Payment Order, Oct. 27, 2015).

sufficient to satisfy the requirements of Form 3 as soon as possible. Then, the applicant can submit more detailed information and evidence to the JFTC later.

The JFTC admits that in some instances, applicants may orally report certain information required by Forms 2 or 3, including entire statements of concerned employees or officers. This may occur, for example, when the applicant faces the potential risk of discovery in U.S. lawsuits concerning the violation.

The leniency applicant may not continue its participation in the violation after a dawn-raid at the latest. The leniency applicant may not disclose that it applied for leniency without any justifiable reason. False reports or materials submitted to the JFTC, or failure to submit additional reports or materials requested by the JFTC, would disqualify an applicant from being granted leniency.

A leniency applicant that has coerced another enterprise to participate in the cartel or bid-rigging, or has prevented participants of a cartel or bid-rigging from ceasing the violation, is ineligible for leniency. This disqualification is distinct from the "major role" factor, which increases the surcharge calculation rate by a factor of 1.5. An enterprise which played a major role in an unreasonable restraint of trade can still be granted leniency, provided it did not engage in the above coercive conduct.[192]

The reduction rate in accordance with the sequence of leniency applications, and the number of leniency slots available for enterprises, are prescribed in the AMA and are not subject to the JFTC's discretion. The JFTC is currently considering revisions to the AMA that would allow for some discretion in leniency programs, based upon the degree of a defendant's cooperation.[193]

---

192. Though the JFTC found Sumitomo Densetsu played a "major role" in the bid-rigging for Overhead Transmission Line Works ordered by KEPCO, and found Takasago Thermal Engineering played a "major role" in the bid-Rigging Concerning Snow-Melting Equipment Engineering Works for the Hokuriku Shinkansen bullet train, it granted leniency for both enterprises (the JFTC Surcharge Payment Order, Jan. 31, 2014 and Oct. 27, 2015).

193. JFTC Study Group on the Antimonopoly Act Released Report (rev. Apr. 25, 2017), *available at* http://www.jftc.go.jp/en/pressreleases/yearly-2017/April/170425.html.

4. *Procedures*

a.   Investigation

The JFTC can conduct two types of investigations into unreasonable restraints of trade: criminal investigations or administrative investigations. When the JFTC plans to file criminal charges for cartel activity or bid-rigging, the criminal investigation department of the JFTC starts its investigation by obtaining a search warrant from a court. With this procedure, the JFTC can inspect, search, and seize materials compulsorily, even without consent from the subject of the investigation. Public prosecutors also conduct investigations in cooperation with the JFTC in order to prosecute the suspected persons and enterprises.

In an administrative investigation, the JFTC also inspects, searches, and seizes materials. This procedure cannot be conducted without consent from the subject of the investigation. However, the JFTC can resort to administrative measures or orders, under which any party who does not obey can be criminally sanctioned (indirect enforcement). Both criminal and administrative investigations are formally commenced by onsite-inspection (dawn-raid). During a dawn-raid in both types of investigations, the JFTC usually interviews officers or employees involved in the cartel or bid-rigging on a voluntary basis.

In the course of the investigation, whether criminal or administrative, the JFTC interviews suspected enterprises' officers or employees who are suspected to be involved in the cartel or bid-rigging, and makes a record of the written statements obtained. It is usual for the JFTC to interview an involved person several dozen times. The JFTC does not allow an attorney to attend the interview. Furthermore, the attorney-client privilege and attorney work-product doctrines are not guaranteed in Japan[194] and the JFTC can seize materials that would not be taken in other jurisdictions. It is not rare that the JFTC searches the legal department of the enterprises, and seizes whatever it finds valuable, including emails between attorneys and clients, and attorneys' work product.

The JFTC issued its "Guidelines on Administrative Investigation Procedures under the Antimonopoly Act" in December 2015, which

---

194.   As of January 2019, it was reported that the JFTC is moving toward an introduction of confidentiality rights which is similar to attorney-client privilege, though only in cartel cases and only once the bill to amend the cartel sanction and leniency system is submitted to and passes the Diet.

governs the JFTC officers in charge of administrative investigations.[195] These guidelines require officers to observe due process, integrity, and confidential duty. They also address some practical matters, such as providing that the JFTC's interview should be limited to eight hours a day, and officers should permit interviewees to take notes or communicate with their counsel during breaks.

b. Prosecution

When, after a criminal investigation, the JFTC believe the suspected individuals and enterprises are guilty of an "unreasonable restraint of trade," the JFTC submits an accusation against the individuals and enterprises to the Public Prosecutor General, and a public prosecutor's office prosecutes them before the criminal court. A public prosecutor's office cannot prosecute anyone for "unreasonable restraint of trade" without the JFTC's accusation. The court in the first instance is the district court governing the relevant district. As Japan has a three-tiered court system, the defendants can appeal the court judgements to the high courts, and then to the Supreme Court.

c. Administrative Orders

When the JFTC plans to issue cease and desist orders and surcharge payment orders as a result of an investigation, the JFTC send drafts of the orders to the prospective subjects and conducts an opinion hearing on the orders. The prospective subjects can review relevant evidence, and make copies of evidence submitted by them or their officers or employees, as well as of their officers' or employees' written statements recorded by the JFTC. At the hearing, which the hearing officer presides over, the investigator explains the contents of the orders. The prospective subjects may ask the investigator questions or deliver opinions about the orders. The hearing officer makes a hearing record and report. After considering the hearing record and report, the JFTC will issue the formal cease and desist order and surcharge payment order. [196]

It usually takes one year or less from the dawn-raid before the JFTC issues the orders.

---

195. Press Release, the JFTC, "Publication of 'Guidelines on Administrative Investigation Procedures under the Antimonopoly Act,'" (Dec. 25, 2015) *available at* http://www.jftc.go.jp/en/pressreleases/yearly-2015/December/151225.html.
196. AMA Art. 49 – 62.

d. JFTC Hearing of Opinion Procedures

The purpose of the hearing of opinion procedure is to provide possible subjects with an opportunity to review evidence relating to future orders, question the fact-finding of the JFTC, and present an opinion as to findings of fact and/or applications of law. It should be noted, however, that the hearing of opinion procedures are not intended to be a full-blown adversarial proceeding. Rather, it is intended to provide the party concerned, namely the possible subject, with a brief opportunity in a fast-tracked proceeding to raise issues and present its opinion to be taken into consideration by the JFTC commissioners before issuing orders. The hearing of opinion proceeding consists of (i) evidence review through reading and photocopying and (ii) a hearing process.

e. Evidence Access Process[197]

A party concerned has the right to review evidence that the JFTC believes supports their fact-finding and application of law.[198] In practice, countervailing evidence that the JFTC possesses is out of the scope of the review. The party concerned applies for a reading with a commitment not to use information contained in the evidence other than for preparation for the hearing of opinion procedure and an action for revocation of the order(s). The party concerned visits the JFTC and, while reading, the party is not allowed to make photocopies or take pictures (with a smartphone or any other device), or take *full* notes of the evidence, including interview statements. Taking summary or partial notes is allowed. In international cases that involve the United States, it would be wise for the party concerned to have its attorney take summary or partial notes of evidence under work-product doctrine to prepare for future discovery in U.S. private actions. Though the work-product doctrine is not recognized under Japanese law and practice as of January 2019, summaries and notes taken by qualified Japanese attorneys could be protected by privilege laws in the U.S.

Information implicating privacy or trade secret concerns will be masked by the JFTC. The JFTC has the right to refuse a party's reading of evidence based on a likelihood of harming interests of third parties, and

---

197. AMA Art. 52.
198. Rules on Hearing of Opinions by the Fair Trade Commission Article 12. For English translation, see
       http://www.jftc.go.jp/en/legislation_gls/antimonopoly_rules.files/hearing ofopinions.pdf.

other reasons.

A separate procedure exists, known as the photocopy evidence process.[199] In this procedure, a party concerned has the right to photocopy only interview statements of its employees and physical evidence that it produced (party's evidence).[200] In other words, a party concerned has no right to take photocopies of interview statements of other entities or their employees, or physical evidence that other entities produced. The rationale behind this is to avoid potential leaks.

For this procedure as well, the party concerned must commit to using the photocopied evidence only for the purpose of preparing for the hearing of opinion and actions for revocation. In practice, the JFTC provides a CD or DVD containing the party's evidence. In international cartel cases, it should be noted that the copy of party's evidence may be subject to discovery in U.S. civil actions. A party concerned may refuse to provide the CD or DVD during U.S. discovery proceedings based on the above commitment to the JFTC, but ultimately, it is the U.S. judge that decides whether it must be produced. Thus, the party concerned needs to bear in mind the risk of U.S. discovery procedures when obtaining copies of evidence from the JFTC.

f.   Hearing of Opinion Process

A hearing officer is designated after notification of the hearing of opinion procedures. After consulting with the party concerned and/or its attorney, a hearing date will be set by the JFTC around one month from the date of notification.[201] At the hearing, investigators explain the content of the draft orders and primary evidence,[202] and the party concerned may ask questions of the investigator subject to the hearing officer's approval. The party concerned may also state opinions and produce evidence.[203] A second hearing may be held upon approval from the hearing officer.[204] These hearing of opinion procedures are still new and it remains to be seen how practices will evolve. The JFTC seems to think it rare that more than two hearings are required. After the conclusion of the hearing process, the hearing officer draws up a record and report of the hearing, which describes the point(s) of controversy for the JFTC commissioners. The

---

199.   Rules on Hearing of Opinions by the Fair Trade Commission Art. 13.
200.   AMA Art. 52(1).
201.   AMA Art. 51(1).
202.   AMA Art. 54(1).
203.   AMA Art. 54(2) (3).
204.   AMA Art. 56.

party concerned may review the record and report.[205] The hearing officer does not have the authority to present his or her own opinion as to the issues raised by the party concerned.

g. Appeal

The recipient of a cease and desist order and/or a surcharge payment order may file an action for revocation of the order, which is an administrative disposition by the JFTC. The period for filing such an action is six months from the date of service of the order.[206] The Tokyo District Court has exclusive jurisdiction over the appellate proceedings relating to the order.[207]

When appealing cease and desist orders or surcharge payment orders in international cartel cases, parties should consider potential adverse effects on U.S. civil discovery. In appellate proceedings, though the JFTC is named as the defendant, the JFTC has the burden of proving the cartel activity at issue. In order to meet this burden, the JFTC is very likely to produce a fair amount of evidence, including confessions and interview statements. Since copies of the evidence will be provided to the plaintiff, the alleged cartel member, this evidence will then be subject to discovery in U.S. civil cases.

h. Commitment/Settlement

(1) Commitment

The JFTC adopted a commitment system similar to that of the European Union as part of its obligation under the Comprehensive and Advanced Agreement on the Conclusion and the Pacific Rim Partnership of the Trans-Pacific Partnership Agreement. The system went into effect as of December 30, 2018. The commitment system is similar to the consent decree system of the U.S. FTC, though it does not need to be approved by a court. The commitment system is expected to correct competition issues at an earlier stage without imposing surcharges and making definitive factual finding of infringement, and to extend the area to address cases based on JFTC and violator collaboration. Though the system is intended to provide both the JFTC and the suspected violator with another enforcement option, the JFTC's guideline concerning the commitment

---

205.   AMA Art. 58.
206.   Administrative Case Litigation Act Art. 14(1).
207.   AMA Art. 85(1).

procedure specifically indicates that the JFTC has no intention to use it in serious cartel cases, including bid-rigging, price cartels, and quantity cartels.

(2) Settlement

As of January 2019, the AMA has not adopted a European Union-type settlement system.

5. Statute of Limitations

In connection with restraint of trade or cartel conduct, the statute of limitations for both cease and desist orders and surcharge payment orders is five years from the date of discontinuation of the violation.[208]

According to Article 250(2)(v) of the Code of Criminal Procedure, the statute of limitations for criminal cartel conduct is five years, and begins running once the criminal act has ended.[209]

6. Extraterritoriality

There is no specific provision relating to territorial limits on application of the AMA. Nevertheless, recent JFTC decisions[210] and the Supreme Court decision[211] in the Cathode-Ray Tube (CRT) cartel case applied the AMA to a price-fixing cartel in which the cartelized products were physically sold and traded within Southeast Asia and few CRTs and final products were exported to Japan. The decisions focused on the location of the "customer" or "counterparties" of the cartel product, holding that the AMA applies to cases where the cartel at issue is aimed at the "customer" in Japan and the market impacted by the cartel includes Japan. Although the cartelized CRTs were sold and traded by manufacturing subsidiaries in Southeast Asia, the subsidiaries were substantially controlled by Japanese parent companies. Major negotiations were directly conducted by the parent companies and they instructed

---

208. AMA Art. 7(2).
209. For reference, as a result of an imprisonment term revision in 2009 and transitional measure, the statute of limitations for cartel conduct which ended before December 31, 2009 was three years.
210. The JFTC Decisions, May 29, 2015. For English information and translation, see http://www.jftc.go.jp/en/pressreleases/yearly-2015/May/150529.html.
211. The Supreme Court Judgement, Dec. 12, 2017.

subsidiaries to purchase CRTs sold by the cartel. Accordingly, the "customers" or "counterparties" of the cartelized CRT products were Japanese CRT-TV companies located in Japan, such that the AMA applied.

Based on the logic of the rulings in the CRT case, the AMA is applicable to cartel agreements formed outside of Japan if the relevant geographic market includes Japan. The definition of the market depends on whether the cartel impairs the competition function of the Japan market where the counterparty exists, for example when a parent company located in Japan conducts economic activity with its subsidiary located outside of Japan in an integrated manner as to a transaction targeted by the cartel.

F. United Kingdom

1. Competition law

The key provisions in the United Kingdom in relation to cartel arrangements are Chapter I of the Competition Act 1998 (CA1998),[212] and Section 188 of the Enterprise Act 2002 (EA2002).

a. Basic Explanation of Law

(1) The Chapter I Prohibition

Chapter I prohibits agreements between undertakings or decisions by associations of undertakings or concerted practices that may affect trade within the U.K. and have as their object or effect the prevention, restriction, or distortion of competition within the United Kingdom.[213]

The prohibition is modeled upon the prohibition contained in Article 101 of the Treaty on the Functioning of the European Union (TFEU). The latter applies where the agreement or concerted practice affects trade between EU Member States rather than within a Member State.

The CA1998 requires that the Chapter I prohibition be interpreted consistently with the EU competition rules.[214] The term "agreements" is therefore broadly interpreted as covering not only formal written agreements between undertakings, but also "gentlemen's agreements," and other types of informal arrangements or understandings, whether oral

---

212. The Chapter I prohibition is set out in Section 2 of the CA1998.
213. A prohibition on the abuse of a dominant position is set out in Chapter II of CA1998.
214. Section 60 of the CA1998. It remains to be seen whether – and, if so, how – the UK decision to leave the EU (Brexit) will affect this obligation.

or in writing, and whether or not intended to be legally enforceable. It also covers decisions of trade associations.

The term "undertakings" encompasses any natural or legal person engaged in economic activity, irrespective of its legal status and the way in which it is financed. Public sector bodies engaging in economic activity can be undertakings for these purposes.

The effect on trade and competition can be actual or potential but must be appreciable.

Some agreements/practices are considered anticompetitive by their very nature. There is no requirement to demonstrate anticompetitive effect for these agreements/practices. Where the analysis of the object of the agreement/practice does not reveal an obvious anticompetitive objective, it is necessary to conduct an extensive analysis of its effect on the market, taking account of the economic context of the agreement.

Examples of the types of agreements considered to breach the Chapter I prohibition by object (i.e., hardcore infringements) are price fixing; exchange of price information; market-sharing; collusive tendering; and resale price maintenance.

(2) The Cartel Offense

Section 188 of the EA2002 makes it a criminal offense for an individual to agree with one or more other persons to make or implement (or to cause to be made or implemented) arrangements relating to at least two undertakings involving the following prohibited cartel activities: price fixing; market sharing; limitation of production or supply; and bid rigging. Vertical agreements (for example, resale price maintenance) fall outside the scope of the offense. The criminal offense operates alongside the regime that imposes civil sanctions on undertakings that breach the Chapter I prohibition in the CA 1998. The civil regime applies to a much wider range of anti-competitive activities than are targeted by the criminal offense.

Under Section 188, as it stood prior to April 1, 2014, an individual was guilty of a criminal offense only if he had engaged in hardcore cartel arrangements with others "dishonestly." The Enterprise and Regulatory Reform Act 2013 (ERRA2013) amended Section 188, with effect from April 1, 2014, to remove the "dishonesty" element from the offense. The main rationale behind this amendment was the government's view that the dishonesty criterion made it harder to prosecute individuals under the offense and that this was weakening the offense's deterrent effect.[215]

The ERRA2013 also introduced new exclusions to the offense and three new defenses to (1) reflect the government's intent that the cartel offense should catch only participation in covert cartels and (2) address concerns that removing the dishonesty element might lower the threshold for prosecution unreasonably. The other elements of the offense and the sanctions remained unchanged.

The revised cartel offense applies to cartel activities entered into on or after April 1, 2014.

b.   Any Major Exemptions/Immunities

(1) The Chapter I Prohibition

There are broadly three categories of exclusions from the Chapter I prohibition:

- mergers and concentrations—generally, the Chapter I prohibition does not apply to merger or joint venture agreements that fall within the scope of the EU or U.K. merger control regime;
- sectors subject to competition scrutiny under other U.K. legislation—in particular, the Broadcasting Act 1990 and the Communications Act 2003; and
- general exclusions, including compliance with legal requirements, avoidance of conflict with international obligations, and public policy.

The CA1998 further provides for exemptions from the prohibitions in Chapter I, broadly speaking, where the competitive advantages or benefits of agreements/practices outweigh the competitive disadvantages. However, hardcore cartel arrangements are unlikely to qualify for such an exemption.

(2) The Cartel Offense

In addition to the (existing) exclusion relating to the notification of bid rigging arrangements, the exclusions from the cartel offense (following

---

215.   Paragraph 3.5 of BIS: Growth, Competition and the Competition Regime, Government Response to Consultation (March 2012).

the ERRA2013) are: (1) the notification exclusion (where customers are provided relevant information before the arrangements are made); and (2) the publication exclusion (where the relevant information is publicized in the manner specified).[216] It also provides that an individual will not be deemed to have committed an offense if the agreement in question is made in order to comply with a legal requirement.[217]

In addition, the EA2002 provides for three substantive defenses to the cartel offense, in particular where:

- there is no intention to conceal the nature of the arrangements from customers;
- there is no intention to conceal the nature of the arrangements from the Competition and Markets Authority (CMA); and
- the defendant "took reasonable steps to ensure that the nature of the arrangements would be disclosed to professional legal advisers for the purpose of obtaining advice about them" before making or implementing them.[218]

c. Standard of Proof

In civil cartel cases, the CMA—on whom the burden of proving an infringement lies—must prove its case according to the normal civil standard (balance of probabilities). However, given the seriousness of the penalties for Competition Act infringements, strong and convincing evidence is required.[219]

In criminal cartel cases, the prosecution must proof its case according to the normal criminal standard, i.e. "beyond reasonable doubt."

d. Whether Information Exchange Is Violative

In some circumstances information exchange between businesses can fall foul of the Chapter I prohibition. In assessing information exchange, parties should analyze whether or not the exchange has the object or effect

---

216. Relevant information about the arrangement must be published, before the arrangements are implemented, by advertising them once in any of THE LONDON GAZETTE, THE EDINBURGH GAZETTE, or THE BELFAST GAZETTE (the Enterprise Act 2002 (Publishing of Relevant Information under Section 188A) Order 2014).
217. Section 188A of EA2002.
218. Section 188B of EA2002.
219 *Napp Pharmaceutical v DGFT* [2002] CAT 1.

of restricting competition. The competition authority will pay particular attention to the legal and economic context in which the information exchange takes place. Exchanges of information about future prices or quantities are more likely to lead to a collusive outcome and are highly likely to infringe the Chapter I prohibition.

Whether or not information exchange will have restrictive *effects* on competition depends on both the characteristics of the market and the nature of the information that is exchanged.

e.   Extraterritorial Application of Competition Law

The CA1998 provides that the Chapter I prohibition applies wherever "the agreement, decision or practice is, or is intended to be, implemented in whole or in part in the United Kingdom." [220] The prohibition can therefore apply to arrangements between undertakings located outside the United Kingdom.

Similarly, the EA2002 provides that proceedings may be brought for a criminal cartel offense in respect of an agreement outside the United Kingdom if it has been implemented in whole or in part in the United Kingdom. [221] The offense can therefore apply to individuals with domicile or place of residence outside the United Kingdom.

It is relatively rare, however, for the CMA (and previously the OFT) to investigate and fine non-U.K. companies for breach of the Chapter I prohibition.

In the cartel offense cases discussed below, all of the individuals pursued were U.K. nationals.

2.   *Enforcement Authority and Actions*

a.   Name/Description of Authority

The CMA is the principal competition enforcement agency in the United Kingdom. In addition to investigating breaches of Chapter I of the CA1998 and bringing criminal proceedings against individuals under the cartel offense, the CMA is able to directly apply Article 101 of the TFEU (in relation to anticompetitive conduct that may affect trade between EU

---

220.   Section 2(3) of CA1998.
221.   Section 190(3) of EA2002.

Member States rather than within the United Kingdom) (*see also* Section 9.3 of this Chapter on the EU regime).[222]

The UK electorate's vote in June 2016 to leave the EU (Brexit) may—depending on the model that is adopted for the UK's future relationship with the EU—result in significant changes to the CMA's role in the enforcement of Article 101 of the TFEU. Until the UK formally leaves the EU (and during the anticipated transition period), however, the current regime is likely to continue to apply.

Certain sectoral regulators have concurrent powers to apply aspects of competition law in the relevant regulated sector, including the power to enforce the U.K. and EU prohibition on anticompetitive agreements.

The concurrent regulators are:

- the Civil Aviation Authority (CAA);
- the Office of Communications (Ofcom);
- the Gas and Electricity Markets Authority (Ofgem);
- the Financial Conduct Authority (FCA) and the Payment Systems Regulator (PSR);
- monitor (part of NHS Improvement);
- the Office of Rail and Road (ORR);
- the Water Services and Regulation Authority (Ofwat); and
- the Northern Ireland Authority for Utility Regulation.

Before taking enforcement action, these sectoral regulators are required to consider whether the use of their competition law powers is more appropriate than the use of their sector-specific regulatory powers.[223]

b.   Whether Investigation and Prosecution Are Bifurcated

The CMA and the concurrent regulators have the power to investigate and prosecute suspected breaches of the civil cartel prohibitions. There is no separate prosecution authority.

---

222.   Article 3(1) of Council Regulation No. 1/2003/EC. Similarly, the CMA is responsible for the enforcement of the Chapter II/Article 102 prohibitions on the abuse of dominance.
223.   THE CMA'S GUIDANCE ON CONCURRENT APPLICATION OF COMPETITION LAW TO REGULATED INDUSTRIES (CMA10) explains the scope of the concurrent powers, and how the concurrent application and enforcement of competition law works in practice.

For criminal cartel cases, the CMA shares its powers of investigation and prosecution in respect of the criminal cartel offense under EA2002 with the Serious Fraud Office (SFO). The SFO is the intended prosecutor for the offense in England, Wales, and Northern Ireland in cases that involve serious or complex fraud. In Scotland, the Lord Advocate is responsible for all prosecutions and exercises the same powers as the SFO through the National Casework Division (NCD) of the Crown Office and Procurator Fiscal Service (COPFS). The CMA and COPFS cooperate to investigate and prosecute criminal cartel cases in Scotland.[224]

c. Investigation Techniques

The CMA's responsibilities are supported by a range of powers of investigation and enforcement set out in the CA1998. Procedural rules apply when it takes investigative or enforcement action.[225] The CMA is also required to carry out its investigations and take decisions in a procedurally fair manner (in accordance with the standards of administrative law), and, as a public body, it must act in a manner that is compatible with the Human Rights Act 1998.

The CMA has adopted guidance on its investigative powers under CA1998, including guidance on its procedures when investigating suspected competition law infringements.[226]

(1) Pre-Investigation Stage Powers

The CMA may conduct a civil investigation if there are "reasonable grounds for suspecting" that the Chapter I/Article 101 prohibition has been infringed (the Section 25 test). The Act gives the CMA discretion as to whether or not to instigate an investigation once this test is satisfied. The corresponding provision for criminal investigations is set out in Section 192 of EA2002 (the Section 192 test).

If the CMA decides not to prioritize a case, where appropriate, it may send the undertaking(s) involved a warning letter, informing them that it is aware of a possible competition law infringement by the undertaking(s)

---

224. Memo. of Understanding between the CMA and the COPFS, July 2014.
225. The Competition Act 1998 (Competition and Markets Authority's Rules) Order 2014 SI 2014/458 (the CA1998 Rules).
226. GUIDANCE ON THE CMA'S INVESTIGATION PROCEDURES IN COMPETITION ACT 1998 CASES (CMA8).

and that, although it is not minded to pursue an investigation at the moment, it may do so in the future if it receives further evidence.

The CMA obtains information about possible competition law infringements in a variety of ways, most notably:

- tip-offs from parties to the cartel (i.e., leniency applications);
- complaints by third parties; and
- its own research and market intelligence function or that of other competition authorities.

In the pre-investigation stage, the CMA typically gathers information informally.

(2) Formal Investigation Powers

As soon as the CMA considers that the Section 25 test (or the Section 192 test for criminal investigations) is met and opens a formal investigation, it will be able to use its formal investigation powers to help it establish whether an infringement has been committed, including the power to:

- issue formal information requests in writing (Section 26 notice) (the notice may be addressed to the undertakings alleged to have infringed the Chapter I/Article 101 prohibition, but also to complainants, suppliers, customers, and competitors);[227]
- conduct formal interviews with any individual connected to an undertaking under investigation, requiring them "to answer questions with respect to any matter relevant to the investigation";[228]
- enter premises with or without a warrant, and with or without notice;[229] and

---

227. For criminal investigations, *see* § 193(2) of EA2002.
228. Section 26A of CA1998. Any person being formally interviewed may request to have a legal adviser present (*see* GUIDANCE ON THE CMA'S INVESTIGATION PROCEDURES IN COMPETITION ACT 1998 CASES (CMA8), ¶ 6.21). This interview power is in addition to the CMA's power under § 193(1) of EA2002 to compulsorily interview individuals during criminal investigations.
229. If the CMA officials have a warrant, they are entitled to (1) use reasonable force to enter any premises specified in the warrant (including residential premises), (2) search and move freely around the premises, (3) use "seize

- fine any business or individual who does not comply with its information gathering powers (*see* further below).

In the case of suspected cartels, the CMA typically uses its formal information gathering powers from the outset (rather than gather information informally) so as not to prejudice the investigation.[230]

While it completes an investigation, the CMA has the power to require an undertaking to comply with temporary directions (interim measures) where it considers it necessary to act urgently either (1) to prevent significant damage to a person or category of persons, or (2) to protect the public interest.[231]

An undertaking that is the subject of a CMA investigation is under a general duty to cooperate. Failure to cooperate may result in the undertaking facing significant fines, and individuals facing imprisonment (of up to two years) and/or fines. The relevant offenses fall into four categories:

- failing to comply with the requirements imposed by a notice, or at an on-site investigation (including "dawn raids");
- intentionally obstructing an officer investigating with or without a warrant;
- intentionally or recklessly destroying, disposing of, falsifying, or concealing documents or causing or permitting those things to happen; and
- knowingly or recklessly supplying information which is false or misleading to the CMA.[232]

In light of the significant potential fines, an undertaking that is subject to an investigation should brief its employees to ensure that they do not obstruct the investigation, for example, by withholding, destroying, or deleting documents.

---

and sift" powers, and (4) bring non-CMA officials or staff to assist the officials during the investigation. Sections 27-29 of CA1998 for civil investigations. For criminal investigations, *see* §§ 194-195 of EA2002 (only power to enter under a warrant).

230. *See* GUIDANCE ON THE CMA'S INVESTIGATION PROCEDURES IN COMPETITION ACT 1998 CASES (CMA8), ¶ 4.6.
231. Section 35 of CA1998.
232. Section 42 of CA1998 and § 201 of EA2002.

Under English law, communications that attract a claim to legal professional privilege may be withheld from the CMA.[233] This includes both (1) communications that attract legal advice privilege,[234] and (2) communications that attract litigation privilege.[235] Unlike the position under EU law, communications between the company and its non-EU-qualified external lawyers, as well as those between the company and its in-house counsel, may be privileged under English law. Establishing a process during an on-site inspection for identifying documents that may be covered by legal privilege (in addition to documents that fall outside the scope of the investigation) before officials see, copy, or take them will therefore be an important task for the undertaking and its legal counsel.

In the case of an unannounced on-site inspection, the CMA will in principle wait "a reasonable time for legal advisers to arrive," provided that there is no in-house lawyer on the premises.[236]

It is also worth noting that the CMA cannot compel an undertaking to provide it with answers that might involve an admission on the undertaking's part of a competition law infringement (privilege against self-incrimination).[237]

Finally, there are strict rules governing the extent to which the CMA is permitted to disclose confidential information relating to both undertakings and individuals.[238]

(3) Investigation Outcomes

The CMA's investigation into alleged cartel practices can be resolved in a number of ways.[239] The CMA:

---

233. GUIDANCE ON THE CMA'S INVESTIGATION PROCEDURES IN COMPETITION ACT 1998 CASES (CMA8), ¶¶ 7.1-7.3.

234. Namely, communications between the company and either in-house or external counsel made for the dominant purpose of seeking or receiving legal advice.

235. Namely, communications between either the company and its counsel, or between the company or counsel and certain third parties (*e.g.*, a witness) made for the dominant purpose of legal proceedings.

236. GUIDANCE ON THE CMA'S INVESTIGATION PROCEDURES IN COMPETITION ACT 1998 CASES (CMA8), ¶ 6.38.

237. *Id.*, ¶¶ 7.4-7.5.

238. *Id.*, ¶¶. 7.6-7.16.

239. *See also id.*, Chapter 10.

- can decide to close an investigation on grounds of administrative priorities;
- can issue a decision that there are no grounds for action if the CMA has not found sufficient evidence of a competition law infringement;
- can accept commitments from an undertaking relating to its future conduct where the CMA is satisfied that these commitments fully address the competition concerns; however, the CMA is "very unlikely to accept commitments in cases involving secret cartels between competitors";[240] and
- will issue a written Statement of Objections where the CMA's provisional view is that the conduct under investigation amounts to a competition law infringement;[241] this document sets out all of the allegations and facts upon which the CMA proposes to base its final decision.

After allowing the undertaking(s) under investigation an opportunity to make representations on the Statement of Objections,[242] if the CMA still considers that it/they have committed an infringement, the CMA can:

- issue an infringement decision against it/them and impose fines, (and/or give directions to bring to an end any ongoing anticompetitive conduct) (*see* further below);[243] and
- apply for a disqualification order to be made against a company director for a period of up to fifteen years (*see* further below).

---

240. *Id.,* ¶ 10.19.
241. It is the CMA's normal practice to publicly announce the issue of the Statement of Objections on its website.
242. The CMA must also offer the undertaking(s) under investigation the opportunity to attend an oral hearing—during which representations may be made—and inspect documents in the CMA's investigation file (excluding certain confidential information and CMA internal documents).
243. The infringement decision will set out the facts on which the CMA relies to prove the infringement and the action that it is taking, and will address any material representations that have been made during the course of the investigation. A non-confidential version of the infringement decision will be published on the CMA's website. The addressee of the decision will have the opportunity to make confidentiality representations.

(4) International Enforcement Cooperation

Within Europe, the CMA cooperates extensively with the European Commission and with the national competition authorities (NCAs) in the other Member States of the EU. The main forum for such cooperation is the European Competition Network (ECN) (*see* further below for cooperation in the context of leniency applications).[244] It is not possible to predict how and when Brexit might affect this cooperation (if at all).

Outside Europe, the United Kingdom is a party to mutual assistance arrangements relating to competition law enforcement with a number of other non-European countries, including the United States, Australia, Canada, China, and New Zealand.

Internationally, the CMA also works to promote enforcement cooperation and the convergence of rules and standards through its work with the Organization for Economic Cooperation and Development (OECD) and the International Competition Network (ICN).

d.   Sanctions/Penalties

(1) The Chapter I Prohibition

In addition to possible private damages actions, diversion of management time to deal with the investigation, advisers' costs, and reputational damage, breach of the Chapter I prohibition may result in civil fines of up to a maximum of 10 percent of the undertaking's worldwide turnover in its previous business year.[245] Individuals found to have breached the prohibition are liable to disqualification from serving as a director for a period of up to fifteen years.

When determining the level of a fine, the CMA has a statutory duty to have regard to the seriousness of the infringement concerned and the

---

244.   The European Commission and the NCAs have a duty to cooperate under Article 11 of Regulation 1/2003 when applying the Community competition rules. The provision also contains various information/document exchange and notification obligations for the Commission and the NCAs in relation to investigative measures and proposed decisions. Further rules/guidance on this cooperation are set out in the *Commission Notice on Cooperation within the Network of Competition Authorities* (2004/C101/03).

245.   Section 36 of CA1998.

desirability of deterring both the undertaking on whom the penalty is imposed and others from entering into anticompetitive arrangements.[246]

Undertakings can appeal against the imposition, or amount, of fines to the Competition Appeal Tribunal (CAT).

The CMA may consider settlement for any CA98 case, provided the evidential standard for giving notice of its proposed infringement decision is met.[247] The settlement option is designed to allow the CMA to achieve efficiencies through the adoption of a streamlined administrative procedure, resulting in earlier adoption of any infringement decision and/or resource savings. For an undertaking involved in cartel activity, it can represent an opportunity to avoid a lengthy and costly investigation and a reduction in fines.[248] Settlement is distinct from leniency. However, the leniency policy and the use of settlements are not mutually exclusive.[249]

Individuals found to have breached the Chapter I prohibition are liable for disqualification from serving as a director for a period of up to fifteen years. It is the CMA that applies to the court for such a disqualification, and the court must make such an order if it considers that the director's conduct was such as to render him unfit to be concerned in the management of a company.[250] A director can be considered unfit for these purposes either because of direct participation in the infringement or on the basis of having turned a blind eye to breaches of the competition rules.

The disqualification order will prevent an individual from being involved (directly or indirectly) in the management of a company without leave from a court.[251]

---

246. Section 38(7A) of CA1998. The CMA is also required to prepare and publish guidance as to the appropriate amount of any penalty (§ 38(1) of CA1998). *See CMA'S GUIDANCE AS TO THE APPROPRIATE AMOUNT OF A PENALTY* (CMA73).

247. GUIDANCE ON THE CMA'S INVESTIGATION PROCEDURES IN COMPETITION ACT 1998 CASES (CMA8), 14.6.

248. The CMA may impose a financial penalty on any settling business, including a settlement discount of a maximum of 20 percent for settlement pre-Statement of Objections and 10 percent for settlement post-Statement of Objections. *Id.*, 14.30.

249. *Id.*, ¶ 14.3.

250. Company Directors Disqualification Act 1986 and OFT GUIDANCE: DIRECTOR DISQUALIFICATION ORDERS IN COMPETITION CASES (OFT510), adopted by the CMA.

251. Breach of a disqualification order is a criminal offense and may lead to imprisonment for up to two years and a fine of up to £5,000.

(2) The Cartel Offense

Participation by an individual in one or more of the prohibited cartel activities may lead to the imposition of a prison sentence of up to five years, unlimited fines, or both.[252]

The U.K. criminal cartel offense has resulted in relatively few successful prosecutions since it was first introduced in 2003:

- In 2008, three U.K. executives pleaded guilty to the U.K. cartel offense in relation to their involvement in the global marine hose cartel, which was investigated by the OFT in parallel with the DOJ and the European Commission. They were sentenced to imprisonment for between two-and-a-half and three years.[253]
- In 2010, the case against four British Airways executives for allegedly fixing prices of transatlantic fuel surcharges collapsed for procedural reasons during trial.[254]
- In 2015, three individuals were prosecuted following an investigation into suspected cartel conduct relating to the supply in the United Kingdom of steel tanks for water storage. One individual pleaded guilty and was sentenced to six months' imprisonment and 120 hours of community service. The other two individuals were acquitted, as the jury was not persuaded that they

---

252. Section 190 of EA2002.
253. The Court of Appeal reduced the sentences to between two-and-a-half years and twenty months, which were the levels equivalent to those of the U.S. plea-bargaining agreements (*R v. Whittle* [2008] EWCA Crim 2560). Under the England and Wales system, there is generally no place for plea-bargaining agreements between the prosecution and the defense. The Court of Appeal therefore expressed its reluctance to follow the plea-bargaining agreements struck in the U.S. In the event, however, it held that it could not otherwise do justice.
254. The OFT decided not to continue the case following discovery, after the trial had begun, of a substantial volume of electronic material that had not been reviewed by either the OFT or the defense. The OFT indicated that continuation of the trial would be potentially unfair to the defendants (OFT press release, "OFT withdraws criminal proceedings against current and former BA executives" (May 10, 2010), *available at* http://webarchive.nationalarchives.gov.uk/20140402142426/http://www.oft.gov.uk/news-and-updates/press/2010/47-10).

had acted dishonestly. These prosecutions are the only U.K. criminal cartel cases in which a trial by jury was completed.[255]

- In 2016, a man was charged with the offense for dishonestly agreeing with others to fix prices, divide customers, and divide supply in the United Kingdom of products for the construction industry. He pleaded guilty on March 21, 2016. In September 2017, he was sentenced to two years' imprisonment, suspended for two years, and made the subject of a six month curfew order. He was also disqualified from acting as a company director for seven years.[256]

All of these cases related to (alleged) cartel conduct prior to April 2014 (when the ERRA2013 amendments came into force) and were therefore prosecuted under the original cartel offense. It remains to be seen to what extent the amendments to the cartel offense, in particular the removal of the dishonesty element, will facilitate prosecutions under this offense in the future.

The cartel offense, attempts to commit the offense, and conspiracy to commit the offense are crimes in relation to which an individual may be extradited to the United Kingdom under the European Convention on Extradition (provided that the extraditing country has a similar provision punishable by at least twelve months' imprisonment). The Extradition Treaty with the United States, which entered into force in 2007, governs extradition of suspected offenders to and from the United States.[257]

Individuals who have participated in a cartel may also be guilty of money laundering under the Proceeds of Crime Act 2002, which is a criminal offense punishable by a prison sentence of up to fourteen years, unlimited fines, or both.

3. Leniency Program

Lenient treatment is available under the CMA's leniency program for undertakings and individuals that provide information to the CMA about a cartel in which they are or were involved and that cooperate proactively

---

255. CMA statement following completion of criminal cartel prosecution (June 24, 2015), *available at* https://www.gov.uk/government/news/cma-statement-following-completion-of-criminal-cartel-prosecution).

256. More details are available on the CMA's case page, *available at* https://www.gov.uk/cma-cases/criminal-investigation-into-the-supply-of-products-to-the-construction-industry.

257. *See also* Extradition Act 2003.

with the CMA to help it bring a successful enforcement action. The program is designed to enhance and facilitate the CMA's enforcement actions against cartel practices.[258]

For purposes of the program, cartel activity is defined as:

Agreements and/or concerted practices which infringe Article 101 of the TFEU and/or the Chapter I prohibition and involve price fixing (including resale price maintenance), bid rigging (collusive tendering), the establishment of output restrictions or quotas and/or market sharing or market-dividing . . . . Leniency in relation to vertical arrangements is limited to price fixing (for example, resale price maintenance cases).[259]

For individuals, immunity (in the form of no-action letters) can relate to any type of activity that would amount to a criminal cartel offense under Section 188 of EA2002.[260]

a. Requirements and Immunity vs. Reduction in Fines

Under the CMA's leniency program, different types of protection are available to an applicant depending on its order in the queue and whether an investigation has already commenced.

Type A immunity is available where: the undertaking is the first to apply (providing the CMA with evidence of cartel activity); there is no pre-existing civil and/or criminal investigation into such activity; and the CMA does not otherwise have sufficient information to establish the existence of the reported cartel activity. Type A immunity provides (1) automatic immunity from civil fines for an undertaking, and (2) criminal immunity (and, where relevant, protection from director disqualification) for all current and former employees and directors who cooperate with the CMA.[261] The information provided by the applicant must, at a minimum, give the CMA a sufficient basis for taking forward a credible investigation.

---

258. The key features of and procedures relating to the CMA's leniency policy are set out in the following publications: GUIDANCE ON APPLICATIONS FOR LENIENCY AND NO-ACTION IN CARTEL CASES (OFT1495), adopted by the CMA; and GUIDANCE AS TO THE APPROPRIATE AMOUNT OF A PENALTY (CMA73).

259. GUIDANCE ON APPLICATIONS FOR LENIENCY AND NO-ACTION IN CARTEL CASES, ¶¶ 2.2 and 2.3.

260. *Id.*, ¶ 2.4.

261. Immunity from criminal prosecution is granted in the form of a no-action letter issued by the CMA. A no-action letter will prevent a prosecution from being brought against an individual in England, Wales, or Northern Ireland. Guarantees of immunity from prosecution cannot be given in

Type B immunity/leniency may be available where the undertaking is the first to apply (providing the CMA with evidence of cartel activity) but there is already a pre-existing civil and/or criminal investigation into such activity. In these circumstances, the CMA has discretion as to whether to provide (1) immunity from civil fines or a reduction in fines (up to 100 percent) to the undertaking, and/or (2) criminal immunity (and, where relevant, protection from director disqualification) to current and former employees and directors who cooperate with the CMA. The key criterion for determining the discount available will be the overall added value of the information provided by the applicant.

Type C leniency may be available where an undertaking provides evidence of cartel activity but another undertaking has already reported the cartel activity, or where the applicant has coerced another undertaking to participate in the cartel activity. The grant of Type C leniency is always discretionary, resulting in (1) discretionary reductions in corporate penalties of up to 50 percent, and/or (2) discretionary criminal immunity to specific individuals (and protection from director disqualification proceedings).

In addition to the above criteria, an undertaking must fulfill the following conditions in order to be granted Type A or Type B immunity/leniency:

- accept that it participated in cartel activity;
- provide the CMA with all information, documents and evidence available to it in relation to the cartel activity;
- maintain continuous and complete cooperation throughout the investigation and until the conclusion of any CMA action arising as a result of the investigation;[262]

---

relation to Scotland. However, cooperation with the CMA will be reported to the Lord Advocate, who will give such cooperation serious weight when considering whether to prosecute the individual in question.

262. GUIDANCE ON APPLICATIONS FOR LENIENCY AND NO-ACTION IN CARTEL CASES ¶ 5.4 indicates that this requirement implies that "the overall approach to the leniency process by an applicant must be a constructive one, designed genuinely to assist the CMA in efficiently and effectively detecting, investigating and taking enforcement action against cartel conduct, so that the public policy objectives of the [CMA's] leniency policy are achieved."

- refrain from further participation in the cartel activity from the time of disclosure of the cartel activity to the CMA (except as may be directed by the CMA); and
- not take steps to coerce another undertaking to take part in the cartel activity.

In order to be granted Type C leniency, an undertaking must also fulfill each of these conditions, except for the non-coercion condition.

b. Procedure

If an undertaking is not aware of a pre-existing investigation, a representative from the undertaking or its legal adviser may contact the CMA on a no-names basis to ascertain whether Type A immunity (guaranteed immunity) is available. The representative/legal adviser will be asked to (1) confirm that (a) he/she has instructions to apply for such immunity, if available, and that the undertaking understands that such an application will include a cooperation duty, (b) there is a "concrete basis" for the suspicion of cartel activity, and (c) the undertaking has a "genuine intention to confess"; and (2) specify the relevant sector, dates and broad nature of the cartel activity, or otherwise provide sufficient information to allow the CMA to determine whether there is a pre-existing civil and/or criminal investigation and/or a pre-existing leniency applicant.[263]

Generally, the CMA will be able to confirm within one or two working days whether Type A immunity is available. If Type A immunity is not available, the applicant is free to consider all the available options, including whether to submit an application for Type B or Type C leniency or whether to withdraw without its identity having been made known to the CMA.[264]

If an undertaking is aware of a pre-existing investigation, a representative from the undertaking or its legal adviser may contact the CMA on a no-names basis to ascertain whether Type B immunity (discretionary immunity) is available. If the CMA indicates that Type B corporate immunity (and/or blanket criminal immunity) is available in principle, the would-be applicant can then seek to establish whether the information it can provide would be sufficient to warrant a marker for Type B immunity in its particular case by specifying the form and substance of the information it expects to be able to provide. The CMA

---

263. *Id.*, ¶ 4.2.
264. *Id.*, ¶ 4.4.

will then advise whether, if such evidence were to be provided, it would be minded to grant immunity (corporate and/or criminal) or only a reduction in fines. The CMA guidance notes that, in principle, there is no reason why this cannot be done on a no-names basis.[265]

If the CMA has one or more previous leniency applications in relation to the cartel activity, only Type C markers will be available.

If immunity/leniency (of whatever type) is available, the legal adviser/representative will have to disclose the identity of the applicant to obtain a preliminary marker (that is, a marker pending consideration of the full application package). The preliminary marker will be operational only from the moment the applicant's identity has been disclosed to the CMA.[266]

During or immediately following the telephone call to grant the preliminary marker, the CMA and the applicant will discuss the timing and process for the applicant's provision of the application package, including a statement (oral or written) and all relevant documentary evidence uncovered so far.[267] If the cartel activity is ongoing, the CMA and the applicant will also discuss cessation of the cartel activity without tipping off others and/or, in exceptional circumstances, a requirement for the applicant to continue to participate in the cartel to protect the CMA's investigation or obtain further evidence.[268]

Once the CMA has had an opportunity to consider the information provided, it will revert to the applicant and:

- confirm the marker but not launch an investigation (e.g., because it has higher priorities for its resources at that point in time);
- confirm the marker and discuss next steps with the applicant;
- reject the preliminary marker (e.g., the information provided may not give reasonable grounds to suspect cartel activity (Type A) or add significant value (Type B or C)); or
- ask for more information before confirming or rejecting the preliminary marker.

Leniency applicants are required to maintain complete confidentiality of the fact that they have applied for leniency (or even that a leniency application is in contemplation) in order to avoid "tipping off" other

---

265. *Id.*, ¶ 4.9.
266. *Id.*, ¶ 4.12.
267. *Id.*, ¶ 4.15.
268. *Id.*, ¶ 4.16.

parties to the reported cartel activity of a possible investigation by the CMA.[269]

Where parallel leniency applications have been made in other jurisdictions, the applicant is not prohibited from informing the competition authorities in those jurisdictions that an application to the CMA is pending or has been made.[270] In such cases, the CMA would in fact expect to be given "waivers" of confidentiality so as to be able to discuss appropriate matters with those other jurisdictions.[271] Generally, any transfer of information in these circumstances is limited to what is necessary to coordinate planned concerted action (such as on-site investigations).[272]

Information supplied by an undertaking as part of a leniency application will not be passed to an overseas agency without the consent of the provider of the information, except in one situation: such information may be disclosed to the Commission and/or another EU NCA (in accordance with the safeguards contained in the European Commission's Notice on Cooperation within the ECN and following consultation with the provider).[273] It remains to be seen whether Brexit will affect these cooperation arrangements.

G. Singapore

1. *Competition law*

a. Basic Explanation of Law

The Competition Act, Chapter 50B, of Singapore (the Competition Act), is the principal statute governing the competition law regime in Singapore. Section 34 of the Competition Act prohibits agreements between undertakings, decisions by associations of undertakings, or concerted practices which have, as their object or effect, the prevention, restriction, or distortion of competition within Singapore (the Section 34 Prohibition) unless excluded by the Third Schedule to the Competition Act or a block exemption. Only agreements with the object or effect of

---

269. *Id.*, ¶ 3.24.
270. *Id.*, ¶ 3.25.
271. The CMA generally considers such waivers to be mandatory (*Id.*, ¶ 4.5 and ¶ 114).
272. *Id.*, ¶ 4.40.
273. *Id.*, ¶ 7.30.

appreciable prevention or restriction or distortion of competition will fall within the scope of the Section 34 Prohibition.

The types of agreements caught by the Section 34 Prohibition include hardcore agreements such as price-fixing, output limitation, bid-rigging, and market sharing, where appreciability is presumed. Section 34 also prohibits other types of agreements, such as fixing trading conditions, joint purchasing or selling, sharing information, exchanging price information, exchanging non-price information, restricting advertising, and setting technical or design standards to the extent that such agreements have the effect of restricting competition to an appreciable extent.

Agreements falling within the Section 34 Prohibition can range from hardcore cartels to concerted practices where no formal agreement or decision was reached. These include formal, informal and oral agreements, as well as "gentlemen's agreements." All that is required is that parties agree on the actions each party will, or will not, take.

b.   Major Exemptions/Immunities

The Third Schedule in the Competition Act sets out exclusions to the prohibition under section 34 of the Competition Act (Section 34 Prohibition), including, but not limited to:

- An agreement made to comply with a legal requirement.
- Specified activities within the supply of postal services, supply of public transport, cargo terminal operations and so on.
- Vertical agreements.
- Agreements with net economic benefits.
- Agreements directly related and necessary to the implementation of mergers, including ancillary restrictions (such as, non-compete clauses).

An agreement will generally have no appreciable adverse effect on competition in the following circumstances:

- If the aggregate market share of the parties to the agreement does not exceed 20 percent in any of the relevant markets affected by the agreement, where the agreement is made between competing undertakings (i.e., actual or potential competitors).
- If the market share of each of the parties to the agreement does not exceed 25 percent in any of the relevant markets affected by the

agreement, where the agreement is made between non-competing undertakings (i.e., actual nor potential competitors).

- In the case of an agreement between undertakings, where each undertaking is a small or medium enterprise (SME).

However, directly or indirectly fixing prices, bid-rigging, sharing of markets, and limiting or controlling production and investment (that is, hardcore prohibitions) will always have an appreciable adverse effect on competition, even if the market share of the parties are below the above threshold levels, and even if the parties to these agreements are SMEs.

The Minister for Trade and Industry, acting on a recommendation of the Competition and Consumer Commission of Singapore (CCCS), can order the exemption of categories of agreements from the prohibition under section 34 of the Competition Act (Chapter 50B of Singapore) (Section 34 Prohibition). Exempted agreements must contribute to either improving production or distribution or

promoting technical or economic progress, in order to meet the criteria for a block exemption.

On July 14, 2006, the Minister for Trade and Industry issued the Competition (Block Exemption for Liner Shipping Agreements) Order, which exempted a category of liner shipping agreements from the Section 34 Prohibition until December 31, 2010. This was subsequently extended until December 31, 2020.

c.   Whether Information Exchange Is Violative

Information exchanges between parties are prohibited under the Section 34 Prohibition to the extent that competitively sensitive information (e.g., pricing, business strategies, etc.) is disclosed.

Even a unilateral provision or receipt of information can result in an infringement of the Section 34 Prohibition. On July 18, 2012, the CCCS imposed fines totaling S$285,766 on two ferry operators for the unilateral transmission of price information.[274]

---

274.   *See* CCS 500/006/09, *CCS Imposes Financial Penalties On Two Competing Ferry Operators For Engaging In Unlawful Sharing Of Price Information.*

d.   Whether Enforced Civilly or Criminally

A financial penalty can be imposed by the CCCS for an infringement of the Section 34 Prohibition, committed intentionally or negligently.

There is no personal liability, except if individuals commit the following offences:

- Knowingly or recklessly providing information that is false or misleading either to the CCCS or to another person such as an employee or legal adviser, in the knowledge that it will be used for the purpose of providing information to the CCCS.
- Obstructing, by refusing to give access to, assaulting, hindering or delaying, any agent of the CCCS.
- Failing to comply with any requirement imposed under sections 61A, 63, 64 or 65 of the Competition Act (which set out the CCCS's formal powers of investigation), including refusal to provide any required document or information, unless such compliance is reasonably not practicable or a reasonable excuse for failing to comply can be provided.
- Intentionally or recklessly destroying or otherwise disposing of or falsifying or concealing a document of which production has been required under sections 61A, 63, 64 or 65 of the Competition Act, or causing or permitting its destruction, disposal, falsification or concealment.

e.   Extraterritorial Application of Competition Law

Even if anticompetitive agreements are entered into outside Singapore, or any party to such agreements is outside Singapore, the Section 34 Prohibition still applies, so long as the agreement has the object or effect of preventing, restricting, or distorting competition in relevant product and geographical market(s), giving rise to competition concerns affecting Singapore. The CCCS has "signal[led] [its] intent to act against international cartels that have an anticompetitive impact in Singapore"[275] (i.e., insofar as their cartel conduct affects or restricts competition in Singapore).

---

275.   CCS Chief Executive Toh Han Li in the Singapore chapter of Global Competition Review's *The Asia-Pacific Antitrust Review 2014.*

To-date, the CCCS has investigated and issued decisions in relation to three international cartels, as set out below.

International cartel	Fines by CCCS (millions)
Capacitor manufactures' cartel	S$19.55
Ball bearing manufacturers' cartel	S$9.31
Freight forwarders' cartel	S$7.15

2. Enforcement Authority and Actions

a. Name/Description of Authority

The CCCS is Singapore's competition authority, and is tasked to administer and enforce the Competition Act as well as the enforcement of rules relating to retailers that persist in unfair trade practices under the Consumer Protection (Fair Trading) Act.

b. Whether Investigation and Prosecution Are Bifurcated

Under the Competition Act, the CCCS may conduct an investigation if there are reasonable grounds for suspecting that the Section 34 Prohibition has been infringed by any agreement.[276]
Where the CCCS has made a decision that an agreement has infringed the Section 34 Prohibition, the CCCS has the power to issue directions to require parties to the agreement to modify or terminate the agreement.[277] The CCCS may also impose financial penalties on parties to the agreement where the infringement has been committed intentionally or negligently, subject to a maximum of 10 percent of the turnover of the infringing party's business in Singapore for each year of the infringement, up to a maximum of three years (Statutory Maximum Financial Penalty).[278]

---

276. *See* § 62(1) of the Competition Act.
277. *See* § 69(2)(a) of the Competition Act.
278. *See* § 69(3) and § 69(4) of the Competition Act.

c. Investigation Techniques

The CCCS has wide-ranging investigative powers to require from any person the production of specified documents or information which the CCCS considers to be relevant to the investigation, to enter premises without a warrant, and to enter and search premises with a warrant. For the purpose of any investigations, the CCCS may appoint inspectors. In addition, investigating officers and other authorized personnel, as required by inspectors, may be authorized by the CCCS where entries to premises are concerned.

d. Sanctions/Penalties

In imposing any financial penalty, the CCCS has two objectives—to reflect the seriousness of the infringement, and to deter undertakings from engaging in anticompetitive practices. As such, the factors that the CCCS takes into account in calculating financial penalties include the seriousness of infringement, the turnover of the business of the undertaking in Singapore for the relevant product and geographic markets affected by the infringement in the undertaking's last business year, the duration of the infringement, other relevant factors such as deterrent value, and any further aggravating[279] or mitigating factors.

The CCCS's methodology for setting the appropriate penalty is as follows:

- Step 1: A "base amount" is determined from relevant turnover and a multiplier for seriousness of infringement.
- Step 2: A "penalty adjusted for duration" is obtained from the "base amount" multiplied by the number of years of infringement.
- Step 3: A "penalty adjusted for aggravating and mitigating factors" is calculated from the "penalty adjusted for duration" multiplied by a percentage increase or decrease for aggravating or mitigating factors respectively.
- Step 4: Further adjustments may be made for any other considerations such as deterrence value.

---

279. *See, e.g.,* CCS 500/003/13, *Infringement of the section 34 prohibition in relation to the distribution of individual life insurance products in Singapore,* where the CCS considered Financial Alliance to have acted as a leader in the infringements, and consequently increased its financial penalty.

- Step 5: A final adjustment is made (if necessary) to prevent the Statutory Maximum Financial Penalty from being exceeded.

The CCCS has been increasing the intensity of its cartel enforcement, which has culminated in more than S$67 million in financial penalties for cartel infringements as of December 2018 (representing a more than 200 percent increase in 2018 over the first 12 years of CCCS' cartel enforcement).For an individual (*see* 1(e) above), sanctions could include a fine of up to S$10,000 and/or imprisonment for a term not exceeding twelve months.

3. *Leniency Program*

The CCCS operates a leniency program applicable to infringements of the Section 34 Prohibition. The details on the leniency program are set out in the CCCS Guidelines on Lenient Treatment for Undertakings Coming Forward with Information on Cartel Activity Cases 2009 (CCCS Leniency Guidelines).

The CCCS's leniency program does not protect undertakings from other consequences of infringing the law, including, for example, that an unenforceable infringing agreement is void. Nor does leniency protect an undertaking from a claim by third parties harmed by the cartel under a private right of action. Leniency also does not provide immunity from any penalty that may be imposed on the undertaking by other competition authorities outside of Singapore.

a. Requirements

Full immunity from administrative penalties is available. An applicant can benefit from full immunity if all the following conditions are met:

- It is the first in line to provide the CCCS with evidence of the cartel activity before an investigation has commenced.
- It has not initiated or coerced another undertaking to take part in the cartel activity.
- The CCCS does not already have sufficient information to establish the existence of the alleged cartel activity.

An investigation is considered to have commenced when the CCCS exercises any of its formal investigative powers under sections 63 to 65 of the Competition Act.

All leniency applicants must satisfy all of the following general conditions:

- Immediately provide the CCCS with all the information, documents and evidence available to them regarding the cartel activity, which must provide the CCCS with a sufficient basis to commence an investigation.
- Grant an appropriate waiver of confidentiality to the CCCS for any jurisdiction where the applicant has also applied for leniency or any other regulatory authority which it has already informed of the conduct.
- Unconditionally admit to the conduct for which leniency is sought and detail the extent to which this had an impact in Singapore by preventing, restricting or distorting competition within Singapore.
- Maintain continuous and complete cooperation with the CCCS throughout the investigation and until the conclusion of any action by the CCCS arising as a result of the investigation.
- Refrain from further participation in the cartel activity from the time of disclosure of the cartel activity to the CCCS (except as may be directed by the CCCS).

b.   Immunity and Reduction in Fines

Leniency applicants can be granted up to a 100 percent reduction in financial penalties.

If an applicant does not qualify for total immunity because CCCS has already commenced an investigation, it can still benefit from a reduction in the financial penalty of up to 100 percent, if all of the following applies:

- The applicant is still the first to provide the CCCS with evidence of the cartel activity.
- This information is provided before the CCCS has sufficient information to issue a proposed infringement decision.
- The information adds significant value to the CCCS's investigation.
- The applicant has not initiated or coerced another undertaking to take part in the cartel activity.

- The applicant also satisfies all of the general conditions (see 3(a) above).

If an applicant is not the first in line, but provides useful evidence before the CCCS issues a proposed infringement decision, or the applicant is a coercer or initiator, the applicant can still be granted a reduction of up to 50 percent of the financial penalty. However, the level of reduction is discretionary, and the CCCS will take into account all of the following factors:

- The stage at which the applicant comes forward.
- The evidence already in the CCCS's possession.
- The quality of the information provided.

c. Procedure (Marker, Cooperation)

A leniency application can be made to the CCCS until:

- For a first-in-line applicant, to benefit from total immunity from financial penalties: before the CCCS has commenced an investigation, and provided that the CCCS does not already have sufficient information to establish the existence of the alleged cartel activity.
- For a first-in-line applicant, to benefit from a reduction of up to 100 percent in the level of financial penalties: before the CCCS has sufficient information to issue a proposed infringement decision in relation to the cartel activity.
- For second-in-line and all subsequent leniency applicants: before the CCCS issues a proposed infringement decision in relation to the cartel activity.

Any person contacting the CCCS on an undertaking's behalf must have power to represent the undertaking. The CCCS allows for initial contact or "feelers" to be made anonymously by potential applicants, or their authorized representatives (for example, external legal counsel), to ascertain if immunity or leniency is available. This is usually made by way of a without prejudice telephone call. The CCCS will typically require a brief description of the market concerned, the conduct involved and the relevant time period before it can respond on whether immunity or leniency is available.

A leniency application can be submitted to the CCCS online (however, the online forms do not support attachments), by e-mail, by mail, or by arranging to meet the CCCS in person by calling the CCCS's hotline to set up an appointment. Oral corporate statements will be recorded and transcribed at the CCCS's premises. Where an oral corporate statement is made, the applicant and/or its legal representatives will be given the opportunity to verify the accuracy of the CCCS's transcript.

If a first-in-line applicant cannot provide the CCCS with all the evidence relating to the suspected infringement available to it at the time of the application, the applicant can apply for a marker to secure its position in the immunity or leniency queue, and discuss the timing and process of perfecting the marker by the prompt provision of relevant information.

The following rules apply in relation to markers:

- A marker protects the first-in-line applicant's place in the queue for a limited period of time specified by the CCCS, to allow it to gather the necessary information and evidence to perfect the marker. The CCCS will grant markers to subsequent leniency applicants to secure their rank, so long as first-in-line immunity or leniency is still available.

- To secure a marker, an applicant must provide its name and a description of the cartel conduct in sufficient detail to allow the CCCS to determine that no other applicant has applied for immunity or a reduction of up to 100 percent for similar conduct.

- If the first-in-line applicant fails to perfect the marker, the next applicant in the marker queue will be allowed to perfect its marker.

- To perfect a marker, the applicant must provide information, documents and evidence that meet the requirements for a grant of conditional immunity or leniency.

- There are no set deadlines for the perfection of a marker in the CCCS Leniency Guidelines. When a first-in-line marker is granted, the applicant will discuss the timing and the process of perfecting the marker with the CCCS. The length of time given by the CCCS can range from two weeks to one month. The CCCS has stated that it will work with leniency applicants, who genuinely cooperate with the CCCS, to set reasonable time frames for providing information and evidence.

- The grant of a marker is discretionary. However, the CCCS has stated in the Leniency Guidelines 2016 that its grant is expected to be the norm rather than the exception. An applicant will only be informed whether it has been the first to come forward.

CCCS Leniency Guidelines set out that, as a minimum to meet the conditions for immunity or leniency, the information provided by the leniency applicant must provide the CCCS with a sufficient basis for taking forward a credible investigation or add significant value to the CCCS's investigation. In practice, this means that the information must be sufficient to allow the CCCS to exercise its formal powers of investigation (that is, to establish reasonable grounds for suspecting an infringement under section 34 of the Competition Act), or to genuinely advance the investigation.

The key applicable procedures and timetable are as follows:

- Optional initial contact or "feelers" to the CCCS on an anonymous basis (for example, by telephone call) to ascertain if immunity or leniency is available for the market concerned, the conduct involved and the relevant time period.
- Apply for immunity or leniency to the CCCS (orally or in writing), providing the applicant's name, in addition to the details provided at the "feeler" stage.
- Immediately provide to the CCCS all evidence relating to the suspected infringement available to the applicant. If this cannot be satisfied immediately, the applicant can alternatively apply for a marker to secure a position in the queue, and discuss the timing and process of perfecting the marker by the prompt provision of relevant information. The marker system will not apply to second-in-line and subsequent leniency applicants.

4. Fast-Track Procedure

The CCCS has implemented a new fast track procedure since December 1, 2016 to expedite the investigative process, including for section 34 infringements under the Competition Act.

The fast track procedure can be initiated by the CCCS at its own discretion, taking into account certain factors such as:

- Whether parties have proactively indicated their willingness to engage in the fast track procedure.
- Foreseeable divergences in parties' relative positions.
- The possibility of parties contradicting their positions.

- Predicted margins for argument.
- The extent to which facts may be contested.

All parties under investigation in a case must unanimously indicate to the CCCS an interest or willingness to utilize the fast track procedure before discussions may commence. Each party must also unequivocally admit liability to the infringement based on an agreed set of facts.

Parties will benefit from a 10 percent reduction in financial penalties under the fast track procedure. CCCS's leniency policy and the fast track procedure are not mutually exclusive, and it is possible for a leniency applicant to benefit from reductions arising from both the leniency policy and the fast track procedure.

5. Notifications

There is no requirement for undertakings to notify agreements to the CCCS. It is up to the parties to an agreement to ensure that their agreements are lawful and decide whether it is appropriate to make a notification for guidance or decision.

For an informal guidance or opinion, parties to an agreement can make a notification to seek guidance from the CCCS on whether an agreement would be likely to infringe the Section 34 Prohibition.

For a decision, parties to an agreement can make a notification for guidance or decision in the event that the undertaking is unsure of whether an agreement is likely to infringe the Section 34 Prohibition.

The relevant forms of notification are Form 1 and Form 2 in Appendix A of the CCCS Guidelines on Filing Notifications for Guidance or Decision. An applicant submitting Form 1 may also submit Form 2 to the CCCS at the same time, noting that information required by Form 2 is more detailed and may not be required in all cases. Concurrent submission of both forms will speed up the process in more complex cases.

H. South Africa

1. Competition Law

Section 4(1)(b) of the Competition Act, No. 89 of 1998 (as amended) (the SA Act) prohibits "an agreement between, or concerted practice by, firms, or a decision by an association of firms" on a *per se* basis if it involves:

- directly or indirectly fixing a purchase or selling price or any other trading condition;
- dividing markets by allocating customers, suppliers, territories, or specific types of goods or services; or
- collusive tendering.

2. Enforcement Authority and Actions

An administrative penalty of up to 10 percent of the firm's annual turnover in South Africa and its exports from South Africa during the firm's preceding financial year may be imposed for a first time offense.[280]

As of May 1, 2016, any director or manager may be held criminally liable if he/she causes a firm to engage in, or knowingly acquiesces[281] in a firm engaging in, any of the above prohibited practices.[282] Any person convicted of an offense under the SA Act is liable to a maximum fine of R500,000 and/or term of imprisonment of up to ten years.[283] The SA Act applies to all economic activity within, or having an effect within South Africa.[284] There is no precedent in South Africa to suggest that the effect has to be direct, substantial and foreseeable in order for the competition authorities to exercise jurisdiction.

a. Name/Description of Authority

The Competition Commission (the Commission) is the body established to investigate alleged contraventions of the SA Act.

The Commission's investigative powers include requesting information, conducting dawn raids, and summoning any person who may be able to furnish information on the subject of the investigation.

It is possible to protect confidential information submitted to the Commission by submitting a written statement in the prescribed form.[285]

---

280. Section 59(1) read with section 59(2) of the SA Act.
281. To "knowingly acquiesce" means to acquiesce while having actual knowledge of the relevant conduct by the firm. There is no provision in the SA Act that deems a director or manager to have knowledge of a prohibited practice.
282. The Competition Act of 1998, Section 73A (S. Afr.).
283. Section 74(a) of the SA Act as amended by section 13 of the Competition Amendment Act, No. 1 of 2009, which was brought into effect by Proclamation No. 36 of 2016, Government Gazette, June 9, 2016.
284. The Competition Act of 1998, Section 3 (S. Afr.).
285. *Id.* at Section 44.

b. Whether Investigation and Prosecution Are Bifurcated

A person questioned by an inspector conducting an investigation or by the Commissioner or other authorized person must answer truthfully and to the best of that person's knowledge, but the person is not obliged to answer any question if the answer is self-incriminating. [286] No self-incriminating answer given or statement made is admissible as evidence against the person who gave the answer or made the statement in criminal proceedings, except in criminal proceedings for perjury or in which the person is tried for an offense of failing to answer fully or truthfully or failing to comply with the SA Act. [287]

Dawn raids are usually conducted with a warrant issued by a judge of the High Court, a regional magistrate, or a magistrate, where there are reasonable grounds to believe that (1) a prohibited practice has taken place, is taking place or is likely to take place on the premises or (2) a person on the premises is in the possession or control of anything of relevance to an investigation under the SA Act. [288] It is possible, however, for a dawn raid to be conducted in a premises (other than a private dwelling) without a warrant if the owner or person in control of the premises provides permission to enter and search the premises or the inspector conducting the investigation believes on reasonable grounds that a warrant would be issued if applied for, and that the delay that would ensue by first obtaining a warrant would defeat the object or purpose of the entry and search. [289] During a dawn raid, a person may refuse to permit the inspection or removal of an article or document on the grounds that it contains privileged information. [290]

If the Commission finds cause for a complaint, it may refer the complaint to the Competition Tribunal (the Tribunal), the body established to adjudicate the SA Act. There would then be a hearing before the Tribunal (similar to a trial) to determine whether the conduct contravenes the SA Act. Any decision by the Tribunal may be appealed to the Competition Appeal Court (the CAC).

The Commission, Tribunal and CAC do not have jurisdiction over criminal conduct. If, following a finding of the Tribunal or CAC, a criminal prosecution is appropriate, this would have to be pursued by the

---

286. *Id.* at Section 49A(2).
287. *Id.* at Section 49A(3).
288. *Id.* at Section 46.
289. *Id.* at Section 47.
290. *Id.* at Section 49(5).

National Prosecuting Authority (NPA). The NPA is the prosecutorial body in relation to criminal conduct in South Africa. The NPA has not been particularly active in prosecuting white collar crimes. Given that the Commission and NPA are independent bodies, it is unclear how criminal prosecutions for cartel conduct will work in practice. The NPA and the Commission are apparently negotiating a memorandum of understanding in this regard.

It is expected that the Commission will advocate for the prosecution by the NPA of hardcore cartel cases, for example those that involve rigging of government tenders.

c.   Sanctions/Penalties

A firm that is found to have contravened section 4(1)(b) of the SA Act may be liable for an administrative penalty. The Tribunal considers a group of firms to be a single economic entity upon which liability resulting from a contravention of section 4(1)(b) by a single firm within the group may be imputed.[291] A specific six-step methodology has been developed by the Tribunal and the CAC to determine administrative penalties[292] and has been incorporated into formal guidelines developed by the Commission.[293]

- Step one: Determine the affected turnover, which is the firm's turnover derived from sales of products and services that can be said to have been affected by the contravention.
- Step two: Calculate the base amount which is a proportion of the affected turnover from a scale of 0 percent to 30 percent. The proportion applied will be based on factors such as: (i) the nature, gravity and extent of the contravention; (ii) any losses or damage suffered as a result of the contravention; (iii) the market circumstances in which the contravention took place; (iv) the nature of the affected product(s); (v) the structure of the market; (vi) the market shares of the firms involved; (vii) the barriers to

---

291. Competition Commission v Delatoy Investments (Pty) Ltd and Others (CR212Feb15) 2016 ZACT 37 (Apr. 14, 2016) (S. Afr.).
292. Competition Commission v. Aveng (Africa) Limited t/a Steeledale, Reinforcing Mesh Solutions (Pty) Ltd, Vulcania Reinforcing (Pty) Ltd and BRC Mesh Reinforcing (Pty) Ltd, (84/CR/Dec09) 2013 ZACAC 4 (Nov. 15, 2013).
293. GUIDELINES FOR THE DETERMINATION OF ADMINISTRATIVE PENALTIES FOR PROHIBITED PRACTICES, effective May 1, 2015.

entry in the market; and (viii) the impact of the contravention on competitors and consumers, and the likely impact on small and medium sized enterprises and low income consumers.

- Step three: Multiply the base amount by the number of years of participation in the contravention. For contraventions lasting less than one year, the Commission will apply a duration multiplier equal to the proportion of the year over which the contravention lasted.

- Step four: Ensure that the amount in step 3 does not exceed the statutory limit of a maximum of 10 percent of the firm's annual turnover during its preceding financial year.

- Step five: Adjust the figure in step 3 based on aggravating and mitigating factors of each firm and its conduct, including factors such as participation of directors and senior management in the contravention, the nature of the firm's involvement in the contravention (i.e., passive or aggressive), whether the firm terminated the conduct as soon as the Commission intervened and the degree of cooperation with the Commission.

- Step six: Adjust the figure calculated in step 5 if necessary so as to not exceed the statutory limit of 10 percent of the firm's annual turnover during its preceding financial year. The financial year considered is the financial year preceding that in which the administrative penalty is imposed. If there is no turnover in that preceding financial year, it shall be the last year in which there is turnover available.

3. Leniency Program

a. Requirements

The Commission has a corporate leniency policy [294] that offers immunity for the first firm to approach the Commission with information relating to a cartel in exchange for cooperation in the prosecution of the other members of the cartel. Other members of the cartel may approach the Commission with additional information in exchange for a reduction in fine, a settlement order, or a consent order.

---

294. CORPORATE LENIENCY POLICY, *available at* http://www.compcom.co.za/corporate-leniency-policy/.

b. Immunity vs Reduction in Fines

The Commission will first grant an applicant conditional immunity which is later converted into total immunity once the applicant's cooperation has played out. Once total immunity is granted, the firm will have complete immunity in relation to administrative penalties. Total immunity does not, however, protect the firm against civil damages claims or protect an individual who caused the firm to engage in, or who knowingly acquiesced in the firm engaging in, cartel conduct from criminal prosecution.

The Commission may grant leniency to an individual who may otherwise be held criminally liable for causing the firm to engage in, or knowingly acquiescing in the firm engaging in, cartel conduct. The Commission may not seek or request the prosecution of a person deserving of leniency and it may make submissions to the NPA in support of leniency for any person prosecuted for an offense in this regard. As the NPA is an independent body, in the absence of a memorandum of understanding with the Commission, it is not clear to what extent reliance can be placed on the Commission's certification.

A leniency grant does not protect an applicant from collateral civil claims. However, there have not yet been any awards of civil damages for cartel conduct.

4. Procedure

It is possible for a firm to apply for a marker (which holds the firm's place as first in line) while it gathers the relevant information.[295] The application must identify the alleged cartel conduct and its participants and justify the need for a marker. The Commission may grant a marker at its discretion. In granting the marker, the Commission will determine the period of time within which the applicant must provide the necessary information, evidence, and documents needed to meet the conditions and requirements for immunity. If the applicant submits an application for immunity along with the necessary information, evidence, and documents within the time limit determined by the Commission, such application for immunity will be deemed to have been made on the date when the marker application was granted by the Commission.

---

295. CORPORATE LENIENCY POLICY, ¶ 12.

I.   Taiwan

1.   Competition Law—Cartel

a.   Basic Explanation of Law

The Fair Trade Act of Taiwan, Republic of China (ROC) (TFTA) became effective on February 4, 1992 and has been amended several times. The latest amendment was made in June 2017.

Cartels are regulated by the provision concerning concerted actions under the TFTA. A concerted action is conduct involving any enterprise by means of contract, agreement, or any other form of mutual understanding with a competing enterprise to jointly determine the price of goods or services, or to limit the terms of quantity, technology, products, facilities, trading counterparts, or trading territory with respect to such goods and services, thereby restricting each other's business activities.[296] A concerted action is limited to a horizontal action that is conducted by enterprises competing at the same production or sale level, and it may interfere with the market mechanism for the production or supply and demand of goods or services.[297]

b.   Major Exemptions/Immunities

Under the TFTA, a concerted action is prohibited unless it meets one of the exemptions stipulated in Article 15 of the TFTA and is beneficial to the economy as a whole and in the public interest. Any enterprise that intends to apply for exemption of a concerted action must submit the required documents to the Taiwan Fair Trade Commission (TFTC) seeking the TFTC's prior approval.

Article 15 of the TFTA provides the following eight requirements for a concerted action to be approved by the TFTC:

> (a) unification: it unifies the specifications or models of goods for the purpose of reducing costs, improving quality or increasing efficiency;
> (b) joint research and development: it entails joint research and development for the purpose of enhancing technology, reducing costs, improving quality or increasing efficiency;

---

296.   TFTA art. 14.
297.   *Id.*

(c) specialisation: it develops a separate and specialised area for the purpose of rationalising operations;

(d) exportation: it is to enter into agreements concerning solely competition in foreign markets for the purpose of securing or promoting exportation;

(e) importation: it is for the importation of foreign goods for the purpose of strengthening trade;

(f) economic downturn: it is to limit the quantity of production and sales, equipment or prices for the purpose of meeting the demand expected during an economic downturn, meaning that the enterprises in a particular industry have difficulties in maintaining their business or face overproduction;

(g) small to medium-sized enterprises: it is for the purpose of improving operational efficiency or strengthening the competitiveness of small to medium-sized enterprises; and

(h) catch-all provision: any other joint acts for the purposes of improving industrial development, technological innovation or operational efficiency.

The TFTC is required to make a decision within three months upon receipt of an application and may only extend the three-month period once. The approval granted by the TFTC shall specify a time limit not exceeding five years for the implementation of a concerted action and may attach conditions thereto. Such approval can be renewed by an application filed before the expiration of the original time limit.

c.   Standard of Proof

Since the TFTA was amended on February 6, 2015,[298] the TFTC is permitted to presume the existence of an agreement on the basis of circumstantial evidence, such as market conditions, characteristics of the products or services involved, and profit and cost considerations. By way of this amendment, the new law substantially shifts the burden of proof regarding the existence of an agreement among competitors from the TFTC to the enterprises that are investigated or penalized.

---

298. *Id.*

d.   Whether Information Exchange Is Violative

Although the TFTA does not explicitly stipulate that information exchange is a type of concerted action, information exchange could be violative if the information being exchanged is sensitive business information that could lead to the parties' coordination on the price, production and sales quantity, etc.

In the 2012 optical disk drive (ODD) case,[299] the TFTC ruled that four ODD manufacturers had conspired during the bidding processes held by Original Equipment Manufacturers and thus had violated the cartel provisions under the TFTA. According to the TFTC, the four ODD manufacturers exchanged their bidding prices and expected bid ranking through e-mails, telephone calls and meetings. Additionally, in several bidding cases, they agreed on the final price and ranking in advance while exchanging other sensitive information such as capacity and amount of production among themselves.

Based on the TFTC's decision in the ODD case, exchanging sensitive business information between competitors could be a violation of cartel prohibition rule.

e.   Whether Enforced Civilly or Criminally

According to the TFTA, cartel violation will be sanctioned first with an administrative fine, followed by criminal liability if the violating enterprise fails to follow the TFTC's order to cease, rectify or take necessary measures to correct its violation or repeats the violation.

f.   Extraterritorial Application of Competition Law

The TFTC's jurisdiction is determined based on the effect of the conduct in question. Coordination between or among foreign enterprises that takes place in either Taiwan or another jurisdiction is subject to the TFTA's jurisdiction if such conduct may affect the Taiwanese market.

---

299.   TFTC decision announced on September 24, 2012. The full content of the decision letter was not published because of protection of the leniency applicant.

2. Enforcement Authority and Actions

a. Name/Description of Authority

The competent authority under the TFTA is the TFTC, which is an independent agency not under the supervision of the Executive Yuan (cabinet). The TFTC is the regulatory body responsible for enforcing, interpreting, and promulgating rules under the TFTA.

b. Whether Investigation and Prosecution Are Bifurcated

The TFTC is only empowered with administrative power under the TFTA, and thus the investigation and prosecution of a cartel violation are handled by different authorities. As a cartel violation is sanctioned first with an administrative fine, followed by criminal liability, the investigation is conducted by the TFTC. If the violating enterprise fails to follow the TFTC's order to cease, rectify or take necessary measures to correct its violation or repeats the violation, the TFTC, at its discretion, may submit the case to the prosecutors' office for prosecution.

c. Investigation Techniques

Under the current legal framework, the TFTC is not entitled to apply for a search warrant with the court because it is not granted judicial power. Therefore, the investigatory powers granted to the TFTC by the TFTA and other administrative regulations is somewhat limited compared with that of other foreign competition authorities or the prosecutors' office. Accordingly, while a dawn raid may be initiated by a prosecutor based on a search warrant, the TFTC cannot take such action.

If the TFTC has carried out unscheduled visits to target enterprises, it may request that the enterprises provide necessary documents and information; however, it cannot compel those enterprises to submit documents and information to it, nor can it search the enterprises' premises to obtain the requested documents and information.

According to the TFTA, the TFTC has the following four types of investigatory tools. It can:

(a) order the parties and any related third parties to appear before the TFTC to make statements;
(b) order relevant agencies, organizations, enterprises or individuals to submit books and records, documents and any other necessary materials or exhibits;

(c) dispatch personnel to conduct any necessary on-site inspection of the office, place of business or other locations of the relevant organization or enterprises; and

(d) seize articles discovered during any of the above-mentioned investigations that may serve as evidence. The articles and period of the seizure should be limited to those necessary for the investigation, inspection, verification or any other purpose of preserving evidence.[300]

In addition, the TFTC has to observe the principles in the Administrative Procedure Act (the Act) just like all other administrative government agencies when conducting an investigation.[301] In particular, the principle of proportionality under the Act requires that the method adopted by a government agency should help achieve the intended objective; where there are several methods that could lead to the same result, the method that causes the least harm to the people concerned should be adopted; and the harm caused by an action should not be disproportionately greater than the benefits from the action.

d.   Sanctions/Penalties

If any enterprise is found to have conducted a concerted action without the TFTC's approval, the TFTC may, pursuant to Article 40 of the TFTA: (i) order it to discontinue the illegal conduct; (ii) set a time limit for it to rectify the conduct or take necessary corrective measures; and (iii) impose an administrative fine of between NT$100,000 and NT$50 million.[302] If the violating party fails to act as ordered, the TFTC may continue to order the violating party to cease the violation or set another time limit for the violating party to comply, and it may impose successive administrative fines of NT$200,000 to NT$100 million until the violating party complies.[303] When assessing fines in accordance with the TFTA, the following items shall be taken into consideration:

(a) motivation, purpose, and expected improper benefit of the act;

(b) the degree of harm to market order caused by the act;

(c) the duration of harm to market order caused by the act;

---

300.   TFTA art. 27.
301.   Administrative Procedure Act (promulgated Feb 3, 1999, effective Jan 1, 2001).
302.   TFTA art. 40.
303.   *Id.*

(d) benefits derived on account of the unlawful act;

(e) scale, operating condition, and market position of the enterprise;

(f) types of, number of, and intervening time between past violations, and the punishment for such violations; and

(g) remorse shown for the act and degree of cooperation in the investigation.[304]

In addition to the administrative punishments mentioned above, a violation of cartel regulations may also carry criminal liability. That is, if any enterprise is ordered by the TFTC to cease, rectify or take necessary measures to correct its violation of the cartel regulations under the TFTA, but fails to follow such order or repeats the violation, the enterprise's responsible person and any employees involved may face a prison term of up to three years.[305] In such circumstances, the enterprise may receive a criminal fine of up to NT$100 million in accordance with Article 34 of the TFTA. If the TFTC considers a concerted action to be serious, however, it may impose a fine of up to 10 percent of the violating enterprise's revenue in the last fiscal year.[306]

A serious concerted action is one that materially affects competition in the relevant market, taking the following factors into account:

(a) the scope and extent of the market competition and order affected;

(b) the duration of the damage to market competition and order;

(c) the market status of the violating enterprise and the structure of the corresponding market;

(d) the total sales and profits obtained from the unlawful conduct during the violation period; and

---

304. Enforcement Rules of the Fair Trade Act (promulgated Jun 24, 1992, effective Jun 24, 1992), art. 36.

305. TFTA art. 34.

306. *Id.* art. 40. In the revenue calculations, revenues from an enterprise's domestic and foreign branches should be included, but those from its subsidiaries are excluded. The reason for this is that the TFTC considers a subsidiary as a separate entity that operates independently. Hence, the TFTC will not consider the consolidated revenues of a conglomerate enterprise but only the revenues of the enterprise that violates the TFTA. Since some enterprises (such as holding companies) do not have actual operation activities, the fine calculated without including the consolidated revenues may be lower than the TFTC's expectation.

(e) the type of concerted cartel: joint price decision on product or service, or restriction on quantity, trading counterpart or trading area.[307]

In the event of either of the following circumstances, the violation should be deemed as serious:

(a) the total amount of turnover of the relevant products or services during the period the cartel is active exceeds NT$100 million; or
(b) the total amount of gains derived from the cartel exceeds the maximum fine under the TFTA (NT$50 million).[308]

According to Regulations for Calculation of Administrative Fines for Serious Violations of Article 9 (monopoly) and 15 (cartel) of the TFTA, the fine imposed on a serious cartel should be based on the basic amount and adjusting factors. The basic amount refers to 30 percent of the total amount of turnover of the relevant products or services during the cartel period. The adjusting factors include aggravating factors and mitigating factors.

The aggravating factors are as follows:

(a) the violating enterprise has organized or encouraged the unlawful conduct;
(b) the violating enterprise has implemented supervision or sanctioning measures to ensure that the concerted action is upheld or executed; and
(c) the violating enterprise has been sanctioned for a violation of monopoly or cartel regulations within the past five years.

The mitigating factors are as follows:

(a) the violating enterprise immediately ceased the unlawful act when the TFTC began the investigation;
(b) the violating enterprise has shown real remorse and cooperated in the investigation;

---

307. Regulations for Calculation of Administrative Fine for Serious Violations of Articles 9 and 15 of the TFTA (promulgated Apr 5, 2012, effective Apr 5, 2012), art. 2.
308. *Id.*

(c) the violating enterprise has established compensation agreements with the victims or has taken remedial measures;
(d) the violating enterprise has participated in the concerted action under coercion; and
(e) other government agencies approve or encourage the fine imposed to be reduced, or the fine reduction can be granted in accordance with other laws.[309]

3. Leniency Program

The TFTC's Leniency Program came into effect on January 6, 2012. The Leniency Program specifies, the requirements for leniency, the maximum number of cartel participants eligible for leniency, the fine reduction percentage, the required evidence, and confidentiality treatment.[310] Adoption of the Leniency Program, which has been active for six years, has significantly affected the enforcement of cartel regulations in Taiwan. The TFTC has, based on the Leniency Program, imposed sanctions on two international cartels, including the capacitor case.[311]

a. Requirements

According to the Leniency Program, an enterprise violating the cartel prohibitions under the TFTA can be exempted from a fine or entitled to a fine reduction if it meets one of the following requirements, and the TFTC agrees in advance that the enterprise qualifies for the immunity or reduction:

(a) before the TFTC knows about the unlawful cartel activities or commences investigation on its own initiative, the enterprise voluntarily reports to the TFTC in writing the details of its unlawful cartel activities, provides key evidence, and assists the TFTC in its subsequent investigation; or

---

309. *Id.* art. 6.
310. Regulations on Immunity and Reduction of Fines in Illegal Concerted Action (promulgated Jan 6, 2012, effective Jan 6, 2012).
311. The TFTC published a press release on its decisions on December 9, 2015. The reference numbers of these decisions are Gong-Chu-Zhi Nos.: 104133 to 104140.

(b) during the TFTC's investigation, the enterprise provides specific evidence that helps prove unlawful cartel activities and assists the TFTC in its subsequent investigation.

b.   Immunity vs. Reduction in Fines

In any case, a maximum of five applicants can be eligible for fine immunity or a fine reduction. The first applicant to file the application can qualify for full immunity from a fine. The fines for the second to fifth applicants can be reduced by 30 to 50 percent, 20 to 30 percent, 10 to 20 percent, and 10 percent or less, respectively. An applicant that has coerced any other enterprise to join or not to exit the cartel cannot be eligible for fine immunity or a reduction of the fine.[312]

The board of directors, representatives or managers of an involved enterprise, or others with the authority to represent the enterprise who should be jointly penalized based on the Republic of China (ROC) Administrative Penalty Act, may be granted immunity or a fine reduction if the following requirements are met:

(a) the enterprise is an applicant that can be granted immunity or a fine reduction;
(b) these persons have provided honest and full statements with regard to the unlawful act; and
(c) these persons have followed the instructions of the TFTC and have provided honest, full and continued assistance to the TFTC during its investigation before the case is concluded.[313]

According to the Leniency Program, when the TFTC grants an applicant immunity or a reduction of the fine, it must take the following steps to protect the confidentiality of the applicant's identity:

(d) not indicate the name of the applicant, the fine imposed, and the amount of fine reduced and the reasons, unless with the consent of the applicant; and
(e) send its decision letter to each violating enterprise, with the main text regarding the fine referring only to the enterprise that receives

---

312.   Regulations on Immunity and Reduction of Fines in Illegal Concerted Action (promulgated Jan 6, 2012, effective Jan 6, 2012), art. 2.
313.   *Id.* art. 9.

the decision letter. The decision letter should not contain information about other violating enterprises.[314]

Unless otherwise stipulated by law, the records or original documents carrying information about the identity of the applicant may not be provided to any agencies, groups or entities other than investigation and judicial agencies. Despite the foregoing, if any injured party files a civil lawsuit for damages against the violating enterprises, the injured party may request that the court ask the TFTC to provide relevant documents according to the ROC Code of Civil Procedure.[315] The applicant will likely be identified during the court procedure.

c.   Procedure

An enterprise that intends to apply for fine immunity, but does not have information and evidence required by the Leniency Program and is therefore unqualified to file the application, may submit a written statement to the TFTC requesting preservation of the priority status for fine immunity (i.e., to obtain a marker), which must contain the following information:

(a) the enterprise's name, paid-in capital, annual revenue, name of its representative, and address and date of company registration;
(b) the product or service involved, the form of the concerted action, the geographic areas affected and the duration of the action; and
(c) the names, company addresses and representatives of other cartel members. An enterprise that has been granted a marker should provide the information and evidence required by the Leniency Program within the period specified by the TFTC, or it will lose the marker. The application for a marker should be made in writing and should follow the format prescribed by the TFTC.[316]

From the time the application is filed until the case is concluded, the enterprise that files the application should withdraw from the cartel immediately or at the time specified by the TFTC, follow the instructions

---

314.   *Id.* art. 18.
315.   ROC Code of Civil Procedure (promulgated Dec 26, 1930, last amended Jun 13, 2018), art. 286.
316.   Regulations on Immunity and Reduction of Fines in Illegal Concerted Action (promulgated Jan 6, 2012, effective Jan 6, 2012), art. 10.

of the TFTC, and provide honest, full and continued assistance to the TFTC during its investigation. The assistance should include the following:

(a) the applicant should, as early as possible, provide the TFTC with all the information and evidence regarding the cartel that it currently possesses or may obtain in the future. For those applying for a fine reduction, the information and evidence provided must be of significant help in the TFTC's investigation into the cartel or enhance the probative value of the evidence the TFTC has already obtained;

(b) the applicant should follow the instructions of the TFTC and provide prompt descriptions or cooperation to help the investigation regarding related facts capable of proving the existence of the cartel;

(c) if necessary, the applicant must allow its staff members or representatives that participated in cartel-related activities to be questioned by the TFTC;

(d) the content of the statements, information or evidence provided may not contain any untruths, and no destruction, forgery, alteration or concealment of any information or evidence related to the cartel will be tolerated; and

(e) without the consent of the TFTC, the applicant may not disclose to any other parties the filing of the application or any content of the application before the case is concluded.[317]

The TFTA was further amended in June 2015 to introduce a whistle-blower reward scheme, which provides that, among other sources, 30 percent of the funds for this reward will come from the amount of penalties collected by the TFTC.[318] As stated in the TFTC's news release, this reward scheme aims to encourage employees to report illegal activities carried out by their employers.[319]

J.　People's Republic of China

1.　Competition Law

317.　*Id.*, art. 6.

318.　Fair Trade Act (promulgated Feb 4, 1991, effective Feb 4, 1992), art. 47-1.

319.　The TFTC published a press release on June 9, 2015. The link to that press release is not currently available.

a. National Law

The Anti-Monopoly Law of the People's Republic of China (AML) is the main legislation that regulates competition domestically.[320] The AML took effect on August 1, 2008. China has a unitary legal system and the AML is a national law of China; it applies to all provinces and administrative municipalities. In terms of application and enforcement, Hong Kong, Macau, and Taiwan are considered separate legal jurisdictions and do not fall under the AML's regulation.

The AML regulates monopoly agreements (both horizontal and vertical); abuse of dominant market position; and concentration of undertakings. Additionally, Chapter 5 of the AML deals with administrative monopoly, a unique feature due to China's socialist market economy.

In the context of horizontal cartel regulation, information exchange is not directly mentioned in the AML's language. But the relevant antitrust enforcement agencies have made it clear that the exchange of sensitive information between competitors is prohibited.

b. No Criminal Liability for Engaging in Cartel Activities

Under the AML, there is no criminal liability for engaging in cartel activities. China's Criminal Law also does not make it a crime to engage in cartel activities. The only exception, per the AML, relates to criminal liability that may arise from obstruction-of-justice type conduct during a government investigation.

c. Administrative and Civil Liability and Corresponding Evidentiary Standards

Engaging in cartel activities triggers administrative liabilities. The fine is between 1 and 10 percent of the perpetrator's revenue for the preceding year.[321] In addition, according to Article 50 of the AML, private plaintiffs

---

320. The Anti-Unfair Competition Law of the People's Republic of China (AUCL) also has some provisions that regulate certain competition behaviors of business operators, and it is recognized as a competition-related law in a broader sense. But this article only discusses the AML.

321. Revenue, as the AML-prescribed basis for calculating penalties, is not limited to the geographical area of China. In penalty decisions issued by the National Development and Reform Commission (NDRC) and the State Administration for Industry and Commerce (SAIC), the cartel perpetrator's

may sue for damages. There is no class action system for private plaintiffs in China.

For civil cases, the general evidentiary standard is "high degree of probability," which is higher than the "preponderance of evidence" standard under common law systems.

For criminal cases, the evidentiary standard requires that "the facts are clear and the evidences are reliable and sufficient." That said, this is a non-issue because typically there is no criminal element in cartel cases, other than obstruction-of-justice type conduct during a government antitrust investigation that may incur criminal liability.

For administrative cases, the law is not clear on the evidentiary standard. The mainstream academic view is that the evidentiary standard for administrative cases falls somewhere between civil cases and criminal cases.

d. Extraterritorial Application

The AML has extraterritorial application. [322]	The key to extraterritorial application is whether the overseas monopoly behavior has an anti-competitive effect on the Chinese domestic market.

2. *Enforcement Authorities and Actions*

a. Enforcement Authorities

Until recently, the National Development and Reform Commission (NDRC) and the State Administration for Industry and Commerce (SAIC) were the two enforcement agencies with the authority to enforce the AML with respect to cartels. The third AML enforcement agency was the Ministry of Commerce (MOFCOM), which reviewed and approved

---

China-derived revenues were used as the base for calculating fines. Theoretically, however, the NDRC and the SAIC could also use global revenue as the base for calculating penalties. It is likely that the recently established unified antitrust enforcement agency SAMR (State Administration for Market Regulation) will take the same approach on this issue.

322. Article 2 of the AML provides that "this Law is applicable to monopolistic conducts in economic activities within the territory of the People's Republic of China; and it is applicable to monopolistic conducts outside the territory of the People's Republic of China, which conducts serve to eliminate or restrict competition on the domestic market of China."

concentration transactions. In March 2018, the National People's Congress passed a bill to institute a major reform of the Chinese central government. Under the reform, the State Administration for Market Regulation (SAMR) was established, which assumed all the AML-related functions of the NDRC, the SAIC and MOFCOM. SAMR is a ministerial level agency that reports to China's State Council. It was officially established on March 21, 2018 as the unified antitrust enforcement agency in China. It issued the first merger clearance decision on May 14, 2018.. While SAMR is not an independent commission with great powers, the fact that SAMR is a single and unified antitrust enforcement agency will certainly enhance the AML enforcement in China.

Under Article 39 of the AML, when conducting investigations into suspected monopolistic conduct, the enforcement authority may take the following measures: (1) inspect the business places or the relevant premises of the undertakings under investigation; (2) inquire into the undertakings under investigation, the interested parties, or other units or individuals involved, and request that they provide relevant explanations; (3) consult and duplicate relevant documents and materials, such as invoices, vouchers, agreements, account books, business correspondence and electronic data, of the undertakings under investigation, the interested parties, and other relevant units and individuals; (4) seal up or seize relevant evidence; and (5) inspect the bank accounts of the undertakings under investigation. What's more, to take these measures and enforce the AML, a written report must be submitted to the principal leading person of the authority for approval.

b.   Enforcement Actions

Because there is no criminal liability under the AML for engaging in cartel activities, there have not been any reported criminal cartel cases in China. In the administrative area, both the former antitrust divisions of the NDRC and the SAIC (which have now been consolidated into SAMR) have been active in enforcing the AML, and on their individual websites have published penalty decisions imposing fines on perpetrators. Since the institutional reform resulting in the unified and combined antitrust enforcement agency SAMR, cartel enforcement is carried out by SAMR.

c.　No Attorney-Client Privilege

There is no concept of attorney-client privilege in China. [323] The Lawyer's Law of China prescribes that lawyers shall maintain the confidentiality of client information obtained during service to clients. But in civil litigation and administrative proceedings, if law enforcement authorities request client information and documents from a lawyer, the lawyer typically has no grounds to refuse.

d.　Transfers of Documents Outside of China

During global cartel investigations, there may be situations where it becomes necessary to transfer documents outside of China. In such cases, Chinese law prohibits the transfer of any documents containing state secrets outside of China. In addition, if the undertaking being investigated for cartel violation is classified as a "critical information infrastructure operator" under the Cybersecurity Law, all personal information generated or collected by such undertaking during its business operation in China may not be transferred outside of China, unless the required security evaluation has been processed.

In addition, on October 26, 2018, the Law of the People's Republic of China on International Judicial Assistance in Criminal Matters took effect. Under Article 4, unless granted approval from the competent Chinese authorities, no foreign institution, organization or individual may conduct criminal litigation activities within China, and "no institution, organization or individual within the territory of the People's Republic of China shall provide any evidentiary materials or assistance described in this law to any foreign country."[324]

e.　Cooperation with Enforcement in Other Jurisdictions

Before SAMR was established, the NDRC and the SAIC have each signed a number of cooperation agreements (or memoranda of cooperation) with foreign antitrust enforcement agencies, allowing the

323.　Criminal defense lawyers have some limited privilege under Article 46 of the Criminal Procedure Law of the People's Republic of China. But since there is no criminal liability under the AML for engaging in cartel activities that limited privilege is inapplicable with respect to the AML.
324.　International Criminal Judicial Assistance Law ("ICJAL"), art. 4, Standing Comm. Nat'l People's Cong. (promulgated and effective October 26, 2018) (China).

agencies to exchange information under certain conditions. These cooperation agreements will be inherited and performed by SAMR.

f. Sanctions/Penalties

Under the AML, the penalties imposed by the enforcement agencies are administrative in nature. For private civil actions, no punitive damages are awarded. For administrative investigation cases involving monopoly agreements and abuse of dominant market position, the penalties include fines (1 to 10 percent of the preceding year's revenue) and confiscation of illegal gains. The agencies will consider factors including the conduct's nature, severity, extent, duration and other factors, such as a major role in condemnable behaviors. Self-rectification or existence of coercion could lead to reduction of penalties.

3. *Leniency Program*

Leniency programs exist under the AML.[325] However, because there is no criminal liability under the AML for engaging in cartel activities, leniency benefits only include exemptions from or reductions in fines. Parties that voluntarily report cartel agreements to the Chinese enforcement authorities and provide important evidence may be granted leniency.

Before SAMR was established, under the respective leniency programs of the NDRC and the SAIC, the first qualifying leniency applicant was granted immunity from fines. The NDRC's leniency program granted a fine reduction of at least 50 percent for the second leniency applicant and a fine reduction of less than 50 percent for subsequent leniency applicants. The SAIC had discretion as to the amount and percentage of any fine reduction for later leniency applicants based on the applicant's cooperativeness. SAMR has not taken a position as to which of the above leniency programs to adopt. It is likely that they will apply the NDRC's program to price-related cases and the SAIC's program to non-price-related cases until SAMR issues its own leniency program.

The Chinese enforcement authorities have broad discretion in deciding whether to grant leniency. In 2016, the NDRC issued a consultation draft of Guidelines for the Application of Leniency Programs

---

325. Article 46 of the AML provides that if the undertaking, on its own initiative, reports to the AML enforcement authority a monopoly agreement that has been reached, and provides material evidence, the authority may, at its discretion, reduce any penalty, or exempt the undertaking from penalties.

in Horizontal Monopoly Agreement Cases, in which the agency proposed more transparency in its leniency program.

K. Australia

Cartels may be prosecuted as indictable criminal offenses in Australia under Division 1 of Part IV of the *Competition and Consumer Act 2010 (Cth)* (CCA). The criminal cartel prohibitions, introduced in July 2009, form part of Australia's bifurcated system of public cartel enforcement, complementing the established civil cartel regime. Cartels are frequently investigated on a potentially criminal basis, and in August 2017, Australia had its first successful prosecution under the criminal cartel provisions,. There have also been many civil prosecutions against companies and individuals under the civil cartel regime.

1. Competition Law

a.   Criminal Cartel Conduct

The elements of Australia's criminal cartel offenses mirror the civil prohibitions; both proscribe making or giving effect to any contract, arrangement or understanding between competitors or potential competitors that contains a "cartel provision."[326] A provision of a contract, arrangement or understanding is a cartel provision if it has the purpose or effect of price fixing, or the purpose of output restriction, market allocation or bid rigging, between two or more parties that are competitive with each other in respect of the goods or services that are subject of the agreement (or would be, but for the agreement).[327] Such conduct is per se prohibited by the CCA.

Criminal liability also requires that two fault elements be established, specifically an intention to make or give effect to the contract, arrangement or understanding, and knowledge or belief that the contract, arrangement or understanding contains a cartel provision.[328]

To establish either an arrangement or understanding, it must be shown that a direct or indirect communication between competitors resulted in a "meeting of the minds" accompanied by a level of commitment by at least one of the parties to act in a proscribed manner. When direct evidence is

---

326.   *Competition and Consumer Act 2010 (Cth)* ("CCA") §§ 45AF, 45AG.
327.   "Cartel provisions" are defined in CCA § 45AD.
328.   CCA §§ 45AF(2), 45AG(2), *Criminal Code 1995 (Cth)* §§ 5.6(1)

not available, circumstantial evidence may be relied upon to infer the existence of an arrangement or understanding.

A corporation will be vicariously liable for cartel conduct committed by an employee, agent or officer acting within the actual or apparent scope of their employment or authority.[329] As a result, individual persons can also be subject to personal liability for cartel offenses.

b. Extraterritorial Application

The criminal cartel offenses and civil prohibitions will apply to conduct occurring outside Australia where it is engaged in by bodies incorporated in or carrying on business in Australia, and by Australian citizens or persons ordinarily resident in Australia.[330]

c. Sanctions/Penalties

Criminal sanctions will apply to individuals and corporations found guilty of knowingly contravening the cartel offenses. A non-exhaustive list of sentencing factors required to be considered by a court is set out in section 16A of the *Crimes Act 1914 (Cth)*, including factors such as the nature and circumstances of the offense and the degree of deterrence that a sentence may have.

Individual cartel offenders may be sentenced by a court to a maximum of ten years' imprisonment and face fines of up to 2,000 penalty units (currently AUD$420,000) per contravention.[331] A corporation may be punished by conviction with a fine not exceeding the greater of AUD$10m, three times the value of the benefit obtained from commission of the offense or, if the attributable benefit cannot be calculated, 10 percent of the corporation's annual turnover.[332]

Other sanctions for criminal cartel conduct include injunctions, declarations, community service, and director disqualification orders.

Related bodies corporate (where the only parties to the cartel conduct are related bodies corporate) and certain joint ventures are exempt from

---

329. CCA § 79.
330. CCA § 5.
331. CCA § 79, currently penalty unit is AUS$210 § 4AA *Crimes Act 1914 (Cth)* (CA)
332. CCA §§ 45AG, 45AF.

the cartel conduct under the CCA.[333] Parties can also seek and obtain prior authorization to engage in cartel conduct from the ACCC.

In August 2017, Australia had its first criminal cartel conviction under laws introduced in 2009. NYK was ordered to pay AUD$25 million (ACCC v NYK), which included a 50 percent discount on its penalty for its early guilty plea and cooperation with the ACCC. [334]

2. Enforcement Authorities and Actions

a. Enforcement Authorities

The Australian Competition and Consumer Commission (ACCC) is the independent federal regulator responsible for general investigation and enforcement of the CCA, including the cartel prohibitions. However, the ACCC does not have the capacity to lay criminal charges and will refer cases involving "serious cartel conduct" to the Commonwealth Director of Public Prosecutions (CDPP) for potential criminal prosecution when the cartel conduct has caused, or has the potential to cause, serious or large-scale economic harm.[335]

In exercising its independent discretion to prosecute, the CDPP must consider whether there is sufficient evidence, a reasonable prospect of conviction, and whether a prosecution is in the public interest.[336]

---

333. CCA § 45AN (related bodies corporate); § 45AO (joint venture–criminal proceedings); § 45AP (joint venture–civil penalty proceedings).

334. Australian Competition and Consumer Commission, *NYK convicted of criminal cartel conduct and fined 25 million* (Aug. 3, 2017) https://www.accc.gov.au/media-release/nyk-convicted-of-criminal-cartel-conduct-and-fined-25-million.

335. *See*, Commonwealth Director of Public Prosecutions and the Australian Competition and Consumer Commission, Memo. of Understanding regarding Serious Cartel Conduct (Aug. 15, 2014), *available at* https://www.cdpp.gov.au/sites/g/files/net2061/f/MR-20140910-MOU-Serious-Cartel-Conduct.pdf.

336. Commonwealth Director of Public Prosecutions, *Prosecution Policy of the Commonwealth* (Sept. 9, 2014), *available at* https://www.cdpp.gov.au/sites/g/files/net2061/f/Prosecution-Policy-of-the-Commonwealth_1.pdf.

b. Investigations

The ACCC is equipped with extensive administrative powers to procure evidence in criminal cartel investigations. Under section 155 of the CCA, the ACCC may compel an individual or corporation to provide information or documents, or appear before the ACCC for examination. Substantial penalties may apply for non-compliance with, or for knowingly providing false or misleading evidence in response to, a section 155 notice. This can include referral to the CDPP for criminal prosecution punishable by up to twelve months imprisonment or a fine of up to twenty penalty units (AUD$21,000).[337]

The ACCC also has search and seizure powers; under section 154X of the CCA, an inspector from the ACCC may apply to a magistrate for a warrant to enter or search premises, or to seize, make copies, or remove evidentiary materials.[338] In criminal cartel investigations, the ACCC may request assistance from the Australian Federal Police (AFP) in relation to the execution of ACCC-issued search warrants or to separately obtain other court-issued warrants related to surveillance, the interception of telephone communications, or search.[339]

The ACCC is party to a number of agreements with international competition law agencies, including with the European Commission and the New Zealand Commerce Commission, facilitating cooperation and information exchange in cartel enforcement cases. A close degree of cooperation between Australia and the United States in respect of antitrust matters is supported by treaties and the 2004 United States-Australia Free Trade Agreement.[340]

c. Actions

A cartel offense may be tried in the Federal Court of Australia (FCA) or in the Supreme Court of an Australian State or Territory where, pursuant to the Commonwealth Constitution, trial by jury is mandatory for a federal

---

337. CCA § 155(6A), current penalty unit is AUD$210 § 4AA CA.
338. *See generally*, CCA pt XID.
339. The Australian Federal Police may be issued a warrant to enter and search premises and seize evidential material under § 3E CA. *See* generally, CA pt IAA div 2.
340. *See*, Mutual Antitrust Enforcement Assistance Agreement, Austl.-U.S., Apr. 1999; and Agreement relating to Cooperation on Antitrust Matters, Austl.-U.S., June 29, 1982.

offense proceeding by way of indictment.[341] At trial, the burden of proof rests with the CDPP to establish its case beyond a reasonable doubt and to obtain the unanimous verdict of a jury.

There is no limitation period for commencing criminal cartel proceedings in Australia. This compares to a limitation period of six years for civil cartel proceedings (both public enforcement and private actions).

3. Leniency Program

a. Immunity Policy

First-in immunity from criminal prosecution for serious cartel offenses is available from the CDPP pursuant to the *Prosecution Policy of the Commonwealth.* [342] However, an application for criminal cartel immunity must be made to the ACCC for an assessment of conditional immunity from civil liability under the ACCC's *Immunity and Cooperation Policy.*[343] Where the criteria for a conditional civil immunity application are met, the ACCC will make a recommendation to the CDPP that immunity from criminal prosecution be conferred to the applicant. A corporation will be eligible for conditional civil immunity when the corporation applies for immunity and the following criteria are satisfied:

- the corporation was a party to the cartel, admits that its conduct may constitute a contravention of the CCA and is the first applicant for immunity under the policy;
- the corporation has not coerced others to participate in the cartel;
- the corporation has ceased involvement in the cartel or indicates that it will cease involvement;
- the corporation's admissions are truly corporate; and
- the corporation has provided full, frank and truthful disclosure and has cooperated fully and expeditiously while making the application and undertakes to continue to do so through the ACCC investigation and any court proceedings.

---

341. *Commonwealth Constitution of Australia Act 1900* (Cth) § 80.
342. Commonwealth Director of Public Prosecutions, *Prosecution Policy of the Commonwealth*, Annexure B: Immunity from Prosecution in Serious Cartel Offences (Sept. 9, 2014).
343. Australian Competition and Consumer Commission, *ACCC Immunity and Cooperation Policy for Cartel Conduct* (Sept. 10, 2014).

The ACCC will only grant conditional civil immunity when it has not received written legal advice that is has reasonable grounds to institute proceedings in relation to at least one contravention of the CCA arising from the conduct.[344]

If the CDPP is independently satisfied that the applicant meets the ACCC's criteria for conditional immunity, the CDPP will issue a "letter of comfort" to the effect that the CDPP intends to grant criminal immunity in the event that a prosecution is commenced. Prior to the commencement of any prosecution, and subject to compliance with any conditions specified in the letter of comfort, the CDPP will issue a written undertaking granting criminal immunity in respect of the disclosed cartel conduct. The applicant must satisfy the conditions of its conditional immunity and they must remain in place in order to be eligible for final immunity. Derivative criminal immunity will also be available for all related corporate entities, and current or former directors, officers, or employees.

A "marker" will be available for the first party to approach the ACCC and seek immunity. From the time a marker is granted, the applicant has a limited period of time to assemble information necessary to substantiate an application for conditional immunity, which may be presented to the ACCC in an oral or written format. Generally, this period is about 28 days, but may be extended in certain circumstances if the ACCC agrees. The marker may be obtained on an anonymous basis.[345]

After obtaining a marker from the ACCC, if a party decides to proceed with an immunity application, it will need to provide a detailed description of the cartel conduct. This is known as a "proffer."

Neither civil nor criminal immunity protects an applicant from third party proceedings for compensatory damages. Third party litigants can rely on any admissions and findings of fact in subsequent proceedings.[346] Actions for damages for loss or damage have a limitation period of six years.[347]

---

344. Australian Competition and Consumer Commission, ACCC Immunity and Cooperation Policy § C (Sept. 10, 2014).

345. Australian Competition and Consumer Commission, *ACCC Immunity and Cooperation Policy* § E (Sept. 10, 2014).

346. CCA § 83.

347. CCA § 82.

b. Cooperation Policy

Once a matter has been referred to the CDPP and charges laid, cooperation will entail a guilty plea to some or all charges brought by the CDPP in exchange for leniency in respect of the quantum and type of other charges. Charge negotiations may be entered into between the defendant and the CDPP pursuant to the *Prosecution Policy of the Commonwealth*. Plea bargaining, as it is understood in the United States, is not permitted in Australia.[348]

In terms of sentencing, the CDPP will identify, by way of submissions to court, any cooperation by the defendant with the ACCC or the CDPP, and the value of that cooperation. The CDPP may require the cooperating party to make submissions, agree to a statement of facts and/or provide evidence in proceedings in respect of the cartel conduct.[349]

In the context of civil cartel proceedings, the ACCC's *Cooperation Policy* may apply to facilitate settlement between individuals and corporations not eligible for full immunity and the ACCC.[350] The ACCC will identify, by way of submission to the court, any cooperation provided by a party, and the value of that cooperation. The ACCC may require the cooperating party to make submissions, agree to a statement of facts and/or provide evidence in proceedings in respect of the cartel conduct.[351]

In both civil and criminal cases, it is for the court to determine the appropriate penalty or sentence on a party who has engaged in cartel conduct, including the extent of any discount for cooperation. For example, in ACCC v. NYK, the maximum penalty was calculated on the basis of 10 percent of NYK's annual turnover in connection with Australia in the 12 months prior to the commencement of the offence. On that basis, NYK's conduct attracted a maximum penalty of AUD$100 million.[352]

---

348. *See,* Commonwealth Director of Public Prosecutions, *Prosecution Policy of the Commonwealth*, Annexure B: Immunity from Prosecution in Serious Cartel Offences § 6.16 (Sept. 9, 2014).

349. *See,* Commonwealth Director of Public Prosecutions, *Prosecution Policy of the Commonwealth*, Annexure B: Immunity from Prosecution in Serious Cartel Offences § 80, 91 (Sept. 9, 2014).

350. *See,* Australian Competition and Consumer Commission, *ACCC Immunity and Cooperation Policy* § H (Sept. 10, 2014).

351. *See,* Australian Competition and Consumer Commission, *ACCC Immunity and Cooperation Policy* §74-76 (Sept. 10, 2014).

352. Australian Competition and Consumer Commission, NYK convicted of criminal cartel conduct and fined $25 million (Aug. 3, 2017)

Justice Wigney stated that the AUD$25 million fine "incorporates a global discount of 50 percent for NYK's early plea of guilty and past and future assistance and cooperation, together with the contrition inherent in the early plea and cooperation: meaning that but for the early plea and past and future cooperation, the fine would have been $50 million."

---

https://www.accc.gov.au/media-release/nyk-convicted-of-criminal-cartel-conduct-and-fined-25-million.